RECUEIL DES COURS

426 (2022)

L'Académie de droit international de La Haye
honorée du prix Wateler de la Paix (1936, 1950), du prix Félix Houphouët-Boigny
pour la recherche de la paix (1992), de l'ordre du Rio Branco, Brésil (1999), et de la
médaille de l'Institut royal d'études européennes, Espagne (2000)

The Hague Academy of International Law
awarded the Wateler Peace Prize (1936, 1950), the Félix Houphouët-Boigny Peace
Prize (1992), the Order of Rio Branco, Brazil (1999), and the Medal of the Royal
Institute of European Studies, Spain (2000)

© Académie de droit international de La Haye, 2022
The Hague Academy of International Law, 2022

Tous droits réservés All rights reserved

ISBN 978-90-04-51771-4

Printed by/Imprimé par Triangle Bleu, 59600 Maubeuge, France

ACADÉMIE DE DROIT INTERNATIONAL

FONDÉE EN 1923 AVEC LE CONCOURS DE LA
DOTATION CARNEGIE POUR LA PAIX INTERNATIONALE

RECUEIL DES COURS

COLLECTED COURSES OF THE HAGUE
ACADEMY OF INTERNATIONAL LAW

2022

Tome 426 de la collection

BRILL | NIJHOFF

Leiden/Boston

COMPOSITION DU CURATORIUM
DE L'ACADÉMIE DE DROIT INTERNATIONAL DE LA HAYE

PRÉSIDENT

Y. DAUDET, professeur émérite de l'Université Paris I (Panthéon-Sorbonne)

VICE-PRÉSIDENT

B. HESS, avocat, docteur en droit

MEMBRES

M. BENNOUNA, juge à la Cour internationale de Justice

K. BOELE-WOELKI, doyenne de la faculté de droit de Bucerius, Hambourg; présidente de l'Académie internationale de droit comparé

H. BUXBAUM, professeure à l'Université de l'Indiana

A. A. CANÇADO TRINDADE, juge à la Cour internationale de Justice; ancien juge et ancien président de la Cour interaméricaine des droits de l'homme

H. CHARLESWORTH, *Laureate Professor* à l'école de droit de l'Université de Melbourne; professeure à l'université nationale australienne

G. CORDERO-MOSS, professeure à l'Université d'Oslo

D. P. FERNANDEZ ARROYO, professeur à l'école de droit de Sciences Po, Paris

B. B. JIA, professeur à l'Université de Tsinghua, Pékin

M. KAMTO, professeur à l'Université de Yaoundé II

M. M. MBENGUE, professeur à l'Université de Genève

D. MOMTAZ, professeur à l'Université de Téhéran

Y. NISHITANI, professeure à l'Université de Kyoto

N. J. SCHRIJVER, professeur émérite de l'Université de Leiden; Conseiller d'Etat au Conseil d'Etat des Pays-Bas

L.-A. SICILIANOS, doyen de la faculté de droit de l'Université d'Athènes; ancien président de la Cour européennne des droits de l'homme

P. TOMKA, juge et ancien président de la Cour internationale de Justice

T. TREVES, professeur émérite de l'Université de Milan; ancien juge au Tribunal international du droit de la mer

SECRÉTAIRE GÉNÉRAL
DE L'ACADÉMIE DE DROIT INTERNATIONAL DE LA HAYE

J.-M. THOUVENIN, professeur à l'Université Paris-Nanterre

COMPOSITION OF THE CURATORIUM
OF THE HAGUE ACADEMY OF INTERNATIONAL LAW

PRESIDENT

Y. DAUDET, Emeritus Professor at Paris I University (Panthéon-Sorbonne)

VICE-PRESIDENT

B. HESS, Attorney-at-Law, Ph.D.

MEMBERS

M. BENNOUNA, Judge at the International Court of Justice

K. BOELE-WOELKI, Dean of Bucerius Law School, Hamburg; President of the International Academy of Comparative Law

H. BUXBAUM, Professor at Indiana University

A. A. CANÇADO TRINDADE, Judge at the International Court of Justice; former President and former Judge at the Inter-American Court of Human Rights

H. CHARLESWORTH, Laureate Professor at Melbourne Law School; Professor at the Australian National University

G. CORDERO-MOSS, Professor at the University of Oslo

D. P. FERNANDEZ ARROYO, Professor at the Sciences Po Law School, Paris

B. B. JIA, Professor at Tsinghua University, Beijing

M. KAMTO, Professor at the University of Yaoundé II

M. M. MBENGUE, Professor at the University of Geneva

D. MOMTAZ, Professor at the University of Tehran

Y. NISHITANI, Professor at Kyoto University

N. J. SCHRIJVER, Emeritus Professor at Leiden University; State Councillor at the Netherlands Council of State

L.-A. SICILIANOS, Dean of the Law Faculty of the University of Athens; former President of the European Court of Human Rights

P. TOMKA, Judge and former President of the International Court of Justice

T. TREVES, Emeritus Professor at the University of Milan; former Judge at the International Tribunal for the Law of the Sea

SECRETARY-GENERAL
OF THE HAGUE ACADEMY OF INTERNATIONAL LAW

J.-M. THOUVENIN, Professor at the University Paris-Nanterre

ACADÉMIE DE DROIT INTERNATIONAL DE LA HAYE
— FONDÉE EN 1923 AVEC LE CONCOURS DE LA DOTATION CARNEGIE —
HONORÉE DU PRIX WATELER DE LA PAIX (1936, 1950), DU PRIX FÉLIX HOUPHOUËT-BOIGNY POUR LA RECHERCHE DE LA PAIX (1992), DE L'ORDRE DU RIO BRANCO, BRÉSIL (1999), ET DE LA MÉDAILLE DE L'INSTITUT ROYAL D'ÉTUDES EUROPÉENNES, ESPAGNE (2000)

L'Académie constitue un centre d'études et d'enseignement du droit international public et privé, et des sciences connexes. Son but est de faciliter l'examen approfondi et impartial des problèmes se rattachant aux rapports juridiques internationaux.

L'enseignement de l'Académie est principalement donné au Palais de la Paix, à La Haye, par des personnalités de différents États. Il porte sur le droit international, sous ses aspects théoriques et pratiques, et sur la jurisprudence internationale. La durée de ses deux principales sessions est en été de six semaines s'étendant sur les mois de juillet et d'août, et partagée en deux périodes, consacrées l'une au droit international public, l'autre aux relations privées internationales, et, en hiver, de trois semaines, consacrée en janvier au droit international. L'enseignement est dispensé en français ou en anglais, avec traduction simultanée dans l'autre langue. Les sessions de l'Académie se déroulent sous l'autorité du Secrétaire général.

L'enseignement de l'Académie est conçu dans un esprit à la fois pratique et hautement scientifique. Nettement différencié des enseignements similaires des universités et écoles nationales, il s'adresse à tous ceux qui possèdent déjà des notions de droit international et ont, par intérêt professionnel ou curiosité d'esprit, le désir de se perfectionner dans cette science.

Il n'existe pas de cadre permanent de professeurs à l'Académie. Le Curatorium, qui est le corps chargé de la direction scientifique de l'institution, et qui se compose de dix-huit membres appartenant statutairement à des nationalités différentes, adresse chaque année, en toute liberté, ses invitations aux personnes qu'il estime qualifiées pour donner un cours ou une conférence à l'Académie. Les personnes ayant donné des cours à l'Académie ne sont donc aucunement fondées à s'intituler professeur de ou à l'Académie de droit international de La Haye.

L'Académie décerne un diplôme à ceux des auditeurs qui, réunissant les qualifications spéciales exigées par le règlement en vigueur, auront subi avec succès des épreuves d'examen devant le jury de la session à laquelle ils se sont inscrits. Elle délivre en outre aux auditeurs un certificat attestant l'assiduité aux cours de l'Académie à la fin de la session suivie.

Toute personne désirant suivre l'enseignement de l'Académie doit faire parvenir par voie électronique au secrétariat de l'Académie, au Palais de la Paix, à La Haye, un formulaire d'inscription dûment rempli. L'Académie perçoit des droits d'inscription fixés par le Conseil d'administration de l'Académie.

Un programme de bourses d'études permettant d'assister aux cours d'été ou d'hiver est institué auprès de l'Académie. Le mode d'attribution de ces bourses fait l'objet d'un règlement disponible sur le site Internet de l'Académie.

Tous les cours professés à l'Académie durant les sessions d'été et d'hiver font, en principe, l'objet d'une publication dans le *Recueil des cours de l'Académie de droit international de La Haye*, ainsi que sur une plateforme Internet, dans la langue dans laquelle ils ont été professés. Certains cours sont également publiés ou réédités dans des collections spéciales.

THE HAGUE ACADEMY OF INTERNATIONAL LAW
— FOUNDED IN 1923 WITH THE SUPPORT OF THE CARNEGIE ENDOWMENT —
AWARDED THE WATELER PEACE PRIZE (1936, 1950), THE FÉLIX HOUPHOUËT-BOIGNY PEACE PRIZE (1992), THE ORDER OF RIO BRANCO, BRAZIL (1999), AND THE MEDAL OF THE ROYAL INSTITUTE OF EUROPEAN STUDIES, SPAIN (2000)

The Academy is an institution devoted to the study and teaching of Public and Private International Law and related fields. Its mission is to further the thorough and impartial examination of issues arising from international legal relations.

The courses of the Academy are dispensed principally at the Peace Palace in The Hague by personalities from different States. They deal with the theoretical and practical aspects of international law, including international jurisprudence. The duration of its two main sessions is, in Summer, of six weeks in July and August, divided into two periods of three weeks each, one devoted to Public International Law and the other to Private International Law, and, in Winter, of three weeks, in January, devoted to international law. They are taught in either English or in French, with simultaneous interpretation into the other language. The Secretary-General is responsible for managing the sessions of the Academy.

The education offered by the Academy is designed to be both practical and highly academically advanced. Clearly distinct from the teachings provided in national universities and law schools, it is intended for those who already possess some notion of international law and who, out of professional interest or intellectual curiosity, desire to deepen their knowledge in this field.

There is no permanent teaching staff at the Academy. The Curatorium, which is the body entrusted with the scientific management of the institution, and which consists of eighteen members of different nationalities, invites each year, in its unfettered discretion, whomsoever it deems best qualified to dispense a course or give a lecture at the Academy. It follows that no one who has lectured at the Academy is entitled to style himself or herself Professor of or at The Hague Academy of International Law.

The Academy awards a Diploma to those attendees who possess special qualifications as set out in the regulations, after having successfully passed examinations before the Jury of the session in which they are registered. It also delivers a certificate of attendance to registered attendees at the end of the session.

Anyone wishing to attend the courses at the Academy must send a completed electronic registration form to the Secretariat of the Academy at the Peace Palace in The Hague. The registration fee for each session of courses is fixed by the Administrative Board of the Academy.

The Academy manages a programme of scholarships to allocate at its discretion to attendees at the Summer and Winter Courses. The regulations governing scholarships are published on the website of the Academy.

All courses taught at the Academy during the Summer and Winter Courses are, in principle, published in the *Collected Courses of The Hague Academy of International Law*, which also exist in electronic format, in the language in which they were delivered. Some courses are also published or reissued in special collections.

GENERAL TABLE OF CONTENTS

Delegation and International Organizations, by P. J. KUIJPER, Emeritus Professor, University of Amsterdam.   9-240

The Evolution of the Law of International Watercourses, by S. C. McCAFFREY, Carol Olson Endowed Professor, University of the Pacific, McGeorge School of Law in Sacramento, California . . .   241-384

DELEGATION AND INTERNATIONAL ORGANIZATIONS

by

PIETER JAN KUIJPER

P. J. KUIJPER

TABLE OF CONTENTS

Chapter I. What inspired this lecture series? 21

Chapter II. Delegation of powers in national legal systems. 27
  A. The United States. 28
    1. A bit of history 28
    2. Since the Second World War 30
  B. France. 35
    1. A hard separation between the legislative and the regulatory domain 35
    2. The Conseil Constitutionnel and the separation between the two domains 37
    3. Article 38 of the Constitution: Legislative regulations 43
  C. Italy 48
    1. Article 76 of the Italian Constitution: Delegation of the legislative function. 48
    2. Early case law of the Corte Costituzionale on the delegation of legislative power 50
    3. Special question of subdelegation of legislative power 51
    4. Margin of maneuver of the (sub)delegated authorities 53
  D. Germany 55
    1. Delegation in the FRG Constitution: Initially a post-Weimar moment? 55
    2. Development of broad constitutional principles and its influence on delegation 58
    3. Application of the broader principles of Article 20 GG to delegation under Article 80 GG 61
  E. National law of delegation in an administrative context: The Dutch example 63
    1. The Dutch system of administrative law delegation as an example   64
    2. Attribution 65
    3. Delegation. 67
    4. Mandate 68
    5. Conclusion 69
  F. Some concluding remarks on national systems of delegation 70
  G. Some remaining loose ends inspired by national law and practice on legislative delegation 72
  H. Some basic notions related to delegation 74
    1. Distinction between attribution and delegation 74
    2. Contrast between commercial and public law notions of delegation 74
    3. Are Roman law parallels helpful? 75
    4. Aversion from self-delegation and subdelegation? 76
    5. Implied powers 77
    6. States and international organizations 77
    7. Outline of the remaining part of this study 78

Chapter III. Delegation within the United Nations: the General Assembly and the secretariat 80
  A. Delegation to a newly created body: The United Nations Administrative Tribunal 80

B. The ICSC and the *Molinier* case: A technical delegation to a newly created body?.................................... 84
C. The Secretary-General's bulletin on delegation of authority..... 89
D. The different powers delegated to the ICSC: Advisory and decisional 92

   1. The judgment of the ILO Administrative Tribunal......... 92
   2. The view of the UN Internal Justice System............ 97

E. The story of Mr Kompass: A well-intentioned civil servant sent on administrative leave........................... 106
F. Conclusions on delegation by the General Assembly and Secretariat. 109

Chapter IV. Delegation by the Security Council............... 113

A. The *Tadić* case.............................. 114
B. The financing of the creation and functioning of the ICTY....... 118
C. Delegation in connection with the application of Chapter VII UN Charter................................... 121
D. The UN mission in Kosovo....................... 124
E. Delegation by the Security Council to sanctions committees..... 128
F. UN delegation to one or more Member States and International Organizations............................... 138

   1. The Beira blockade......................... 139
   2. Kosovo............................... 141
   3. East Timor cases of 1999 and 2006................ 142

      (a) 1999: From UNAMET to UNTAET............. 142
      (b) 2006: To UNMIT...................... 145

   4. Coalitions of the willing...................... 146

      (a) Korea............................. 146
      (b) The Iraq-Kuwait war..................... 146
      (c) Other examples........................ 148

         (i) Bosnia........................... 148
         (ii) Afghanistan....................... 149
         (iii) Libya........................... 150

G. Conclusions on delegation by the Security Council.......... 152

Chapter V. Delegation in the European Union................ 155

A. Introduction: The *Meroni* case..................... 155
B. The Rome Treaty and management committees............ 161
C. The Single European Act of 1987 and the codification of the implementing committees............................ 165
D. From the Treaty of Amsterdam and the second comitology decision to the Treaty of Nice............................ 171
E. After the Treaty of Nice and up until the Treaty of Lisbon...... 177

   1. The amendment of the second comitology decision....... 178
   2. Some interim conclusions..................... 181

F. The Treaty of Lisbon, delegation of legislative powers and the third comitology decision............................ 182

   1. Jurisdiction of the Court of Justice................ 182
   2. Delegated acts........................... 182
   3. Implementing measures....................... 185
   4. Some preliminary questions and conclusions........... 188

G. The post-Lisbon cases and the present state of the law of delegation in the EU................................. 191

   1. The borderline between delegated acts and implementing acts.. 191
   2. Delegated powers.......................... 195

Delegation and International Organizations 15

    3. Implementing powers. 197
    4. Some conclusions on the post-Lisbon state of the law of delegation 202
  H. Administrative delegation within the Commission and other institutions. 204
    1. The rules on administrative delegation 204
    2. Case law on administrative delegation within the Commission . 208
    3. Some concluding remarks 212
  I. Delegation to EU agencies 213
    1. Introduction 213
    2. Classification of agencies 215
    3. The *ESMA* case. 217
  J. Some final remarks on delegation in the EU. 225

Chapter VI. Concluding remarks. 229

BIOGRAPHICAL NOTE

Pieter Jan Kuijper, born in Olst, Netherlands, on 5 October 1946.
Education: Law degree *cum laude*, University of Leiden (1970). MA in International Relations with distinction, Johns Hopkins School of Advanced International Studies, Washington DC (1971). PhD in Law, University of Amsterdam (UvA) (1978), with doctoral dissertation: "The Implementation of International Sanctions: The Netherlands and Rhodesia".

Academic posts: Lecturer in the Law of International Organizations, Law Faculty, University of Leiden (1972-1979). Fellowship, Netherlands Institute for Academic Studies in the Humanities and the Social Sciences in Wassenaar (1977-1978). Professor of International Law, International Relations Department, Faculty of Social Sciences, UvA (1984-1987). Visiting Professor, Université Catholique de Louvain-la-Neuve (1987-1991), University of Michigan (1994), UvA (1995-2007), and Université Libre de Bruxelles (2004-2007). Emeritus Professor of the Law of International (Economic) Organizations, Faculty of Law, UvA (since 2018). Former editor of *Common Market Law Review*, *Legal Issues of Economic Integration* and the *Journal of International Economic Law*. Recipient of the Maastricht Prize for International Law (2015).

Professional roles: Member of the Legal Service of the Commission of the European Communities (1979-1984, 1987-1999, 2002-2007). Director of the Legal Affairs Division of the Secretariat of the World Trade Organization (1999-2002). Legal Adviser and Director of the External Relations and International Trade team, Legal Service of the European Commission (2002-2007).

PRINCIPAL PUBLICATIONS

A. Books

The Law of the European Union, 5th ed., Alphen aan den Rijn, Wolters Kluwer, 2018 (Coeditor).
The Law of EU External Relations: Cases, Materials, and Commentary on the EU as an International Legal Actor, 2nd rev. ed., Oxford, Oxford University Press, 2015 (Coeditor).
From Treaty-Making to Treaty-Breaking: Models for ASEAN Free-Trade Agreements, Cambridge, Cambridge University Press, 2014 (Coeditor).
Essays on the Development of the International Legal Order: In memory of Haro F. Van Panhuys, Alphen aan den Rijn, Sijthoff & Noordhoff, 1980 (Coeditor).
The Implementation of International Sanctions: The Netherlands and Rhodesia, Alphen aan den Rijn, Sijthoff & Noordhoff, 1978.

B. Articles and volume contributions

"The European Union and the Multilateral Trade Regime: Reciprocal Influences" (with G. Vidigal), in M. Hahn and G. van der Loo (eds.), *Law and Practice of the Common Commercial Policy* (Studies in EU External Relations 18), Leiden, Brill Nijhoff, 2020, pp. 434-458.
"Recent Tendencies in the Separation of Powers in EU Foreign Relations: An Essay", in E. Neframi and M. Gatti (eds.), *Constitutional Issues of EU External Relations Law* (Luxemburger Juristische Studien 16), Baden-Baden, Nomos, 2018, pp. 201-229.
"The Court of Justice of the European Union", in R. Howse, H. Ruiz-Fabri, G. Ulfstein and M. Q. Zang (eds.), *The Legitimacy of International Trade Courts and Tribunals* (Studies on International Courts and Tribunals), Cambridge, Cambridge University Press, 2018, pp. 70-137.
"The Court and the New EU Foreign Relations Law: Institutional Balance?", in J. Czuczai and F. Naert (eds.), *The EU as a Global Actor: Bridging Legal Theory and Practice: Liber Amicorum in Hounour of Ricardo Gosalbo Bono* (Studies in EU External Relations 13), Leiden, Brill Nijhoff, 2017, pp. 48-64.
"The Case Law of the Court of Justice of the EU and the Allocation of External Relations Powers: Whither the Traditional Role of the Executive in EU Foreign Relations?" in M. Cremona and A. Thies (eds.), *The European Court of Justice and External Relations Law: Constitutional Challenges*, Oxford, Hart, 2014, pp. ???.
"Attribution – Responsibility – Remedy: Some Comments on the EU in Different International Regimes", *Revue belge de droit international*, Vol. 47, No. 1 (2013), pp. 57-77.
"EU International Responsibility and its Attribution: From the Inside Looking Out" (with E. Paasivirta), in M. Evans and P. Koutrakos (eds.), *The International Responsibility of the European Union: European and International Perspectives*, Oxford, Hart, 2013, pp. 35-71.
"WTO Influence on EU Law: Too Close for Comfort?" (with Frank Hoffmeister), in R. A. Wessel and S. Blockmans (eds.), *Between Autonomy and Dependence: The EU Legal Order Under the Influence of International Organisations*, The Hague, TMC Asser, 2013, pp. 131-158.
"'It Shall Contribute to . . . the Strict Observance and Development of International Law . . .': The Role of the Court of Justice", in A. Rosas, E. Levits and Y. Bot (eds.), *The Court of Justice and the Construction of Europe / La Cour de Justice et la construction de l'Europe*, The Hague, TMC Asser, 2012, pp. 589-613.
"La politique commerciale commune de l'Union européenne dans le cadre de l'OMC: quelques enjeux juridiques (1)", in M. Le Barbier-Le Bris (ed.), *L'Union européenne*

et la gouvernance mondiale: quel apport avec quels acteurs? (Rencontres européennes 16), Brussels: Bruylant, 2012, pp. 191-204.
"Mr. Kadi and Mrs. Prost: Is the UN Ombudsperson Going to Find Herself Between a Rock and a Hard Place?" (with L. Boisson de Chazournes), in E. Rieter and H. de Waele (eds.), *Evolving Principles of International Law: Studies in Honour of Karel C. Wellens* (Queen Mary Studies in International Law 5), Leiden, Nijhoff, 2012, pp. 71-90.
"The Court and the Appellate Body: Between Constitutionalism and Dispute Settlement", in S. E. Gaines, B. Egelund Olsen and K. E. Sørensen (eds.), *Liberalising Trade in the EU and the WTO: A Legal Comparison*, Cambridge, Cambridge University Press, 2012, pp. 99-137.
"La Jurisprudence Usine MOX, Est-elle symptomatique d'un Dialogue de Sourds Entre la CJCE et les Autres Juridictions Internationales?" / "The MOX Plant Case, is it Symptomatic of a Dialog of the Deaf Between the ECJ and the other International Jurisdictions?", in Y. Kerbrat (ed.), *Forum shopping et concurrence des procédures dans le contentieux international*, Brussels, Larcier / Bruylant, 2011, pp. ???.
"The Court of Justice and Unrecognized Entities Under International Law", in I. Govaere, R. Quick and M. Bronckers (eds.), *Trade and Competition Law in the EU and Beyond*, Cheltenham, Edward Elgar, 2011, pp. 257-275.
"The European Courts and the Law of Treaties: The Continuing Story", in E. Cannizzaro (ed.), *The Law of Treaties Beyond The Vienna Convention*, Oxford, Oxford University Press, 2011, pp. 256-278.
"Conflicting Rules and Clashing Courts: The Case of Multilateral Environmental Agreements, Free Trade Agreements and the WTO", Issue Paper No. 10, ICTSD, Geneva, September 2010.
"International Responsibility for EU Mixed Agreement", in C. Hillion and P. Koutrakos (eds.), *Mixed Agreements Revisited*, Oxford, Hart, 2010.
"Super-Power Frustrated? The Costs of Non-Lisbon in the Field of External Relations", *German Yearbook of International Law*, Vol. 51 (2008), pp. 9-37.
"WTO Institutional Issues", in D. Bethlehem, D. McRae, R. Neufeld and I. van Damme (eds.), *The Oxford Handbook of International Trade Law*, Oxford, Oxford University Press, 2009, pp. 79-128.
"Customary International Law, Decisions of International Organisations and Other Techniques for Ensuring Respect for International Legal Rules in European Community Law", in A. Nollkaemper, E. de Wet and J. Wouters (eds.), *The Europeanisation of International Law*, The Hague, TMC Asser, 2008, pp. 87-106.
"Does the World Trade Organization Prohibit Retorsions and Reprisals? Legitimate 'Contracting out' or 'Clinical Isolation' Again?", in M. E. Janow, V. Donaldson and A. Yanovich (eds.), *The WTO: Governance, Dispute Settlement and Developing Countries*, New York, Juris, 2008, pp. 695-708.
"Does One Size Fit All? The European Community and the "Codification" of the Responsibility of International Organizations" (with E. Paasivirta), *Netherlands Yearbook of International Law*, Vol. 36 (2005), pp. 169-226.
"Les Mesures Commerciales à l'Encontre d'Etats Tiers: Tendances de la Pratique" / "Commercial Measures Against Non-Member States: Practical Tendencies", in I. Pingel (ed.) *Les Sanctions Contre les Etats en Droit Communautaire*, Paris, Pedone, 2006, pp. 82-98.
"WTO Law in the European Court of Justice" (with M. Bronckers), *Common Market Law Review*, Vol. 42 (2005), pp. 1313-1355.
"Further Exploring International Responsibility: The European Community and the ILC's Project on the Responsibility of International Organizations" (with E. Paasivirta), *International Organizations Law Review*, Vol. 1 (2004), pp. 111-138.
"The Evolution of the Third Pillar from Maastricht to the European Constitution", *Common Market Law Review*, Vol. 41 (2004), pp. 609-626.
"From Dyestuffs to Kosovo Wine: From Avoidance to Acceptance by the Community Courts of Customary International Law as Limit to Community Action", in I. F. Dekker and H. H. G. Post (eds.), *On the Foundations and Sources of*

Delegation and International Organizations 19

International Law: Essays in Memory of Herman Meijers, The Hague, TMC Asser, 2003, pp. 151-171.
"Some Institutional Issues Presently before the WTO", in D. L. M. Kennedy and J. Southwick (eds.), *The Political Economy of International Trade: Essays in Honor of Robert E. Hudec*, Cambridge, Cambridge University Press, 2002, pp. 81-110.
"Some Legal Problems Associated with the Communitarization of Policy on Visas, Asylum and Immigration under the Amsterdam Treaty and Incorporation of the Schengen Acquis", *Common Market Law Review*, Vol. 37, No. 2 (2000), pp. 345-366.
"The Appellate Body and the Facts", in M. Bronckers and R. Quick (eds.), *New Directions in International Trade Law: Essays in Honour of John. H. Jackson*, The Hague, Kluwer, 2000, pp. 309-323.
"The Court and Tribunal of the EC and the Vienna Convention on the Law of Treaties 1969", *Legal Issues of European Integration*, Vol. 25, No. 1 (1998), pp. 1-24.
"Booze and Fast Cars: Tax Discrimination Under GATT and the EC", *Legal Issues of European Integration: Special Issue in Honour of Prof. Richard Lauwaars* (1996), pp. 129-144.
"The Conclusion and Implementation of the Uruguay Round Results by the European Community", *European Journal of International Law*, Vol. 6, 1995, pp. 222-244.
"The New WTO Dispute Settlement System: The Impact on the Community", in J. H. J. Bourgeois, F. Berrod and E. Gippini Fournier (eds.), *The Uruguay Round Results, A European Lawyers' Perspective: Proceedings of an International Conference Held at the College of Europe, Bruges*, Bruges, College of Europe, 1995, pp. 87-114.
"The Community and State Succession in Respect of Treaties", in D. Curtin and T. Heukels (eds.), *Institutional Dynamics of European Integration: Essays in Honour of Henry G. Schermers*, Vol. 2, Dordrecht, Martinus Nijhoff, 1994, pp. 619-640.
"The Law of GATT as Special Field of International Law: Ignorance, Further Refinement or Self-Contained System of International Law?", *Netherlands Yearbook of International Law*, Vol. 25 (1994), pp. 227-257.
"Trade Sanctions, Security and Human Rights and Commercial Policy", in M. Maresceau (ed.), *The European Community's Commercial Policy after 1992: The Legal Dimension*, Dordrecht, Martinus Nijhoff, 1993, pp. 387-422.
"European Economic Community", in K. M. Meessen (ed.), *International Law of Export Control*, London, Graham and Trotman, 1992, pp. 57-78.
"Netherlands", in Karl M. Meessen (ed.), *International Law of Export Control*, London, Graham and Trotman, 1992, pp. 117-146.
"The Influence of the Elimination of Physical Frontiers in the Community on Trade in Goods with Third States", in M. Hilf and C. Tomuschat (eds.), *EG und Drittstaatsbeziehungen nach 1992*, Baden-Baden, Nomos, 1992, pp. 51-67.
"International Legal Aspects of Economic Sanctions", in P. Sarcevic and H. van Houtte (eds.), *Legal Issues in International Trade*, Dordrecht, Martinus Nijhoff, 1990, pp. 145-175.
"Deployment of Cruise Missiles in Europe: The Legal Battles in the Netherlands, the Federal Republic of Germany and Belgium" (with K. C. Wellens), *Netherlands Yearbook of International Law*, Vol. 18 (1987), pp. 145-218.
"European Community Law and Extraterritoriality: Some Trends and New Developments", *International and Comparative Law Quarterly*, Vol. 33 (1984), pp. 1013-1022.
"The European Community and the US Pipeline Embargo, Comments on Comments", *German Yearbook of International Law*, Vol. 27 (1984), pp. 72-96.
"Airline Fare-fixing and Competition: An English Lord, Commission Proposals and US Parallels", *Common Market Law Review*, Vol. 20 (1983), pp. 203-231.
"Community Sanctions Against Argentina: Lawfulness under Community and International Law", in D. O'Keeffe and H. G. Schermers (eds.) *Essays in European Law and Integration, to Mark the Silver Jubilee of the Europa Institute Leiden*, Deventer, Kluwer, 1982, pp. 141-166.

"A Colonial Power as Champion of Self-determination: Netherlands State Practice in the Period 1945-1975" (with P. J. G. Kapteyn), in H. F. van Panhuys, W. P. Heere, J. W. Josephus Jitta, Ko Swan Sik and A. M. Stuyt (eds.), *International Law in the Netherlands*, Vol. 3, Alphen aan den Rijn, Sijthoff & Noordhoff, 1980, pp. 149-218.

"The Netherlands and International Organizations", in H. F. van Panhuys, W. P. Heere, J. W. Josephus Jitta, Ko Swan Sik and A. M. Stuyt (eds.), *International Law in the Netherlands*, Vol. 2, Alphen aan den Rijn, Sijthoff & Noordhoff, 1979, pp. 3-41.

"Recognition: Netherlands Theory and State Practice", in H. F. van Panhuys, W. P. Heere, J. W. Josephus Jitta, Ko Swan Sik and A. M. Stuyt (eds.), *International Law in the Netherlands*, Vol. 1, Alphen aan den Rijn, Sijthoff & Noordhoff, 1978, pp. 371-403.

"The Limits of Supervision: The Security Council Watchdog Committee on Rhodesian Sanctions", *Netherlands International Law Review*, Vol. 25 (1978), pp. 159-194.

"Sanctions Against Rhodesia: The EEC and the Implementation of General International Legal Rules", *Common Market Law Review*, Vol. 12 (1975), pp. 231-244.

"De Akkoorden van Genève" / "The Geneva Agreements on Vietnam", *Ars Aequi*, Vol. 17, No. 7 (1968), pp. 254-260.

The author, in addition to the above listed works, has written many other shorter articles, editorials, blogs and annotations of judgments of international courts.

CHAPTER I

WHAT INSPIRED THIS LECTURE SERIES?

The subject of these courses for the Hague Academy of International Law was inspired by a sense of wonder [1]. Returning from a life as a practitioner of international law within such international organizations as the World Trade Organization (WTO) and the European Union to devote myself again to academic study of certain practices of these organizations, including also the United Nations and the specialized agencies, I was struck by the seeming insouciance with which, in worldwide organizations, powers were passed on from major organs to other organs or to (sometimes newly created) subordinate bodies. It seemed that not much attention was given to whether the conditions for decision-making needed to be equally stringent in the delegated bodies as in the delegating organs or whether certain powers could or should be delegated at all.

This lightheartedness in relation to delegation in the UN, and in the Security Council in particular, also seemed to contribute to the difficulties caused by the policy of targeted sanctions. Such relative neglect of the problematic side of delegation or transfer of powers within an organization like the UN contrasted sharply with the almost obsessive attention given to the phenomenon of delegation of powers and its legality in the EU and its predecessor organizations. Almost from the beginning, the European Coal and Steel Community (ECSC) and the European Economic Community (EEC, now the EU) were hamstrung by a very stringent approach to delegation of powers imposed by its Court, the so-called *Meroni* doctrine, which limited delegation to

---

1. The original course that lies at the basis of this written version was construed for the students around a limited number of judgments of international courts, including those of the EU. This written version follows the same approach, referring to a larger selection of cases, with the judgments of national constitutional courts added. The emphasis is thus very much on constitutional texts, national and international, and their interpretation by the courts, i.e. on the primary sources; literature plays a somewhat secondary role. Thanks are due, for their help and advice, to C. Brölmann, M. Chamon, Y. Daudet, M. Dougan, T. Eijsbouts, G. Nolte, P. Palchetti, D. Petrovič, B. Smulders and T. Staal, as well as from my former research assistant at the University of Amsterdam's Law Faculty, Niamh Deery. As always invaluable sustenance in and beyond the field of law was forthcoming from Laurence Boisson de Chazournes.

a very restricted set of measures, allowing the delegated body hardly any discretionary powers [2].

By the early 2000s a growing wariness made itself felt within the European Commission relating to the question of whether the many agencies that the Commission and Council had been spawning over the years could still be fitted within the legal "Procrustean bed" that the *Meroni* doctrine had become. By the time of writing this sentiment had been subsided under the influence of the entry into force of the Lisbon Treaty and how it was being interpreted by the European Court of Justice. Such new developments have only sharpened the feeling of wonder at the different approaches to delegation in different organizations and increased the urgency to describe and analyze what has been happening in this field since then and to see whether the two main streams of international organizations – the UN and other worldwide organizations on the one side, the EU and other regional organizations that pursue deeper integration on the other – continue to diverge or learn from each other. The UN and the EU are seen in this study as ideal types.

Before building further on existing work in the field of delegation in international organizations [3] it is important, by taking a stab at defining delegation of powers, to raise a number of questions about the nature and scope of the problem. A working definition could be the following: *Delegation is the transfer of a power from an organ of an international organization to another existing organ or a newly created body of this organization, or of another organization (of a Member State), or a private party.* It is important to keep in mind that this "big tent" definition of delegation may fall into different categories of delegation, one of which may also be called "delegation" in order to distinguish it from other categories of delegation. Moreover, there are many other questions hiding behind this definition. Is delegation to the organ of another organization even legally possible? Is delegation to organs of a (or all) Member State(s) a delegation within the organization or outside

---

2. Case 10/56, *Meroni* v. *High Authority*, ECLI:EU:C:1958:8, p. 157 ff.
3. Everyone working on this subject is to some extent indebted to Dan Sarooshi's pathbreaking work on the subject. See his *The United Nations and the Development of Collective Security: The Delegation by the UN Security Council of its Chapter VII Powers*, Oxford, Oxford University Press, 1999, and his *International Organizations and their Exercise of Sovereign Powers*, Oxford, Oxford University Press, 2005. This is also true for the present writer, and insofar as the Security Council is covered in this course, there is clearly some overlap. However, the terrain covered in the following chapters is broader and comparative in approach between the UN and the EU and with national approaches to delegation.

the organization? Does that depend on the kind of organization? Why is it that many lawyers would regard delegation by EU institutions to organs of one or more Member States at first sight as delegation *within* the organization, whereas they would be more inclined to see delegation from the Security Council of peace enforcement or peacekeeping tasks to certain Member States, forming a so-called coalition of the willing, as a delegation *outside* the organization?

Given that there is delegation from organs of the organization to (institutions of) the Member States, or even third States, is it also possible to speak of delegation from the Member States to the organization? Can the founding treaty by which States create a treaty body or an international organization, and give it certain powers, itself be considered an act of delegation? And if so, is it then an act of delegation under national or under international law? If it is a delegation under national law, is it possibly an illegal delegation under that national law? Or is the granting of powers by States to a treaty body or an international organization to be regarded as an exercise of their treatymaking power on the international level and, therefore, as an act of attribution of powers under international law, in the same way a national constitution vests powers in certain institutions of government [4]? Only a passing on of these powers from the organs of the organization, to which they have been originally attributed, to another organ or a body specially created for this purpose inside or outside the organization can then rightfully be qualified as an act of delegation within that organization. That is the position from which this course starts.

There is still a further question. Organs of international organizations consist of representatives of Member States, and the decisions, by which such organs exercise attributed powers or delegate them to other organs or specially created bodies, or even to Member States, are thus sometimes referred to as "international delegations". Hence recourse to the UN Security Council, or to the decisions of multilateral environmental agreements (or MEAs), is often portrayed as an international delegation by States. These decisions, however, from a legal point of view, are taken by organs of the relevant international organization and not by the Member States of these organizations. Indeed, on a more principled level, what is seen as a transfer (or delegation) of sovereign powers by

---

4. In many national systems of public law such a distinction between the (original) attribution of powers and the (further) delegation of powers is made. For an example in the Dutch literature, see W. Voermans, *Toedeling van Bevoegdheid*, The Hague, Boom, 2004, at chaps. 2 and 3.

States is actually a matter of the State using its treaty power together with other States to found an international organization. This organization is equipped by the founding States with certain powers. The international organization in question may then use what have become its powers to bind its Member States. This is what Jan Klabbers has called the "Frankenstein problem" of international organizations [5] and this dilemma is inherent in international organizations, and perennial. It cannot be undone by calling a decision of an organ of an international organization an (il)legal delegation of powers by one or more Member States participating in that decision (and possibly being outvoted in the process) [6].

The contradictory perspectives on the problem of delegation lightly sketched above find their roots in whether one looks upon international organizations with political science eyes or legal eyes. From a political science point of view, it may be attractive and have a certain explanatory power to regard the creation of a treaty body or an international organization as a cession or delegation of powers from the founding States. They were there first and always had the plenitude of powers internally and externally. And the powers bestowed on these international bodies came from them collectively. The same State-centered approach may also be attractive to apply to *decisions* of organs of international organizations. According to that view, States are the principals and the plenary organ of an international organization, or a treaty body is their mere agent. Indeed, principal-agent theory has become an explanatory tool in the political science approach to international organizations [7].

Real problems arise when the two approaches are used simultaneously or are mixed up. This happens when national *legal* approaches restricting, for instance, the delegation of national legislative powers to executive or judicial organs of the State in question are applied to a *political science* approach to delegation from a State to an international organization. As a consequence, such a national legal rule is applied to something that, in law, is not a delegation at all. Even from the national legal standpoint it

---

5. See J. Klabbers, *An Introduction to International Institutional Law*, Cambridge, Cambridge University Press, 2002. All editions of this book since 2002 have this motto taken from Mary Shelley's book: "You are my creator, but I am your master; Obey!"

6. This would amount to invoking a rule of national law on delegation as an excuse to invalidate a lawful decision of an international organization. This is obviously contrary to Article 27 of the 1969 Vienna Convention on the Law of Treaties.

7. On principal-agent theory in international organizations, see e.g. M. Elsig, "Principal-Agent Theory and the World Trade Organization: Complex Agency and 'Missing Delegation'", *European Journal of International Relations*, Vol. 17, No. 3 (2010), pp. 496-517.

is not a delegation, but – as was stated above – an exercise of the State's treaty power [8]. From the international legal viewpoint, it is the creation *ex nihilo* of a new international personality to which certain powers are *attributed* by States that under international law by definition have the power to do so. It is for these reasons that this course will pay no attention to what are called "international delegations" in the literature (see the relevant section of the bibliography included at the end of these lectures).

In the following, an international law approach to delegation of powers in international organizations will be taken. That is not to say that national law will be left out of consideration altogether. To the contrary because, as will be shown below, the ideas that inspired questions of delegation – and the answers to them – in international organizations inevitably were not conceived totally anew. The representatives of Member States and the international civil servants working in international organizations and the judges of international courts and tribunals, when confronted with questions concerning delegation or with situations closely resembling delegation, instinctively fell back on the notions of delegation that they knew from their national systems of constitutional and administrative law. These national public law rules on delegation, in turn, often borrowed terminology from civil and commercial law harking back to old notions of Roman law, such as mandate and agency.

That is why this course in Chapter II turns first to the delegation of powers in selected systems of national law and to a comparative study of the evolution of the doctrine governing the law on the delegation of (quasi-)legislative and/or regulatory powers in four such systems, as well as a brief descriptive analysis of the legislation governing delegation of a fifth country. It is hoped that such analysis will yield a number of common traits which may prove to have some explanatory power as to whence came certain approaches to delegation of powers in international organizations.

In Chapter III the course goes on to an analysis of the practice and case law in the field of delegation of powers within the UN. First, the

---

8. It may be argued, of course, that in national constitutional law the treaty power may not be as unfettered as in principle it is in international law, where *ius cogens* is at least one limit. It may be hemmed in by constitutional principles inherent in the structure of the constitution, such as the separation of powers, or by explicit constitutional rules about delegation of legislative power, but this is a question of national and not of international law. It could give rise to a reservation to certain treaty provisions or to a request for a renegotiation of parts of the treaty.

delegation of judicial powers from the UN General Assembly to judicial organs such as the two generations of UN administrative tribunals and from the General Assembly of advisory and decision-making powers to the International Civil Service Commission will be described and analyzed. A look at the Secretary-General's bulletin on the delegation of authority will clarify the distinction between delegation of a constitutional nature and delegation of an administrative law character within one institution, primarily the Secretariat.

In Chapter IV different types of delegation practiced by the Security Council will be analyzed. These include, as in the case of the General Assembly, the delegation of judicial tasks to a newly created humanitarian law tribunal for the former Yugoslavia, the International Criminal Tribunal, or ICTY. Moreover, delegation to specially created sanctions committees and to the function of the Ombudsperson also raise questions as to their legality, since the rules of decision-making of the Council are modified, although return to the treaty rules on this point remains possible.

The treatment of the delegation of (quasi-)legislative, regulatory and implementing powers in the European Union – the subject of Chapter V – is analyzed at some length, both as to its codification in legislation and as to its development through the case law of the EU Court of Justice (EUCJ). It will become clear that the role of the EUCJ is of prime importance in the development of the EU doctrine in the field of delegation, but that the Treaty of Lisbon, in particular the Treaty on the Functioning of the EU (TFEU), has probably radically changed the EUCJ's approach to the problem.

The approach followed in all these chapters is inductive. By looking from all sides at the law determining the delegation of powers in national legal systems and in the UN and EU legal systems, it is hoped that in the final Chapter VI it will be possible to come to a synthesis that will show the common points and the divergences between the different ways delegation of powers is handled in the UN and the EU and can explain why this should be the case.

CHAPTER II

DELEGATION OF POWERS
IN NATIONAL LEGAL SYSTEMS

In the following, the constitutional provisions relating to delegation, if any, and their application by the constitutional courts of a limited number of countries will be briefly described and analyzed. It is recalled that the purpose of this section is merely to give the reader some insight into which national law principles those that dealt with problems of delegation in international organizations after the Second World War might have been influenced. In the light of the study's focus on the UN system and the EU, it seemed reasonable to choose two important founding UN Member States, the United States (Sec. A) and France (Sec. B), and two additional founding members, next to France, of what is now the European Union: Italy (Sec. C) and the Federal Republic of Germany (FRG) (Sec. D). All these countries have constitutional courts that have interpreted the respective constitutional texts and principles. They are all democracies, the US of the presidential type, Italy and the FRG of the parliamentary type, while France is a somewhat mixed system under the Fifth Republic [9]. The analysis of the law of delegation of these four legal systems will be complemented by a brief sketch of the system of delegation under administrative law of the Netherlands (Sec. E). This is a country that has no constitutional court or constitutional review of its laws, but is still interesting because of the rigorous way in which delegation is treated by its relatively recent General Administrative Law Act. In this way, it may shine a light on delegation in other national and international legal systems.

At the end of the chapter, and on the basis of the material presented in it, a number of general questions and issues relating to the delegation of powers will be raised and a sketch of the further research undertaken for this course will be set out (Secs. F–H).

---

9. The United Kingdom was omitted from this selection because there is no written constitution, and the sovereignty of parliament makes delegation much less of a fraught problem.

A. The United States

1. A bit of history

From the early days of the American republic, it was clear that the explicit vesting of the legislative power in Article I of the Constitution in Congress and the underlying separation of powers were to be important factors in a "fundamental rejection" of the delegation of legislative powers. However, the case of *Wayman* v. *Southard* of 1825 [10] also showed that the Supreme Court immediately balked at applying it without nuance. Federal statutes in force at the time allowed the federal courts to regulate "their own practice" [11]. The Supreme Court saw that its task was not simple:

> "The line has not been exactly drawn which separates those important subjects which must be entirely regulated by the legislature itself from those of less interest in which a general provision may be made and power given to those who are to act under such general provisions to fill up the details." [12]

Nevertheless, it found without undue difficulty that Congress could leave to the federal courts, overseen by the Supreme Court, the task of fixing their own procedural rules, given the clear way in which the pertinent legislative text had been drafted. Still Chief Justice Marshall, who was the author of the judgment, included the following oft-quoted word of caution in the text:

> "The difference between the departments undoubtedly is that the legislature makes, the executive executes, and the judiciary construes the law; but the maker of the law may commit something to the discretion of the other departments, and the precise boundary of this power is a subject of delicate and difficult inquiry, into which a court will not enter unnecessarily." [13]

The modern US history of delegation begins in 1928 with a case concerning a federal law by which Congress delegated its powers to impose tariffs on the trade with foreign countries to the President, who would be advised in this matter by the Tariff Commission. In *Hampton*

---

10. *Wayman* v. *Southard*, 23 US (10 Wheat) 1.
11. That is, their own procedures, including those concerning the execution of court judgments ordering the sale of the possessions of those who were in debtor's prison.
12. *Wayman, supra* footnote 10, at 43.
13. *Ibid.*, at 46.

v. *US*, the Supreme Court bases itself again firmly on the separation of powers [14], but it also referred approvingly to a judgment of the Ohio Supreme Court that made a distinction between delegation of power to make the law, "which necessarily involved a discretion as to what it shall be and conferring an authority", and delegation which involved only a discretion as to the law's execution, "to be exercised under and in pursuance of the law". To the latter no objection could be made [15]. Thus "the exercise under and in pursuance of the law" – and how it has been laid down in the law in question by Congress – becomes decisive for the lawfulness of the delegation. And it so happened that Congress had laid down in the Tariff Act clear provisions for imposing or adapting tariffs in function of the difference between the costs of production abroad and in the US. Hence the Court came to the conclusion that

"if Congress shall lay down by legislative act *an intelligible principle* to which the person or the body authorized to fix such rates is directed to conform, such legislative action is not a forbidden delegation of legislative power" [16].

Later on, the words "an intelligible principle" have been much derided in US practice and doctrine as setting virtually no meaningful barrier to the delegation of legislative power [17]. And indeed, at first sight Chief Justice Taft's formula seemed to suffer from an unbearable lightness, but in reality, the principle on the basis of which the Tariff Commission was to advise the President about the level of tariffs to be imposed or adapted was simple and very clear: the difference in costs of production between the US and foreign countries. Indeed "an intelligible principle", but not at all vague or flexible or capable of overbroad interpretation.

This would seem to be borne out by *Schechter Poultry Corp.* v. *US* of 1935 [18], which led the Supreme Court to strike down the delegation of powers from Congress to the executive, but actually largely to representatives of the different economic sectors (who were supposed to create codes containing "fair rules of conduct" for their sector, in the

---

14. *Hampton* v. *US*, 276 US 394 (1928), at 406.
15. *Ibid.*, at 407, referring to *Cincinnati, Wilmington & Zanesville Railroad Co.* v. *Commissioners*, 1 Ohio St. 77, 88.
16. *Ibid.*, at 409.
17. The most recent criticism from practice is Justice Gorsuch's dissent in *Gundy* v. *US*, *infra* footnote 35 and accompanying text. In the doctrine, ridiculing the words "intelligible principle" has become commonplace.
18. *ALA Schechter Poultry Corp.* v. *US*, 295 US 495 (1935).

case at hand the live poultry sector) contained in the National Industry Recovery Act. The Court, through the pen of its then Chief Justice Charles Evans Hughes, distinguished *Schechter* from *Hampton* in no uncertain terms:

> "To summarize and conclude upon this point: Section 3 of the Recovery Act is without precedent. It supplies no standards for any trade, industry, or activity. It does not undertake to prescribe rules of conduct to be applied to particular states of fact determined by appropriate administrative procedure. Instead of prescribing rules of conduct, it authorizes the making of codes to prescribe them. For that legislative undertaking, paragraph 3 sets up no standards, aside from the statement of the general aims of rehabilitation, correction and expansion described in section one. In view of the scope of that broad declaration, and of the nature of the few restrictions that are imposed, the discretion of the President in approving or prescribing codes . . . is virtually unfettered. We think that the code-making authority this conferred is an unconstitutional delegation of legislative power." [19]

It is likely that the fact that the delegation of "code-making" was one to private bodies and supposed to lead to self-regulation, without much governmental oversight, also played a role in condemning it as unconstitutional.

2. Since the Second World War

Since 1935, however, the Supreme Court has never again found an opportunity to censure an act of Congress for overstepping the limits set in *Hampton* and *Schechter*. This was extensively documented in the case of *Mistretta*, a detainee who attacked his sentence before the courts because it had been decided under sentencing guidelines promulgated by the independent US Sentencing Commission, newly established under the Sentencing Reform Act 1984 [20]. The Sentencing Commission

---

19. *Ibid.*, 294-295. In the same year the Supreme Court also struck down a delegation of legislative power relating to the transportation in inter-State and foreign commerce of petroleum and petroleum products produced or withdrawn from storage in excess of the amounts permitted by State authority. That delegation was ruled plainly void, because nowhere in the statute had Congress declared or indicated any policy or standard to guide or limit the President when acting under such legislative delegation. *Panama Refining Co.* v. *Ryan*, 293 US 388, at 414 ff.

20. *Mistretta* v. *US*, 488 US 361 (1988).

was placed in the judicial branch of government and consisted of at least three federal judges and other experts in the field of criminal law and criminology. It was charged with making guidelines that would reestablish fairness and consistency in sentencing, which had been lost under the old system, but would still leave room for individualized sentences. However, Mistretta argued that the Sentencing Reform Act was much too lax in giving guidance to the Sentencing Commission and thus gave the Commission broad legislative discretion in violation of the nondelegation doctrine [21].

With Justice Blackmun writing for the majority, the Supreme Court made an effort first to return to the basics of nondelegation mostly in pre-World War II cases, then briefly to give an overview of a series of cases handed down during the war and immediately thereafter, and finally, in the light of the preceding jurisprudential overview, to conclude on the basis of the Act at hand, whether Congress had given such light instructions as to grant the Sentencing Commission actual legislative discretion. In the first phase the Court returns to the tripartite separation of powers as the basis of nondelegation, but mentions that this system is also based on an indispensable cooperation and mutual assistance between the branches of government. It refers to *Hampton* and its "intelligible principle" and claims that in applying it "in our increasingly complex society replete with ever-changing and more technical problems, Congress simply cannot do its job absent an ability to delegate power under broad general directives" [22]. The Court recalls that it has decided that in such situations it is constitutionally sufficient, if Congress clearly delineates the general policy, the public agency that is to apply it and the boundaries of this delegated authority [23].

In the second phase the Court sums up in one page a series of delegations of authorities granted to various bodies subject to instructions formulated in such broad language ("determining excessive profits" – *Lichter* [24]; "fixing fair and equitable commodity prices" – *Yakus* [25];

---

21. *Ibid.*, at 371.
22. *Ibid.*, at 372, referring to *Opp Cotton Mills Inc. v. Administrator, Wage and Hours Div. of Dept. of Labor*, 312 US 126, at 145. It is important to note that the case law of the EU courts, as will be shown below, also attaches equal importance to what it calls the "balance between the Institutions" and the duty of sincere cooperation between the EU institutions (and also with the State authorities of the Member States). See *supra* Chap. V.
23. *Ibid.*, at 372-373, quoting *American Power & Light Co. v. SEC*, 329 US 90 (1946), at 105.
24. *Lichter v. US*, 334 US 742 (1948).
25. *Yakus v. US*, 321 US 414 (1944).

"prevent unfair or inequitable distribution of voting power among security holders" – *American Power and Light* [26]; "upholding just and reasonable rates" in electricity pricing – *Hope* [27]; regulate broadcast licensing "as public interest, convenience, or necessity" require – *National Broadcast Corporation* [28]) that it makes one wonder whether the wartime period, including price controls, must have influenced the Supreme Court at the time to approve of all these delegations in the light of the *Hampton* criteria [29]. Another element may have been that some of these delegations were made to agencies with high expertise in their field, such as the Securities and Exchange Commission, the Federal Power Commission and the Federal Communications Commission. If anyone evenhandedly could say what was fair and equitable, just and reasonable, or would serve the public interest in these specialized domains, it was these institutions, which were supposed to be largely beyond direct political influence. However, none of these elements were put forward frankly by the Supreme Court in order to distinguish these cases from a case like *Hampton*, which was after all a bit more demanding than only the sobriquet "intelligible principle" would make one believe [30].

To the contrary, Blackmun continued with an easy rhetorical ploy:

"In the light of these broad delegations, we harbor no doubt that Congress' delegation of authority to the Sentencing Commission is sufficiently specific and detailed to meet constitutional requirements."

However, the Court next proceeded with a thorough vetting of the multiple and layered instructions and conditions that Congress imposed on the US Sentencing Commission in the exercise of its tasks. Moreover, in passing, the Court also recalled that, in its past case law, it was considered no objection that the delegated body, in the determination of the facts and the inferences to be drawn from them in the light of the statutory standards and declaration of policy, might need to exercise its judgment and to formulate subsidiary administrative policy within the

---

26. See *infra* footnote 23.
27. *Federal Power Commission* v. *Hope Natural Gas Co.*, 320 US 591 (1944).
28. *National Broadcast Corporation* v. *US*, 319 US 190 (1943).
29. Especially the *Lichter, Yakus and Hope* cases were closely linked to wartime price and other economic measures.
30. On this point, see the text following *supra* footnote 15 and also the dissent of Justice Gorsuch in *Gundy* v. *US*, 588 US__ Slip Op. at 16-18.

prescribed statutory framework [31]. The Court concluded by approvingly citing a lower court: "the Statute outlines the policies which prompted establishment of the Commission, explains what the Commission should do and how it should do it, and sets out particular directives to govern particular situations" [32]. And the Court goes on to conclude that "proportionate penalties for hundreds of different crimes by a virtually limitless array of offenders is precisely the sort of intricate, labor-intensive task for which delegation to an *expert* body is especially appropriate" [33]. And thus at least some importance is still given to the expertise of the delegated body at the very end in determining the fate of a controversial delegation of legislative power.

Since *Mistretta*'s attempted reconstitution of the (non-)delegation doctrine, a few other cases followed over the years, which did not fundamentally change anything, except that there was growing disenchantment from the originalist interpreters on the Court, such as Justices Scalia and Thomas, with the prevailing restrictive interpretation, but lax treatment of nondelegation [34]. With the successive arrivals of Justices Gorsuch, Kavanaugh and, lately, Coney Barrett on the Court, change might be in the offing. In the most recent (2019) nondelegation case, *Gundy* v. *US* [35], a plurality of the justices was able to maintain the traditional view of nondelegation. Justice Kagan wrote the opinion for the plurality and spent more arguments on the interpretation of the transitional provisions from the earlier patchwork of registration systems for sexual offenders to the new system under the Sexual Offenders Registration and Notification Act (SORNA) than on the actual question of whether these transitional provisions included an unconstitutional delegation of legislative powers by Congress to the executive power. Basically, the Court followed the same scheme as in *Mistretta*, referring back to *Hampton* and then briefly mentioning the same cases as listed in *Mistretta*, while adding the case of *Whitman*

---

31. Justice Scalia in his dissent agreed that "a certain degree of discretion and thus of lawmaking inheres in most executive or judicial action", *Mistretta, supra* footnote 30, at 417.
32. *Ibid.*, at 379.
33. *Ibid.*, at 379.
34. Further on that dissenting opinion and Justice Scalia's ambiguous objections to the majority's view of the nondelegation doctrine, see W. K. Kelley, "Justice Scalia, the Non-delegation Doctrine and Constitutional Argument", *Notre Dame L. Rev.*, Vol. 92 (2017), p. 2107 ff. However, he was the author of the Court's judgment in *Whitman, Administrator of the EPA* v. *American Trucking Association*, 531 US 457 [2001]. Thomas concurred in that judgment, while indicating that he did not agree with the Court's standard approach to nondelegation.
35. *Gundy* v. *US*, 588 US___ (2019).

v. *American Trucking Association* handed down in 2001 [36]. After that summing up, the conclusion was near-identical to the one in *Mistretta*: in the light of all these earlier decisions, SORNA easily passes muster [37]. The additional reference to *Whitman* is interesting because that case reveals in slightly greater detail why the Court believes that, except in two cases, it has felt unable to second-guess Congress when it set broad criteria for delegation to the executive or the judicial branch of government. Namely because in modern times it is often inevitable that certain aspects of laws need such a degree of technical detail and expertise in their implementation that the legislative branch cannot possibly take care of that beyond fairly general guidelines [38].

That is why Justice Kagan, approaching the end of her opinion for the Court and with an almost audible sigh, wrote:

> "Indeed if SORNA's delegation is unconstitutional, then most of government is unconstitutional – dependent as Congress is on the need to give discretion to executive officials to implement its programs." [39]

In itself that is probably true, but it also shows what political minefield delegation risks becoming in the future [40]. The strong dissent by Justice Gorsuch in the *Gundy* case may announce a change in the approach to delegation of the Supreme Court.

The whole edifice of case law created by the Supreme Court on (non-)delegation rests essentially on the separation of powers and the conviction that the clause of the Constitution vesting the legislative power in Congress in principle implies the impossibility of delegating

---

36. *Whitman*, *supra* footnote 34.
37. *Gundy* v. *US*, Slip op. 16.
38. *Whitman*, at 475. "[E]ven in sweeping regulatory schemes we have never demanded, as the Court of Appeals did here, that statutes provide a 'determinate criterion' for saying 'how much [of the regulated harm] is too much'." And the Supreme Court, referring to the other cases listed in *Mistretta*, continued "how imminent was too imminent", "how necessary was necessary enough", "how hazardous was "too hazardous" and, in the case of excess profits, "how much profit was enough?" Hence it was not constitutionally intolerable that the EPA (Environmental Protection Agency) was pushed by the relevant statute to make judgments of degree on air pollution, according to the Court, referring back to Justice Scalia's statement of the obvious in his dissent in *Mistretta*, see *supra* footnotes 31 and 32.
39. *Gundy* v. *US*, Slip op. 17.
40. A more restrictive approach to delegation in line with Justice Gorsuch's dissent is seen by many as a direct threat to many agencies and their tasks dating back to the New Deal. See E. Chemerinsky, "How the Roberts Court could alter the Administrative State", *ABA Journal*, 4 September 2019, retrieved at https://www.abajournal.com/news/article/chemerinsky-the-roberts-court-could-alter-the-administrative-state.

the legislative power to other organs inside or outside the US government, unless Congress is capable of writing clear conditions into a delegating law that strictly circumscribe the delegation. As indicated above, it is probably justified to reevaluate the precedent of *Hampton* and the words "intelligible principle" that have been made to bear too much weight in subsequent case law, while neglecting that the principle of *Hampton* was indeed easy to understand but at the same time very clear as an instruction from the legislator to the Tariff Commission, namely that tariffs had to be based on the difference between foreign and US costs of production [41]. It is probably necessary to do away with the phrase "intelligible principle" and to concentrate on what the Supreme Court actually looked at in the various delegation cases which it believed were acceptable. That might also stimulate the Court to look for better foundations for the expertise and depoliticization arguments that often underlie delegation to specialized government departments and to independent agencies.

B. France

1. A hard separation between the legislative and the regulatory domain

Until the proclamation of the Fifth Republic (1958), the legislative domain *(domaine de la loi)* was bounded by a purely formal criterion: anything adopted by Parliament and subsequently promulgated by the President was a law. With the advent of the Fifth Republic the legislative domain was defined not just by formal criteria but also

---

41. According to the "Gorsuch camp", greater vagueness is acceptable when the delegation falls within the field of foreign relations, since they are primarily within the President's remit under Article II of the Constitution and the President needs broad powers in that field. This is invariably accompanied by a reference to *US v. Curtiss-Wright Export Corp.*, 299 US 304 (1936). It should be noted that tariffs fall under "trade with foreign nations", which falls squarely within the power of Congress which, as we saw in *Hampton* above, delegated its powers in this field in large measure to the President and continues to do so under recurring so-called *fast track authorities* for bilateral and multilateral trade negotiations, often within the WTO framework. See "Notes: Nondelegation's Unprincipled Foreign Affairs Exceptionalism", *Harvard Law Review*, Vol. 134:1132:2001. The latest development in the Supreme Court's search for a new approach to the delegation of rulemaking to agencies may be foreshadowed by a number of judgments deciding not to vacate the suspension ordered by two lower courts of the so-called vaccine mandates provisionally imposed by the Departments of Labor's Occupational Safety and Health Administration (OSHA) on all employers with more than 100 employees. See *National Federation of independent business et al. v. Department of Labor, Occupational Safety and Health Administration et al.* and *Ohio et al. v. Department of Labor, Occupational Safety and Health Administration et al.*, issued on 13 January 2022.

by a substantive requirement [42]: the subjects that must be laid down by law are summed up in a long list in Article 34 of the Constitution (Const.). This is quite exceptional in Western European Constitutions. The Parliament, consisting of the House of Representatives and the Senate adopts the laws (Art. 24 Const.). Anything that does not fall in the legislative domain falls in the regulatory domain pursuant to Article 37 Const. *(domaine réglementaire)*. The power to adopt regulatory acts falls to the President only for the most important subjects (summed up in Art. 13 Const.) and to the Prime Minister for all other matters, but in practice all Cabinet members have acquired some regulatory powers related to their ministerial portfolios. A distinction is made between autonomous regulations and regulations adopted for the execution of the laws. The latter are promulgated pursuant to the power granted by Article 21 Const. to the Prime Minister and the ministers to execute the laws. For the former, mostly concerning the organization of State organs and procedures, no preexisting legal basis is required and they are directly enacted by the President or Prime Minister [43].

There is, therefore, a strong boundary between the legislative and the regulatory domain, which at first sight seems, fixed as it is in the Constitution, to be totally watertight. In reality, the legislative domain has been extended by so-called organic laws and constitutional laws, both of which need to follow a special procedure and special majorities be adopted. This was foreseen in the Constitution of 1958 itself, but the new Constitutional Council (Conseil Constitutionnel, hereinafter CC), also created by that Constitution, has by its case law further extended the legislative domain. It has developed a number of "constitutional values" *(valeurs constitutionnelles)* that are most often based on the famous Déclaration des droits de l'homme et du citoyen of 1789 and the Preamble to the Constitution of 1946, which contains human rights but also social rights – which was very progressive for that era [44]. These texts are explicitly referred to in the Preamble to the 1958

---

42. D. Chagnollaud de Sabouret and A. Baudu, *La Constitution de la Ve République*, 9th ed., Paris, Dalloz, 2019, p. 269 ff. and B. Plessix, *Droit administratif général*, 3rd ed., Paris, LexisNexis, 2020, p. 765 ff. and 1500 ff. The following is broadly based on these sources and a search of the case law of the Constitutional Court on its easily accessible and searchable website.

43. *Ibid.*, at p. 290 ff. An example of an autonomous regulation concerning the organization of State organs is the *ordonnance* of 7 November 1958 containing the organic law on the Conseil Constitutionnel.

44. On the basis of this Preamble the Constitutional Court developed the category of "Fundamental Principles recognized by the Laws of the Republic", such as the respect

Constitution [45]. Moreover, the Charter of the Environment *(Charte de l'Environnement)* was adopted as a constitutional law in 2005 and was soon afterward recognized by the CC as having constitutional value [46]. These developments show that the CC has considerably widened the scope of its terrain of action. Moreover, since 2008 the Court's jurisdiction is no longer limited to cases of *a priori* control of specific categories of laws between the high institutions of the State but has been extended to so-called Constitutional Priority Questions (*Questions Prioritaires de Constitutionalité*, or QPC), which are addressed to it by the administrative and civil courts through respectively the *Conseil d'Etat* (Council of State) and the *Cour de Cassation* (Court of Cassation), the highest courts in each domain. In this way, individuals and companies have acquired access to the CC, which thus has arrived as a true constitutional court [47].

2. The Conseil Constitutionnel and the separation between the two domains

The CC watches over the separation between the legislative and regulatory domains, as laid down in Articles 34 and 37 of the Constitution. Below follows a brief overview of the most important case law on this subject. This case law often cannot but concentrate on the question whether or not an act of the Parliament or the government falls in the legislative domain as defined by Article 34 Const., since anything that does not automatically fall in the regulatory domain. However, since what belongs to the legislative domain is defined *ratione materiae*

---

of the rights of the defense, the right of personal liberty and the liberty of conscience, the freedom of education, etc.

45. Sometimes these "constitutional values" can be derived only indirectly from these texts (for instance, the equal access of men and women to civil service jobs and political appointments is derived from the equality between the sexes), sometimes they are rooted deeply in French social and educational traditions (like the *laïcité*), and finally, they may be almost self-evident (for instance, certain fundamental procedural rights).

46. This encompasses, *inter alia*, the duty to prevent pollution and to pay for the damage, the precautionary principle, the access to information and the promotion of sustainable development.

47. It has helped that the composition of the CC has evolved from a club of former Presidents of the Republic and other former politicians, few with serious academic knowledge of constitutional law, most with only limited practical knowledge of the matter, to a real college, in which former Presidents wisely do not occupy their seats any longer and legal expertise is clearly valued, and where recently the initially excessively apodictic style of deciding cases has given way to well-argued judgments, most of which can be understood by the average, educated French citizen.

only (the subject question), the CC cannot escape a second question as well, namely what part of all the subject matters of government listed in Article 34 should be reserved to a law adopted by Parliament and what can be left to regulations enacted by the government pursuant to its Article 21 authority to execute the laws (the quality question). Article 34 does not contain any indications on this second question and the CC's reactions to that question are therefore just as much judge-made law as the judgments of the US Supreme Court discussed above.

Two early cases decided by the CC at the end of 1959 made the distinction between the legislative domain and the regulatory domain (as a quality question) immediately clear as being globally a matter of principles versus details. They also made clear that the government would normally act as protector of the regulatory domain, as it was in both cases the Prime Minister who initiated the procedure before the CC to this end.

The first case concerned the legislation on the RATP, an abbreviation that any tourist who has ever traveled on the Paris metros or buses knows well. This is a public enterprise and Article 34 of the Constitution put the founding of such enterprises in the legislative domain. Obviously, it has a rather special character, given that its network covers many towns and villages around Paris proper, which all need to be represented in some way on its *conseil d'administration* (governing board). This representation itself was a question of principle, which should be laid down in a law within the meaning of Article 34 of the Constitution. How many members that board should have and how they should be divided among the different municipalities of the wider Parisian region, to the contrary, in the eyes of the CC was a question of detail and should be laid down in a *réglement*[48].

A judgment of the same date related to a proposal of a law, put forward by two Senators, concerned the method of how land rents for agricultural land should be calculated: by reference to wheat yield per hectare only, or by a combination of the yield of wheat and other agricultural products. This proposed law also aimed to set aside the government regulation that already existed, since in the Senators' view the government could not interfere by decree in the methodology of calculating the level of land rents, as this was contrary to the right to property and/or the freedom of contract. Therefore, a law was necessary. The CC did not agree. The interference in the price setting

---

48. Decision No. 59-1 L, 27 November 1959, at paras. 2 and 3.

between individuals remained very limited and was particularly well suited to land rents. Moreover, it merely modified one aspect of one of the elements which had always served to calculate land rents in earlier government decrees on this matter and did not amount to a fundamental change in the basic principles relating to fixing the level of land rents. Hence, they were and remained in the regulatory domain and making a law on this matter was unconstitutional [49].

Another early case that shed light on the boundary between laws and regulatory measures concerned a delegation foreseen in the organic law on judicial organization, which was subject to the CC's *ex ante* control of the constitutionality of such laws with a special rank in the French constitutional system, called *organic laws*. It turned out that the fundamental provision on the irrevocability of judges, laid down in Article 64 Const., was repeated in the proposed organic law and expanded to include the right of a fully qualified judge to refuse even a transfer that amounted to a promotion. There was an exception foreseen for judges who served as counselors to the judges of the *Cour de Cassation* and who, after a maximum of ten years, could be moved to another post in the Court system, according to further rules to be laid down in a government decree on the French public administration. The CC reacted emphatically to what it saw as a breach of the Constitution. How to reconcile the fundamental principle of the irrevocability of judges with the reasonable idea that judges assisting the *Cour de Cassation* should not do this for longer than ten years? This should be laid down in the organic law itself and not in some government decree [50]. The CC was not specific on which provision of the Constitution was breached here, Article 64 on the irrevocability of judges or Article 34 on the scope of the legislative domain. That matters little, however, given the clarity with which the CC drew a line between what belongs in an (organic) law and what in a decree.

A decision of 1975 [51] shows that the CC can also conclude that the legislative domain, of which matters of criminal procedure are an integral part pursuant to Article 34 Const., can be adversely affected by a decision of the legislative power to leave to another authority – *in casu* a judicial authority – a decision touching such a fundamental matter as the equality of citizens before the law. A new provision in the law on criminal procedure charged the President of the *Tribunal*

---
49. Decision No. 59-1 FNR, 27 November 1959, at paras. 4 and 5.
50. Decision No. 67-31 DC, 26 February 1967, at paras. 3 and 4.
51. Decision No. 75-56 DC, 23 July 1975.

de Grande Instance with deciding freely and without appeal in all cases coming under the jurisdiction of the lower criminal courts *(tribunaux correctionnels)*, whether to allocate cases to judges sitting alone or to tribunals of three. According to the CC this could lead to cases coming before either a single judge or a tribunal of three, even if they were highly similar. This was incompatible with the principle of equality before justice, which is part and parcel of equality before the law. The latter principle is included in the *Déclaration des droits de l'homme et du citoyen* (Declaration of the Rights of Man and the Citizen), which was adopted by the Constituante (Assembly) during the revolution in August 1789 and solemnly reaffirmed by the Preamble to the Constitution of 1958 [52]. Thus there was, also in this case, a double breach of the Constitution: of Article 34 by an attempted illegal escape from the *domaine de la loi* by delegation to the judiciary (presumably without setting any standards for the decision to be taken by that branch of government), and also of a fundamental right, equality before the law, as reconfirmed in the Preamble to the Constitution.

What happens if the legislator impinges upon the regulatory realm without meeting any resistance from the government [53]? In that case the "absolute" nature of the boundary between the legislative and regulatory domains has to be analyzed in the context of two other relevant articles of the Constitution, which give the government the possibility to oppose such a trespass of the legislative power on the regulatory domain, according to the CC. First, Article 41 Const. gives the government or the President of either the Assembly or the Senate the possibility to oppose any provision of a proposal or any amendment that in their opinion does not belong in the legislative domain. In case of lack of agreement between the government and the President of the relevant assembly, the question will be decided by the CC within a week. Second, even after adoption of the contested provision, the President of the Republic can start a so-called procedure for *déclassement* of (parts of) the contested law before the CC under Article 37 (2) Const., by which the law can be declared in part or in whole to fall in the regulatory domain [54]. If the government fails to use either of these two procedures, which are

---

52. *Ibid.*, at paras. 3-6.
53. Decision No. 82-143 DC, 30 July 1982.
54. These cases on *déclassement* occur with great regularity – Chagnollaud de Sabouret and Baudu, *supra* footnote 42, have counted 277 such cases between 1959 and 2019 – and are treated usually without much reasoning along the lines of the first cases discussed above. Two recent examples are Decision No. 2020-228 L and Decision No. 2021-293 L.

not obligatory, it loses the right to plead the illegality of the legislator impinging on the regulatory domain. Therefore, the boundary between the two domains is not as impermeable as all that [55].

What happens if the legislator (or the government) does not fully use its power or has a mistaken view of its own power, considering it narrower than it is [56]? This is called "negative incompetence" *(incompétence négative)* [57] in French public law, and occurs when the legislator delegates an aspect of a law to the government or the judiciary which it should have reserved to itself [58]. To give an example: the General Tax Code *(Code général des impôts)* delegated the task of determining the deadlines, within which certain deductions from the VAT had to be made, to the government, acting by decree *(ordonnance)* and subject to control by the Conseil d'Etat. The Kimberly Clark company considered that this decree was affected by negative incompetence, briefly after the jurisdiction of the CC had been extended to QPCs [59]. It argued that this was contrary to Article 14 of the 1789 Declaration of the Rights of Man and the Citizen and that fixing the deductions from the VAT could not be left to a government decree. This article read:

> "All citizens have the right to ascertain, by themselves, or through their representatives, the need for a public tax, to consent to it freely, to watch over its use, and to determine its proportion, basis, collection and duration."

In its decision, the CC first determined that natural or moral persons could only successfully complain of a failure by the legislature to exercise its competence in case a constitutional right or a freedom appertaining to them had been affected thereby. This was not the case, since Article 14 of the 1789 Declaration may speak of the citizens, but from legal historical research it could be deduced that this referred rather to the representatives of the citizens; that is, to Parliament [60].

---

55. Decision No. 82-143 DC, 30 July 1982, at para. 11.
56. Both aspects are present in the French term *méconnaissance*, as in "méconnaissance de son propre pouvoir".
57. In contrast to *incompétence positive*, which occurs when an authority goes beyond the limits of its powers.
58. Decision No. 75-56 DC is already an example of such an *incompétence negative*, see *supra* footnote 52 and accompanying text.
59. Decision No. 2010-5 QPC Kimberly Clark, 18/6 2010, at para. 2.
60. *Ibid.*, at para. 4. Much of this cannot be found in para. 4 but only in Commentaire de la décision no. 2010-5 QPC, in *Les Cahiers du Conseil constitutionnel No. 29*. In the early days of the QPC, the staff of the CC in this way provided much of the underlying arguments for its decisions to the general public. Now that the CC has

Hence Article 14's function in 1789 is nowadays assured by Article 34 Const., which ensures that taxes and everything pertaining to it belong to the *domaine de la loi* and thus Kimberly Clark could not pretend to be protected by Article 14 of the 1789 Declaration [61].

Two years later, after a similar decision on the protection that the Constitution should provide for special systems of social security [62], the floodgates began to open and the cases on *incompétence négative* became frequent also in the domain of QPC. They evolved more and more beyond the original idea behind this action, namely that the legislator had not cared to exercise the fullness of its powers and thereby had encouraged others (the executive, the judges, local authorities or even private individuals or companies) to enter the legislative domain and assume the mantle of the lawgiver. There were quite some indications that the CC was binding up *incompétence négative* inextricably (not to say, confusing it) with such notions as the protection of acquired rights, the upholding of minimum standards of good legislation (sanctioning "vagueness", lack of accessibility of the law, lack of the necessary guidelines to the executive or to the judicial branch, when delegating tasks to them, etc.) [63]. Let us leave to one side for now the question whether the CC is improving its ways in response to internal and outside criticism of having made of the *incompétence négative* an almost meaningless container concept [64], and turn to an

---

proved increasingly willing to be more elaborate in its decisions, this may be no longer necessary.

61. And, one might add, Kimberly Clark could not have been protected by Article 34 either, since that article does not exactly read as a provision for the protection of natural and moral persons. Perhaps the question of *compétence négative* should remain reserved to cases between the different branches of government and should not have been transplanted to the QPC procedure. More on this in: Ariane Vidal-Naquet, "L'état de la jurisprudence du Conseil constitutionnel sur l'incompétence négative", *Nouveaux Cahiers du Conseil constitutionnel No. 46 (Incompétence et droit constitutionnel)*, 7-20 January 2015, https://www.conseil-constitutionnel.fr/nouveaux-cahiers-du-conseil-constitutionnel/l-etat-de-la-jurisprudence-du-conseil-constitutionnel-sur-l-incompetence-negative, consulted 25 April 2021.

62. Decision No. 2012-254 QPC, 18 June 2012.

63. See on this, Vidal-Naquet, *supra* footnote 61. Decision No. 75-56, discussed above, can also be interpreted as an example of this confusion.

64. Vidal-Naquet, *supra* footnote 61, uses the telling French term *fourre-tout* in this connection. The most interesting implication of the doctrine of *incompétence négative*, especially in QPC actions by moral and natural persons, is that it may bring about a duty to legislate in relation to citizens. This is unknown in most constitutional systems in Western Europe, except in very exceptional situations, for instance when the government does not fulfill its duty of care under human rights law derived from the European Convention on Human Rights in respect of groups of people or even the people as a whole, cf. the *Urgenda* litigation on climate change, *Staat der Nederlanden v. Urgenda*, ECLI:NL:HR:2019:2006. Note that the *Hoge Raad* gave the State some

area where the *domaine de la loi* and the *domaine réglementaire* have been intermingled on purpose by the French Constitution, namely in its Article 38.

3. Article 38 of the Constitution: Legislative regulations

Article 38 Const. grants the government the power, with a view to the implementation of its program, to request Parliament to authorize the executive to adopt measures, which would normally fall in the legislative domain, by promulgating regulations *(ordonnances)* for a limited period of time. The government proposes the authorization and is the intended beneficiary of it. The regulations based on the authorization are to be adopted by the Council of Ministers, after advice from the Conseil d'Etat, and enter into force immediately. They must contain a deadline within which the government will present the so-called ratification law to Parliament and expire automatically if the government does not respect its self-imposed deadline (which may be prolonged by a new request to Parliament)[65]. Step by step the procedure proceeds as follows. First, the government proposes the so-called habilitation law *(loi d'habilitation)* to Parliament. Once that law is adopted, the government, within a deadline set in the habilitation law, adopts one or more *ordonnances*, dependent on what it asked for in the habilitation law. These are published and enter into force immediately. The last step is the presentation to Parliament of the "ratification law" within the self-set deadline proposed by the government in the habilitation law[66]. The two laws at the beginning and at the end of the procedure are true laws; they fall within the *domaine de la loi*. The *ordonnance(s)* in the middle, however, fall(s) fully within the *domaine réglementaire* for as long as they are *ordonnances*[67]. Once "ratified",

---

choice of means to achieve 25 percent reduction of greenhouse gases by 2020, but legislation was not excluded.

65. Chagnollaud de Sabouret and Baudu, *supra* footnote 42, at p. 296 have signaled that in reality many statutory instruments based on Article 38 have never been ratified. Note that only the government may propose the "habilitation" and "ratification" laws.

66. A "ratification law", for some time, was not the exclusive instrument by which the conversion of the *ordonnance* under Article 38 Const. into a law must take place. The wish to "ratify" such an instrument could also be expressed in a broader law, as long as this intention is clearly expressed by Parliament, see CC Decision No. 72-73 L, at para. 3 *in fine*. However, a constitutional law would seem to have put an end to this "implicit ratification" and inserted the requirement of an explicit ratification at the end of the second para. of Article 38. See D. Chagnollaud de Sabouret and Baudu, *supra* footnote 42, at pp. 301-303.

67. CC Decision No. 72-73 L, beginning of para. 3. Note that the *ordonnances* remain in force as long as a proposal for their conversion into law is pending; this

the *ordonnance(s)* formally become law in their entirety, at least as long as Parliament does not amend them in the process. However, there may be provisions of these new laws that do not fall in the domain of Article 34 and therefore ought to come under Article 37 *(domaine réglementaire)*. *De iure* this effect is automatic, but the government still needs to activate the procedure of *déclassement* – mentioned earlier – in respect of such provisions [68]. One author has characterized the constant flow of procedures of *déclassement* as the "controlled fluctuations" in the division of powers between law and regulation [69] – that is to say, better controlled than in the so-called decree-laws *(décrets-lois)* during the Third Republic, when this way of legislating was legal, but much maligned, and under the Fourth Republic, when *décrets-lois* were prohibited by the Constitution but nevertheless practiced in other forms [70]. In the new guise of Article 38 Const., the Parliament does not merely authorize the government to make, within a limited time span, *ordonnances* having the force of law, but after the initial authorization, must have reconfirmed them into law within a certain deadline, with the possibility of amendments both from the government and the Parliament. In this way, the government is held to two deadlines and the Parliament has two votes, on the habilitation law and on the ratification law. Thus one may hope that there are sufficient safeguards built into the procedure to avoid a renewed abuse of the delegation of legislative powers to the government [71].

The crucial instrument in the sequence is the habilitation law. That law is most often contested before the CC, initially by the Parliament and, after QPC, also by natural and moral persons. It falls to the CC once again to judge whether the habilitation law fulfills all the conditions explicitly or implicitly laid down in Article 38 Const. The most obvious

---

means that when the deadline for conversion set in the habilitation law is so near that it risks expiring, a new draft ratification law may be filed to keep the *ordonnances* alive for another period. Nevertheless, many *ordonnances* expire peacefully at this moment.

68. See *supra* footnote 54 and accompanying text.

69. M. Verpeaux, "Les ordonnances de l'article 38 ou les fluctuations contrôlées de la répartition des compétences entre la loi et le règlement", in *Cahiers du Conseil constitutionnel No. 19*, January 2006, https://www.conseil-constitutionnel.fr/decisions-de-nomination/les-ordonnances-de-l-article-38-ou-les-fluctuations-controlees-de-la-repartition-des-competences, last consulted 26 April 2021.

70. Plessix, *supra* footnote 42, at p. 784.

71. But there are worrying signs again, such as the increased recourse to including delegations through *ordonnances* in normal legislation instead of proposing a separate habilitation law under Article 38, thus avoiding the scrutiny in advance of the Conseil d'Etat foreseen in that article. See Chagnollaud de Sabouret and Baudu, *supra* footnote 42, at p. 297.

condition is that the proposal for a habilitation law must be linked to the implementation of the program of the government. When the CC got to rule on this question in 1976, it rejected a link with Article 49 Const., where the terms "program of the government" and "general political declaration" of the government were used in connection with the government obtaining a vote of confidence from the majority of Parliament. The CC felt that relying on such a link would leave no room for recourse to Article 38 for unforeseen circumstances and other situations requiring urgent measures and that, moreover, there was a risk that a reference to the government's program might be too broad [72]. It therefore stated that the first paragraph of Article 38 should be understood to impose on the government an obligation to indicate with precision, at the moment of putting a proposal for a habilitation law before Parliament, what the objective is it will be pursuing thereby [73].

Over the years the CC developed this notion into a formula that by 1999 read as follows:

"[Even] if Article 38, first paragraph, imposes on the government an obligation to indicate with precision, at the moment of putting a proposal for a habilitation law before Parliament, what the objective is of the measures it is seeking to take by way of *ordonnances,* as well as their field of application, that provision does not oblige the government to let Parliament know [already] the broad contents of the *ordonnances* that it will take on the basis of this habilitation." [74]

This formula has been repeated many times since then with slight variations [75] and can be found again in recent cases relating to urgent measures taken by *ordonnance* under Article 38 in relation to the Covid-19 pandemic [76]. In these cases the formula is followed immediately by explanations from the CC, which seem to have been

---

72. Decision No. 76-72, at para. 3.
73. *Ibid.*, at para. 2.
74. Decision No. 99/421 DC, at para. 12, translation by the author. It should be noted in passing that this decision also accepts that urgency in itself can be a (partial) justification for recourse to the procedure of Article 38.
75. A quick perusal of the relevant decisions of the CC yielded the following nonexhaustive list of cases: 2003-473 DC; 2004-506 DC; 2006-189 DC; 2008-373 DC; 2010-618 DC; 201 -687 DC; 2015-710 DC; 2016-732 DC; and four other recent cases mentioned in the text.
76. Decision No. 2020-851/852 QPC (Sofiane A. et autre. Habilitation à prolonger la durée des détentions provisoires dans un contexte d'urgence sanitaire), at para. 8; Decision No. 2020-808 DC (loi autorisant la prorogation de l'état d'urgence sanitaire), at paras. 28-29.

inspired by didactic considerations, to the effect that the recourse to the procedure of Article 38 Const. does neither by itself nor by the consequences that follow from it necessarily imply a breach of a rule or principle with constitutional value. Moreover, it could not have the objective or the effect of freeing the government, in its exercise of the powers that are conferred on it by the recourse to Article 38, from respecting the rules and principles with constitutional value. Only the reasoning, by which the CC then sets out why in the individual cases the requirement that the government explain fully the objectives of the measures sought by it and the domain(s) of their application are satisfied or not, still differs widely in thoroughness. It varies between extremes of the old-fashioned apodictic affirmation that this is simply the case [77] and (fairly) elaborate arguments, which are so precisely geared to the case in point that they do not seem to represent a particularly consistent trend in the case law [78].

The delegation of legislative powers as foreseen in Article 38 of the Constitution of 1958 seems to have functioned quite well and has been kept well within its boundaries by the Conseil Constitutionnel. Recently (since the 1990s), however, there has been a considerable increase in the frequency of the government's recourse to this instrument [79], and this has led to increasing numbers of cases brought before the CC by groups of MPs who have complained of abuses of the procedure and of having too little time to verify all the ratification laws presented and to debate them with the requisite seriousness [80]. It has been pointed out that the growing recourse to Article 38 is caused by three problems: reorganizing the status and government of French Polynesia and New Caledonia; pressure for quick progress with codification activities that will improve the accessibility and clarity of the law; and arrears with implementing EU directives [81]. These are certainly very necessary and laudable goals, which at a certain moment will be reached, when arrears with codification and implementation of EU directives will have been eliminated, and the status and government structure of the French

---

77. Decision No. 2017-752 (loi pour la confiance dans la vie politique), at para. 77.
78. Decision No. 2017-751 (loi pour le renforcement du dialogue social), *passim*; Decision No. 2020-851/852 QPC (Sofiane A et autre), *supra* footnote 76, at para. 10 ff.
79. See Chagnollaud de Sabouret and Baudu, *supra* footnote 42, at p. 296, which mention figures, for example that in the ten years from 2004 to 2013 the government had recourse to the article 38,257 times, i.e. 2.3 times as often in the preceding twenty years.
80. *Ibid.*
81. Plessix, *supra* footnote 42, at pp. 787-788.

Pacific will have been placed on an even keel. It also shows that speed of enactment has indeed become a major element in the government decision to have recourse to Article 38.

From the overview of the French law on delegation laid out above, it is clear that the French Constitutional Court had more support in the text of the Constitution than the US Supreme Court. Nevertheless, on the qualitative question, when in the fields covered by Article 34 Const. a measure falls in the legislative or the regulatory domain, the CC largely had to find its own way, broadly based on a distinction between the principal aspects and the less important details of a legal regime. This is not a very surprising criterion. More surprising is that the CC, based on the strict division between legislative and regulatory domains, developed the idea of negative incompetence of the legislator, in cases in which the legislator had not fully occupied the legislative space relating to an Art. 34 subject and thus also made it more difficult for the government to produce appropriate decrees without sufficient legislative guidance and/or to avoid invading the legislative domain. But the legal logic behind this approach falls partially away if one reminds oneself, once again, that the exclusivity of the legislative domain in Article 34 is based on the different terrains of government activity *(ratione materiae)* alone, and not on the qualitative distinction between legislation and regulation. It is perhaps in relation to that problem that the CC has started to mix up the choice between legislation and regulation with questions related to where fundamental rights, the rule of law and other basic requirements of good legislation belong to be decided: in regulations or legislation [82]? The answer to that question is self-evident, namely in legislation, but cannot be found on the basis of the text of Article 34 Const.

Where Article 38 Const. is concerned, the transfer of legislative power from the Parliament to the executive is, in the final analysis, only transitory, between the habilitation law and the "ratification" of a decree-law. Especially the second parliamentary check on the proposed decree-law, gives the CC the leeway to be not too demanding on the precision of the habilitation law starting the process.

---

82. See *supra* footnote 63 and accompanying text. What seems confusion now may still develop into a more elaborate integration between the interpretation of Article 38 Const. and the elements that in the view of the CC determine France's existence as an *état de droit* comparable to the development in the case law of the German Constitutional Court on Article 80 of the German Constitution; see *infra* footnote 120 and accompanying text.

48   Pieter Jan Kuijper

C. Italy

1. Article 76 of the Italian Constitution: Delegation of the legislative function

In Italy, Article 70 of the Constitution of 1948 *(Costituzione italiana)* (Cost.) allocates the legislative power to the two Chambers of Parliament (the Senate and the Chamber of Representatives)[83]. Article 76 Cost. explicitly states that the exercise of the legislative function cannot be delegated to the government unless the delegating law lays down the principles and criteria that should drive that delegation, and even then, only for a limited period and for well-defined objectives[84]. It is clear that the intention of these provisions is to let Parliament keep control of the legislative power, even at a distance. And even without giving an exhaustive listing of matters that fall under the legislative power, as Article 34 of the French Constitution does, by implication all the rest is seen as belonging to the regulatory domain. In what the French constitutional system regards as the domain of regulation *(domaine de réglementation)*, in the Italian system the executive clearly has the upper hand. According to Article 89 of the Constitution, ministers alone or together write ministerial decrees in their area of competence, which are promulgated by signature of the President and the minister(s) concerned. The decree-laws of Article 76 (and 77) Cost. need the signature of the President and the Prime Minister. This double signature is also necessary for other decrees that are based on a law. This last category of decrees is comparable to the French decrees for the execution of the laws based on Article 21 Const. However, the further discussion will concentrate on Article 76 Cost.[85].

---

83. This section is principally based on R. Nevola and D. Diaco, *Delega della funzione legislativa nella giurisprudenza costituzionale*, Corte Costituzionale, Servizio studi 2018, https://www.cortecostituzionale.it/documenti/convegni_seminari/stu_309.pdf, last consulted 28 April 2021. It consists of an introduction of twenty pages, "Premessa" (pp. 7-27) and over 600 pages of long fragments of the case law of the Corte Costituzionale on Article 76 of the Constitution, logically arranged into different chapters. I am very grateful to the two authors, since their collection of the relevant material up to 2018 has enabled me to choose the cases discussed below on the basis of their selection and to revert to the full text of each case on the website of the CCost. for further study: https://www.cortecostituzionale.it/actionPronuncia.do.

84. The second exception to the Parliament's exclusive power to legislate is laid down in Article 77 on decree-laws, but that exception is clearly limited to emergency measures and will not be further discussed here. Note, however, that the first para. of that article confirms that the government cannot issue a decree having the force of law without an enabling act from both houses of Parliament.

85. It should be noted that this category of decrees in principle does not fall within the jurisdiction of the CCost., according to Article 134 Cost. That explains why there

Although Article 38 Const. and Article 76 Cost. look very much like each other – for instance, both articles leave no doubt that only the government can be the proposer and the recipient of the legislative delegation. There are, however, important differences. Article 76 provides for a two-step procedure: the Parliament, at the initiative of the government, proposes a delegating law and, after its adoption, the government produces the delegated law (formally a decree which has the force of law), which will expire after a certain period. The middle stage in the French procedure – when the government produces an *ordonnance*, which needs to be adopted by Parliament as law before the date set in the delegating law, and is immediately in force – is absent [86]. The delegating law follows the normal legislative procedure, as is explicitly confirmed in Article 72 (4) Cost. Article 76 Cost. is clearly presented as one of only two exceptions to the normal reservation of the exercise of legislative power to Parliament, but the permitted delegation is – even a bit more explicit than in Article 38 Const. – one of normal legislative power. In Article 76 Cost. there is no indication that the delegated law is in any way formally different from the delegating law, even if the prescriptions contained in the delegating law have to be followed. The nature of the prescriptions has been laid down, with a certain clarity, in the constitutional article itself, whereas in the case of Article 38 Const. it was the CC that had to give substance to very meager indications in that article. The Italian *Corte Costituzionale* (CCost.) clearly had more indications to work with than the French CC: the delegating law has to contain specified purposes, for which principles and criteria have to be established, and an expiration date has to be set. The delegated law is time-limited, unlike the law resulting from the procedure of Article 38 Const., but on the other hand it remains a product of the executive alone and the Parliament does not adopt it.

---

is hardly any case law of the CCost. on the question whether such decrees might have crossed the line into the legislative domain. The author is indebted to Dr Riccardo Evola for confirmation of this view. It cannot be excluded that there are such cases that have been decided in the lower courts, but it proved impracticable to extend the research that far.

86. Urgency is, in principle, not an element that plays a role in Article 76; that is left to Article 77. Nevertheless, it is well known that in practice the procedure of Article 76 is often used to implement EU directives with a view to respecting an (urgent) implementing deadline, just as Article 38 Const in France. Also comparable to the French situation is the recourse to the procedure of Article 76 for codification and similar purposes.

2. Early case law of the Corte Costituzionale on the delegation of legislative power

In the early days of the case law of the CCost. concerning Article 76 Cost, the Court was still preoccupied by basic questions about the relation between the delegating and the delegated law and its own role as the purveyor of constitutionality tests. In a 1957 case, which concerned the question whether an accountant could inscribe himself in more than one professional register – which was forbidden in a new provision in a delegated law – the CCost. gave short shrift to the accountant's allegations that this was contrary to Articles 3 Cost. (equality before the law) and 4 Cost. (right to work and hold a job corresponding to one's choice and ability), but dwelled a bit longer on the question whether the delegated law as such might be unconstitutional [87]. This was necessary because if the delegating law and the decree carrying the delegated law were to be seen respectively as a normal law and a special kind of implementing decree, or as two successive laws of equal rank, it could be argued that such a situation was a normal public law problem that would not fall under the jurisdiction of the CCost., but under that of the normal courts [88]. The CCost. rejected this view: the delegating law had to be in conformity with the requirements mentioned in Article 76 and the delegated decree-law in turn had to be in conformity with the delegating law and with other constitutional prescriptions as well. This was the expression of the ground rule that the Parliament alone was the legislator in the Italian constitutional system. The CCost. thus considered that it was competent to rule on the question of the constitutionality of the delegated act and, on the basis of a simple analysis of the provisions of the delegating and delegated acts, it concluded that the delegating law contained the necessary principles and criteria, as well as a clear objective, and that the delegated law was in harmony therewith [89].

As far as the delegating law is concerned, not only does it need to respect the criteria mentioned in Article 76 Cost. and thus, by setting the objective for the delegation and by laying down the principles and the criteria that the government has to follow, firmly and clearly circumscribe how far the government can go. It should also avoid broad

---

87. Sentenza 3/1957 (rel. Gabrieli). NB. Early judgments of the Italian Corte Costituzionale do not yet have numbered paragraphs.
88. The jurisdiction of the CCost. is restricted to assuring the conformity with the Constitution of any law and any instrument having the power of law, according to Article 134 of Cost. The delegated act falls clearly within the latter category of instruments having the power of law.
89. Sentenza 3/1957, *supra* footnote 87.

general statements and should not give guidelines that are unhelpful to the delegated legislator (i.e. the government or specific government authority). On the other hand, it must leave the authority to which it has delegated powers a certain room for maneuver and even a certain level for discretion in the way it wants to implement the delegation granted by Parliament.

A delegating law cannot eliminate all room for choice in the exercise of the delegation [90]. This is considered important in the case law of the CCost. and we will return to this rather specific concern. In practice a lot seems to depend on the subject matter of the delegation and the context into which the delegation is going to be embedded. Some delegations are used, for instance, to transpose a whole group of EU directives into Italian law and can be very broad, which the CCost. accepts. At the same time, however, the Court puts the government on notice that, insofar as penal sanctions are needed for implementing the directives, the delegating legislation should be as specific and clear as possible [91].

In another context, the CCost. accepts the near total absence of the principles and criteria that Article 76 Cost. demands for a delegating law because the delegation aims to integrate certain measures into a sector of the law that needs to be adapted to, in the case in question, the new rules of criminal procedure. In such situations the stated objective speaks for itself and is sufficient [92]. The context in which the delegated law has to function can count for a lot. For instance, in a case on delegation relating to rules for limits to the length of television publicity spots, the lower court had stated that the delegated act was totally innovative, not justified by any express provision or implicit motive contained in the delegating act. The CCost., in contrast, was quite prepared to refer to an EU directive (and a judgment of the EU Court of Justice relating to it), to which the delegating act did not refer explicitly, but in the light of which elements that were present in that act could be interpreted and made sense of [93].

3. Special question of subdelegation of legislative power

Precisely because the Italian approach to delegation attaches relatively more importance to the delegating and delegated laws both

---
90. See Ordinanza 8/1999 (red. Marini) and Sentenza 107/2017 (red. Cartabia) at para. 3.1.
91. Sentenza 53/1997 (red. Onida), at para. 3.
92. Sentenza 299/1993 (red. Greco), at para. 3.
93. Sentenza 210/2015 (red. Amato), at para. 5.3.

being laws in the formal sense [94], even if the government adopts the latter by decree, subdelegation seems to be less of a problem than in other regimes of delegation discussed in this chapter. The delegating law can charge the delegated legislator with devolving to a lower level of government the power to further develop norms laid down in that delegating law. Sometimes such norms have already been given greater precision in the delegated law. As long as such subdelegations are of a technical nature and remain within the parameters set by the delegating and delegated acts, they are acceptable [95].

This problem has arisen in at least two cases. The first was one in which the regions claimed the right to be informed of the implementation of complicated multilevel procedures setup for issuing permits for selecting sites and for the actual construction of nuclear electricity generating plants. The second concerned the broad reorganization of the chambers of commerce throughout Italy. How far down in the decision-making chain had the regions the right to intervene? Should they also be heard down to the level of subdelegation, where interministerial decrees are made? That seemed unlikely, and hence the regions' position that subdelegation was not in conformity with Article 76 Cost.

In the procedure on the delegation concerning permits for nuclear plant construction, the CCost. cites extensively from the text of an article in the delegated law in order to show that it was already quite detailed on the requirements that the operators of nuclear installations had to fulfill in respect of their technical and professional qualities, also in respect of security. Moreover, the operators needed to show that they had the necessary human and financial resources to be devoted to the planning, construction and exploitation of the installation, including stocking and managing its nuclear waste, as well as being capable of following the recommendations of International Atomic Energy Agency. Given these detailed directives in the delegated law, it was clear in the mind of the Court that the subdelegation to an interministerial decree could only go into further detail on all these requirements, which is exactly as it should be. Hence the subdelegation was acceptable to the CCost. [96].

This was later presented as standing case law in the procedure concerning the reorganization of the chambers of commerce, even though it was arguable that the latter case left a wider mandate for subdelegation to the level of an interministerial decree than the first

---

94. Sentenza 3/1957, *supra* footnote 87.
95. Sentenza 261/2017 (red. Barbera), at para. 11.1.1.
96. Sentenza 33/2011 (red. De Siervo), at 6.3.1.3.

one. The mandate for subdelegation merely mentioned the possible development of "criteria for the redefinition" of the territorial boundaries between different chambers of commerce, without much more precision than that [97].

4. *Margin of maneuver of the (sub)delegated authorities*

However, it is quite possible that for subdelegation one should apply the same approach that was already approved by the CCost. in 1993 for the application of Article 76 to the first level of delegation, namely that a delegating law did not need to be so detailed that the criteria imposed on the delegated authority were, so to say, *autoapplicativa* (self-applying), but that the Parliament could merely impose on the delegated authority a criterion that was strongly goal-oriented *("un criterio a valenza essenzialmente finalistica")*, which would be better in line with the normal approach of leaving a certain discretion to the (delegated) legislator[98]. In the same vein the CCost. stated in an order of 1988 that a delegation is not intended to remove from the delegated legislator any margin for exercising its own discretion, but merely to circumscribe it [99]. In more modern terms the delegated legislator should not just carry out a scan of the terms of the delegating law *("una scansione linguistica")* in drafting its delegated law; there should be room for a coherent development and complementing of the delegating law [100].

The room for maneuver that the delegated legislator has in the Italian constitutional system is fairly exceptional but in the end remains a "shackled liberty" since the outer bounds of his "freedom" or "discretion" are determined in the first place by the principles and criteria that the delegating act imposes. These – it is true – should not be too stringent, according to the constant case law of the CCost. In addition, the delegated act is constrained by the Constitution; not just by Article 76, but by all of the Constitution. At the same time, the delegating act and the Constitution are a source of interpretation. If at all possible, the delegated act has to be interpreted harmoniously in the

---

97. Sentenza 216/2017, at 11.1.1 *in fine*, in which Sentenza 33/2011 is referred to as authority.
98. Sentenza 44/1993 (red. Catavola), at para. 2, *"secondo l'ordinaria sfera della discrezionalità legislativa"*.
99. Ordinanza 21/1988 (red. Borzellino), at para. 7.
100. Sentenza 250/2016 (red. Barbera), at para. 5.1 and Sentenza 362/1995 (red. Granata), at para. 3.1.

light of the delegating act and the Constitution [101]. If that is not possible, the threshold of the excess of the delegating act or of unconstitutionality is reached.

The process by which the CCost. in the end comes to the conclusion that there is some constitutional flaw (or not) in a concrete case relating to delegation has been described in a standard formula that is repeated, with small variations here and there, as follows:

> "According to the consolidated case law of this Court, the constitutional review of legislative delegation can be understood as a confrontation between the outcomes of two parallel hermeneutic processes: one relating to the norms which determine the object, the principles and leading criteria mentioned in the delegating act, taking account of the global context of norms in which they co-exist and distinguish themselves and in which the reasons and the final objective serve as the basis of the delegating legislation; the other, relating to the norms laid down by the delegated legislation, seeking to interpret them for their compatibility with the principles and leading directives of the delegating legislation." [102]

It is obvious that this repeated "incantation" helps to bring some regularity in the steps to be taken by the members of the Court in analyzing questions of delegation, but says very little about the likely outcome. What is important to note is that the legal and factual context in which the delegated law must find its place becomes more and more important, which is visible for instance in the case concerning time reserved for publicity spots on television mentioned above, in which that context was decisive [103]. This confirms the tendency to use delegation in domains where (technical) expertise is an important element in favor of delegation to a more expert government department, or even of the creation of (new) expert organs or committees. There is a similar tendency to put greater emphasis on the final objective sought by means of the delegating law. Together with the legal and factual context in which that law will have to function, the final objective is important as

---

101. Sentenza 278/2011 (red. De Siervo), at para. 13, where the Court points to the necessary interpretation of the contested delegation in the light of the Constitution as a means to lay to rest the concerns of the complainants.
102. Sentenza 170/2007 (red. Tesauro), at para. 4. Author's translation. A fairly recent example of (almost) the same formula is Sentenza 10/2018 (red. Barbera), at para. 9.
103. See *supra* footnote 90 and accompanying text.

a redeeming element if the delegating legislator has been vague or even silent on other elements that determine the lawfulness of the delegation.

The question of vagueness or silence of the delegating law is tricky because these may also be instruments for the government to leave room for the legitimate discretion that the delegated legislator should be able to exercise, possibly on the basis of its technical expertise. Hence probably the tendency of the CCost. to seek for the final objective of the delegation and the context in which the delegation has been used as a solution to cases presenting these problems.

Obviously, the Italian law on the delegation of powers through the decree-laws of Article 76 Cost. is pretty close to the French law on the subject, especially to Article 38 Const. Both systems are impregnated by the risk of abuse, especially by the executive power, and of the possibility that the Parliament will inflict "self-harm" by delegating too much power for too long. Historical episodes in both countries have contributed to this. Hence, in the Italian, as in the French, constitutional system the constitutional courts, unlike the US Supreme Court, remain willing to condemn "bad" cases of delegation as unconstitutional. There is little doubt that the Italian CCost. is more watchful where the delegating law is concerned because the Italian Parliament, unlike the French Parliament under Article 38 Const., has no second bite at the apple. The Italian system is rather unique for its attachment to a certain measure of discretion retained by the delegated legislator, when implementing an Article 76 decree-law. However, the US Supreme Court, as we have seen, is also aware that the executive or an agency needs certain room for exercising a modicum of discretion when applying a delegated power [104].

D. Germany

1. Delegation in the FRG Constitution: Initially a post-Weimar moment?

The danger of parliamentary "self-harm" under pressure of an over-mighty executive, as illustrated by the final moments of the Weimar Republic, lies at the root of the present-day constitutional law on the subject of delegation in the FRG. Article 80 of the Basic Law (*Grundgesetz*; hereafter GG) enables the legislature (the House of Representatives – *Bundestag* – and the Senate – *Bundesrat*) to

---

104. See *Mistretta, supra* footnote 20 and accompanying text.

authorize the Federal Government, an individual Federal Minister or the governments of the *Länder* to issue "statutory instruments" *(Rechtsverordnungen)*. The "content, purpose and scope of the authority conferred shall be specified in the [delegating] law". And "each statutory instrument shall contain a statement of its legal basis"[105]. Finally, if the delegating law so provides, subdelegation is possible and shall be effected by the delegated statutory instrument[106]. As is immediately clear from the text of Article 80 (1) GG, there is no time limit built in anywhere in this provision, whether between the moment of the granting of the authority and its effective usage by the government (as in France) or as far as the life of the delegated statutory instrument itself is concerned (as in Italy).

The negative experience of the Weimar Republic was still very much alive in the very first years of the Federal Republic, as the first case relating to Article 80 (1) demonstrated. The case concerned complicated legislation relating to the question how the *Länder* Baden and Württemberg would be (re)organized, depending on whether or not, after a referendum, they would be united or stay apart. One of the acts counted twenty-six articles and the Article 27 authorized the Minister of Home Affairs of the Federation "to issue the statutory instruments *necessary* for the execution of the act". Given the words of Article 80 (1) GG, it is not surprising that the Constitutional Court (Bundesverfassungsgericht, hereafter BVerfGe) wanted to teach a lesson to the government and to Parliament. In its view, that wording, which required that any and all delegated statutory instruments should be explicitly circumscribed as to their "contents, purpose and scope", had been drafted in "deliberate revulsion" *(in bewußter Abkehr)* from the practice of Weimar. Here, as elsewhere in the GG, the BVerfGe argued, the choice had been made for a more stringent separation of powers. Parliament could not evade its responsibility as legislative organ by transferring legislative powers to the government without having seriously thought about, and laid down the limits to, the powers it wanted to transfer. On the other hand, the government should not

---

105. Article 80 GG (1), first three sentences.
106. *Ibid.*, fourth sentence. The other three paragraphs of Article 80 GG are of lesser importance for the purpose of this course. Paragraph 2 gives the Senate a right of approval of delegated statutory instruments, when these relate to a number of specific subjects or have been adopted according to specific procedures. Paragraph 3 entitles the Senate to provide the government with drafts of those statutory instruments that require its approval. Paragraph 4 gives the *Länder*, if they so wish, the right to execute powers delegated to them by laws of each *Land* instead of by statutory instrument.

de facto take the place of Parliament by issuing statutory instruments based on vague delegations. Whether the empowerment of the government to issue statutory instruments under Article 80 GG was sufficiently delimited as to its contents, purpose and scope was to be based on a case-by-case analysis. However, there were cases where the authorization was so loosely formulated that it was impossible to foresee in which cases and with which objective it would be used and what the actual contents of the statutory instruments in question would be [107]. This was obviously the case at hand, where the drafters of the delegating law and Parliament had believed that "necessary" would suffice to characterize the content, purpose and scope of the instruments of implementation of the twenty-six substantive articles of the law. That was then, but not under the new German Constitution and its Article 80. The threesome of "objective, content and scope" had to be in the delegating law *with the necessary clarity*. The *Bestimmtheitsklausel* had been born [108].

After this first, fairly easy rejection of a delegation based on Article 80 GG, it was unlikely that future cases would be that simple. And indeed, in subsequent cases, the BVerfGe had to adapt its method of analyzing the delegating laws that were subjected to its scrutiny. A good example is the case concerning one of the annual prolongations of the postwar price control laws that had initially been promulgated by the occupying powers and had been continued in the form of annual prolongation laws of the (then) West German authorities [109]. In that case it was not so easy to find a clear expression of "objective, content and scope" of the delegation on the face of the law on price control. The highest administrative court in Germany (the Bundesverwaltungsgericht) had been in great difficulty on this point and this had been one of the reasons to put the case before the BVerfGe. The latter court found a simple solution to this problem: "objective, content and scope" of the delegation did not need to be explicitly present on the face of the delegating law as long as they could be deduced from the context, the connection with other legal texts and the overall objective pursued by the *system of rules* as a whole. The legislative history of the provisions in question could also play a role in all of this. This was, after all, the

---

107. BVerfGe 1, 14, *Südweststaat*, 23 October 1951, at para. E 15.
108. *Bestimmtheit* can best be translated as a mix of clarity, certainty and specificity; it is also used in German law for the *nulla poena* rule in criminal law. *Klausel* means clause.
109. BVerfGe 8, 274, *Preisgesetz*, 12 November 1958, at para. C, V, 2c.

normal way in which courts sought for the meaning of legal clauses that were obscure and difficult to understand [110].

The BVerfGe indeed proceeded with this intensive analysis of the Price Control Law and did not quite succeed in arriving at full clarity as far as the objective of the delegation was concerned, but concluded that "sufficient" *Bestimmtheit* was enough for Article 80, even if that qualification could not be found in the text of that provision [111]. However, the BVerfGe went along with the Bundesverwaltungsgericht in its historical interpretation of the development of the Price Law as a transitional law that meant to proceed from strict price control in nearly all sectors of the economy immediately after the end of the war to a gradual relaxation of price controls in more and more economic sectors, with the aim of arriving at a normal market situation, where demand and offer would determine prices again [112]. The *Bestimmtheit* of the objective of a delegation, therefore, could also be found in the development of the law and its application over time – an approach that can only work if the delegated law in question has been in existence for some time already.

2. *Development of broad constitutional principles and its influence on delegation*

Earlier in the same year (1958) another development in the case law on Article 80 began to take root, namely the intertwining with the "rule of law" *(Rechtsstaatprinzip)* and, closely linked to that, the notion of "parliamentary primacy" *(Gesetzesvorbehalt)* and reservation of the essential elements of a coherent complex of legal rules to the legislature *(Wesentlichkeitstheorie)*, which the BVerfGe had begun to derive from Article 20 GG [113]. This was particularly important, in

---

110. *Ibid.*, at para. C.V.1.
111. *Ibid.*, at para. C.V. 2 *b in fine*. The other extreme advanced by the Court in its discussion of the problem, "as *bestimmt* as at all possible", was not inscribed in the text of Art. 80 GG either, but it must be very doubtful if the absence of these words justifies the Court's opting for "hinreichend [sufficiently] bestimmt".
112. *Ibid.*, at paras. C.V.2 *c, d* and *e*.
113. Article 20 GG reads as follows:

"(1) The Federal Republic of Germany is a democratic and social federal state.
(2) All state authority is derived from the people. It shall be exercised by the people through elections and other votes and through specific legislative, executive, and judicial bodies. (3) The legislature shall be bound by the constitutional order, the executive and the judiciary by law and justice. (4) All Germans shall have the right to resist any person seeking to abolish this constitutional order if no other remedy is available."

the view of the Court, when German citizens were directly touched by the consequences of particular delegations. This was the case with the law on the (pre-VAT) turnover tax [114]. Such "old" turnover taxes were nearly always unfair or unequal in their consequences depending on whether the companies concerned were more or less vertically integrated. Already on that point the terminology of the law was bereft of any clarity, according to the Court. Moreover, the solution for this unfairness, a so-called supplementary turnover tax, was totally undefined in the law, but nevertheless left to implementation through a law-decree *(Rechtsverordnung)* to be adopted under Article 80 GG. This was unacceptable to the Court: the rule of law required that the delegation must be so clearly and precisely circumscribed that it is clear from the delegating law itself, and not from the implementing statutory instrument, what it is exactly that citizens will have to abide by. Moreover, this was in conformity with the idea that Parliament, and not the executive, had to decide, after due deliberation among the representatives of the people, the "essential" *(wesentliche)* aspects [115] that should determine the implementing measures of the law. This justified the imposition of strong demands of *Bestimmtheit* on the legislative power when determining delegations under Article 80 GG, to the point of adding the requirement of "predictability" with respect to the cases in which the delegation would be used, in which direction their use would go and what content the implementing statutory instruments might have [116].

In a case concerning the Act on the Administration of Justice [117] the BVerfGe in 1975 developed its approach laid down in the turnover tax case in a long *obiter dictum* broadly as follows. The principle of the primacy of the law, the idea that certain subjects can only be regulated by a formal law adopted by the legislature *(Gesetzesvorbehalt)*, is not laid down in so many words in Article 20 GG, but flows from the logic of its third paragraph [118]. The prescription that the executive and the judiciary are bound by law and justice would lose its meaning if the Constitution would not require that State action in certain fundamental domains is lawful only if it is legitimized by a formal law. Which domains are we talking about? The fundamental rights and freedoms laid down in the

---

114. BVerfGe 7, 282, *Lex Salamander*, 5 March 1958.
115. See *ibid.*, at para. C II, 5. Hence the term *Wesentlichkeitstheorie*.
116. *Ibid.*, at C III.
117. BVerfGe 40, 237, *Justizverwaltungsakt*, 28 October 1975.
118. For the text see *supra* footnote 113.

Constitution give some indication. In any case, the nineteenth-century idea that formal laws are necessary only when citizens are touched by interventions affecting their physical liberty and material assets is no longer satisfactory. A modern State offers its citizens services (think, for example: education, cultural, financial support, public health) and opportunities that are equally, if not more, important than freedom from dictatorial interventions in their worldly possessions or their physical integrity, for a "good" and fulfilling life. Hence the need for granting a primacy of the legislature also for protecting such values. All this, according to the BVerfGe, speaks in favor of an expansion of the *Gezetzesvorbehalt* beyond its black letter boundaries. Also, outside the domain of Article 80 GG the delegating legislator itself should decide and assume the responsibility for taking the fundamental decisions governing a delegation [119].

This raises the question whether the general *Gesetzesvorbehalt* (inspired by fundamental rights and comparable advantages for citizens) and the *ratio* of Article 80 GG (primarily a question of maintaining the appropriate balance between the main institutions of the State) remain separate matters or will mutually influence each other and will become more and more intertwined? A good example is the way in which the BVerfGe has handled the problem of the disciplinary removal of pupils from secondary schools [120]. First, it recalled certain elements from earlier case law, in particular the case on the law on price controls [121]. On the one hand, the delegation should be well defined, and accordingly should circumscribe the delegated powers in such a way that the empowerment alone makes clear and predictable what will be expected from the citizens. On the other hand, the empowerment does not need to be as precise as possible; it merely needs to be sufficiently defined *(bestimmt)* and can be interpreted in accordance with the usual techniques of interpretation, which also take account of the context, not just of the law itself, but also of other relevant legal rules and the goal that is pursued by the whole complex of legal rules in which the delegation is embedded. Second, the BVerfGe recalled that the intensity of the different requirements of "objective, contents and scope" of the delegation could vary, dependent on the specificity of the object of the regulation and the detail of the measures delegated to the administration. Finally, the Court took a new and wider turn, asserting

---

119. See *supra* footnote 109, at B I, 2 *a*.
120. BVerfGe 58, 257, *Schulentlassung,* 20 October 1981.
121. See *supra* footnote 109 and accompanying text.

that the requirement of sufficient *Bestimmtheit* of the conditions laid down in Article 80 GG constituted a complement to, and a concrete application of, the primacy of the law *(Gesetzesvorbehalt)* that followed from the constitutional ground rules of *Rechtsstaat* and democracy (as laid down in Article 20 GG).

3. Application of the broader principles of Article 20 GG to delegation under Article 80 GG

In the case concerning disciplinary removal of secondary school pupils, the BVerfGe used the terms of Article 80 GG in a domain, education, where (young) citizens enjoy a certain protection of fundamental rights or even of their important interests. As a consequence, the position of the person in question should be governed by rules, the basic principles of which have been decided by the legislature, and not by mere decrees adopted by the administration. Given that education is a matter for the *Länder*, the Court did not (and could not) pretend that Article 80 applied directly to the decrees that some *Länder* had adopted in this matter. It based itself instead on the general principle of the primacy of the Federal Parliament *(Gesetzesvorbehalt)* and combined that with an analogous application of Article 80 and its principal requirements, such as the one demanding that "object, contents and scope" of the delegation should be determined with sufficient clarity and predictability in the delegating law [122]. In this way the governments and parliaments of the *Länder* were coaxed into following the requirements of Article 80, but on the basis of the general constitutional principle of the primacy of the Parliament and the important way in which a pupil's life could be affected by not receiving the education he/she could reasonably have expected in an environment which was suitable to the needs of the pupil. The yardsticks by which delegating laws of the *Länder* should be measured were finally set out by the BVerfGe along the lines of the then available precedents on Article 80 GG, important examples of which have been highlighted above [123]. This also shows that by 1981 the lines by which Article 80 cases should be decided had been sufficiently settled to be transferred to the broader domain of the general primacy of the formal law, even at the level of the *Länder*.

Another important formal requirement that any delegation has to fulfill is the *Zitiergebot*, the requirement that a clear reference to the

---

122. *Ibid.*, at C V 1, 2 *b.*
123. *Ibid.*, at C V 2 *b.*

legal basis of the delegation in the delegated law is necessary [124]. That is to say that the delegated act must refer to the provision(s) in the delegating law(s), which state(s) that certain further rules implementing that law shall be taken by statutory instrument *(Rechtsverordnung)* under Article 80 GG. However, precise mention of the article of the Constitution and the nature of the secondary law instrument is not obligatory as long as the requirements of Article 80 in a more general sense are fulfilled [125]. However, the *Zitiergebot* is essential: for democratic control by the legislature, which will be able to see that its empowerment has been used in accordance with the terms of the delegation; for control by those who are affected by the delegated act, and for the same reasons; and finally for judicial control in case of a complaint [126]. A failure to respect the *Zitiergebot* infringes "an essential element of the democratic *Rechtsstaat*" (rule of law), according to the BVerfGe, and entails the nullity of the statutory instrument [127].

More recent case law on delegation confirms the impression that the position of the BVerfGe is by now well settled. Neither a case concerning a delegation that enables the *Länder* to close certain areas to prostitution for reasons of public morality, which proved to be acceptable to the Court [128], nor a case on a delegation that enabled the Ministry of Agriculture to determine penal sanctions for infringing EU legislation on the labeling of meat of young bovines [129], which was unacceptable to the Court, showed any further development in the criteria and the method applied by the German Constitutional Court in delegation cases. What it did show was that the BVerfGe, rather more than the Supreme Court, remains willing, with a certain regularity, to

---

124. See Article 80 (1), third sentence, GG.
125. This flexibility was especially necessary in the early days of the FRG, when old laws and instruments inherited from the occupation regime were often the basis for delegations, which obviously could not refer to Article 80, and often used words other than *Rechtsverordnung* for delegated instruments.
126. BVerfGe 101 1, *Hennenhaltungsverordnug*, 6 June 1999, at D I, 1-2.
127. *Ibid.*, at D I, 4. The actual reasons for declaring the statutory instrument on keeping laying hens null and void are given in D II. The *Zitiergebot* is essential also in cases of subdelegation and applies between the delegated statutory instrument and the subdelegated decree. See BVerfGe 151, 173 *Subdelegierte Verordnung*, at C I, 1*a-b* and *cc*.
128. BVerfGe, *Sperrbezirksverordnungen*, 28 April 2009, 1 BvR 224/07. The delegation was okay as long as a breach of public morality was interpreted, not as against prostitution itself – which was, by that time, legal in Germany – but as directed at its accompanying antisocial dimension.
129. BVerfGe, *Rindfleischetikettierungsgesetz*, 21 September 2016, 2 BvL 1/15.

condemn delegations of legislative power that do not live up to its well-established standards as unconstitutional [130].

The BVerfGe has construed an important edifice of case law on the basis of Article 80 GG, initially mainly based on the requirement of the sufficiently defined character *(Bestimmtheit)* of the words "object, content and scope" of that article. The normal means of interpretation of any law, namely text, context (including the whole system of rules in which the delegation was intended to be embedded) and legislative history, of course, also played a role. The *Zitiergebot*, as we just saw, is inscribed in Article 80 itself and essential. Finally, the Constitutional Court began the movement to integrate its interpretation of Article 80 into the major elements that it had distilled from Article 20 GG, namely the rule of law, parliamentary primacy and that the essential elements of any body of legal rules be laid down in a formal law, and that together make the FRG into a *Rechtsstaat*. That was necessary as Article 80 GG lacks the additional safeguards on delegated *Rechtsverordnungen* that are laid down in the corresponding French and Italian constitutional provisions: the additional parliamentary check on the delegated law-decree in France, or the limited validity of such decrees in Italy. This circumstance may also be an element that helps to explain why the German Constitutional Court (BVerfGe) has made a central point of the completeness and thoroughness of the delegating law in explaining object, content and scope of the delegation, without paying much, or even any, attention to the delegated *Verordnung*, especially in comparison to the Italian CCost., and to a lesser extent the US Supreme Court.

E. National law of delegation in an administrative context: The Dutch example

Thus far the delegation most intensely discussed in this course is the delegation of a "constitutional nature"; that is, between the different branches of government, in practice mainly the question of delegation of legislative or quasi-legislative power. This was the focus in all four of the national constitutional systems that have been discussed above, also because in three of these four systems the constitution contains provisions which "organize" such delegation. What has been left out

---

130. G. Nolte, "Ermächtigung der Exekutive zur Rechtsetzung: Lehren aus der deutschen und amerikanischen Erfahrung", *Archiv des öffentichen Rechts*, Vol. 118 (1993), p. 378 ff, at 402 *et seq.*

of consideration altogether is the delegation that is practiced in these countries, not between the branches of government, but inside the government bureaucracy.

Such delegation within (a branch of) the government is not without interest or importance, but is – it cannot be denied – of a more pedestrian nature. It is of great importance for the proper functioning of national government bureaucracies, not only for the execution of government tasks but also for the maintenance of national civil service law and the proper execution of the budget of the State. Laws or regulations covering internal delegation within the government are normally considered to be part of administrative law. Similarly, international civil service law and the law governing the execution of the budget of an international organization have also been inspired, with very important adaptations, by national civil service law and national rules relating to public accounts. Hence the rules of delegation that have been borrowed from national law are also of an administrative law nature and are, as will be further explained below, of a different kind and sometimes even directly the opposite of the rules on delegation of a constitutional nature.

1. The Dutch system of administrative law delegation as an example

For the purpose of this research, it seemed useful to take the Dutch system for a good example of delegation as an administrative law phenomenon. The Netherlands does not have a constitutional court that has the right to review the laws in the light of the Dutch Constitution, but all courts may review laws in the light of directly effective provisions of international agreements to which the Netherlands is a party; this includes the European Convention on Human Rights. This makes the Strasbourg Court *de facto* the highest instance for fundamental rights cases. For the rest, however, the Netherlands is not very different from the other administrative law systems of delegation of continental Europe, many of which have been strongly influenced by the French system [131]. It seems that the Netherlands system of administrative law might serve as a good example because of its systematic treatment of

---

131. Thanks to Napoleon and his occupation of large parts of continental Europe in the early nineteenth century. The French administrative law presently looks at delegation very much as a question of (possible) incompetence of the authority that has exercised a "delegated" power (in the broadest meaning of the word). See Plessix, *supra* footnote 42, at p. 1505 ff.

the different modes of delegation in the broad sense, which was part of a fairly recent systemic legislative overhaul of Dutch administrative law [132]. It is certainly not fully representative of the treatment of delegation in other continental legal systems, but it rigorously touches upon virtually all the questions that arise when discussing "delegation" in its broadest sense and covers principally delegation within the Dutch State administration.

2. Attribution

Dutch administrative law makes a firm distinction between attribution and various forms of delegation, notably delegation proper and mandate. Attribution is the creation of a new power and bestowing it on a specific administrative authority. The principle of legality implies that attribution can only flow directly from the Constitution or from a formal law. Attribution of a power is, therefore, a constitutional or legislative act and hence not covered by the Dutch General Administrative Law Act (GALA) [133].

Such attribution can be granted by law directly to a minister, for instance the Minister of Education, and also to a special service of a ministry, for instance the Inspector-General of Education. Such powers are granted by the laws relating to different types of education. The Provinces Act and the Municipalities Act [134] bestow specific powers on the provincial and municipal authorities, that is to say to their councils or the colleges that are charged with the day-to-day administration, or to both in cooperation. In the same way, the mayor is tasked with

---

132. Algemene Wet Bestuursrecht (1992) [General Administrative Law Act, GALA], English text at https://www.acm.nl/sites/default/files/old_publication/publicaties/15446_dutch-general-administrative-law-act.pdf. This overhaul of the Dutch system of administrative law seems to have become semipermanent; since the enactment thirty years ago of the first stage of this systemic reform, numerous amendments and additions have been made, including the long Article 10 discussed here.
133. *Ibid.* See H. E. Bröring and K. J. De Graaf *et al.*, *Bestuursrecht 1*, 6th ed., The Hague, Boom, 2019, at p. 135.
134. Just as in the French constitutional system, such laws organizing the branches of government and the territorial decentralization of the country are called "organic laws", a term that is broadly used for all laws that have to be enacted according to the Constitution. On the constitutional level there is no strict boundary line between the legislative and the regulatory domain in the Netherlands, as in France, although the Hoge Raad (the Dutch court of cassation) has given clear indications that rules that interfere significantly with the domain of individual rights can only be laid down by law. See C. W. van der Pot, *Handboek van het Nederlandse Staatsrecht*, D. J. Elzinga, R. de Lange and H. G. Hoogers (eds.), 16th ed., Deventer, Kluwer, 2014, at pp. 687-690.

the full responsibility for the maintenance of public order in his/her municipality. Some laws even attribute powers directly to individual civil servants; the commonsense examples are to be found in the areas of income taxes, customs and excise (where large numbers of binding individual decisions have to be taken by midlevel officials), and the police, in such cases as drunken driving and disorderly conduct – which are in need of immediate orders, backed up by the force of law, to desist from further driving and to disperse quietly. The common factor in all these forms of attribution is that there is direct or indirect political control exercised by national, regional or local representative bodies.

Another example of attribution occurs in the case of (semi)-autonomous public authorities, such as the Authority Financial Markets, the Authority Consumer and Market (i.e. antitrust and consumer protection), the Commissioner for the Media (i.e. supervision of the implementation of legislation on radio and TV) and the National Bank. In most cases these are purely public bodies, and historically often spun off from ministries, but still strongly linked to "their" ministry for budgetary and financial matters, as well as for democratic accountability [135]. "Their" minister can issue, at arm's length, policy directives to them and quash decisions they take. He or she can directly intervene, only if the authority in question has committed gross dereliction of duty. In other instances, such semiautonomous bodies have been newly created and sometimes given the legal form of a foundation under civil law [136]. They may have received attributed powers of execution, supervision or decision in legislation covering specific sectors of government and of the economy. The one thing that they have in common is that (with exceptions) they fall under the Framework Law of Independent Public Authorities, which is an attempt to make them respond at least somewhat to a common model, while maintaining their autonomy and also preserving proper financial management and a minimum of democratic accountability [137]. The number and variety of these autonomous agencies is simply

---

135. Kaderwet Zelfstandige Bestuursorganen (2006) [Autonomous Administrative Authorities Framework Act], see esp. Articles 10-16. There are authorities that are not linked to a ministry but that are still part of the State machinery. Only the agencies that are part of the State can be charged with exercising public authority.

136. The Authority Financial Markets (AFM) is an example of such an Autonomous Administrative Authority constituted as a foundation – which obviously is also not part of the State but still has to abide by the most important rules, including the budgetary rules, of the Framework Act.

137. The autonomy (note: *not* independence) of the agencies is guaranteed mainly by the provisions relating to the "members" (i.e. of the Board) of the agency and its staff, who are outside any ministerial authority.

stunning. There must be close to 150 such agencies and they go from the Police Academy, the Council for Pensions and Benefits, the public notaries and the Netherlands Literary Fund to various certification authorities for different categories of products and the Authority on Personal Data Protection [138]. This foreshadows what we will see in the EU later.

After this brief digression into the attribution of powers to Dutch autonomous authorities, let us recall that in the Dutch system, attribution precedes the matters covered in the GALA. Attribution is considered to be part of constitutional law and not of administrative law as regulated by GALA. The various forms of delegation and mandate are covered in Chapter 10 of the Act [139].

3. Delegation

Delegation in Dutch modern administrative law is the transfer by an administrative authority of part or all of its power in a particular domain to another person or administrative organ. The latter assumes full responsibility for the exercise of the delegated power (Arts. 10.13 and 10.14 GALA). The transfer is a real transfer, and the delegating authority may no longer exercise that power itself; at best it may still give policy orientations to the delegated authority, which may also ask for such directives, if necessary (Arts. 10.16.1 and 10.17 GALA). In principle, however, the delegated authority can and should exercise the delegated powers independently. Delegation needs a statutory basis – that is, a law in the formal sense (Art. 10.15 GALA) – precisely because it implies a shift of attributed powers, which derive from the Constitution or a law in the formal sense and now are transferred by delegation to another administrative authority than foreseen in the original attribution. This is also the reason why subdelegation, which is allowed, also needs a statutory basis [140]. The decision by which the delegation is made effective also must indicate its outer limits, for instance by setting conditions, listing maximum amounts of money, the rank of the person executing the delegation, and so forth. This, in turn, entails the obligation for the delegated authority or person that it

---

138. https://organisaties.overheid.nl/Zelfstandige_bestuursorganen/.
139. The following is based on Chapter 10 of GALA, *supra* footnote 132, and on the comments on that chapter in Bröring and De Graaf, *supra* footnote 133, at pp. 141-154. Chapter 10 was later added to GALA with a view to bringing a bit of order to the system of delegation in Dutch administrative law.
140. See Bröring and De Graaf *supra* footnote 133, at p. 141 and 144.

indicates in any decision executing the delegation the act by which the delegation was authorized and where it has been published (Art. 10.19 GALA). They may also be subjected to an obligation to provide the delegating authority or person with information on their exercise of the delegated powers (Art. 10.16.2 GALA).

This type of delegation can take place at all levels of government: the State of the Netherlands, the provinces and the municipalities. The ultimate sanction for not faithfully carrying out a delegation is its revocation by the delegating authority. The nature of delegation, that it is a true transfer of powers, also carries the consequence that it is unsuitable, even prohibited, to delegate powers to natural persons or public authorities that have a hierarchical relationship to the delegating authority or person. One cannot independently exercise a delegated power on one's own responsibility and be subject to the hierarchical authority of the delegating power.

4. Mandate

"Mandate means the power to make orders in the name of an administrative authority" (Art. 10.1 GALA). It is typically the way in which an administrative authority empowers certain civil servants who are part of its hierarchy to act in its name and under its responsibility. A mandate under Dutch administrative law, therefore, does not shift authority and responsibility to another public law actor, as delegation does. An order by the mandatory (within the limits of its powers) is an order of the mandator (Art. 10.2 GALA).

In principle any public authority has the right to grant mandates in accordance with the powers attributed to it unless a statutory provision states the opposite [141] or unless the nature of the powers is incompatible with the granting of a mandate. The administrative law courts normally decide which powers are inherently incompatible with granting a mandate on the basis of their onerousness, that is, the burden they are likely to impose on the property rights or other fundamental rights of the citizens concerned [142].

A mandate may be as broad or as narrow in scope as the mandatory wishes, but normally there are two tastes: a mandate to take certain

---

141. Article 10.3.2 mentions a few instances, but so too does the Law on Municipalities (Gemeentewet).
142. See Bröring and De Graaf, *supra* footnote 133, at pp. 147-149.

decisions or a mandate to sign decisions taken by the mandatory [143]. A mandate of a general nature has to be made public in written form and has to be withdrawn in the same way. Most public authorities maintain a register of the mandates they have issued [144]. The "right to know" of the citizen is thus protected. Mandates in specific cases may be made orally; no written decision is necessary. Mandates are the instruments of choice for delegation within a hierarchical bureaucratic structure. On this point mandate is fundamentally different from delegation, as defined by GALA. Mandates can be easily reinforced or nuanced by instructions down the hierarchical line. Nevertheless, a mandate granted to persons outside the hierarchy is not entirely excluded if certain conditions are fulfilled, in particular a written decision and, again, if there is no inherent incompatibility with the nature of the power so delegated.

5. Conclusion

The clear conceptual distinctions that Dutch administrative law makes between the trio of attribution, delegation and mandate is useful as an ideal type that helps us to make sharper distinctions than we might otherwise do when analyzing delegation within States and international organizations. Distinguishing *attribution*, granting a new power (i.e. a power that the attributing authority does not necessarily itself have but can create in favor of another organ of the State on the basis of the Constitution or a formal law) from *delegation* (transferring a power that the delegator possessed to another State organ) is very helpful. It actually avoids a lot of misunderstandings in public law, which are caused by old (Roman) civil law principles, as will be shown in Section H.3 below. Similarly, the clear conceptual distinction between *delegation* – which transfers power and responsibility to the delegate and allows the delegator only to give arms-length directives to the delegate, who must be outside the hierarchical authority of the delegator – and *mandate* – which transfers power down the hierarchical line, but not authority and responsibility, which stay with the delegator, who can issue prescriptions to the delegate at any moment – also helps to make clear distinctions. Also, because delegation must be law-based and mandate not, it demonstrates that delegation is semipolitical but

---

143. *Ibid.*, at p. 145. This is the equivalent of the French *délégation de signature*.
144. *Ibid.*, at p. 152.

mandate is strictly bureaucratic. In the same way *attribution* can be regarded as semiconstitutional as it is based directly on the constitution or on a law in the formal sense.

F. Some concluding remarks on national systems of delegation

The short overviews of the national law with respect to (non)-delegation of legislative powers in the US, France, Italy and Germany, as interpreted by their national constitutional courts, show a considerable diversity, which is only logical given the different ages of their constitutions, their national histories and different legal systems. Nevertheless, there are important, even fundamental, common points that result from the description and analysis above.

The main and most important common points are obviously a concern (1) for the separation of powers and (2) for keeping those matters of government that belong to the legislative domain in principle firmly in the hands of the legislature. This is, after all, the organ of the State that in all these countries is legitimized by direct and indirect elections; it thus legitimizes the legislation adopted by it. This is laid down in more or less detailed constitutional articles that directly address the question of second order legislation through a strict separation between the legislative domain and the regulatory domain (each defined by a list of categories of government interest), as in France. Or, as in Italy, by a strict prohibition of delegation of legislative powers unless firm conditions are fulfilled and by imposing a time limit on the validity of the delegated law. In France the conditions for the constitutionally lawful delegation of legislative powers had to be teased out by the CC. There are stringent conditions on the procedure for enacting delegated legislation, but there is no time limit on the validity of delegated legislation. In Germany there is no time limit on the enactment and the validity of the delegated legislation, but the conditions for the delegation of legislative power are strict and have been made stricter still by the BVerfGe. In the US, with only the "vesting" clause of Article I of the Constitution and the discussion among the founding fathers on the separation of powers to base itself on, the Supreme Court has created a jurisprudential edifice that is somewhat comparable to the Italian system: no legislative delegation unless strict conditions are satisfied. Only the conditions, probably due to the extraordinary circumstances – the Great Depression and World War II – under which they had to be developed and applied, have not coalesced into a doctrine that lends itself easily to nuanced application, certainly not now that nearly every nook and cranny of the US constitutional edifice is heavily ideologized. In all these legal systems the (non)-delegation of legislative powers doctrine has been intermingled to a greater or lesser extent with the protection of the basic rights, and even the important protected interests, of citizens. Any government measure that was likely to affect citizens in those rights and interests had to be laid down in a formal law that, if it delegated powers to other State organs, had to be of good legislative quality, that is, capable of being understood by, and predictable in its effects for, the average citizen. All these elements can be recognized to a greater or lesser degree in the case law of the constitutional courts of the four legal systems discussed above [145]. There are clearly diverging approaches among these countries on whether their courts come to the conclusion that the delegating law is all-important, or nearly so, and must, independently from later developments and the practice of the delegated authorities and their delegated decrees or laws, clearly spell out the objectives, the contents and the scope of the delegated powers (the German BVerfGe). Or whether their constitutional courts are content to grant more leeway to the autonomy and expertise of the implementing authorities and are willing to accept that their delegating laws leave greater leeway to these authorities (the Italian CCost. in particular) and that the practice of these implementing authorities can have a certain (corrective) influence on their view of the constitutionality of the delegating law (the US Supreme Court and the Italian CCost.). As to the stringency of enforcement of the (non)-delegation doctrine, it has been shown that the European constitutional courts regularly pronounce a judgment of "unconstitutional" on delegations of legislative power, while the US Supreme Court has not done so since the 1930s.

Finally, in respect of the French, Italian and German constitutional systems, one should not forget that Articles 38 of the French Const., 76 of the Italian Cost. and 80 of the German GG are all provisions that deal with what one can call roughly decree-laws, where the delegation of legislative power by parliament to the executive and its dangers are at their sharpest, with strong negative historical overtones. It is important to realize that all three constitutions also contain provisions on normal implementing or executive ministerial decrees taken pursuant to a great variety of laws adopted by parliament, such as laid down in Article

---

145. It is also present in the prohibition of granting a mandate in case the nature of the powers so delegated is incompatible with it in Articles 10.3.1 and 2 GALA in the Netherlands. See *supra* footnote 139 and accompanying text.

21 French Const. and Article 86 of the Italian Cost., or implementing measures taken by the German *Länder* in the framework of cooperative federalism. France has always the special barrier, by which the major State institutions can ask the CC to reclassify measures adopted as a law as falling into the *domaine réglementaire*. Insofar as the constitutional courts have developed or are developing specific criteria linked to the requirements inherent in the fact that, for instance, Germany is a democratic country under the rule of law (derived from Article 20 GG) and that all legislation, regulation and implementing measures have to respond to these requirements, the difference between "normal" implementing measures and exceptional decree-laws that entail an "exceptional" delegation of legislative power to the executive will be whittled away. It was already mentioned above that the French CC might be moving in this direction as well.

G. *Some remaining loose ends inspired by national law and practice on legislative delegation*

As has been shown above, for States the central problem of delegation as a constitutional question is the relation between the legislative and the executive power and where the line has to be drawn as to what is properly in the legislative domain and where the legislature enters the executive domain and *vice versa* [146]. Less frequent and less prominent are the questions of delegation that touch upon the relations of the legislature and the executive on the one hand and the court system on the other hand. Nevertheless, the first US case on delegation discussed above [147] was preoccupied by the relation between the legislature's right to make laws on the (overall) organization of the courts and the courts' right (under a delegation) to regulate their own activities when judging cases and everything related thereto. Such issues may indeed be less frequent, but they are of great importance.

Another type of delegation that was inspired by national law and institutions and was adopted by international organizations was based on the idea that expert advice was important for lawmaking or government decision-making in certain sectors of the economy or on certain markets where the government lacked such specialized knowledge. The first such examples at the national level were the agencies created in the

---

146. As G. Nolte has remarked, this question has to be answered over and over again in any parliamentary democracy, see Nolte, *supra* footnote 130, at p. 401.
147. *Wayman, supra* footnote 10.

US during the Great Depression [148]. They could give important advice to the government or even be granted delegated decision-making and rulemaking powers. The *Schechter* case, discussed earlier, is one of the few cases in which the Supreme Court found that such delegation went too far [149]. Historically, in the European Union there has been more of a mutual influence between the Member States and the EU. From the 1970s onward, the EU and its Member States started to spin off from the central government and from the Commission more and more semiautonomous bodies, or to create such bodies *ex nihilo* with quite diverse tasks: giving advice, setting standards, drafting rules and sometimes even adopting them. The Union created so-called network agencies that actually pushed some Member States into creating national bodies or agencies where they did not yet exist [150]. Where these bodies did already exist and the EU agencies were created later, the Member States have tried (sometimes with success) to keep the EU bodies or agencies small and to limit their powers [151].

Apart from the need for specific expertise as motive for the creation of independent agencies, there is sometimes the additional consideration that certain expertise ought to be isolated from politics. For example, the question of whether or not a medicine is safe for use and has the positive effects it is claimed it has should not be decided while being subject to political influence or lobbying. It should principally, or even entirely, be decided on the basis of scientific considerations and hence independent national medicines agencies, and later the European Medicines Agency (EMA), should be charged with this task. Such national and international agencies narrow the political arena, but that is considered desirable. This raises difficult questions of political and democratic accountability, also, because there are some indications that

---

148. See the cases mentioned in *supra* footnotes 24, 25 and 27.
149. See *supra* footnote 18 and accompanying text. The Supreme Court in the end accepted the delegation of powers to several other such agencies.
150. A well-known result of the so-called decentralization of competition/antitrust policy was the creation of national authorities in this domain in Member States, such as France and the Netherlands, and in nearly all the new "eastern" Member States that acceded in 2004.
151. According to the literature, in Europe the Agency for the Cooperation of Energy Regulators (ACER) and the Body of European Regulators of Electronic Communications (BEREC) are two such network agencies that have arguably been exposed to client and Member State capture. See for instance M. Zinzani, "Market Integration Through 'Network Governance': The Role of European Agencies and Network of Regulators", PhD thesis, Maastricht University, 2012, https://cris.maastrichtuniversity.nl/en/publi cations/market-integration-through-network-governance-the-role-of-europea. Zinzani is, however, on the whole rather sanguine about this risk of capture.

precisely such agencies may become captive to the lobby of national stakeholders and the pressures of Member State regulators, especially when the latter have participated in the creation of so-called network agencies [152].

H. Some basic notions related to delegation

The case law of the national courts and the literature discussing the cases rely often on concepts and notions that hail from private and even Roman law and have passed through the public law cooking pot for subtle changes. There is, in some cases, serious reason to believe *ab initio* that these concepts and notions are of limited use when applied to international organizations.

1. Distinction between attribution and delegation

First of all, in a legal course, it is important to make a clear distinction between attribution and delegation. For our purposes it bears repeating explicitly that attribution is the constitutional grant of power to an organ of a State or an international organization [153]. In the latter case this grant of power is laid down in the founding treaty of an international organization or in a treaty that merely sets up a light treaty body for the administration of the treaty, instead of leaving this to the parties to the treaty. Such a grant of power may contain an authorization for its delegation, including conditions for such delegation, which may be more or less demanding.

2. Contrast between commercial and public law notions of delegation

The notion of agency *(agence)* comes originally from commercial law, where it indicates the relationship between a principal and an agent, in which the agent is essentially the instrument of the principal. The agent must perform exactly what he/she has agreed in an agency contract with the principal. If this proves impossible, the agent must return to the principal for a further mandate and cannot act on his/her

---

152. For examples at the worldwide level, see A. Berman, "Industry, Regulatory Capture and Transnational Standard Setting", *AJIL Unbound*, Vol. 111 (2017), pp. 112-118. On the International Maritime Organization (IMO), see M. Apuzzo and S. Hurtes, "Tasked to Fight Climate Change, a Secretive UN Agency Does the Opposite", *New York Times*, 3 June 2021, https://www.nytimes.com/2021/06/03/world/europe/climate-change-un-international-maritime-organization.html.
153. See Voermans, *supra* footnote 4, at p. 19 ff.

own. If the agent acts beyond the contract with the principal, the latter in principle is not responsible, but the agent is [154]. Indeed, the principal-agent relation is broadly identical in its stringency to the relation between a mandator and his/her mandatory. In the public law sphere of States, however, the terms linked to "mandate" are often preferred [155]. Delegation *(délégation)* in a narrow sense covers the situation in which a delegator has delegated (part of) his authority or power to a delegate, who has a certain freedom to act. This freedom, as already suggested above, may be (and in most instances is) circumscribed by certain conditions in the act of delegation. Delegation in most instances is a true transfer of powers and responsibility, but it is reversible: the delegator may take back the delegated powers or at the outset may decide not to exercise the power of delegation [156]. Finally, conferral constitutes a true transfer of power to another body or organ of the State or international organization, where such transfer is definitive and cannot be undone or taken back, unless in extreme situations, such as the state of emergency or comparable circumstances. It is a form of nonconstitutional attribution.

3. Are Roman law parallels helpful?

A classic rule from Roman law that is often cited is that no one can transfer more powers or rights than he or she already has. *Nemo plus iuris transferre potest quam ipse habet.* It is a typical private law rule that is of very limited use in respect of delegation in the public law sphere since political organs of the State or of an international organization mostly exercise very broadly defined powers and transfer only a limited part of them. If this maxim is used in order to restrict the powers of political organs to create bodies that exercise powers not larger than, but different from, their own, for instance executive or judicial powers, such attempts to curtail their delegation will also fail as such delegating organs normally have a very broad remit according to national constitutions and the founding treaties of international

---

154. The law of agency in different legal systems is full of nuances and refinements in cases where the agent acted outside his/her instructions, but broadly in the interest of the principal, but it is not necessary to go into that here.

155. As explained earlier, this is especially clear in Dutch public law. See *supra* Sec. E and Bröring and De Graaf, *supra* footnote 133, at p. 145 ff.

156. It is recalled that in the French legal system, nonuse of a delegation, especially if delegation is necessary to make a law fully effective, gives rise to a so-called *incompétence négative* and will be sanctioned as such by the Constitutional Court. We will see that in the EU system this has also led to problems.

organizations. It is a rule that has some traction, however, in delegation of the administrative law type within State organs. When powers concerning personnel policy or the execution of the budget have to be delegated two or three levels down the line within the administration, it is of great importance that these powers do not inadvertently "grow" or "change" with each step.

Another classic Roman law ditty is *delegatus delegare non potest*, that is, a delegate cannot delegate the power he/she has received from a delegator further down the line. This rule is strongly reflected in the law of agency, which was briefly discussed above, given the strong link between principal and agent. However, once again such a private law rule proves of little consequence when applied to the domain of public law. It may create enormous difficulties in those national constitutional systems where the sovereignty is situated in the people. If the prevailing view in such a legal system is that through elections the people have delegated their sovereign power to the legislature, the latter theoretically would be blocked from delegating parts of that power to other State organs. The modern administrative State could not exist if this rule was strictly applied. However, even if this Roman law rule is not fully applied nowadays in public law, there still exists in many national constitutional systems a fairly strong presumption against delegating legislative powers. This is often linked to other constitutional principles, such as the separation of powers, especially if the constitution lays down a stringent allocation of powers to different State institutions, or within an international organization.

4. Aversion from self-delegation and subdelegation?

Another prevalent tendency that hangs together with the separation of powers in many constitutional systems is the aversion from self-delegation, especially by the legislature. If parliament decides to retain certain aspects of what can fairly be described as the implementation of a law to a committee of itself, this will have two problematic consequences. Such work ought to have been done by the executive, *and* the action of a parliamentary committee will not follow the same rules as the full parliament in adopting a piece of legislation. The separation of powers is distorted and even if what the committee decides could conceivably have been characterized as legislation, the decision-making procedure in the committee is naturally not the same as in the plenary legislature, and thus also does not give the same guarantees of legitimacy.

As was already mentioned above, the so-called principle of *delegatus delegare non potest* would be an enormous obstacle to the existence of the modern administrative State if it were taken literally. Notably in the field of the execution of the budgets of the State organs at various levels of government and in the management of large government bureaucracies, it is absolutely necessary to delegate authority to lower and lower levels of government. And this entails other requirements that are important for the verification of the government accounts and the lawfulness of nominations of members of the civil service: clarity and transparency of the delegations granted. In some national systems of government this has led to a distinction being made between a true delegation of power and a *delegation of signature* (also interpreted as the delegation of the exercise of power). This distinction seems to have seeped also into the case law of administrative tribunals of international organizations, as we will see in Chapter III.

5. Implied powers

Another notion that is found in national constitutional orders as well as in the law of international organizations and that plays an important role in the discussion about delegation is the concept of implied powers. The theory of implied powers consists of the argument that in order to reach the objectives of a nation State or of an international organization or to exercise the powers given to an institution or an organ of the State effectively, it may be necessary to have recourse to powers that have not been explicitly foreseen in the founding documents of the State or the international organization concerned. Such implied powers are deemed to have been granted by implication since they are indispensable in order to achieve the objectives that have been granted explicitly by the founding documents concerned. Implied powers are therefore closely linked to the effectiveness of the action of the State or an international organization. Implied powers exert a direct influence on the division of powers between the organs of a State or an international organization and thus on the separation of powers.

6. States and international organizations

It is obvious that such notions about delegation as have been developed in States are not directly applicable in international organizations. Nevertheless, it has become quite usual to think about international organizations in constitutional terms and this can be quite helpful as long as the differences are clearly kept in mind. Since international organizations are not based on the presumption of full sovereignty, as States are, the precise attribution of powers to the organization and their distribution over the different organs of the organization is of great importance. As a consequence, it is difficult, if not impossible, to speak of a true separation of powers, as with States. Nevertheless, in virtually all international organizations a kind of "balance between the institutions", as the EUCJ has characterized it in the case of the EU [157], can be recognized by carefully considering the founding treaty and the way it is being applied. If the founding treaty is amended or newly constituted, as has happened several times with the EEC and EU treaties, the balance between the institutions is likely to change as well. This is an important element to take into account when studying delegation in international organizations and in particular its evolution over time.

7. Outline of the remaining part of this study

In the following chapters (III-V) we will first analyze the evolution of delegation in the UN General Assembly and the UN bodies dependent on the Assembly (Chap. III). By discussing a number of exemplary cases an attempt will be made to sketch the way in which the Assembly has developed an approach to delegation in connection with the creation of new UN bodies. The International Court of Justice (ICJ) and the United Nations administrative tribunals (old and new) have had a certain influence on the Assembly in this matter, and their role will be analyzed as well.

Second, it is necessary to have a look at delegation by the Security Council (Chap. IV). The Security Council encounters problems related to delegation in three ways. In the field of sanctions ordered by the Security Council, the Council has created different subordinate bodies that are tasked with helping the Council on the details of the imposition of sanctions and of their execution. This has led to peculiar problems related to the decision-making in the Council and in these subordinate bodies. Moreover, the Council has encountered problems related to delegation after it had ordered peacekeeping or peace enforcement

---

157. On balance between the institutions, see among many others, J.-P. Jacqué, "The Principle of Institutional Balance", *CMLRev*, Vol. 41 (2004), pp. 383-391.

operations. If these operations were carried out by UN forces – that is to say, forces to which Member States had contributed contingents which were considered part of the UN Secretariat – it has happened fairly regularly that problems arose at the point where delegation within the organization and responsibility of the organization met. Such problems caused by the interaction between delegation and responsibility are often even more serious when the United Nations carries out peacekeeping operations in collaboration with other organizations like the African Union or the North Atlantic Treaty Organization (NATO). Finally, there is the peculiar problem in cases where the Security Council leaves the implementation of a Chapter VII operation to so-called coalitions of the willing constituted by Member States. Such operations are rare but run a strong risk of mission creep or even straightforward breach of the conditions set for the mission by the Council.

Third, delegation within the EU, and in particular the historical evolution of the doctrine of delegation in that organization, will be discussed (Chap. V). The case law of the EUCJ in the so-called *Meroni* and *Romano* cases [158] will be set out in some detail. These cases, which date back to the period between the late 1950s and the early 1980s, have had a restrictive effect on the possibilities to delegate powers within the European Communities and, later, the European Union. However, the question may be asked whether the Union institutions in the end did much more than paying lip service to this case law. In any case, the modifications to the provisions on the implementation of Union law and the inclusion of new provisions on the delegation of legislative powers in the new Lisbon Treaty, as well as making acts of the EU agencies subject to the jurisdiction of the Court, have all probably had a salutary effect on the case law of the Court of Justice. The political organs of the EU thus have somewhat greater freedom to delegate legislative and implementing powers to existing or newly created bodies.

---

158. Case 10/56, *Meroni*, *supra* footnote 2; Case 98/80, *Romano* v. *INAMI (Brussels)*, ECLI:EU:C:181:104, at para. 20 ff.

CHAPTER III

DELEGATION WITHIN THE UNITED NATIONS: THE GENERAL ASSEMBLY AND THE SECRETARIAT

A. Delegation to a newly created body: The United Nations Administrative Tribunal

The UN was strongly confronted early in his existence by the question of delegation in a conflict between a Member State, the United States, and the United Nations and the UN Educational, Scientific and Cultural Organization (UNESCO). This conflict was the international dimension of what in the United States was called the period of McCarthyism [159]. During this period American civil servants who in the past had allegedly been members of or linked in any way to the American Communist Party and its affiliated organizations were strongly questioned as to their loyalty to the US government and sometimes hounded out of office, fired and prosecuted for espionage. This campaign also affected certain US nationals in the service of the United Nations and its specialized agencies, in particular UNESCO. Considerable American pressure was brought to bear on the UN Secretariat, and from time to time on the Secretary-General himself, to expel such US nationals from the Secretariat and the specialized agencies where they worked since in the view of the US government or the US Congress – this was not always clear – they had been disloyal to the US because of their – often past – affiliation with the communist movement.

When considerable numbers of them were indeed let go by the administration of the organization they belonged to, they turned to the United Nations Administrative Tribunal (UNAT) with a plea for reinstatement and/or damages. UNAT – created a few years earlier by the General Assembly [160] – decided that the UN Secretary-General had

---

159. This includes the hearings before the House Committee on Un-American Activities (HUAC) of which Senator McCarthy for obvious reasons was not a member. For a good overview of what was also called the "Red Scare", see J. Michaels, *McCarthyism. The Realities, Delusions and Politics behind the 1950s Red Scare*, New York, Routledge, 1971.
160. UN General Assembly (UNGA) Res. 351A (IV) of 24 November 1949, Establishment of a UN Administrative Tribunal. Note that there are two UNATs, the single-level United Nations Administrative Tribunal created by the resolution mentioned above (hereinafter UNAT-old), and the second-level United Nations Appeals Tribunal

acted in defiance of the Staff Regulations by firing these persons and that compensation was due [161]. Such compensation had to be paid by the Secretariat out of the budget of the United Nations. That led to discussions among the Member States when the budget in which these compensations were listed as expenses of the UN came up for approval in the General Assembly. In short, the right of the fired UN civil servants to receive their compensation came up against the power of the General Assembly under Article 17 (1) Charter to "consider and approve" the budget of the organization. Obviously, it was in particular the United States that had stoked this controversy. In the end a compromise was reached in the General Assembly, which consisted of putting the question of whether that organ was obliged to include the compensation in the budget of the UN as a consequence of the judgment of UNAT-old to the ICJ in the form of a request for an advisory opinion [162].

This well-known case, the so-called *Effect of Awards* case, will be discussed here at some length because it illustrates a large number of crucial questions that arise when an organ of an international organization, in this case the General Assembly of the UN, creates a new body, in this case the UNAT, to which it delegates certain tasks [163].

The first question that arose was whether UNAT-old should be regarded primarily as a mere subordinate organ of the General Assembly or as a judicial institution. The ICJ looked for an answer to this question in the Statute of UNAT-old that was included in the relevant resolution of the General Assembly [164]. Article 1 of that Statute clearly mentioned that the resolution created a tribunal and Article 2 (1) stated that UNAT-old would pass judgment on the cases submitted to it. Moreover, Article 2 (3) affirmed that the decisions of UNAT-old would be final and without appeal. From the combination of these provisions the ICJ derived the conclusion that UNAT-old had the power to determine its own competence, a capacity that is typical of all courts [165].

---

created by the reform of the UN Internal Justice System in 2007, see *infra* footnote 169 (hereinafter called UNAT-new).

161. See for instance UNAT Case 29, *Gordon* v. *Secretary-General*, https://untreaty.un.org/unat/UNAT_Judgements/Judgements_E/UNAT_00029_E.pdf; UNAT Case 30, *Shevchansky* v. *Secretary-General*, https://untreaty.un.org/unat/UNAT_Judgements/Judgements_E/UNAT_00030_E.pdf.

162. UNGA Res. 785 (VIII) of 9 December 1953, Supplementary estimates for the financial year 1953.

163. *Effect of Awards of Compensation made by the United Nations Administrative Tribunal, ICJ Reports 1954*, at 47 ff.

164. See UNGA Res. 351A (IV), *supra* footnote 160.

165. See *Effect of Awards*, *supra* footnote 163, at 51-52.

From the conclusion of the ICJ to the effect that the UNAT was a true court immediately the next dilemma arose, namely whether the General Assembly had the power to create a judicial body. Was it conceivable that a political organ like the General Assembly had the power to create a judicial body that had capacities that the General Assembly itself lacked? Here we encounter the problem (already briefly touched upon in Chapter I) that in private law a person cannot bestow on another person powers that he/she himself lacks. And, as we already surmised in Chapter I, in public international law such a rule does not hold given the broad powers that an organ like the General Assembly of the UN has been granted by the UN Charter. In addition, the willingness of the ICJ to apply the implied powers doctrine to the UN Charter, as shown almost from the beginning in the *Reparations for Injuries* case [166], also played an important role in accepting a rather broad power to create new UN bodies and to charge them with judicial power if necessary for a proper functioning of the organization. In the *Effect of Awards* case the ICJ found it necessary for the good functioning of the Secretariat that such a judicial body be created by the General Assembly. The Court reasoned that given the complexities that would inevitably arise in managing a multinational Secretariat like that of the UN, litigation was almost inevitable. Hence the broad powers that had been given by the Charter to the Secretary-General to manage the Secretariat should be interpreted so as to include the possibility of creating a judicial organ charged with deciding conflicts within the Secretariat between the management and the individual staff members of the Secretariat [167].

The third question that came up, namely whether decisions rendered by UNAT-old should be considered *res judicata*, was easy to answer. Since the Court had decided that UNAT-old was a judicial organ and, as it appeared from its Statute, its decisions were final and without appeal, there could be no doubt about their status as *res judicata* [168].

This conclusion had direct consequences for the answer to the fourth question that arose before the ICJ: does the United Nations have the duty to pay damages ordered by UNAT-old? The answer was obviously in the affirmative given the Court's view on *res judicata*.

In the pleadings before the ICJ a fifth question was put forward, namely whether there was no possibility of escaping the payment. Was

---

166. *Reparations for Injuries suffered in the Service of the United Nations, ICJ Reports 1949*, at 174 ff.
167. See *Effect of Awards, supra* footnote 163, at 57-58.
168. *Ibid.*, at 59.

there some possibility of review after a sentence of UNAT-old? Or could an appeal be lodged against this judgment? The answer given by the ICJ was in the negative for the simple reason that if these possibilities had been desired, they would have been included in the Statute of UNAT-old and this was not (yet) the case [169].

Once these four questions, which discussed the consequences of the fact that the UN General Assembly could create a judicial body, had been dealt with, the truly crucial question came to the fore. That was the question whether the power of UNAT-old of ordering damages to be paid to personnel of the United Nations by the organization could be overridden by the General Assembly's own power to approve the budget. And once again, basing itself on the provision in the Statute that laid down that the judgments of UNAT-old would be final and without appeal, and by recalling its view about *res judicata* and its consequences, the ICJ came rather easily to the conclusion that this was obviously not possible. Hence the General Assembly's power to decide about the budget was circumscribed by the judgments of the organ that the General Assembly itself had created, UNAT-old [170].

There is little doubt that many delegations in the UN General Assembly at the time must have asked themselves the question how it was possible that they had created a subsidiary body that they now had to follow when deciding about the budget of the United Nations, the approval of which clearly was the prerogative of the Assembly. The principal turned out to be bound by the decisions of its agent. How was this possible? In the eyes of the ICJ this was simple. The General Assembly, because of its broad powers to ensure the proper functioning of the UN, and in particular of its Secretariat, could create a judicial organ for internal justice purposes, but this was clearly not an organ intended to help the General Assembly in the exercise of its own functions, the advice of which could be put aside [171]. In a way, this is another manifestation of Klabbers's Frankenstein problem mentioned in Chapter I. Just as Doctor Frankenstein imparted to the

---

169. At this time the special appeals procedure from UNAT-old to the ICJ had not yet been established (see H. G. Schermers and N. M. Blokker, *International Institutional Law*, 6th ed., Leiden, Brill, 2020, at para. 642) and only the establishment of the new Internal Justice System of the UN established by UNGA Res. 62/228 (Administration of Justice at the United Nations of 22 December 2007, https://undocs.org/en/A/RES/62/228) would create a regular appeals procedure: see Helmut Buss, *et al.*, *Handbook on the Internal Justice System at the United Nations*, UN E-book, 2014, https://www.un-ilibrary.org/content/books/9789210566636.
170. See *Effect of Awards*, *supra* footnote 163, at 59-60.
171. *Ibid.*, at 61.

monster certain physical and character traits that he himself lacked, so the General Assembly had imparted judicial powers to its creation, the UNAT-old, that it itself lacked. It simply had to bear the consequences of the particular way in which it had itself used its broad powers.

B. The ICSC and the Molinier case:
A technical delegation to a newly created body?

Case No. 370 of the UNAT-old was brought by Cécile Molinier and five other staff members of the UN Secretariat against the Secretary-General of the United Nations in 1985 [172]. The subject matter of the case related to the remuneration of the personnel of the UN and to their post adjustment, subjects that belong to the core of the law of the civil service of not only the United Nations but also of those organizations that are within the UN Common System [173]. The case was (and still is) illustrative of several problems inherent in delegation in the UN.

An important principle determining the remuneration of members of the international civil service is the so-called Noblemaire principle [174]. This principle was named after the French diplomat Georges Noblemaire who at the Versailles Peace Conference headed a commission in charge of the principles that should govern the level of remuneration of future international civil servants of the League of Nations, the International Labour Organization (ILO) and other international bodies. His commission took the view that if an international Secretariat was supposed to provide services of high quality to the organization and its Member States, it should be in a position to attract civil servants of a high quality from all the Member States. In practice this would only be possible if the remuneration of international civil servants was sufficiently better than the remuneration of the best paid civil servants in equivalent employment in the civil service of the Member State who offered the best salaries and working conditions to its public servants.

This so-called comparator State was originally the United Kingdom and, since the creation of the UN has been, and still is, the United States for nearly all worldwide organizations, including the United

---

172. UNAT Judgment 370 *Molinier et al.* v. Secretary-General, 6 June 1986, retrieved at https://untreaty.un.org/unat/UNAT_Judgements/Judgements_E/UNAT_00370_E.pdf.
173. The organizations that are part of the common system are listed at https://icsc.un.org/Home/CommonSystem.
174. On the Noblemaire principle, see Schermers and Blokker, *supra* footnote 169, at para. 512; M. Ogwezzy, "Noblemaire Principle in the Context of International Civil Service", *Cosmopolitan Law Journal*, Vol. 2, No. 2-Vol. 4, No. 2 (2014-2016), pp. 14-28.

Nations. The Noblemaire principle was so applied as to maintain a margin of 10 to 20 percent, ideally around 15 percent, between United Nations salaries and conditions and those prevalent in the US civil service. As mentioned above, this guaranteed two important conditions for the proper functioning of an international Secretariat, namely its truly international character and the quality of its services. Another important condition for the proper functioning of an international Secretariat is that its employees, who are often active and stationed in different areas of the world, receive not just nominally equal salaries but salaries that are approximatively equal in purchasing power. To this end the UN Secretariat and other international secretariats (and national diplomatic services) use the so-called technique of post adjustment. Post adjustment means that salaries are indexed dependent on a civil servant's duty station in terms of cost of living and purchasing power. Ideally this entails that UN personnel of a certain rank in New York, Nairobi and Geneva (to name only the three main UN offices in the world) can all afford to buy the same package of goods and services that they need, independent of their duty station.

In order to deal with questions of remuneration and post adjustment the General Assembly in 1972 created the so-called International Civil Service Commission (ICSC) as a subsidiary organ under Article 22 Charter [175]. According to its Statute, the ICSC consists of fifteen members appointed by the General Assembly. These members shall act in their personal capacity and be individuals of recognized competence and experience in public administration and related fields, in particular personnel management. They shall serve full time, for a term of four years. The ICSC is responsible as a body to the General Assembly. The members perform their task in full independence and impartiality and may not seek or receive instructions from any government or from any secretariat or staff association of an organization in the UN Common System [176]. The ICSC is thus a classic example of delegation to an independent expert body that provides the Assembly with information in the form of advice or decisions based on expertise that the Assembly itself does not have. The underlying objective is to arrive at a single unified international civil service for the UN and the international organizations that are part of the UN Common System

---

175. UNGA Res. 3042 (XXVII), United Nations Salary System, https://undocs.org/en/A/RES/3042%20(XXVII).
176. See Articles 3, 5 and 6 of the ICSC Statute, Annex to UNGA Res. 3357 (XXIX), Statute of the International Civil Service Commission, https://undocs.org/en/A/RES/3357(XXIX).

of salaries, pensions and benefits, through the application of common personnel standards, methods and arrangements [177].

One of the tasks of the ICSC is, on the one hand, to make recommendations to the General Assembly on the scales of salaries and post adjustments for staff in the professional category, that is to say the higher civil servants in the UN Common System. On the other hand, the ICSC was also charged with establishing the classification of duty stations for the purpose of applying post adjustments. In its turn the ICSC created a subcommittee, the so-called Advisory Committee on Post Adjustment Questions (ACPAQ), which was tasked with advising the ICSC itself on questions of post adjustment. Thus the General Assembly had delegated an advisory task to the ICSC, namely the one relating to scales of salary and post adjustments, and thus had retained its decision-making power in the matter [178]. However, it had transferred a decision-making power fully to the ICSC, namely the classification of duty stations for the application of post adjustments. On the latter issue the ICSC in its turn was advised by the ACPAQ [179]. Hence the General Assembly remained in control of the elements that governed the application of the Noblemaire principle, namely the level of salaries and post adjustments. Moreover, in a later resolution [180] the General Assembly enjoined the ICSC to follow closely the elements that could influence a proper application of the Noblemaire principle. Such elements also included post adjustment and the resulting changes in the classification of duty stations. Although in theory the Noblemaire principle could and should be respected by the salary scale of the UN professional staff simply following that of the comparator country, in reality the change in *class* of a duty station as a consequence of post adjustment, in particular of New York, had to be manipulated in order not to fall behind or move ahead too much of the US civil service salary scale.

The above serves primarily as background for UNAT-old Case 370 which was brought by a number of UN personnel against the post adjustment and resulting reclassification of the New York duty station. In the early 1980s there were indications that the evolution of the costs

---

177. Article 9 ICSC Statute, *ibid.*
178. Article 10 *(b)* ICSC Statute, *ibid.*
179. Article 11 *(c)* ICSC Statute, ibid. The "classes" of duty stations were later abolished by the General Assembly, but this was never reflected in the text of Article 11 *(c)* ICSC Statute.
180. UNGA Res. 31/141B, Report of the International Civil Service Commission, 17 December 1976, https://undocs.org/en/A/RES/31/141.

of living at the New York duty station had possibly been understated. The ACPAQ was charged with undertaking a study, and indeed arrived at the conclusion that the post adjustment for New York had to rise by 9.6 percent. This implied a reclassification of the New York duty station from class XI to class XII. The ICSC decided to follow the ACPAQ, and in its report to the General Assembly in November 1984 announced the post adjustment of 9.6 percent and the reclassification for the New York duty station. In that report it was also mentioned that the difference between the salary scales of the comparator country and those of the United Nations in New York would thus rise to the level of 24 percent, which was well above the "ideal" differential of 15 percent. Moreover, the ICSC also advised that the new, adjusted salary scale of the UN professional staff should only be applied as from 1 August 1984.

In reaction to the ICSC's report, the General Assembly adopted a resolution [181] on 30 November 1984 stating that the differential of 24 percent in favor of the UN remuneration in comparison to US civil service salary scales was too high and that therefore the entry into force of the new UN salary scale should be put off until the next meeting of the General Assembly in the autumn of 1985, that is to say after a new session of the ICSC and an opportunity for the General Assembly to react to the ICSC's decisions. Subsequently the matter was considerably complicated further by the fact that the special emergency rules for deciding urgent matters during a period that the ICSC was not in formal session (as it was not between mid-December 1984 and early 1985) were not properly followed by its chair. Later this alleged illegality was effectively superseded by a renewed decision of the ICSC during its spring meeting of 1985, when it reconfirmed its earlier decision, that is to say the decision taken according to the emergency procedures regarding the suspension of the ICSC decision reclassifying duty station New York to class XII, as desired by the General Assembly. The UNAT-old agreed with the complaining staff members that the special emergency rules for taking decisions during a period that the

---

181. UNGA Res. 39/27, United Nations Common System, Report of the ICSC, 30 November 1984, https://undocs.org/en/A/RES/39/27. In its operative paragraphs, this resolution requested the ICSC in highly technical terms to find a solution to the reasons why the post adjustment for New York led to the overall remuneration of New York staff going far over the level required for the maintenance of the Noblemaire principle. This was due to the very high cost of living in New York in the 1980s compared to that of the rest of the US, including the District of Columbia, which served as the basis for determining US federal government salaries.

ICSC was not in session had indeed been improperly applied, but the consequences of that decision remained limited [182].

Much more important for our study of delegation was the second plea brought forward by the complainants, namely that once the General Assembly had decided to delegate a certain task to a new subordinate organ, the Assembly was no longer authorized to meddle in the exercise of those delegated powers by the organ in question, that is to say that it was a full delegation [183]. The complainants bolstered this argument by referring to the case about the creation and the powers of UNAT-old itself before the ICJ, which was discussed in the previous section. In this connection they referred to the decision of the ICJ that the General Assembly had to abide by the decision on damages issued by the body that the General Assembly itself had created. UNAT rejected that claim in no uncertain terms by pointing out that it constituted a judicial body, which was not the case of the ICSC. The latter was an advisory body, to which also some decision-making tasks had been delegated by the General Assembly, while the latter had reserved other such tasks to itself – which as "the legislative sovereign", it was free to do [184]. In such circumstances, according to UNAT-old, it was entirely acceptable that the UN General Assembly could modify the delegation granted to the ICSC, or modulate its exercise, as it had done in its resolution of 30 November 1984, which, in addition, the ICSC had validly followed on 25 March 1985 [185].

It is interesting that UNAT-old espoused a quite narrow approach to delegation. It is obvious that the ICSC cannot be compared to UNAT itself as far as its independence and its tasks are concerned. It is also true that a delegation can be taken back and that the delegator may give directives to the delegate. The problem in this case was precisely that the General Assembly did not care to take back the delegation of decision-making in Article 11 *(c)* – and has not done so to this day – and that the directives were issued after the ICSC had taken the

---

182. The effects of this illegality were limited to the period of three months between the illegal decision of December 1984 and its reconfirmation at the end of March 1985 and meant a right to a rise in salary in conformity with class XII pay for New York for the complainants during those months. See UNAT Judgment No. 370, *supra* footnote 172, at paras. XXIII-XXXVIII.
183. Cf. the notion of delegation in Dutch administrative law under GALA Article 10, see *supra* Chap. II.E.3.
184. UNAT-old Judgment No. 370, *supra* footnote 172, at paras. IX and XIII. This position was later also adopted by the Office of Legal Affairs of the UN Secretariat; see *UN Juridical Yearbook*...
185. UNAT-old Judgment No. 370, *supra* footnote 172, at paras. X-XXII.

"wrong decision" on class XII for the New York duty station and that the ICSC was forced to "redo" its "wrong classification" – which, in spite of procedural errors, it did. But could this view of delegation be brought in conformity with the nature of a body that had been created by the Assembly on the basis of the independence and the expertise of its members [186] ? That is a question that would come back to haunt the United Nations thirty-five years later.

Before continuing with this recurring problem in the history of the UN, it may be useful to pay some attention to the rules that the Secretary-General promulgated in respect of the delegation of authority in the administration of the Staff Regulations and Rules and the Financial Regulations and Rules.

C. *The Secretary-General's bulletin on delegation of authority*

It is obvious that the rules included in this bulletin [187] are rules of delegation of an administrative law character; they deal exclusively with delegation from the Secretary-General to so-called heads of entity [188] and subdelegation from thereon down through the hierarchy. They do not cover what has been called earlier "delegation of a constitutional character" between the principal organs of the UN, such as the General Assembly, the Security Council and the Secretary-General, including the Secretariat that he heads. The delegation of authority covers the administration of staff and the application of the budgetary rules. The most important aspects of this bulletin are sections 2 and 4 covering respectively the general principles of delegation and the management of authorities delegated to heads of entities.

First of all, it is important to signal that all delegations of authority, including any limitations, will be available through an online portal,

---

186. The ICSC may not be based on legal expertise and the necessary independence flowing therefrom, but it was created by the General Assembly as an independent body of experts and accordingly would have deserved some restraint on the part of its creator.

187. Secretary-General's bulletin, Delegation of authority in the Administration of the Staff Regulations and Rules and the Financial Regulations and Rules, ST/SGB/2019/2, 17 December 2018. This bulletin superseded two predecessor bulletins, one for delegation relating to the Staff Regulations and Rules (ST/SGB/2015/1) and the other for delegation relating to the Financial Regulations and Rules (ST/AI/2016/7), which were much less detailed, especially on the *nature of delegation*.

188. "'Head of entity' means the head of a department or an office, including an office away from Headquarters; the head of a special political or peacekeeping mission; the head of a regional commission; a resident or regional coordinator; or the head of any other unit tasked with programmed activities." Delegation bulletin, ST/SGB/2019/2, *supra* footnote 187, at p. 1, n. 1.

which presumably is accessible to each UN civil servant so as to enable him/her to be informed on the delegations that affect him/her. Transparency is thus a ground rule of the system. If no delegation is listed in a certain domain, this means that the Secretary-General has reserved that authority to himself [189].

The objective of delegation within the Secretariat is to situate decision-making closer to the point of service delivery. The actual execution of the decision based on a delegated authority may be in the hands of another entity that has the requisite operational capacity (which will be designated by the Under-Secretary-General for Operational Support). In this way delegation should not lead to duplication of decision points or of operational capacities [190]. Delegation from the S-G on downwards is always to a specific function, not to the person occupying the function, which simplifies matters when a function is exercised by a temporary replacement from inside or outside the UN civil service [191]. Since accountability cannot inhere in a function, the natural person occupying that function is personally accountable for incorrectly applying or failing to discharge the delegated authority in the appropriate way [192].

A delegate may proceed to subdelegate (part of) the delegated authority unless subdelegation is excluded by the delegator in the (sub)-delegation decision. On the other hand, delegators remain accountable and responsible for the delegated authority that they have (sub)-delegated. In the UN system there is no true transfer of power to the lower level, only transfer of *the exercise* of power. The delegate shall comply with reporting obligations imposed on him by the delegator (and presumably any other obligations laid down in the delegation decision). Any (sub)-delegate shall carry out the (sub)-delegation with the utmost professionalism and integrity, in conformity with the applicable Staff and Financial Regulations. The delegation bulletin also contains an extensive definition of accountability [193].

The Secretary-General may suspend, amend or even revoke any delegation to a head of entity at any moment. In these decisions he is advised by the Under-Secretary-General for Management Strategy, Policy and Compliance in consultation with the Under-Secretary-

---

189. *Ibid.*, at Points 1.2 and 1.3.
190. *Ibid.*, at Points 2.3.
191. *Ibid.*, at Points 2.4 and 2.6. The Secretary-General may in specific cases nevertheless expressly delegate authority on a personal basis.
192. *Ibid.*, at Points 2.7 and 4.3.
193. *Ibid.*, at Points 2.8-2.11.

General for Operational Support. Such measures may have a disciplinary aspect to them and in such a case are accompanied by the necessary disciplinary action. All this will be recorded in the online portal [194].

It is important to point out that many of the core rules laid out in the delegation bulletin were based on the existing case law of the administrative tribunals of the UN [195]. It is also obvious that the system of (sub)-delegation applying internally in the UN Secretariat is characterized by certain features that hardly leave any serious independent responsibility to the delegates functioning within this system. The relevant features are: the rather extreme power to suspend, amend or revoke the (sub)-delegation at *any* time; and the fact that (sub)-delegators remain accountable for the powers they have (sub)-delegated to the delegate, which entails that delegates in practice may be subject to constant instructions from the delegator.

These features characterize a system of agency or mandate rather than any true delegation which, because there is a *real transfer* of power to the delegate and not only *of its exercise*, normally entails a certain autonomy of application or implementation of the delegated authority on the part of the delegate and regards revocation of the delegation as an *ultimum remedium*. As explained earlier, that was a pronounced aspect of the Italian doctrine on delegation. That, however, was a constitutional approach to delegation, between coequal branches of government [196]. Therefore, it is both not surprising and legitimate for a system of administrative law delegation *within* the hierarchical UN Secretariat to be based on a more stringent approach to delegation, founded on the transfer of the *exercise* of authority, which is close to

---

194. *Ibid.*, at Points 4.4-4.5.
195. A good, recent example, handed down a few months before the delegation bulletin, is UNDT's Judgment 2018/29, *Finiss* v. *Secretary-General* some ten months before the delegation bulletin was published in December of 2018:

> "[D]elegation does not equate to the delegator definitively ridding himself/ herself of the powers and authority that he or she delegates. Legally, a delegator continues to maintain the powers and authority that he or she has delegated, and such delegation is thus revocable at any time. Therefore, both parties' arguments that the USG/OIOS could or should have "surrendered" her delegation back to the Secretary-General are flawed. Rather, the Secretary-General may simply revoke a prior delegation at any time. The delegation of powers to hierarchically subordinated organs (as in the present case) presents several defining juridical features: *(a)* It is an entitlement established and delimited by legislation whereby an organ or an authority is enabled to transfer (partially) the exercise of its competencies to a subordinated organ; *(b)* . . . ; *(c)* The delegator continues to be the authority legally bestowed with the competence, not the delegate, who can only exercise the authority on behalf of the delegator."

196. See *supra* Chap. II.C.2 and 4.

the notion of delegation of signature mentioned earlier. However, the question is to what extent this model has also influenced the relation between the General Assembly and the Secretary-General in the domain of personnel and budgetary policy and implementation and whether that is justifiable and desirable in the light of the relevant text of the Charter, that is to say, in the UN *constitutional* setting. The same question can also be asked about the relation between the General Assembly and the subsidiary bodies it has created itself and given a special Statute, such as the successive administrative tribunals and the ICSC. These questions will be discussed after further description and analysis of the recent case law concerning the relation between the ICSC, the Assembly and the Secretary-General.

D. *The different powers delegated to the ICSC: Advisory and decisional*

1. *The judgment of the ILO Administrative Tribunal*

Recently the ILO Administrative Tribunal (ILO AT) has had to deal with a problem closely related to that discussed earlier in relation to the *Molinier* case: the relationship between the advisory powers and decision-making powers of the ICSC [197]. The discussion above of UNAT Judgment 370 has already shown [198] that there is a close connection between a decision of the ICSC under Article 11 *(c)* of its Statute on the classification of duty stations for the application of post adjustment on the one hand, and its advisory powers on the scales of salaries and post adjustments themselves on the other. The latter powers, laid down in Article 10 *(b)* of the Statute of the ICSC, serve to help the General Assembly take its final decision on these matters, while the former is a true delegated decision-making power that, however, is bound to have an important influence on the ICSC's final advice to the General Assembly and therefore also on the subsequent decision of the General Assembly itself. As a matter of fact, the General Assembly has come to regard the advice of the ICSC on the scales of salaries and post adjustments more and more as a decision by which it was bound itself. Oddly enough, at the same time, the General Assembly implicitly took the view that as delegator, it was free to exercise strong pressure on the

---

197. Judgment No. 4134 and other similar cases of the ILO AT, 3 July 2019, https://www.ilo.org/dyn/triblex/triblexmain.detail?p_judgment_no=4134.
198. See *supra* Sec. B.

delegate, the ICSC, both in the period leading up to an ICSC advice and decision, as well as in the period of implementation of its advice and decision [199].

Over recent decades the United Nations has been under increasing budgetary pressures from its Member States. There was a strong tendency in the political organs of the organization to cut costs at all duty stations of the UN. In this connection Geneva was a favorite target because of its relatively high cost of living. Hence the Member States were looking for a reassessment of the Geneva post adjustment on the basis of a new cost of living survey for Geneva. Hopefully this would lead to a reduction of the overall remuneration of personnel of the United Nations and of the specialized agencies in Geneva, which were part of the UN system of salaries and benefits [200]. On the other hand, UN staff and the personnel of UN specialized agencies in Geneva were of the view that cost of living had rather gone up, especially as far as housing was concerned. The ICSC and its ACPAQ subcommittee were charged with carrying out this reassessment. The outcome of their work was that the post adjustment for Geneva would in any case not rise; in the end the result, according to the complainants, was to reduce the post adjustment for Geneva by more than 4 percent. While even some of the Geneva-based UN organizations and specialized agencies balked at implementing this reduction, a large number of their staff members started a case against the ILO and other UN specialized agencies and UN offices in Geneva about the way in which the post adjustment for Geneva had been fixed. This case was brought initially before the ILO AT, which traditionally had continued to serve as the administrative tribunal for the ILO and other UN specialized agencies domiciled in Geneva – for example, the World Health Organization (WHO), the International Telecommunication Union (ITU), the World Meteorological Organization (WMO), and so on – and for smaller non-EU international organizations in Europe, such as the European Free Trade Association (EFTA), CERN (the European Organization

---

199. As will be shown below (see *infra* footnotes 208 through 210 and accompanying text), UNGA Resolutions 67/641, 72/255 and 74/255 are notorious for attempts to confirm that the ICSC is subservient to the General Assembly, and that the UNDT and UNAT-new should be too.

200. There were and are certainly many international civil servants of the UN and its specialized agencies at Geneva that would regard the qualification "hopefully" here as much too soft. They remain convinced that the intended objective of the reassessment from the beginning was to bring the overall salary of the Geneva-based civil servants down, and that the reassessment was construed accordingly, notably by neglecting the considerable increase in housing costs.

for Nuclear Research), and so on [201] [202]. The staff members of the UN in Geneva had to bring the case before the United Nations Disputes Tribunal (UNDT) [203]. The ILO AT was the first to decide of these two.

Since its creation in 1973 the ICSC had become a very important suborgan of the General Assembly that fulfilled a central role in personnel matters and salary questions. During the case before the ILO AT, it transpired that the UN General Assembly increasingly left not just the technical questions concerning salaries, benefits and post adjustments to the ICSC, but also trusted the ICSC to follow the political mood of the Assembly. As a consequence, the General Assembly itself began to forget the difference between the advisory powers that it had delegated to the ICSC under Article 10 *(b)* of its Statute and the rather preparatory matters in which it had delegated decision-making powers to that body under Article 11 *(c)*. In the case before it, the ILO AT demonstrated that the General Assembly had taken the action of the ICSC under Article 10 *(b)*, which was of an advisory character, as a definitive decision:

> "On any reasonable view, the General Assembly did not consider and act on a recommendation [of the ICSC] in adopting its Resolution 72/255. . . . It is not apparent that the General Assembly exercised any discretionary decision-making power whether to act on a recommendation, but assumed . . . the decision had already been made." [204]

The ILO administration responded with the argument that this had become the current practice of the General Assembly and had to be recognized as such. This raised the question whether customary practice of an organization can change the existing written rules established by the organization itself, in this case the founding resolution and the

---

201. The cases concerned are ILO AT Judgments No. 4134, *B. et al., A-M et al., A-U et al.* v. *ILO*; No. 4135, *K, A et al., A.M et al.* v. *WHO*; No. 4136, *A, G, P and R* v. *IOM*; No. 4137, *CB (No. 2), d. AP, M and R* v. *ITU*; No. 4138, *G et al., K and W, A et al.* v. *WIPO*. See https://www.ilo.org/dyn/triblex/triblexmain.showlist. These judgments substantially follow the same lines of arguments and reach the same conclusions. The text below is primarily based on the first case, No. 4134, *supra* footnote 197.

202. A full list of the organizations that have elected the ILO AT as administrative tribunal can be found at https://www.ilo.org/tribunal/membership/lang--en/index.htm.

203. UNDT Judgment, 30 June 2020, UNDT/2020/106, *Abd Al Shakour et al.* v. *Secretary-General*, https://www.un.org/en/internaljustice/files/undt/judgments/undt-2020-106-EN.pdf. Discussed at *infra* footnote 217 and accompanying text.

204. ILO AT Judgment No. 4134, *supra* footnote 197, at paras. 31-34. Indeed, Res/A/72/225 under the title "The Common System" thanks the ICSC for its report and its work, mentions the Assembly's view of Articles 10 and 11 of the ICSC Statute in terms that are far from clear, and in Section II C on Post Adjustment does not take any clear decision.

Statute of the ICSC, in particular its Articles 10 and 11. The ILO AT took the position that such a modification of preexisting written rules by later customary practice that is clearly incompatible with these rules, is not possible. This is a long-standing principle in the case law of the ILO AT, a principle which is in turn "a manifestation of a more fundamental requirement namely the creation of stability and predictability and certainty" in the relation between the organization and its civil servants. "To accept the contention of the ILO concerning the legal effect of practice is to invite instability, unpredictability and uncertainty and must be rejected." [205]

One may well wonder how this view of the ILO AT can be squared with what the ICJ has said about the effect of a constant practice of the organization on the interpretation of articles of the Charter in its advisory opinion on *Namibia* [206]. The first question that arose in that case was that of the competence of the Court, since the Security Council resolution asking for the opinion had been adopted by the requisite number of nine votes and with the voluntary abstentions of two permanent members. Could such abstentions be regarded as "concurring votes" within the meaning of Article 27 (3) of the Charter? The Court accepted that in this way valid resolutions of the Security Council could be adopted on the strength of a long-standing practice of the members of the Council, and in particular its permanent members, and on the basis of numerous rulings from the Chair. All this had been generally accepted by members of the United Nations and "evidenced a general practice of that organization" [207]. However, a closer look both at Judgment 4134 of the ILO AT and the *Namibia* opinion of the ICJ, as well as their context, may give valuable insights into how both judgments might coexist.

Both cases concern the creation of a customary way of taking decisions by respectively the General Assembly and the Security Council, which goes against written rules determining the way these decisions normally ought to be made. In the case of the General Assembly, this process seems to have taken place in a much less conscious way than in the Security Council, where there is a solid record of rulings by the

---

205. ILO AT Judgment No. 4134, *supra* footnote 197, at paras. 37-41.
206. ICJ Advisory Opinion, *Legal Consequences for States of the Continued Presence of South Africa in Namibia (South-West Africa) notwithstanding Security Council Resolution 276 (1970)*, *ICJ Reports 1971*, p. 16.
207. *Ibid.*, at p. 22. How such a general practice could modify the wording of Article 27 of the Charter – a treaty with the special rank in international law conferred by its Article 103 – remains somewhat mysterious but is not directly relevant to the argument here.

President and instances where the permanent members have accepted that their abstention constitutes no veto. In a way, one might say that the General Assembly has blundered into its own practice of regarding advice by the ICSC as a delegated decision [208], while the practice of the treatment of abstention by permanent members in the Security Council has been carefully fashioned by all participants over the years. That is perhaps also a reflection of the fact that the practice in the Security Council went against the primary law of the organization, which the members of the Security Council cannot change, whereas the practice of the General Assembly was contrary only to secondary law of the organization, the ICSC Statute, which the General Assembly itself adopted, but has never seen fit to adapt to its own practice to this day [209].

The major difference between the two attempts to create new customary rules prevailing over written provisions of UN law, however, probably depends on who are the immediate subjects of these pretended customary rules of decision-making. In the case of the Security Council the members of the Council, and in particular the permanent members, fashioned the rules over the years into custom and at the same time they were the main subjects of these rules, both as members of the Council and as possible addressees of Council resolutions taken according to the new decision-making rules. Seen in this light it is easier to understand how the ICJ could come to the conclusion that it should not disturb the customary rules of decision-making created by the Security Council and accepted by the UN membership at large. By contrast, it is equally easy to see how the ILO AT could not accept the purported amended decision-making procedure of the General Assembly, where the subjects of the decisions made were not the Member States themselves, but the civil servants of the different specialized agencies, notably the ILO and other Geneva-based UN entities [210]. According to the unchanged Articles 10

---

208. As it appears from the cases before the UN internal justice tribunals discussed below, this shift in the GA's practice was helped along by the fact that the "classes" of UN bureaus and specialized agencies determined by the level of the post adjustment index were abolished after 1984. Thus Article 11 *(c)* of the ICSC Statute became obsolete whereupon that index for each city/country where the UN was present became decisive for post adjustment.

209. The ILO AT did not forget to mention that: "Article 30 of the ICSC Statute provides that amendments to it are to be made by the General Assembly and are subject to the same acceptance procedure 'as the present statute'." ILO AT Judgment No. 4134, *supra* footnote 197, at para. 37 *in fine*.

210. It is important to recall that the Geneva-based specialized agencies of the UN are part of the UN Common System, but are subject to the jurisdiction of the ILO AT, which in a paragraph that is common to all the cases mentioned in footnote 197 states the following:

and 11 of the ICSC Statute, these civil servants had the fullest right to expect that these rules still applied and that there was a need for the General Assembly formally to accept or overrule the advice of the ICSC before the effects of the new post adjustment index would be brought to bear upon them. Not doing so has created a situation which is characterized by at the minimum a lack of transparency, probably an absence of good government and possibly a breach of the rule of law, all rolled into one [211].

2. The view of the UN Internal Justice System

As mentioned above, the UN civil servants affected by the new post adjustment for Geneva had to file their own complaint with the UN Internal Justice System, in the first place with the UNDT. In the meantime, in reaction to the initial hesitation of some Geneva-based UN specialized agencies and the judgment of the ILO AT, the reaction at the UN Headquarters in New York had been pretty strong. The Secretary-General expressed his concern that ILO and some other organizations had decided not immediately to implement the decisions of the ICSC regarding the results of the cost of living survey for Geneva, and the UN General Assembly followed suit [212]. From their point of view a breakdown of the unity in the common system of salaries, pensions and benefits was a very serious matter. At the same time the General Assembly attempted to rectify belatedly its neglect of properly amending Articles 10 and 11 of the ICSC Statute to bring them into conformity with the actual practice of the ICSC and General Assembly, reaffirming its own role under these two articles, as well as the "the

---

"Some principles in the case law of the Tribunal should be noted. . . . The first is, as observed in Judgment 1266, consideration 24, that:

'. . . by incorporating the standards of the common system in its own rules the [organization] has assumed responsibility towards its staff for any unlawful elements that those standards may contain or entail. Insofar as such standards are found to be flawed, they may not be imposed on the staff and [the organization] must, if need be, replace them with provisions that comply with the law of the international civil service. That is an essential feature of the principles governing the international legal system the Tribunal is called upon to safeguard'".

This implies, of course, that there may be limits to the commonness of the UN Common System.

211. See ST/SGB/2019/2, *supra* footnote 187, which requires that all delegations and subdelegations in a new online portal be accessible to all staff.

212. UNGA Res. 72/255, United Nations Common System, 12 January 2018, at paras. 5-8.

central role" of the ICSC "in regulating and coordinating conditions of service for all staff" serving under the UN Common System [213].

After the ILO AT handed down its judgment in the course of 2019, the reaction from the General Assembly became even stronger. Not only was the language of the preceding resolution repeated, but the Assembly explicitly reaffirmed (twice) the authority of the ICSC to continue to establish post adjustment multipliers for duty stations in the UN Common System under Article 11 *(c)* of the ICSC Statute. It also recalled that in older resolutions it had abolished the post adjustment scales in Article 10 *(b)* of the Statute [214]. These resolutions were to have a considerable impact on the cases that were brought against the reduction of the post adjustment for the Geneva duty station before the UNDT and subsequently appealed to the UNAT-new.

The UNDT case, next to the issue of delegation, treats a large number of questions of great importance for the UN administrative court system and its future viability, such as the question of admissibility (or "receivability", as it is called in the UN system) of complaints, in particular if they are *de facto* a mass claim or class action; and the question of how far the UNDT's jurisdiction reaches in the face of decisions of the General Assembly on the conditions of service and pay of the UN's civil servants. The issues related to admissibility will be left entirely to one side in the following. However, for the question of the scope of the jurisdiction of the UNDT this is not completely possible as it is historically linked to the question of delegation, which is very prominent in the execution of human resources policy and budgetary matters regarding pay and other benefits. This is glaringly clear from a General Assembly Resolution adopted eight years before the Geneva post adjustment conflict. In this resolution the General Assembly makes a number of strong statements, such as:

– The resolutions of the General Assembly and the decisions of the ICSC are binding on the Secretary-General and the UN Organization.
– All elements of the system of administration of justice must work in accordance with the UN Charter and the legal and regulatory framework approved by the General Assembly.

---

213. *Ibid.*, at paras. 3-4. The text is far from clear and an actual amendment of Articles 10 and 11 ICSC Statute did not (yet) take place.
214. UNGA Res. 74/255 A-B, United Nations Common System, 27 December 2019, at paras. A 1-2 and B 3-4.

- The decisions of the General Assembly related to administrative and budgetary matters are subject to review by the Assembly alone.
- Recourse to general principles of law and the Charter by the tribunals is to take place within the context of and consistent with their status and the relevant General Assembly resolutions, regulations, rules and administrative issuances.
- Some decisions taken by UNDT and UNAT-new may have contradicted the provisions of General Assembly resolutions on human resources management.
- There is a need to carefully monitor the implementation of the Internal Justice System of the UN and to ensure that it remains within the parameters set by the General Assembly [215].

Further on in the same resolution, the General Assembly showed that it might not be prepared to fully respect the independence of the Internal Justice System of the UN:

"[T]he General Assembly also notes that the authority of judges and the applicability of their judgments derive from decisions of the General Assembly, including the Statute[s] of the Disputes Tribunal ... and of the Appeals Tribunal." [216]

This was language that was difficult to reconcile with the position taken by the ICJ in *The Reparations for Injuries* and *The Effect of Awards* cases, as mentioned earlier, and with the relative restraint with which the General Assembly at the time had ultimately accepted the judgment and its financial consequences in the *Effect of Awards* case.

It is obvious from these pronouncements of the General Assembly that the relations between that leading organ and its new creation, the Internal Justice System of the UN, was fragile and that the new resolutions from the General Assembly of late 2019 and 2020 had to be seen in the light of this older resolution of 2012 and the adverse judgment of the ILO AT. It was in this atmosphere that the UNDT, in the person of Judge Agnieszka Klonowiecka-Milart, had to pronounce itself on the complaint of many UN civil servants, and others falling under the common system and stationed in Geneva [217].

---

215. UNGA Res. 67/241 Administration of Justice at the United Nations, 24 December 2012, at paras. 3, 4, 6, 7, 8 and 11.
216. *Ibid.*, at para. 38.
217. UNDT Judgment 2020/106, *supra* footnote 203.

On the issue of delegation, the UNDT sets out to arrive at an interpretation of Articles 10 and 11 of the ICSC Statute in order to clarify the ICSC's statutory powers of decision. Since certain terms in these provisions – "scales" (of salaries and post adjustments) in Article 10 and "classification" (of duty stations) – are not clear on their face and probably have an unexpressed technical meaning, they have to be interpreted by recourse to the practice of the parties. The UNDT then sketches how the two bodies involved, the General Assembly and the ICSC, step by step changed the process of determining post adjustment indices (which in its view never fully functioned as it had been set out in Articles 10 and 11 of the ICSC Statute, although the abolishing of "scales" in 1989 by a resolution of the General Assembly was an important step) until the process between the General Assembly and the ICSC works as it does now, namely as recalled in General Assembly Resolution 74/255 of December 2019[218]. And yet the UNDT admitted that this was different from the procedure envisaged in Articles 10 and 11. Although Judge Klonowiecka said that this was confusing and nontransparent, she nevertheless decided that the changes were approved by the General Assembly, either expressly or by reference to ICSC reports. Moreover, the UNDT was in a different position than the ILO AT, since the ILO, unlike the UN, had the option of not accepting the ICSC's authority under Article 1 (2) of its Statute[219].

Although the UNDT seemed to have rejected the argument relating to the invalidity of the delegation from the General Assembly to the ICSC, it went on, nevertheless, to confront the question of the scope of its review. As is clear from its Resolution 67/241 discussed above, the General Assembly showed a high degree of anxiety for any decision from the Internal Justice System of the UN that might threaten the smooth implementation of any of its resolutions on budgetary or HR matters.

During the pleadings before the UNDT, and later the UNAT-new, it was even mentioned that the administrative tribunals were on the verge of assuming the mantle of a constitutional court, if they were to

---

218. See *supra* footnote 214 and *ibid.*, at paras. 70-71.
219. *Ibid.*, at paras. 73-74. The UNDT never clarified whether the ILO indeed had failed to accept the authority of the ICSC in a way that was irrelevant, as the ILO AT in its Judgment No. 2134 referred to its standing case law that it had the right to review rules of the common system for conformity with the law, as that was part of its remit. See *supra* footnote 204.

follow the example of the ILO AT [220]. Ever since the advisory opinion of the ICJ about a possible excess of jurisdiction by the UNAT-old in 1982, however, it was clear that there was no such risk. The ICJ itself admitted that it had no powers of judicial review over General Assembly resolutions, and, in its view, there was "no question" that the UNAT-old possessed any powers of judicial review or appeal in respect of decisions taken by the General Assembly. Moreover, the ICJ broadly argued that UNAT's decision in the case in question amounted to a simple protection of a civil servant's acquired right without casting aspersion on the relevant provision of the General Assembly's Staff Regulations or the implementing Staff Rules adopted by the Secretary-General [221]. The UNDT did not deviate from this ruling by the ICJ but was of the view that in deciding individual cases, there should be room for the administrative tribunals "incidentally" to look into the legality of the underlying general legislative act, without having the power to rescind such acts [222]. European administrative lawyers would recognize this as being akin to the *exception d'illégalité*, which originated in French administrative law and was adopted by many other systems of administrative law, including by that of the EU [223]. However, the

---

220. It is perhaps useful to point out that the ILO AT's judgment merely implied that the General Assembly should finally do what it should have done some time in the early 1990s, after the practice of the interaction between itself and the ICSC had changed, namely adapting Articles 10 and 11 of the ICSC Statute to this reality. That is a simple question of good governance or even rule of law, which should be observed by all principal organs of the UN, including the General Assembly, and *not* a question of constitutional review.

221. *Application for Review of Judgment No. 273 of the United Nations Administrative Tribunal*, Advisory Opinion, *ICJ Reports 1982*, p. 325, at para. 76.

222. UNDT Judgment 2020/106, *supra* footnote 203, at paras. 83-85.

223. See Plessix, *supra* footnote 42, at para. 168 ff. It should be noted that this "exception of illegality" existed long before France had a constitutional court and was a recognized way of criticizing legislative texts without going so far as to annul them – annulment of laws being totally unheard of in France before its *Conseil Constitutionnel* came on the scene in 1958 and developed into more of a real constitutional court after access to it was broadened in 2008 by the introduction of the *Questions Prioritaires de Constitutionalité (QPC)*; see *supra* footnote 45 and accompanying text. Before the EUCJ parties have invoked the exception (Art. 277 TFEU) sparingly, but regularly, since the early days until the present, now that the Court has become more of a constitutional court, next to its continuing load of administrative court cases. As to its adoption by the European Union, it should be noted that it was read into ECSC law in the famous *Meroni* case on delegation of quasi-legislative powers as a principle of general administrative law that was confirmed by its inclusion in Article 184 of the EEC Treaty, which at that moment had not yet entered into force. See Case 10/56, *Meroni*, *supra* footnote 2, at pp. 140-141. In the European Commission it was not unusual, in case the Commission or one of the other institutions lost a case based on the exception of illegality, for the Legal Service to address a note to the Commission, certainly if the result risked affecting many other individuals or companies in the same way as the complainant, advising it to propose a modification of the legislation concerned to

UNDT seemed to want to restrict such cases to situations in which there were two conflicting rules emanating from the General Assembly [224]. This is untenable since general principles of administrative law such as good governance, nondiscrimination, transparency, the protection of acquired rights or the "undisputed principles of international labor law" [225] ought at least to be available to the administrative tribunals with a view to decisions on compensation in individual cases when the General Assembly or the Secretary-General choose not to respect such principles, even if they are not laid down explicitly in the Staff Regulations or Staff Rules.

The strong link between delegation and the scope of the review that the administrative tribunals were allowed to exercise comes to the fore again when the UNDT draws attention to the close supervision that the General Assembly maintains over the ICSC: "[The ICSC] remains subordinated to the ... General Assembly who [*sic!*] may intervene and indeed does so, mainly in the policy stage but also after the ICSC decision has been taken." After which the UNDT gives a considerable number of examples of the Assembly's interfering with and *de facto* changing the ICSC's decisions after they had been taken [226]. Once again, as in the discussion of UNAT-old Case 370 *Molinier* [227], one may

---

the legislature, even if this was formally not required because there was no annulment (personal professional experience of the author).

224. UNDT Judgment 2020/106, *supra* footnote 203, at paras. 89-91 and 93. This idea implicitly refers to UNAT-old Judgment 273, *Mortished* v. *Secretary-General*, which was the subject of the ICJ advisory opinion of 1982, *supra* footnote 204. In that case the UNAT-old determined that Mr Mortished, who lost the right to a (controversial) repatriation grant upon retirement, was entitled to damages for breach of his acquired rights, even though the right to protection of acquired rights had been removed from the Staff Rules after a resolution to this effect by the General Assembly during the procedure before UNAT. Given the timing of the last-mentioned act of the General Assembly, UNAT was able to say that Mortished could still enjoy the protection of this clause. Does that mean that the protection of acquired rights, a general principle of law broadly recognized by UN Member States, now that it has been removed from the Staff Rules, can no longer be applied by the UN's internal justice system in individual cases if that right would have been breached by a resolution of the General Assembly? Would that still be a "justice" system? The UNDT was not of that opinion, as will appear from the text below.

225. For one such principle of international labor law, see Judgment No. 2015-UNAT-55, *Pedicelli* v. *Secretary-General*, at para. 29:

"[I]t is an undisputed principle of international labour law and indeed our own jurisprudence that where a decision of general application negatively affects the terms of appointment or contract of employment of a staff member, such decision shall be treated as an 'administrative decision' falling within the scope of Article 2 (1) of the Statute of the Dispute Tribunal and a staff member who is adversely affected is entitled to contest that decision."

226. UNDT Judgment 2020/106, *supra* footnote 203, at para. 93.
227. See *supra* Sec. B in this chapter.

well ask whether there is still any serious delegation there. In addition, several Assembly resolutions have been adopted that decide that the Secretary-General and the UN Organization are bound by the decisions of the ICSC and the resolutions of the Assembly [228] and that "the decisions of the Assembly related to human resources management and administrative and budgetary matters are subject to review by the Assembly alone" [229]. Nevertheless, the UNDT in the end arrived at the point where, since acquired rights were involved, it felt obliged to test the reasonableness of the restriction of these rights against certain criteria. It added:

> "[A]s previously explained, this is done in order to evaluate the legality of the individual decisions based on [the regulatory decision] and not to hold the ICSC 'answerable' or exercise a constitutional court-type jurisdiction over its decisions." [230]

The aspect of the ICSC decision that worried the UNDT most was its effect on the viability of the international civil service (including the Noblemaire principle).

However, in the light of such elements as "the consistency of procedure with internal rules, high complexity, multiple alternatives, absence of... arbitrariness in the methodology, the mitigation applied and, above all, the temporary character", the decision was not unreasonable "in risking the deterioration of the international civil service" [231]. Although far from satisfactory, the UNDT thus at least made a creditable attempt to escape from a difficult situation, while saving some shadow of the *exception d'illégalité* and nevertheless rejecting the claim.

However, the UN Appeals Tribunal came down much more openly on the side of the General Assembly than the Disputes Tribunal [232]. In its view, the General Assembly is "the legislative sovereign" of the UN [233] and it can by *fiat* straighten out everything that was possibly crooked in the determination of matters of human resources and budgetary policy by giving "a clear command" to carry out any decision the

---

228. UNGA Res. 67/241, *supra* footnote 215, at para. 3, among others.
229. UNGA Res. 73/276, Administration of Justice at the United Nations, at para. 44.
230. UNDT Judgment 2020/106, *supra* footnote 203, at para. 118.
231. *Ibid.*, at para. 131.
232. UNAT Judgment No. 2021-UNAT-1107, *Abd Al-Shakour et al. & Aksioutine et al. v. Secretary-General.*
233. *Ibid.*, at para. 59. This term was already used in UNAT-old Judgment 370 *Molinier*, see *supra* footnote 172.

General Assembly has taken [234]. This is equally true for the two aspects of the case, delegation and the scope of the review of General Assembly resolutions. In respect of the first question, the UNAT-new brushed away the period of over twenty-five years during which the Assembly did not care to adapt the Statute of the ICSC to "the usual practice", as "simply a formality" [235]. At the same time, it admitted that the resolutions had not modified Articles 10 and 11 of the Statute as such but argued that they constituted an authentic interpretation of the evolutionary practice of the ICSC and the General Assembly. Since this was an interpretation by the same lawmaking authority that had adopted the ICSC Statute, this interpretation was authoritative [236]. Nevertheless, the UNAT-new also tried to save some semblance of a possible "exception of illegality", but it believed that it was restricted to cases in which the General Assembly and the ICSC, separately or together, had adopted contradictory decisions, or when the Secretary-General had erred in the implementation of decisions of the General Assembly, assuming that he had any leeway in such implementation – which was not the case here [237].

Let it be said just in passing here that such a self-limitation of this action by those national and EU courts that apply the "exception of illegality" would be revolutionary. There can be little doubt that the position of the ILO AT is right: the administrative courts of the UN and other international organizations are there precisely to protect civil servants of the organizations against breaches of basic rights of all kinds, even if these have crept inadvertently into a general decision of the "sovereign lawgiver" of that organization, as long as that general decision causes damage to individual international civil servants. This includes the rights that decisions be taken according to the existing lawful procedures and that these procedures are unambiguously knowable by those who are affected by them.

Moreover, the UNAT-new seemed to step away from its own attempt to maintain at least some minimum of effectiveness for the two

---

234. *Ibid.*, at para. 51 and the list of resolutions mentioned in para. 59.
235. *Ibid.*, at para. 54. See also the ILO AT case on the same subject, discussed in *supra* footnote 197 and accompagnying text, which qualifies this lack of timely amendment as a failure of good governance or even a breach of the rule of law, since for the personnel of the UN and its specialized agencies in Geneva it was simply impossible to have an unequivocal answer to the question of how the new rules governing their post adjustment ought to have been adopted.
236. *Ibid.*, at para. 53. UNAT-new failed to confront ILO AT's argument that such a *de facto* modification of the law governing benefits by interpretation between two UN organs could not be opposed to the average UN civil servant.
237. *Ibid.*, at para. 52.

administrative tribunals when in the end it accepted that the General Assembly by way of its resolutions could intervene validly in cases while they are before the tribunals, and to do so with retroactive effect by invoking the command theory and the self-review that the General Assembly had assumed (not to say arrogated to itself) in the domains of human resources management and budgetary powers [238]. This would simply be regarded as an egregious breach of the separation of powers and of the judicial character of the work of the administrative courts in any country that maintains such a separation (and cared about it).

The end result of the procedures before the two administrative courts is that there are now two methods for calculating post adjustments for Geneva: one for the UN and those agencies that are formally part of the UN, such as the Conference on Trade and Development (UNCTAD), the High Commissioner for Refugees (UNHCR) and the Office of the High Commissioner for Human Rights (OHCHR), and another for the UN specialized agencies in Geneva and other organizations that fall under the ILO AT's jurisdiction, for example the International Organization for Migration (IOM). Unequal treatment in the same duty station is the result.

The end result for delegation is that it is acceptable for the General Assembly to change the terms of a delegation of powers to a body of independent and expert individuals by practice only, without ever needing to modify the terms of the delegation as laid down in the statute of that body, as annexed to General Assembly Resolution 3357 (XXIX) of 18 December 1974. The practice, by which the terms of delegation are changed fundamentally, modifies the division of decision-making and responsibilities between the General Assembly as delegator and the delegate (ICSC), with the result that the delegate seemingly has the full decision-making power and the delegator has no responsibility at all anymore in respect of decisions concerning staff policy and the budget. In reality, the UN administrative tribunals have accepted that the delegator not only has the right to give directives but may intervene at any time in the work of the delegate body, and that the delegator may not only formally overrule a decision of the delegate but may retroactively change decisions of the delegate at any moment. In short, the delegator has all the power, but no visible responsibility. As the ILO AT implied in its judgment [239], it would be much healthier for

---

238. *Ibid.*, at paras. 59-62, see the discussion of UNGA Resolutions 67/241, 72/255 and 74/255 A-B at *supra* footnote 199.
239. See *supra* footnote 197 and accompanying text.

the relations between delegator and delegate if the relevant General Assembly resolutions were drafted as reactions to the relevant decisions of the ICSC and resulted in acceptances, modifications and overrulings of these (draft) decisions.

Finally, in the light of the aversion that exists in the national doctrines discussed above, and in the EUCJ case law discussed further below, from delegation by the legislator of its own powers to another organ, of which the decision-making procedures are different from its own, it is quite remarkable that nobody has ever raised the question whether the delegation of decision-making powers from the General Assembly to the ICSC was legal in the first place. As indicated earlier, the matters on which the ICSC had decision-making power were minor and everything that touched on the Noblemaire principle and other fundamental questions remained in the hands of the General Assembly. However, after the abolition of "classes of post adjustment" and the blanket way in which the Assembly decided that the decisions of the ICSC were binding on the Secretary-General and the organization as a whole, this distinction between major and minor issues was wiped out. This almost forced the General Assembly into its meddlesome attitude with respect to the ICSC, as sketched above and recognized by the two UN tribunals – at the same time exposing it to the justified criticism of the ILO AT.

E. *The story of Mr Kompass: A well-intentioned civil servant sent on administrative leave*

Mr Kompass was a civil servant working for the United Nations High Commissioner for Human Rights; he was the director of the Field Operations and Technical Cooperation division. In that responsibility he received a report that contained serious accusations of pedophilia, allegedly committed in the Central African Republic by French military personnel who were part of the UN peacekeeping operation in that country [240]. This was in July 2014 and later that month he passed this information on to the Deputy Ambassador of France to the United Nations Office at Geneva (UNOG). He believed it was the best course of action to warn the French authorities as soon as possible of these

---

240. See S. Laville, "UN Aid Worker Suspended for Leaking Report on Child Abuse by French Troops", *The Guardian*, 29 April 2015; T. Berthemet, "Des soldats français accusés de viols sur des enfants en Centrafrique", *Le Figaro*, 29 April 2015.

allegations, thus putting them in a position to begin an investigation of the French units concerned right away. He said that he also spoke to his superiors about having passed on the report to the French Deputy Ambassador. He realized that technically he had "leaked" the document, but he believed he had acted in the best interests of the protection of future possible victims. However, his superiors contested that he had "advised" them of his passing on the documents to the French diplomatic mission in Geneva.

As a consequence, Kompass was advised that the High Commissioner for Human Rights had requested an investigation into the allegations of misconduct raised against him and that pending this investigation he had been placed on administrative leave with pay. In short, he was suspended from his job during the time that the investigation would last. The official decision to place him on administrative leave had been taken by the Head of the UNOG in April 2015, after discussion with the High Commissioner and more than nine months after he allegedly had leaked the report. Kompass reacted immediately to these measures by asking for their provisional suspension since in his view he had done nothing wrong and moreover the Head of UNOG had no authority to take the decision to place him on administrative leave with pay.

The UNDT treated his request for provisional suspension almost immediately, while the Secretariat investigation into his actions was continuing. It appears from the order made by Judge Thomas Laker of the UNDT [241] that the main problem was the lack of a clear delegation of authority to take disciplinary measures from the UN Assistant Secretary-General for personnel matters to the Head of the UNOG, also in respect of the branches of the UN Organization that had their main seat in Geneva. A careful parsing of the relevant documents establishing the relations between the Headquarters in New York, the UN organizations and specialized agencies in Geneva and the Head of UNOG led Judge Laker to the provisional conclusion that although UNOG was to service offices, such as those of the High Commissioner for Refugees and the High Commissioner for Human Rights, in personnel matters there was no explicit delegation of authority in disciplinary matters regarding the personnel of these offices in favor of the Head of the UNOG [242]. This

---

241. See UNDT Order No. 99 (GVA/2015), *Kompass*, https://www.un.org/en/internaljustice/files/undt/orders/gva-2015-099.pdf.
242. *Ibid.*, at paras. 24-34, with reference to para. 49 of Judgment No. 2015-UNAT-511, *Bastet* v. *Secretary-General* of the UN Appeals Tribunal, which stated that

was enough for Judge Laker to establish *prima facie* unlawfulness of the suspension, one of the conditions for the UNDT taking provisional measures. In addition, as far as the substance of the case was concerned, the alleged danger that Kompass would destroy proof or cause harm to his colleagues also suffered *prima facie* from a lack of credibility according to Judge Laker, given Kompass's openness about what he had done and the lack of adequacy of the sanction of administrative leave with pay to prevent him from concealing or destroying elements of proof[243]. Judge Laker, therefore, ordered the reinstatement of Kompass in his functions during the continuing administrative investigation of his acts surrounding the passing on of the documents in question to the French delegation in Geneva. That investigation did not lead to any measures.

The case of Kompass ended well in many respects. As far as delegation was concerned, it clarified that if a delegation affected decisions with consequences for individuals, it could take many forms and be established in different ways, but that it had to be absolutely certain that such a delegation had been lawfully established and was verifiable. That is a result that is, without any doubt, appropriate for delegation within a branch of government (here the UN Secretariat in a broad sense) and in tune with the delegation bulletin of the Secretary-General that would be published not too long after this order from Judge Laker. The UN would do well to heed it in constitutional cases of delegation as well; unfortunately, the saga of the delegation to the ICSC tells us otherwise.

"[a]ny adequate mechanism can be used for the purpose of delegation, provided that it contains a clear transmission of authority to the grantee concerning the matter being delegated". See https://www.un.org/en/internaljustice/files/unat/judgments/2015-UNAT-511.pdf. Actually, it was highly impracticable to grant such a delegation given that these offices, especially the UNHCR, in turn had many field offices. That would mean that the power of deciding important questions of a disciplinary nature was going to be shared between many local administrative offices of the UN and UNOG instead of being centralized in the hands of the High Commissioner or Director-General of each of these organizations. It is also remarkable, given that there was an "adequate mechanism ... contain[ing] a clear transmission of authority to" the ICSC in Articles 10 and 11 of its Statute, that a few years later this counted for very little in UNAT's Judgment No. 2021-UNAT-1107, *Abd Al-Shakour et al. and Aksioutine et al.* v. *Secretary-General*, see *supra* footnote 232 and accompanying text. That was, however, a delegation in the constitutional or at least the political domain and not in the domain of personnel policy, but that does not seem a reason to approach these two cases differently since those who shouldered the consequences of the delegation at issue in the UNDT and UNAT cases on post adjustment were civil servants of the UN and specialized agencies in Geneva.

243. *Ibid.*, at paras. 36-42.

*F. Conclusions on delegation
by the General Assembly and Secretariat*

An evaluation of the material presented above on delegation by the General Assembly unfortunately cannot be very positive. The General Assembly has a formal delegation relationship with the ICSC and with the successive administrative tribunals. Both were instituted by the General Assembly under Article 22 of the Charter. Both are delegations based on independence and expertise that the Assembly lacks. The independence of the administrative tribunals (the UNAT-old, the UNDT and the UNAT-new) is ideally greater than that of the ICSC as they were, and are, judicial institutions pronouncing judgments based on the internal administrative law of the UN, which has been enacted largely by the General Assembly and, in addition, by the Secretary-General. The ICJ has confirmed that the UN organs, including the General Assembly, in the exercise of its budgetary powers under Article 17 Charter, and the Secretary-General, as appointment authority of the Staff under Article 101 Charter, are bound by the judgments of the administrative tribunals. The ICSC, on the other hand, can only rely on its independence and expertise, as recognized by its founding Statute.

The relationship between the General Assembly and the Secretary-General, however, cannot be easily characterized as a mere delegation relationship, although the General Assembly recently has acted more and more as if this is so, especially in the field of budget and personnel policy. Basically, the Secretary-General and the Secretariat together form one of the principal organs of the UN, on an equal footing with the other principal organs, such the Security Council, the General Assembly, the Economic and Social Council, and the International Court. Obviously, the Secretary-General must carry out the tasks that the Security Council and the General Assembly ask him to perform, but he and the Secretariat have their own responsibility in doing so. On the implementation of budgetary restrictions and changes in personnel policies that the General Assembly imposes on the Secretary-General, he must be able to bring to bear general principles of fairness, equal treatment, proportionality, transparency and acquired rights – that is to say, principles of good governance and even the rule of law – that any administration should apply in order to maintain a minimum of fairness and morale, which is conducive to the proper functioning of the Secretariat. That is an independent responsibility that the Secretary-

General, as chief administrative officer of the UN [244], has to maintain and that the General Assembly should leave to him, as a coequal branch of the UN government. We are here in the constitutional phase of delegation, not in the administrative law phase, where mandate and agency apply and any small deviation by the agent or the mandate is basically null and void (in the private law view of agency). It is clear that the General Assembly, in matters of delegation, does not attach the same value to the notion of separation of powers, or even a "balance between the institutions", as do national courts, and as will be shown below, indeed the courts of other international organizations. In fact, the General Assembly has recently worked hard to make it clear in its resolutions on justice at the UN and on the Common System, that it will not tolerate the new administrative courts of the UN, even in indirect fashion, creating the slightest doubt about the legality of the Assembly's decisions in the field of the budget and personnel policy through the application of the exception of illegality or the application of the principle of acquired rights, and thus support the Secretary-General in taking his own responsibility as chief administrative officer [245].

This raises the question whether the General Assembly, after creating subsidiary organs and delegating certain functions to them and providing them with a statute, which at first sight grants them a certain independence *vis-à-vis* the Assembly itself, still has the freedom to modify, restrict or in practice reduce to (next to) naught this independence, by adopting resolutions, bringing to bear all kinds of pressure, without changing anything to the statute itself. The answer to this is in the negative, as the ILO AT decided in its well-reasoned judgment, as long the clearly applicable rules of delegation to the ICSC have not been modified in accordance with the existing rules. It is regrettable that, on the other hand, the old and the new UNATs have weakened the convincing judgment of the ILO AT by giving credence to the General Assembly as the "legislative sovereign" from as early as 1986 [246] and by shrinking their ever smaller possibility to maintain an indirect appreciation in individual civil service cases of the legality of

---

244. See Articles 98 and 99 Charter.
245. See the resolutions discussed at *supra* footnotes 213 through 216, and the recent resolution of the General Assembly on the Common System: A/Res/75/245.
246. See UNAT-old Case 370, *Molinier*, at *supra* Sec. B of this chapter. It is interesting to note that the ICTY Appeals Chamber in *Prosecutor* v. *Dusko Tadić*, *Decision on the Defence Motion for Interlocutory Appeal on Jurisdiction*, 2 October 1995, https://www.icty.org/x/cases/tadic/acdec/en/51002.htm, emphatically rejects the idea that the General Assembly is the legislator of the UN system, at paras. 43 and 44.

an underlying general decision by the Assembly under the assault of ever more critical resolutions by the Assembly since 2012 [247].

The independence and special judicial expertise of the new administrative courts and, in the case of the ICSC, the independence and special budgetary and public accounting expertise of its members, seems to count for very little. The subordination of a "subsidiary organ" will become evident and the delegation of certain powers to such an organ will just become a kind of working arrangement between the General Assembly and such organs. Delegation will be interpreted as it is interpreted by the Secretary-General in his delegation bulletin within the Secretariat, namely as a mandate shifting execution of certain decisions down the administrative line. The General Assembly certainly has specific powers to adopt regulations in the field of the budget and personnel policy and it is the "representative body" of the UN. Under increasing budgetary pressure from Member States, the General Assembly has given priority to this representative role and has given up the self-restraint that allowed for some serious room for delegation to subsidiary organs that were supposed to have some independence and special expertise. It has thus attached more value to the phrase from Article 98 Charter that the Secretary-General "shall perform such . . . functions as are entrusted to him" and to the subordinate character of the subsidiary organs it may create under Article 22 of the Charter than to any other (at least equally valid) consideration, such as independence and expertise.

In spite of the term "legislative sovereign" used by the administrative tribunals and the General Assembly itself, it is not yet the case that the General Assembly has become a kind of *Rex legibus solutus*. In cases concerning disciplinary matters, promotion and so on, the UNAT-new operates more or less normally [248]. However, there is little doubt that the Assembly, helped by the recent UNAT judgments, has freed itself to a large extent from constraints imposed by its delegation to the ICSC and by the administrative tribunals where budgetary and personnel policy are concerned, especially when these are interconnected.

From a normative legal point of view this is regrettable, even wrong, since it goes against the constitutional structure of the UN where the relation between the General Assembly and the Secretary-General is concerned. The latter is not a footman to the former; true delegation

---

247. See the resolutions discussed in the text accompanying *supra* footnotes 212 through 215.
248. See cases like *Kompass*, *supra* Sec. E, and *Finiss*, at *supra* footnote 195.

requires some freedom of action from the latter; and a modicum of loyal cooperation should prevail between these two principal organs of the UN. And in those cases where the value of the independence and the expertise of subsidiary bodies, like UNAT and ICSC, to which certain specific tasks have been delegated is at issue, their subordination by the Assembly is equally regrettable from a normative angle since it severely limits, without serious deliberation or transparency, the values that the Assembly had solemnly included in the statutes of those subsidiary organs. Moreover, in the case of UNAT (both old and new) there are the specific judicial powers which have been bestowed on it, and which give it the power to define its own competence, like any judicial organ, whether formally a subsidiary to the General Assembly or not [249]. This clearly leaves the UNDT and UNAT the possibility in cases that squarely fall within their competence to decide UN administrative law cases while looking incidentally into the lawfulness of acts of the principal organs of the UN that have determined or influenced the legal situation of the complainant before it [250].

---

249. See on this point the ICTY Appeals Chamber in *Tadič*, *supra* footnote 246, at paras. 14-22. In that case the subsidiary relationship was to the Security Council. It is discussed in some detail in *infra* Chap. IV.A.

250. *Ibid.*, at para. 21. The Appeals Chamber of the ICTY refers here to the *Namibia* advisory opinion (*supra* footnote 206) and to the *Effect of Awards* opinion (*supra* footnote 163) of the ICJ in order to bolster its viewpoint on this question. See also earlier references to the "exception of illegality" at *supra* footnote 223.

CHAPTER IV

DELEGATION BY THE SECURITY COUNCIL

In this chapter we will discuss delegation by the Security Council in its different forms and guises. First of all, there will be a discussion of the so-called *Tadić* case. This is a well-known case decided by the International Criminal Tribunal for the former Yugoslavia (the ICTY), which was created by a Security Council resolution in order to decide cases concerning war crimes, crimes against humanity and genocide during the war in the former Yugoslavia [251]. The central issue in the *Tadić* case was whether the Security Council, like the General Assembly, had the capacity to create an organ of a judicial nature. Moreover, the way in which the Security Council established the ICTY called into question the relative powers of the Council in its relation to the General Assembly, especially where the Assembly's budgetary power was concerned. Second, this chapter will turn to the creation of peacekeeping forces by the Security Council and the way in which the Council delegated powers in this respect to the Secretary-General. These problems will be illustrated by a discussion of the United Nations Mission in Kosovo (UNMIK). This example will also show how other international organizations become implicated in such delegation by the Security Council. Third, there will be a discussion of delegation by the Security Council to a subsidiary body created within the framework of the Council itself and the questions that such delegation may raise about the safeguarding of the appropriate decision-making procedures of the Council itself. This type of delegation is illustrated by discussing the so-called sanctions committees that the Council has created in order to carry out certain detailed aspects of a sanctions regime and the way in which these sanctions regimes are being implemented by the Member States of the UN and some international organizations, such as the European Union. Finally, this chapter will look into the delegation to Member States with a view to directly carrying out certain Security Council resolutions. The examples will range from a very early and rather simple case as the Beira blockade in the 1960s to recent cases of empowering so-called coalitions of the willing.

---

251. See S/Res 808 (1993) and S/Res 827 (1993). The Statute of the ICTY appears in S/25704 and Add. 1, Report by the Secretary-General.

A. The Tadič *case*

Mr Dusko Tadič, also known as "Dule", was involved in running several concentration camps in Omarska, Trnopolje and Keraterm during various periods of the war in former Yugoslavia. He was accused of having committed several crimes mentioned in the Statute of the ICTY. As he was the first person being tried by the ICTY, it was no surprise that he raised a number of objections against its jurisdiction. The ICTY Trial Chamber that was in charge of the procedure against Tadič decided that these objections should be treated in a separate, preliminary procedure. Insofar as these objections concerned the competence of the ICTY under its Statute, they are of no interest here. The two remaining objections related to the ICTY's power to determine its own jurisdiction and to its competence to interpret the resolution of the Security Council by which the ICTY was created. The Trial Chamber ruled that the crimes Tadič was accused of fell well within the terms of the Statute of the ICTY. However, the ICTY declared itself incompetent to rule on the other two questions of jurisdiction. Subsequently Tadič lodged an appeal against this interim judgment of the Trial Chamber to the Appeals Chamber of the ICTY [252].

For an answer to the first of these remaining objections to the jurisdiction of the ICTY it is important to recall that the UNAT-old had explicitly been given the power to determine its own jurisdiction by an article in the Statute that established it [253]. This power is presently found in Article 2 (6) of the Statute of the UNDT, the successor to UNAT. The Appeals Chamber of the ICTY, however, went further than drawing merely a parallel with this provision of the Statute of the UNAT-old. It argued that deciding its own competence was inherently part of the powers of any tribunal, whether national or international. This so-called *compétence de la compétence* (or *Kompetenzkompetenz* in German) is simply part and parcel of the judicial function; any court of law must inherently be able to determine the extent of its jurisdiction. Therefore, according to the Appeals Chamber, any limitations on a court's power to determine its own jurisdiction cannot be inferred without textual support – which was lacking in this case [254].

---

252. *Tadič, supra* footnote 246.
253. Article 2 (3) of the Statute of the UNAT-old, https://untreaty.un.org/unat/Statute.htm.
254. *Ibid.*, at para. 19.

As far as the Appeals Chamber's power to rule on the Security Council resolution establishing the ICTY was concerned, the Chamber quite naturally referred to a number of precedents. The *Effect of Awards* case, discussed in the previous chapter, was of course the most important of these. Confronted by the further argument advanced by Tadić's lawyers that the Appeals Chamber should abstain from giving a judgment in this case because thus it would inevitably decide a political question, the Chamber referred to the case law of the ICJ, which has generally rejected the political question doctrine. It referred in particular to the *Advisory Opinion on Certain Expenses of the United Nations*, in which the ICJ pointed out that even if most interpretations of the Charter will have political significance, great or small, this is only natural. However, the ICJ refused to attribute a political character to a request that invited it to undertake "an essentially judicial task, namely the interpretation of a treaty provision" [255]. Hence the Appeals Chamber firmly rejected the view that it was barred from entertaining the *Tadić* case for reasons related to its political or nonjusticiable nature.

After thus having disposed of the political question argument, the Appeals Chamber went on to analyze what it called the issue of the constitutionality of the decision of the Security Council to create the ICTY. To this end it split up the question of constitutionality into three subquestions. First, was there really a threat to the peace justifying the invocation of Chapter VII of the Charter? Second, if there was indeed such a threat to the peace, was the Security Council mandated to take any measure that could arguably help the maintenance of peace and security or was it bound by the measures expressly provided for in Articles 41 and 42 of the Charter, and possibly Article 40 as well? Third, how can the establishment of an international criminal tribunal be justified, since it does not figure among the measures mentioned in those articles and is of a different nature [256] ?

In its analysis of the first question the Appeals Chamber accepted that the Security Council is bound by the specific powers given to it by Articles 24 and 39 of the Charter. However, the Security Council plays the central role in the application notably of the two parts of Article 39, while being bounded by the limits of the purposes and principles of the Charter as set out in Paragraph 24 [2] of the UN Charter. In the end the Appeals Chamber saw very few difficulties since it is obvious

---

255. *Certain Expenses of the United Nations*, 1962, *ICJ Reports 1962*, 151, at 155, as quoted by the ICTY Appeals Chamber in para. 24 of *Tadić*, *supra* footnote 246.
256. *Tadić*, *supra* footnote 246, at para. 27.

that if the armed conflict on the territory of the former Yugoslavia is considered as an international conflict, there certainly is a threat to the peace as mentioned in Article 39. And even if this armed conflict were to be seen as an internal armed conflict, there is ample precedent in the practice of the Security Council in which it has regarded cases of civil war or internal strife as a threat to the peace and dealt with them under Chapter VII of the Charter. The Congo crisis of the early 1960s and more recently the UN interventions in Somalia and Liberia are mentioned by the Appeals Chamber [257].

The second issue raised on behalf of Tadič could be easily disposed of by the Appeals Chamber on the basis that the measures set out in Article 41 of the Charter are obviously intended to be illustrative examples which do not exclude other measures, as long as they do not involve the use of force. This is the case for the creation of a tribunal. It did not matter, in the view of the Appeals Chamber, that the ICTY had not been successful, at least in the short run, in contributing to the reestablishment of peace and security in the former Yugoslavia. What *was* important was that the Security Council had clearly motivated the creation of the ICTY as a contribution to peace and security in that territory. This also served to rebut the arguments of the appellant under the third issue mentioned above [258].

However, there was a further dimension to the creation of the ICTY, advanced on behalf of the appellant, namely whether it was properly "established by law", a criterion laid down in Article 14 of the International Convention of Civil and Political Rights (ICCPR), and whether it was bound to apply the fundamental rules of fair trial and due process of law mentioned in that article. In this connection the appellant fell back on the classical argument already discussed in Chapter I above to the effect that a delegator cannot transfer powers that it does not have itself to the delegate. The Security Council, as primarily a political body, cannot invest the newly created suborgan – in this case the ICTY – with judicial powers. The Appeals Chamber countered this argument by advancing the argument of attribution:

> "It does not follow from the fact that the United Nations has no legislature that the Security Council is not empowered to set up this international tribunal if it is acting pursuant to an authority found within its Constitution, the United Nations Charter. As set

---
257. *Ibid.*, at para. 29.
258. *Ibid.*, at para. 35.

out above . . . we are of the view that the Security Council was endowed with the power to create this international tribunal as a measure under Chapter VII in the light of its determination that there exists a threat to the peace." [259]

The Appeals Chamber, however, was willing to go further and to contemplate that the expression "established by law" also means that the establishment of the ICTY must be in accordance with "the rule of law". This it characterized as the most sensible and most likely meaning of the term in the context of international law. Returning to the drafting history of Article 14 of the ICCPR, the Appeals Chamber pointed out that a conscious decision was taken not to use the term "preestablished" instead of "established" by law. (This in order to shed no doubt on the judicial character of the Nuremberg and Tokyo courts, which were set up after the Second World War but considered to be true courts of law and not mere dispensers of "victor's justice".) Furthermore, the Appeals Chamber demonstrated that the fair trial guarantees laid down in Article 14 ICCPR had been taken up almost word for word in Article 21 of the Statute of the ICTY adopted by the Security Council. In addition, it pointed out that other fair trial guarantees equally appear in the Statute and also in the Rules of Procedure and evidence of the ICTY. In conclusion, the Appeals Chamber found that the ICTY had been established according to the appropriate procedures under the UN Charter and that it provides all the necessary safeguards for a fair trial. It is therefore "established by law" [260].

As far as our subject of delegation is concerned, it is possible to say that the Security Council has a wide latitude to create new suborgans in order to carry out its Charter mandate of maintaining peace and security. These suborgans can have wholly different powers than the Council itself. Such powers, in the Tadić case judicial powers, must be exercised, however, in conformity with other rules of international law that fall broadly within the UN's remit. In this case the rules concerned were the rules of human and fundamental rights, as laid down in the ICCPR. Moreover, the Security Council cannot just pretend to create a court of law but must make sure that the suborgan it calls into existence walks and talks like a court and thus is, indeed, a court. In sum, the

---

259. *Ibid.*, at para. 44. Note that the Appeals Chamber here implicitly rejects the view of the UN administrative tribunals that the General Assembly is the "legislative sovereign" of the UN.
260. *Ibid.*, at paras. 46 and 47.

interlocutory judgment of the Appeals Chamber of the ICTY represents a confirmation and a strengthening of the ICJ's advisory opinion in the *Effect of Award* case [261]. There is no doubt that, along with the General Assembly, the Security Council can also confer judicial powers on a newly created organ, on the condition that it is, in all aspects, clearly a court of international law and organized as such. Inversely, it is also true that if the General Assembly, in its resolutions, sows more and more doubt about the independence and the scope of the jurisdiction of the UN administrative courts, as has been the case for several years now, the conferral of judicial power on these courts may at some moment first lose its legitimacy, next its validity, and finally these courts would cease to be regarded as true courts, established by law, within the meaning of the *Tadić* case.

B. *The financing of the creation and functioning of the ICTY*

Another aspect of the delegation of powers to the newly created ICTY was its financing. There was a certain urgency in setting up the new court for war crimes committed in the former Yugoslavia and this included the question of how the functioning and establishment of the ICTY was going to be funded. The resolution of the Security Council establishing the future ICTY was based on a report by the Secretary-General and included, as an annex, the statute of the new international tribunal for the prosecution of persons responsible for serious violations of international humanitarian law committed in the territory of the former Yugoslavia since 1991 [262]. The annex had been the subject of informal discussions between the Secretariat and the Security Council. It included a provision on the funding of the setting up and subsequent functioning of the ICTY. This provision, Article 32, stated that the expenses of the ICTY "shall be borne by the regular budget of the United Nations in accordance with Article 17 of the Charter of the United Nations" [263]. Given that Article 17 states that the expenses of the Organization shall be borne by the Member States as apportioned by the General Assembly and that it is the Assembly that considers and approves the budget of the Organization, the backlash from the side of the General Assembly and its suborgans preparing the budget was considerable.

---

261. *Ibid.*, at para. 38.
262. For the relevant documents, see *supra* footnote 252.
263. UN Doc. S/25704.

The Secretariat tried to explain in a note to the General Assembly why it had been necessary to include Article 32 in the (draft) Statute of the ICTY. First of all, the Secretary-General had been asked by the Security Council to submit a report on all aspects of the matter of the creation of the new international tribunal. From informal contacts between the Secretary-General and the members of the Security Council it resulted that the report and the Statute had to include also the financial arrangements that would make the creation and the functioning of the ICTY possible. Second, since the ICTY had to be set up in an effective and expeditious manner, the Secretary-General had concluded that its funding, in whole or in part, through voluntary contributions would not contribute to such an effective and expeditious implementation of the decision to establish the ICTY. Moreover, the Secretary-General considered that while the Security Council had set up the international tribunal under Chapter VII as a measure to maintain and restore international peace and security, it was not comparable to a peacekeeping operation. The ICTY might meet problems, being recognized as an impartial and independent judicial authority, were it to become dependent on the financial largesse of a limited number of Member States. That was another reason why the Secretary-General decided that the expenses of the international tribunal ought to be borne by the regular budget of the Organization. In his view, the Security Council was free to reach its own conclusions as to the appropriate financing of the international tribunal and, accordingly include a provision on the matter in the ICTY Statute. These conclusions could be reached without causing "prejudice to the authority of the General Assembly under the Charter to consider and approve the budget of the organization and to apportion the expenses of the organization among its members"[264].

In spite of all these explanations from the side of the Secretariat, the General Assembly was, to put it mildly, "not amused". The first resolution that it adopted on the financing of the new international tribunal for the prosecution of serious violations of international humanitarian law in the former Yugoslavia strongly reaffirmed "the role of the General Assembly as set out in Article 17 of the Charter of the United Nations, as the organ to consider and approve the budget of the organization, as well as the apportionment of its expenses

---

264. UN doc. A/47/1002, Note by the Secretariat of 20 August 1993, at para. 12.

among Member States" [265]. Furthermore, it also expressed concern that "advice given to the Security Council by the Secretariat on the nature of the financing of the international tribunal did not respect the role of the General Assembly as set out in Article 17 of the Charter" [266]. It decided to finance the activities of the ICTY through a separate account outside the regular budget, pending a decision on the matter of apportioning its expenses. Finally, and contrary to the explicit wish of the Secretary-General, the General Assembly invited "member states and other interested parties to make voluntary contributions to the international tribunal" [267]. Nevertheless, the General Assembly decided to find provisional funding for the new international tribunal. In later financing resolutions of the ICTY it even came to the realization that voluntary contributions must be consistent with the need to ensure the impartiality and independence of the international tribunal at all times and that such contributions should be considered supplementary to the assessed contributions [268]. In short, the General Assembly admitted that the Security Council and the Secretariat had a point when they saw risks in financing the ICTY primarily from voluntary contributions.

In conclusion and with the benefit of hindsight, it is obvious that the General Assembly was constrained to follow the Security Council and to recognize that voluntary contributions would never play a major role in the financing of the ICTY. This stands to reason: in the normal life of the United Nations, it is only natural that the Security Council will from time to time be confronted by emergency situations that may require a response that can only be financed from the ordinary budget of the Organization, assessed according to the normal method as decided, and adjusted when necessary, by the General Assembly. Moreover, the clash between the Security Council and the General Assembly briefly described above also demonstrates that new delegations/conferrals of power to a new body deemed necessary by one main organ of an international organization should be respectful of the balance between the institutions as laid down in the founding treaty of that organization. Viewed from this perspective, the position of the General Assembly *vis-à-vis* the Security Council on the problem of financing the ICTY is inconsistent with its position in respect of delegation on budget and

---

265. A/Res. 47/235, at para. 2.
266. *Ibid.*, at para. 3.
267. *Ibid.*, at paras. 6-7.
268. A/Res/48/251, at para. 5.

personnel policy to the Secretary-General [269]. In the latter case it insisted on imposing its position completely on the Secretary-General and denying him his own responsibility for a well-functioning Secretariat that ought to be run according to rule of law and good governance and respect of acquired rights.

C. Delegation in connection with the application of Chapter VII UN Charter

There is no doubt that in the UN system the Security Council originally is the principal organ charged with, if necessary, using force or other forcible means against States whose actions constitute a threat to the peace, a breach of the peace or an act of aggression. The Security Council is master over the question of which measures to take whether they be an interruption of economic relations or other sanctions or whether the use of counterforce is necessary. As is well known, the principal organs of the UN have also devised an intermediate way of taking action by creating so-called peacekeeping forces after it had become clear that the standing forces of the UN that were foreseen in Article 43 of the Charter would not come into being. It is equally common knowledge that the UN General Assembly occasionally has taken it upon itself – in cases where there appears to be a threat to the peace, or a breach of the peace, or an act of aggression, and the Security Council, owing to the veto of permanent members, is not capable of exercising its primary responsibility for the maintenance of peace and security – to take charge of this responsibility and to address appropriate recommendations to the members of the UN with a view to maintaining international peace and security. This was laid down by the General Assembly in its so-called Uniting for Peace Resolution, to which it has had recourse intermittently during the 1950s and 1960s [270].

Both the Security Council and the General Assembly, when exercising their respective powers with a view to maintaining peace and security, have had recourse to various forms of delegation. The first time that the Security Council saw a need to use its enforcement powers under

---

269. See the developments since UNGA Res. 67/241, *supra* footnote 215 and the subsequent text.
270. For an overview of the "Uniting for Peace Resolution" and the history of its application, see L. D. Johnson *et al.*, "Symposium on the Uniting for Peace Resolution", *AJIL Unbound*, Vol. 108 (2014), pp. 106-140, https://www.cambridge.org/core/journals/american-journal-of-international-law/article/comment-on-larry-johnson-uniting-for-peace/6DD035637D.

Chapter VII was when North Korean forces crossed the 38th parallel, the provisional boundary line between North and South Korea. In a number of successive resolutions adopted in late June and July 1950, in the absence of representatives of the USSR, the Security Council first decided that there had been an armed attack which constituted a breach of the peace by the action of the forces from North Korea and demanded that these forces should withdraw forthwith to north of the 38th parallel. The Security Council also called upon all members to render every assistance to the United Nations in the execution of this resolution [271]. Shortly afterward the Security Council recommended that the members of the UN furnish assistance to the Republic of Korea as would be necessary to repel the armed attack and restore peace in the area [272]. In yet another resolution the Security Council later recommended that all members that were providing military forces and other assistance to South Korea make such forces available to a unified command under the United States [273]. It is not too far-fetched to say that this rather crude delegation of power to an international military coalition under the command of the US with a view to reestablishing the boundary between the two Koreas at the 38th parallel constituted, in present-day parlance, the first "coalition of the willing". When the USSR returned to the Security Council later in 1950, it proved no longer possible for the Security Council to direct the operations of the international force in Korea. This brought about the adoption of the Uniting for Peace Resolution in early November 1950 [274].

That resolution was subsequently used to convoke the first Emergency Special Session of the General Assembly after the Security Council had sought in vain to deal with the outbreak of the Suez war on 5 October 1956 [275]. It was then that the General Assembly, in cooperation with the Secretary-General and the Secretariat, created the model of "the peacekeeping force" that, in different guises, has served the United Nations so well ever since [276]. The General Assembly requested the Secretary-General to urgently study the establishing, with the consent of the nations concerned (that is, both the parties to

---

271. S/Res. 82 (1950).
272. S/Res. 83 (1950).
273. S/Res. 84 (1950).
274. A/Res. 377 (V) Uniting for Peace.
275. See the successive resolutions 997-1002 (ES-I).
276. From the very beginning of its existence the UN has also been involved in peace observation through the mentioned UNTSO (Middle East) and the UN Military Observer Group in India and Pakistan, or UNMOGIP (India-Pakistan).

the conflict and the States that would contribute troops to the force), of an emergency international UN force to secure and supervise the cessation of hostilities in accordance with earlier resolutions [277]. The Secretary-General indeed succeeded to produce a first report within a few days [278] and as a consequence the General Assembly adopted the resolution that established the United Nations Emergency Force (UNEF I), which was placed under the command of Major-General Burns, who was already in place as chief of the United Nations Truce Supervision Organization (UNTSO) on the ground in the Middle East [279]. In a further resolution the General Assembly also delegated to the Secretary-General all powers necessary to find troop-contributing countries and to establish the rulebook for this and future international peacekeeping forces. It also established an Advisory Committee composed of the troop-contributing countries involved in the operation. That committee was charged with assisting the Secretary-General in furtherance of the relevant resolutions adopted and to be adopted by the General Assembly [280]. Thus, what was later called UNEF I created a model for the future, which was also embraced by the Security Council when, after the so-called Yom Kippur war in 1973, it fell once again to that UN organ to reestablish a second UNEF [281]. This model was, and is, based on three well-known principles: consent from the parties to the dispute; strict impartiality of the UN peacekeeping troops; and no use of armed force by the UN troops, except in self-defense and in defense of the mandate.

What is of prime interest for the subject of delegation is according to which pattern the authorizing resolutions for peacekeeping forces have been drafted. It is mostly the Security Council, and only in a few exceptional cases the General Assembly, that establishes a peacekeeping force and sets the limits within which it has to do its work and keeps a broad political control over its operations. However, all operational aspects of establishing the force and its functioning in the field are delegated to the Secretary-General [282] in close cooperation with the Advisory Committee of troop-contributing countries (as soon as these have been selected). In the subsequent long history of

---

277. A/Res. 998 (ES-I), 4 November 1956.
278. UN Doc. A/3289.
279. A/Res. 1000 (ES-I), 5 November 1956.
280. A/Res. 1001 (ES-I), 7 November 1956.
281. A/Res. 340, 25 October 1973; A/Res. 341, 27 October 1973.
282. The Department of Peace Operations, always working closely with the Department of Field Support, together constitute the largest part of the UN Secretariat.

peacekeeping, the Secretariat on the basis of its long experience has worked assiduously to regulate, standardize and codify many aspects of peacekeeping [283] and, if necessary, to reform its own practice [284]. In this system of delegation of powers, according to which the different forces have been set up, and where the essential, "political aspects" of these forces are reserved to the Security Council (or exceptionally the General Assembly) and necessitate the Secretary-General to return to the Council if anything needs to be changed to them, but where the myriad practical aspects of selecting the nationality of the troops and their day-to-day operation in the field are left to the Secretary-General, recalls the model of delegation in several Member States operating along the distinction between "legislative" and "regulatory powers".

D. The UN mission in Kosovo

It is unnecessary for the purposes of this work to recall the complete background to the Kosovo crisis. Let it suffice to say that after the military action of Yugoslav/Serbian troops starting in 1998 against the then autonomous province of Kosovo and after NATO bombardments on these troops and on Yugoslav/Serbian territory in reaction, discussions between the former Finnish President Martti Ahtisaari and the Russian representative Victor Chernomyrdin led to the adoption of two sets of principles with a view to moving to a resolution of the Kosovo crisis. There were seven political principles agreed between the G8 Foreign Ministers at Petersberg (Germany) on 6 May 1999. In addition, there were nine additional principles on the practical implementation of the political principles on the ground, to which also the Yugoslav/Serbian government had declared its agreement [285].

Subsequently the Security Council adopted a resolution in which it noted, first of all, that the Federal Republic of Yugoslavia/Serbia had

---

283. The core elements of peacekeeping have been laid down in the so-called Capstone doctrine: United Nations Peacekeeping Operations: Principles and Guidelines, https://peacekeeping.un.org/sites/default/files/capstone_eng_0.pdf, issued in 2008 but kept up to date. In addition a Uniform Code of Conduct for Peace-Keeping Forces has been adopted (see https://peacekeeping.un.org/en/standards-of-conduct) and a common core on rules of engagement of peacekeeping forces has been developed (which may vary for each mission and are not normally published).

284. Examples are the Brahimi Report, UN doc A/55/305; S/2000/809, Report of the Panel on United Nations Peace Operations (2000); and the Secretariat's A New Partnership, Charting a New Horizon for UN Peace-keeping (2009).

285. These two lists of principles were annexed to S/Res/1244 (1999) of 10 June 1999.

accepted these principles and demanded its full cooperation in putting these principles into effect. Further, the Security Council decided on the deployment in Kosovo of both an international civil presence and an international security presence under the auspices of the United Nations and noted that the Federal Republic of Yugoslavia had agreed to that. According to the resolution, it was the task of the Secretary-General to take care of the actual establishment of the civil presence and to appoint a Special Representative at the head of it who should ensure the close coordination with the security side of the operation. The latter, the Kosovo Force, was brought into the field by NATO and called KFOR. It was charged with tasks which ranged from truly military tasks, like deterring hostilities and preventing the return of Yugoslav troops and police into the Kosovo province and demilitarizing the Kosovo Liberation Army, to public order tasks and border monitoring. On the civilian side there were a number of core tasks for which the assistance of other international organizations was crucial. The political process toward the establishment of an interim political framework agreement providing for substantial self-government for Kosovo was to be helped along by the Organization for Security and Co-operation in Europe (OSCE). The UNHCR was charged with overseeing the safe and free return of all refugees and displaced persons to Kosovo. Finally, the European Community was charged with devising a comprehensive approach to the economic development and stabilization of the crisis region, including a broader stability pact for Southeastern Europe. All this was supposed to serve the gradual transfer of healthy and robust institutions in the political, economic, administrative, police and judicial fields to the newly to be created authorities of Kosovo, which was to have a large degree of autonomy [286]. When Ahtisaari in a later report had to arrive at the conclusion that autonomy for Kosovo within the Federal Republic of Yugoslavia was not a viable option, the Kosovo Assembly and the President unilaterally declared independence on 17 February 2008 [287].

---

286. All this was developed *in extenso* in S/Res/1244 (1999).
287. In its advisory opinion of 22 July 2010 on *Accordance with International Law of the Unilateral Declaration of Independence in Respect of Kosovo*, *ICJ Reports 2010*, p. 403 ff., the ICJ stated that the declaration of independence was contrary neither to international law nor to S/Res/1244. There was no rule of international law prohibiting the making of declarations of independence (paras. 79-82) and the persons making the declaration of independence did not act as members of any of the bodies bound by the Resolution (para. 83 ff.).

Viewed from the perspective of delegation, there are three points that call for comment. In the first place, the delegation to the Secretary-General contained in Paragraph 10 of Resolution 1244 authorized him to set up an international civil presence "with the assistance of relevant international organizations". This broad formulation made it possible for the Secretary-General to collaborate not only with other UN agencies like UNHCR but also with specifically European organizations like OSCE and the European Community, as well as a broad regional military organization like NATO, when establishing the military and civil presences in Kosovo. Even under Chapter VII of the Charter, therefore, the UN Security Council and the Secretary-General have the faculty to delegate tasks of peace enforcement and peacekeeping not only to UN Member States but also to other international organizations – which, of course, have to respect the conditions for such delegation laid down by the Security Council.

Second, the Security Council implicitly included in the delegation to the Secretary-General the power to exercise administrative and judicial powers, while enhancing the capacity of Kosovar institutions to take over these functions of government in the course of the mandate of UNMIK. It was also inevitable that UNMIK would need to exercise rulemaking and even legislative functions in order to properly do its work. As a matter of fact, the first Special Representative for Kosovo, Bernard Kouchner, started his mandate by issuing UNMIK Regulation 1999/1, assuming legislative and executive authority, as well as the administration of the judiciary, and later Regulation 1999/24 on the law applicable in Kosovo, which was defined as consisting of the regulations promulgated by Kouchner and of old Kosovar law, insofar as it was not in conflict with the Universal Declaration of Human Rights and seven other major regional and worldwide conventions on human and fundamental rights [288].

Similar powers in the field of legislative, administrative and judicial functions were given shortly afterward to the United Nations Transitional Administration in East Timor (UNTAET), this time in a much more explicit manner than in the Kosovo case [289]. There has been considerable critical discussion in the literature of these grants of "internal powers" of administrative, legislative and judicial nature, and it is not necessary to rehearse these discussions at length here. The criticism relies again

---

288. See https://unmik.unmissions.org/sites/default/files/regulations/02english/E1999regs/E1999regs.htm.
289. S/Res. 1272(1999).

on the argument that the Security Council cannot delegate powers that it does not itself have. However, in the circumstances prevailing on the island of Timor and in the former Yugoslavia, it was reasonable to say that the exercise of such powers by the UN mission established by the Security Council would serve the maintenance of international peace and security, not only in the State or the territory in question, but also in relation to neighboring territories or States. Hence, there is no question that the Security Council acted *ultra vires*[290]. The criticism cuts closer to the bone when it is based on the absence of any guarantee that the UN administration of a territory like Kosovo or East Timor will always be in conformity with the rule of law and fundamental rights. It is not unreasonable to say that the UN administration will be bound not only by the Security Council resolution establishing it but also by the principles of the UN Charter and by the provisions of the UN human rights conventions. However, the main problem then is: who will see to it that these lofty rules are respected by a UN administration in the field? The classic question of *Quis custodiet ipsos custodes?* raises its head. It is not trite to point out that future resolutions establishing such interim UN administrations ought to provide for some quasi-judicial administrative law procedure that could take care of complaints of maladministration, abuse of powers given under the mandate and in breach of the principles of the UN Charter. It may be efficient to charge the existing UN Appeals Tribunal of the UN Internal Justice System with this task[291].

Third, the case of UNMIK also illustrates the broad possibilities that the Secretary-General of the UN has to determine the composition of the UN mission or UN forces once he has been given the task to send them into the field. It is well known from the practice of peacekeeping forces of the UN that the Secretary-General must shop around for troop contributions or administrators among the Member States. Moreover, if a Member State withdraws its contingent from a UN peacekeeping force, it is necessary for the Secretary-General to seek a replacement. In the case of UNMIK, it became necessary at a certain point in time to transfer the economic section of the mission to the Kosovar authorities and on the other hand to increase substantially the assistance in respect

---

290. See *supra* Sec. A on the *Tadić* case.
291. See on these problems, primarily in relation to UNTAET, A. J. J. de Hoogh, "Attribution or Delegation of (Legislative) Power by the Security Council? The Case of the United Nations Transitional Administration in East Timor (UNTAET)", in M. Bothe and B. Kondoch (eds.), *International Peacekeeping: The Yearbook of International Peace Operations 2001*, The Hague, Kluwer Law International, 2002, 1-41.

of police work, the public ministry and the courts. At that point in time the European Union was ready to withdraw its contribution to the economics department of UNMIK and to replace it by a much more ambitious program of assistance to the Kosovar authorities in the domains of police work and the judicial authorities, under the name EULEX Kosovo (European Union Rule of Law Mission in Kosovo). This was bound up with complicated political problems relating to autonomy and independence for Kosovo and a possible change in the mandate of UNMIK. In the end the solution was found in using the broad delegated power of the Secretary-General to (re)organize a UN mission, whether in the field of peacekeeping or of interim administration, and simply accept that his policy space, together with the broad phrase "with the assistance of relevant international organizations" from SC Resolution 1244, allowed the Secretary-General comprehensively to change the tasks of one of these organizations, the EU, within the framework of UNMIK [292]. This episode, once again, confirms the far-reaching delegated powers the Secretary-General routinely receives from the Security Council in connection with the organizational matters of the setting up of a peacekeeping mission.

E. *Delegation by the Security Council to sanctions committees*

The UN Security Council has created quite a large number of suborgans. All peacekeeping forces and other forces in the field are formally suborgans of the Security Council. As is well known, ever since the 1990s the Security Council has had recourse increasingly to international economic sanctions in its efforts to maintain international peace and security. However, the experience of the Security Council with classic sanctions, directed against a State or a territory, beginning with the sanctions against Southern Rhodesia during the 1970s, was not felicitous. For instance, the sanctions imposed on the Iraq of Saddam Hussein in the 1990s after its invasion of Kuwait was repelled and led to widespread disenchantment because its negative effects were felt primarily by ordinary citizens while Iraqi government circles and the upper classes of the country were capable of largely isolating

---

292. For more detail on this change in the Kosovo mandate without changing the basic Security Council resolution, see E. Milano, "Il Trasferimento di Funzioni da UNMIK a EULEX in Kosovo", *Rivista di Diritto Internazionale*, Vol. 91, No. 4 (2008), pp. 967-990; see also, "Editorial Comments", *Common Market Law Review*, Vol. 46 (2009), pp. 377-382.

themselves from them. This so-called Oil for Food Scandal [293] led the Security Council to draft sanctions measures in such a way that they were directed against those in government, those closely related to the government and other specific individuals and their economic interests. That was also the approach followed after 9/11 in order to target a group like Al-Qaida, its leaders and its financial supporters, and other such terrorist groupings and organizations, such as the Islamic State of Iraq and the Levant (ISIL) or Da'esh (hereafter ISIL (Da'esh)).

After it laid down sanctions against Southern Rhodesia after the latter's unilateral declaration of independence, the Security Council soon created a so-called sanctions committee. This was basically a committee of the Security Council, on which all members of the Council were represented and which was charged with monitoring the extent to which UN members implemented the sanctions against Rhodesia in the legislation and actually executed them on the ground. The Rhodesian Sanctions Committee could also place new products on the lists of prohibited products attached to the successive Rhodesian sanctions resolutions [294]. This model was followed when creating sanctions committees for every regime of economic sanctions that was imposed by the Security Council during the 1990s and the early 2000s and is still used today. As a consequence there are now quite a large number of sanctions committees. Nowadays the chair of a sanctions committee is appointed by the Security Council and, though normally a diplomat, chairs the committee in his/her personal capacity. The sanctions committee is supported by a monitoring team within the Secretariat serving the Security Council. The monitoring unit is charged with collecting trade, financial and legal information relevant to the regimes and assisting Member States in finding such information. In the following we will concentrate on the powers delegated to and the functioning of the Sanctions Committee for Al-Qaida and the Taliban, to which was later added the responsibility for supervising the sanctions against ISIL (Da'esh). Under the pressure of circumstances

---

293. This scandal led to a series of reports issued in course of 2005 by and an Independent Inquiry Committee under the chairmanship of Paul Volcker, a former Head of the US Federal Reserve, unveiling considerable graft and kickbacks paid in the course of the execution of the Security Council mandated "Oil for Food" program. See https://www.un.org/press/en/2005/sc8492.doc.htm for the presentation of the fifth and final report.

294. S/Res/253 (1968). See also P. J. Kuyper, "The Limits of Supervision: The Security Council Watchdog Committee on Rhodesian Sanctions", *Netherlands International Law Review*, Vol. 25 (1978), pp. 159-194.

this particular Committee has become the one with the most extensive practice and the most refined procedures.

In its successive resolutions on the matter the Security Council has delegated the power to place persons or groups of persons, undertakings or entities associated with Al-Qaida and the Taliban on the relevant sanctions list, which is attached to those resolutions. Such persons, groups, undertakings or entities are considered to be associated with Al-Qaida and the Taliban if they participate in the financing, planning, facilitating, preparing or perpetrating of acts or activities of these terrorist movements. In addition, supplying, selling or transferring arms and related material to these terrorist movements and recruiting for them, or otherwise supporting their activities, also make persons or groups liable to be placed on the relevant sanctions list. How does the sanctions committee make such a decision? Normally any UN member may propose to place a certain person, group, undertaking or entity on the sanctions list. That member will advance certain elements in order to justify its request, and these will be discussed by the Committee. In reality, most proposals for placing names on the sanctions list were advanced by countries with an important intelligence capacity. According to the relevant resolutions, the preferred decision-making procedure is consensus [295]. According to the practice of the United Nations, consensus exists when there is no active expression of opposition by a member of the sanctions committee. If no consensus can be reached, a member of the sanctions committee could opt to bring the matter to the Security Council itself, where the normal voting rule of a qualified majority of nine affirmative votes, including the votes of the permanent members, will apply. We will return later to the question whether or not the consensus rule is more stringent or weaker than the normal majority requirement of nine members of the Council, subject to the veto of the five permanent members.

It is certain, however, that the Security Council has delegated to the Sanctions Committee quasi-legislative tasks, namely extending the scope *ratione personae* of the relevant resolutions, while following a

---

295. The Sanctions Committee for Al-Qaida and Associated Individuals and Entities laid down its consolidated working procedures for the first time on 7 November 2002. Since then it has gone through more than a dozen versions, has been extended to cover sanctions against ISIL (Da'esh) and the latest version is dated 5 September 2018 and bears the title Guidelines of the Committee for the Conduct of its Work, see https://www.un.org/securitycouncil/sanctions/1267/committee-guidelines. These Guidelines are based on all the relevant Security Council sanctions resolutions, complemented by provisions and standard documents adopted by the Sanctions Committee itself.

decision-making procedure that is different from that of the Security Council itself. As we have seen in Chapter II, containing the brief comparative law study on delegation in national public law, such delegation of (quasi-)legislative powers to a lower body, while modifying the conditions of decision-making in the process, was normally frowned upon in national systems of constitutional and administrative law as an inadmissible self-delegation [296].

Originally, the procedure for delisting persons, groups, companies or organizations was the same as for listing them: the Sanctions Committee could decide by consensus to delist and, if consensus was not forthcoming, a member of the committee could bring the request for delisting back to the Council and it could follow the normal decision procedure there. The main problem with delisting some person, organization or company, initially was not linked to the decision-making procedure but to the question of whom a person or organization or company that was listed could rely on to ask for his/her or its delisting. The resolutions provided for the State that had requested the listing in the first place or for the State of nationality of the person or entity listed making this request; only later was this facility extended to all Member States [297]. Obviously the State that had proposed the listing would only undo it if it was crystal clear that a gross error had been made, such as mistaken identity. And, unfortunately, most States of which nationals had been listed could not be bothered to request delisting, even in cases where doubts about the correctness of the listing might be justified; they did not want to be associated with such people. Hence, at the level of the United Nations, there initially was in reality hardly any legal recourse to undo a listing.

As a consequence, many people, organizations or companies sought relief from Security Council listings before national courts, including the EU courts in cases where the listings had been implemented by the European Union under Article 215 of the TFEU [298]. Some of the cases

---

296. See *supra* Chap. II.F.
297. The Guidelines mentioned in *supra* footnote 295 now mention three delisting procedures, initiated respectively by Member States in general, by designating States and those made by targeted persons themselves through the Office of the Ombudsperson. See Guidelines, at pp. 7-11.
298. Article 215 TFEU reads as follows:

"1. Where a decision, adopted in accordance with Chapter 2 of Title V of the Treaty on European Union, provides for the interruption or reduction, in part or completely, of economic and financial relations with one or more third countries, the Council, acting by a qualified majority on a joint proposal from the High Representative of the Union for Foreign Affairs and Security Policy and the

before national courts, after exhaustion of the local remedies, ended up before regional human rights courts, such as the European Court of Human Rights [299]. In nearly all of these cases, both at the national and international level, another fundamental problem arose, namely that the Sanctions Committee of the Security Council had adopted decisions to list certain persons, organizations or companies on the basis of the work of national intelligence agencies that for security reasons had not been shown to the persons and entities that had been listed and could not be passed on to the courts of other UN members or to a court of an international organization which did not belong to the UN system. National (and EU) courts were ready broadly to accept that the first decision to impose sanctions, such as asset freezes, on natural and moral persons did not need to be preceded by an appropriate procedure since an element of surprise was necessary for their effectiveness. After some duration, however, fundamental rights that have to be respected in criminal and administrative procedures against moral and natural persons should be observed. Hence the targeted persons or entities had a right to know what they were accused of and on which factual basis they continued to be subject to sanctions. Otherwise sanctions had to be lifted [300].

The Security Council sought to find a solution to both problems by the creation, next to the Sanctions Committee, of the Office of the Ombudsperson [301]. The Ombudsperson was going to be the linchpin of an attempt to deal with both problems mentioned above. For the sake of our argument, we will concentrate on the first problem: the representation of those whose State of nationality (or at a later stage, any Member State) was not willing to make a request to delist them.

Commission, shall adopt the necessary measures. It shall inform the European Parliament thereof.
2. Where a decision adopted in accordance with Chapter 2 of Title V of the Treaty on European Union so provides, the Council may adopt restrictive measures under the procedure referred to in paragraph 1 against natural or legal persons and groups or non-State entities."

299. See European Court of Human Rights, Grand Chamber, *Nada* v. *Switzerland*, Judgment No. 10593, 12 September 2012, https://hudoc.echr.coe.int/fre?i=002-6434.
300. See *inter alia* the so-called *Kadi I* cases before the Court of First Instance and the Court of Justice of the EU: Case T-315/01, *Kadi* v. *Council and Commission*, ECLI:EU:T:2005:332 and Case C-402/05 P, *Kadi and Al-Barakaat International Foundation* v. *Council and Commission*, ECLI:EU:C:2008:461, at paras. 280-327.
301. See S/Res/1904 (2009). Before that resolution, the Security Council had encouraged listed persons to file their request for delisting with a so-called focal point, see S/Res/1730(2006) and S/Res/1735(2006), but this quickly proved inadequate as it was too much part of the Security Council machinery. The Office of the Ombudsperson, by its name alone, exuded a certain independence. See S/Res/1904 (2009).

They could appeal directly to the Ombudsperson and explain to him/her why they should not have been listed at all or should be removed from the list. It would then be up to the Ombudsperson, after a direct discussion with the person or organization concerned, further research into the case by the staff of the Ombudsperson and direct discussion with the State that made the listed the person or entity in question, to decide whether indeed the listing should be terminated or confirmed and to issue a comprehensive report on that question to the Sanctions Committee [302]. However, the first occupant of the function of the Ombudsperson, Kimberly Prost, soon came to the conviction that any attempt on her part to actually obtain the delisting of natural or moral persons that in her view deserved to be delisted would remain an uphill battle as long as the Sanctions Committee held on to the consensus approach of decision-making in these cases.

In the meantime, smart sanctions came under increased pressure of several national and EUCJ judgments that supported complainants who did not succeed to have themselves delisted by the Sanctions Committee. EU and/or the Member State courts annulled their listing under EU or national law on the ground either that not enough proof of their activities in favor of Al-Qaida had been disclosed to the Court, or that the procedure was contrary to minimum procedural rights [303]. This risked undermining the effectiveness and/or the legitimacy of smart sanctions.

After long discussions with the Sanctions Committee and its Member States, Prost obtained the following decision-making procedure for cases in which she had investigated delisting requests. In cases where she decided negatively so that the listing would continue, the Sanctions Committee would automatically follow her conclusions. In cases where she proposed to terminate the listing the Sanctions Committee would have sixty days to study the proposal, after which it would automatically

---

302. This often entailed efforts to come to agreements with the States that listed many persons and/or entities about the Ombudsperson's access to classified documents. See First Report of the Ombudsperson, S/2011/29, at para. 33 ff.

303. There was a considerable practice of immediate relisting of certain persons after they had won favorable rulings from courts in the EU; Mr Kadi was an example of this. See the Kadi II cases: Case T-85/09, *Kadi v. Commission*, ECLI:EU:T:2010:418 and Cases C-584/10, C-593/10 P and C-595/10 P, *Commission and Others v. Kadi*, ECLI:EU:C:2013:518, at paras. 103-137. In this appeals case the Court developed a number of procedural minimum requirements that a listing had to respect. However, the Security Council continued to repeat that sanctions against individuals and entities were "preventative in nature and . . . not reliant upon criminal standards set out under national law", S/Res/2161 (2014), at para. 45.

stand if the Committee did not reject it during that period. Such rejection would require a consensus (the so-called negative consensus). If such a negative consensus was not forthcoming, any member of the Committee could bring the matter before the Security Council, subject to its normal procedures for decision-making [304]. If the State that had broken the negative consensus was a permanent member (in practice mostly the UK or the US), such return to the Council was without hope.

In a later phase, Prost's successor as Ombudsperson, Catherine Marchi-Uhel, obtained another decision-making procedure from the Security Council, which was again slightly more in favor of cases where she had come to the conviction that a natural or moral person ought to be delisted, compared to the original consensus in delisting cases. First of all, a delisting proposal from the Ombudsperson would be subject to a ten-day no objection procedure in the Sanctions Committee; that is, delisting would go ahead unless one or more objections were made (in writing) within the ten-day deadline. If at least one objection was made, the sixty-day period, as obtained by Prost, would kick in and again would result in the proposal for delisting to stand, unless a consensus among the members reversed the Ombudsperson's proposal or, in case the proposal was referred to the Security Council at the request of one or more members, the proposal would not be supported by the normal qualified majority, including the affirmative votes of the permanent members [305].

This procedure was identical to the treatment reserved to a delisting request from a "designating State"; that is, a State that had proposed the blacklisted person for inclusion on the sanctions list. This stands to reason as both the Ombudsperson and the State that initially designated the blacklisted person must be considered to have particularly good reason to propose a person's delisting. By contrast, a proposal for delisting from any other UN Member State would have to go through the ten-day waiting period and if an objection was made by a member of the Sanctions Committee, the requesting Member State would have to ask for the request to be put on the agenda of a future Security Council meeting.

Should the self-delegation from the Security Council to the Sanctions Committee on Al-Qaida and ISIL (Da'esh) and the concomitant change

---

304. Guidelines of the Committee for the Conduct of its Work, version of 15 April 2013, https://www.un.org/securitycouncil/sites/www.un.org.securitycouncil/files/guidelines_of_the_committee_for_the_conduct_of_its_work_0.pdf.
305. *Ibid.*, in the version of 5 September 2018.

in the decision-making procedures be considered objectionable? Before discussing that question, it is useful to mention one additional element of the Office of the Ombudsperson that made national and EU courts and international human rights courts wary of its functioning in delisting cases, and that is its "independent" character. There is no doubt that the intention of the Security Council was to create an Office that was at a minimum at arm's length, but at the maximum independent, from the Council itself, but still somehow integrated in its decision-making process on smart sanctions. There is also no doubt that the three persons who have led this Office [306] have always had the ambition to be and to appear as fully independent from the Council and that substantively they have largely succeeded in living up to this standard. However, they have until this day been handicapped by the fact the United Nations was incapable of fashioning a status for them that would demonstrate that independence in a convincing manner. They have always been hired and paid as "consultants" of the UN Secretariat and, in spite of their constant insistence, it has proved impossible to change this. This formal characterization of the relation with the UN Secretariat has remained an obstacle among others to treating the Ombudsperson procedure as a (quasi-)judicial one, which otherwise might have stimulated national and EU courts to show greater deference to its decisions [307].

Leaving aside the evolution over time of to what extent and by which modifications of its decision-making procedure the Security Council delegated to the Sanctions Committee the task of listing and delisting individuals, organizations and companies as subject to the Security

---

306. Marchi-Uhel was appointed by the Secretary-General on 3 July 2017 as head of the "International, Impartial and Independent Mechanism to Assist in the Investigation and Prosecution of Persons Responsible for the Most Serious Crimes under International Law Committed in the Syrian Arab Republic since March 2011". She filed the fourteenth report of the Office of the Ombudsperson on 7 August 2017 (S/2017/685) and left that same day. She was succeeded nearly a year later by Daniel Kipfer-Fasciati, who took up his duties as Ombudsperson on 18 July 2018 and filed his first and overall the fifteenth report of the Office of the Ombudsperson (S/2018/579) on 8 August 2018. He announced his resignation as per 17 December 2021 in the twenty-first report of the Office (S/2021/676).

307. Prost still complained of the problem of her independent status in her last report, having done so in her three preceding reports; see UN doc. S/2015/533, at paras. 55-69. Marchi-Uhel also raised this problem in her reports and Kipfer-Fasciati went on to raise the problem regularly until his last report, from which it transpires that the lack of action by the Security Council and Secretariat in respect of this matter was an important reason for his departure; see UN doc. S/2021/676, at paras. 38-49, also his letter of resignation to S-G António Guterres, https://www.un.org/securitycouncil/sites/www.un.org.securitycouncil/files/20210603_letter_to_secretary-general_0.pdf. The description of the different procedures is again based on the Guidelines mentioned in supra footnote 304.

Council's sanctions against Al-Qaida and the Taliban and later ISIL (Da'esh), the present modifications in the normal decision-making of the Security Council can be summarized in two forms as follows.

The first one is the form applicable to listing and delisting decisions initiated by "normal" UN Member States. A request to list or delist a person, organization or company from such Member States follows a written procedure. The State makes its application for listing or delisting by filling out certain forms that demand the production of certain information, and if necessary, the Monitoring Team provides assistance. The application is put before the Sanctions Committee during a ten-day waiting period and if no objection is received during that period, the listing or delisting is carried out. If there is an objection, the Member State can ask for the case to be put on the agenda of the Security Council, where the normal qualified majority, including the permanent members (who may abstain), will be applied to the proposed listing or delisting decision. If none of the five permanent members is among the objecting Member States, there is a good chance that the listing or delisting will pass in the Security Council.

The second form applies to the delisting applications introduced in the Sanctions Committee by a designating Member State – that is, the same State that had somebody placed on the list by the Sanctions Committee now seeks to take the same person off the list – or by the Ombudsperson assisting a listed person, organization or company. This decision-making procedure starts with the same ten-day waiting period. If there is an objection during this period, a second waiting period of sixty days begins, during which a negative consensus in opposition to the proposed delisting has to be formed or the matter may be brought to the Security Council itself and be exposed to the normal qualified majority for an adoption of the delisting. It is clear that if it appears during the sixty days that a negative consensus is likely out of reach, in particular permanent members opposing delisting have an incentive to request a Security Council meeting in order to cast their veto.

As we have seen in Chapter II, the problematic aspect of the delegation of (quasi-)legislative tasks by legislative organs to a committee of these organs or to other institutions or bodies is that the voting rules are changed or do not give the same guarantees. For simplicity's sake we have started this section on the assumption that extending the group of persons, organizations or companies is a (quasi-)legislative activity. However, this assumption may not withstand closer scrutiny, especially not when the criteria for applying sanctions to the possible targets have been clearly laid out in the Security Council resolution concerned, as seems to be the case. In that case, it can be argued that listing and delisting is simply a question of the application of these criteria (as they have been developed in later resolutions and in the Guidelines as developed by the Sanctions Committee)[308].

There is no doubt that the voting rules of the Sanctions Committee as applied to the listing and delisting of names at first sight deviate from the normal voting rules of the Security Council. They add additional written procedures that require either positive or negative consensus to be achieved during a ten-day or sixty-day period, always keeping open the possibility of a recourse to the normal voting requirements for decisions of the Security Council. In the case of the voting rules applicable to listing and delisting requests made by any Member State, however, the additional burden of the ten-day silence procedure for establishing consensus in the Sanctions Committee is a very limited additional burden on the States making the request, and serves mainly to prevent these States from always going directly to the Security Council, so as to ensure that the Sanctions Committee can fulfill its role as subcommittee of the Security Council. The sixty-day period that is added, if the ten-day period has not led to consensus, is an additional deviation from the usual decision-making procedure. On the other hand, as it is a period during which a negative consensus against the delisting proposal must be created, it is also the expression of the extra weight that the sanctions system of the UN is willing to grant to the special knowledge that the designating State and the Ombudsperson have acquired of the persons, organizations or companies for which they propose the lifting of sanctions. Finally, these two equivalent decision-making procedures could end in the application of the normal qualified majority of the Security Council. Granting additional weight to the findings of the designating State and of the Ombudsperson was considered of great importance for the credibility of UN smart sanctions in the eyes of the national courts of the Member States as well as the EU courts and international human rights courts. As we have seen, the result of all this in the end was not very positive, not least because the UN

---

308. In this connection it is not without interest that, within the EU, the inclusion or withdrawal of names in or from the list attached to a sanctions regulation of the EU Council of Ministers, even in the case of autonomous sanctions, is often left to the Commission as an exercise of its powers of implementation. See also *infra* footnote 402 and accompanying text.

has so far not succeeded in giving to the Office of the Ombudsperson a genuinely independent status.

After weighing up the different elements, on the one hand, it is hard to maintain a formalistic approach to the question and conclude that the decision-making procedures of the Sanctions Committee by their additions to the normal voting rules of the Security Council amount to an illegal delegation of legislative powers by the latter to the former. This is mainly due to the fact that all additions allow for a return to the normal voting rules of the Council in the end and by the objective pursued by some of these additions, namely a fairer chance for some hit by these "smart sanctions" to demonstrate their "innocence". On the other hand, applying the normal voting rules of the Security Council to the lifting of sanctions always creates a problem of asymmetry, also in the case of collective sanctions. This was demonstrated when an increasing number of Security Council members sought to lift the very strict regime of economic sanctions against Iraq, which continued after the Iraqi aggression against Kuwait and which entailed enormous suffering for ordinary Iraqis all through the 1990s, in spite of the introduction of the "Oil for Food" program. Throughout this period, the US could and indeed did stop any lifting or reduction of the sanctions by brandishing its veto power, most of the time behind the scenes. Viewed from this perspective, the special procedures, which aim to make a so-called reverse veto of a permanent member (as in the Iraqi sanctions case) less likely, without it seeming too obvious, grapple with a real problem. The real problem is: too much self-delegation versus the asymmetry effect of the veto in lifting sanctions. The ultimate possibility of returning to the normal qualified majority resurrects the "reverse veto", with all its perverse effects for the individuals and companies that have been listed for doubtful or no good reasons. Tempering the nondelegation doctrine in this context seems the better course of action.

F. *UN delegation to one or more Member States and International Organizations*

There are several examples of the United Nations delegating certain tasks in the field of the maintenance of international peace and security to their Member States. When discussing delegation from international organizations to Member States, it is important to make a distinction between the implementation and execution of binding decisions of international organizations as required by the treaty of such organizations and instances where the organization specifically authorizes or charges a State or group of States with carrying out a particular task. Examples of the latter situation are, first, the obligation in accordance with Article 25 of the UN Charter to accept and carry out the decisions of the Security Council that impose sanctions on a particular State or group of States, and second, the obligation of Member States of the European Union to adopt all measures of national law necessary to implement legally binding Union acts, as laid down in Article 291 of the TFEU. The oldest example of the first situation in the United Nations is the case of the so-called Beira blockade. Below we will discuss this case, as well as a much more recent one involving Libya. Chronologically in between there are two other cases, involving East Timor and Kosovo, which may not amount to real delegation from the UN to one or more Member States, but in which the UN operates in concert with one or more Member States that began an action on their own which is approved or at least accepted as a fact by the Security Council and on which the Council then builds its own action of peacekeeping and transitional government. Finally, the authorization to several Member States to take action in Libya in 2011 will be analyzed.

1. The Beira blockade

When in November 1965 the white minority government of Ian Smith in Southern Rhodesia unilaterally declared its independence from the United Kingdom, this move was immediately condemned by the Security Council on the request of the UK itself. In two resolutions of that month the Security Council called upon all States not to recognize the "illegal racist minority regime in Southern Rhodesia" and to refrain from assisting and encouraging the illegal regime, to desist from providing it with arms and "to do their utmost in order to break all economic relations with Southern Rhodesia, including an embargo on oil and petroleum products" [309].

When in early April 1966 an oil tanker by the name of *Joanna V* approached the Port of Beira in Mozambique, which was then still under Portuguese colonial rule, the Security Council intervened again, and much more forcefully this time. This was because the oil pipeline from the Port of Beira to Southern Rhodesia had been closed for some time and might now reopen again since Portugal did not support the

---

309. S/Res/216 and 217 (1965).

negative attitude of the UK and the UN to Southern Rhodesia's unilateral declaration of independence. This would increase in all probability the capacity of Southern Rhodesia to prolong its independent existence, as indeed it did. Hence the Security Council this time decided that the resulting situation constituted a threat to the peace. Accordingly, it called upon all States "to ensure the diversion of any of their vessels reasonably believed to be carrying oil destined for Southern Rhodesia" which may be on its way to Beira. What is more, the Council also called upon the UK to prevent "by the use of force if necessary" the arrival at Beira of any oil tankers that might be carrying oil destined for Southern Rhodesia. And finally, it empowered the UK to arrest and detain the ship *Joanna V* upon its departure from Beira in the event its oil cargo would be discharged there [310].

Even from this short summary of the Security Council decision, it is clear that its resolutions in these early days of the unilateral declaration of independence of Southern Rhodesia were still highly ambiguous, no doubt also at the request of the United Kingdom – which did not need to remind the other members of the Council that it had the veto, if necessary. Nevertheless, it is impossible to deny, particularly in the light of the determination that there was "a threat to the peace", that the actions indicated by the Security Council fall under Chapter VII of the Charter. Moreover, in spite of the soft words "call upon", the UK in reality received the Security Council's full authorization to put the Port of Beira under a maritime blockade, with a view to preventing the delivery of oil to Southern Rhodesia. This, as the Security Council recognized, necessarily would entail the use of force if a ship were to try to run the blockade. Thus the United Kingdom was authorized by the competent organ of the United Nations to use force, which is normally forbidden by Article 2 (4) of the UN Charter, but, in the particular circumstances, fulfilled a higher purpose of the Organization [311].

Later in 1966 and again in 1968, the embargo on goods originating in Southern Rhodesia was gradually expanded and unambiguously made fully binding [312], but the UK remained the only country that was explicitly authorized to maintain a blockade of Beira harbor by force,

---

310. S/Res/221 (1966), at paras. 1 and 5. Moreover, Portugal was called upon not to discharge the *Joanna V* and not to pump oil through the Beira pipeline to Rhodesia.

311. The higher purpose being the repression of a threat to the peace consisting in the internal situation prevailing in Southern Rhodesia. In that situation the rule of Article 2 (7) of the Charter did not apply.

312. S/Res/232 (1966), at paras. 1 and 2 and S/Res/253 (1968), at paras. 3, 4 and 20 (also creating the first Sanctions Committee).

if necessary, to prevent the discharge of oil there. The powers that the UK received from the Security Council thus went beyond its normal obligations to implement the embargo under Article 25 Charter, and the Council's permission to let UK naval vessels use force was a true delegation of a power that the UK itself formally did not possess, in the face of absence of UN forces under Article 43 Charter. It was a delegation that was not precisely circumscribed ("if necessary"), but one that the UK obviously had agreed to (or even asked for) beforehand. This is a pattern that was to recur regularly in other such delegations that will be briefly analyzed below, and which finally resulted in "coalitions of the willing".

2. Kosovo

The last remaining hot conflict of the war in the former Yugoslavia was between the Federal Republic of Yugoslavia (in reality Serbia and Montenegro) and the province of Kosovo. This province was populated largely by people of Albanian descent, who strove to gain at least autonomy but preferably independence from Serbia. This conflict flared up again in early 1999 and as the Serbian Army progressed further and further into Kosovar territory, the fear grew that the world would be confronted once again with genocide and large-scale war crimes, as it had witnessed in Bosnia-Herzegovina. This fear gave rise to an intervention by NATO under leadership of the United States. A bombing campaign was started originally directed at the Serbian troops moving toward and entering Kosovo, but later also sought out strategic and infrastructural objectives inside Serbia, causing "collateral" civilian loss of life.

A series of difficult negotiations between the parties to the dispute ensued. They faltered and failed and, when they led to a result at the Castle of Rambouillet in France, the Serbian parliament rejected the outcome. In the end, on 2 June 1999, the special Russian envoy and former Prime Minister Viktor Chernomyrdin and Finnish President Martti Ahtisaari managed to convince the Serbian Prime Minister Slobodan Milosevic to agree to a ten-point paper[313] that served as a complement to the general principles of the political solution to the Kosovo crisis agreed between the G8 Foreign Ministers at Petersberg

---

313. UN doc. S/1999/649, including the positive Yugoslav reaction to nine points mentioned therein.

on 6 May 1999 [314]. The ten-point paper foresaw *inter alia* the creation of an international civilian mission and an international security presence under the auspices of the United Nations.

The Security Council resolution that then founded the UNMIK [315] does not approve the unilateral use of force by NATO but takes the consequences of this use of force, as laid down in the Petersberg principles and the ten-point paper agreed between Ahtisaari, Chernomyrdin and Milosevic, as the basis on which UNMIK is established, by explicitly welcoming these documents in one of the preambular paragraphs [316]. In that way Serbia also gave its permission to the creation of the new peacekeeping force in Kosovo. All this is not enough to conclude that the United Nations *de facto* delegated peacemaking and peacekeeping tasks that are normally UN attributes to NATO before it intervened in the conflict itself by creating UNMIK. In the following discussion of two operations in East Timor we will see many of the same ingredients at work as in the Kosovo case, but in a slightly different mixture.

3. East Timor cases of 1999 and 2006

(a) *1999: From UNAMET to UNTAET*

Indonesia invaded and annexed the Portuguese colony of East Timor in 1975. This annexation was not widely recognized but also not vigorously opposed by the international community in the prevailing Cold War atmosphere of the time. But in occupied East Timor an important independence movement emerged under the leadership of Xanana Gusmao. After the downfall of the long-serving, dictatorial Indonesian President Suharto, his successor B. J. Habibie not only began a movement toward internal democracy but also gave indications that he would be ready to consider a plebiscite in East Timor about the future of the territory. In the summer of 1999, he suddenly proceeded very quickly to call for a referendum, where the choice was between autonomy within the Indonesian Republic and independence. The Security Council decided almost at the same time to establish the United Nations Mission in East Timor (UNAMET), which was created to organize such a plebiscite [317]. This news created great unrest in East Timor, mostly stimulated by pro-Indonesian militias. In the end,

---

314. UN doc. S/1999/516.
315. S/Res/1244 (1999).
316. *Ibid.*, at preambular para. 9.
317. S/Res/1246 (1999), at para. 1

however, the Indonesian government agreed that the referendum would take place on 30 August under the auspices of UNAMET [318]. When the result was overwhelmingly in favor of independence, serious unrest broke out, once again, between the pro-Indonesian militias and the independence movement, which led to what the Security Council called "systematic, widespread and flagrant violations of international humanitarian and human rights law" [319]. There were many indications, reported by UNAMET, that the systematic destruction and killings perpetrated by militias took place with the connivance of the Indonesian army and police present in East Timor [320].

In response to these developments, Australia started to mobilize its military, first with a view to evacuating and bringing to safety the members of UNAMET, and second in preparation of a possible intervention with a view to stopping the internecine killing going on in East Timor. In a very short time, the Prime Minister of Australia, John Howard, was able to gain support for this idea, first from New Zealand and Southeast Asian nations such as Malaysia, the Philippines and Singapore, which all promised to send troops as well, and subsequently from the US President Bill Clinton and UN Secretary-General Kofi Annan. Under this combined pressure President Habibie had no choice but to accept that "international peacekeeping forces *through* the United Nations from friendly nations [would] restore peace and security in East Timor" [321].

The offer of organizing such a force consisting of an Australian core with contributions from others was conveyed to the UN and formally welcomed by the Security Council, just as it welcomed the readiness of Indonesia to accept an international peacekeeping force *through* the United Nations in East Timor and reaffirmed its respect for Indonesia's sovereignty and territorial integrity [322]. The force, called the International Force East Timor (INTERFET) was explicitly not a UN force (note the words "*through* the UN" above). In paragraph 3 of the resolution it was called, once again, a "multinational force under a unified command structure, pursuant to the request of the government of Indonesia". It

---

318. S/Res/1262 (1999). Para. 1 prolonged the mandate of UNAMET until 30 November 1999, well after the referendum on 30 August 1999.
319. S/Res/1264 (1999), 15 September 1999, at preambular para. 13.
320. See the annex titled "The Destruction of East Timor Since 4 September 1999: Prepared by UNAMET on 11 September 1999" to Report of the Security Council Mission to Jakarta and Dili, 8 to 12 September 1999, UN doc. S/1999/976.
321. Statement quoted in *ibid.*, at para. 12, italics added.
322. S/Res/1264 (1999), at preambular paras. 10-12.

was charged with important military, security and protection tasks. The operative clauses of Resolution 1264 were preceded by the legal basis of the action of the Security Council with the words "determining that the present situation in East Timor constitutes a threat to peace and security" and "acting under Chapter VII of the Charter of the United Nations". This legal basis shows some uncertainty on the part of the Security Council about the reality of the Indonesian invitation and the assurances of the Indonesian government that it would cooperate with the multinational force [323] since that invitation in principle made reliance on enforcement action under Chapter VII of the Charter superfluous. This is not surprising when one thinks back to the rather unstable situation inside Indonesia after the fall of Suharto; it was far from certain that the military, from which Suharto originated, was following the line of President Habibie on the ground in East Timor – rather to the contrary [324]. Hence the double legal lock on the Security Council action: Chapter VII and the invitation of the Indonesian government. The resolution also agreed that INTERFET should be replaced as soon as possible by a normal UN peacekeeping operation, for which the Secretary-General should make recommendations promptly and which should be part of a broader UN transitional administration [325].

A weaker double legal lock was repeated in the subsequent Security Council resolution [326]. Once again, the cooperation of the Indonesian government, this time in the form of the decision of the Indonesian parliament (to accept the outcome of the vote of 30 August) concerning East Timor was recalled in the fourth preambular paragraph, but obviously there was no longer any reason to mention respect for Indonesia's territorial integrity. The operative part of the resolution, including the creation of the UNTAET, was based once again on the determination that the continuing situation in East Timor constituted a threat to peace and security and that hence the Security Council acted under Chapter VII of the Charter [327]. There was therefore no doubt that UNTAET was a purely UN peacekeeping and administrative operation and that the non-UN multinational force INTERFET was terminated. UNTAET fully transferred governmental powers, after elections, to a new government of East Timor in May 2003. Important successive

---

323. These assurances were repeated in para. 4 of S/Res/1264 (1999).
324. See the report and its annex, *supra* footnote 320.
325. S/Res/1264 (1999), paras. 10 and 11.
326. S/Res/1272 (1999) of 25 October 1999.
327. *Ibid.*, last two preambular paragraphs.

UN missions – the United Nations Mission of Support to East Timor (UNMISET) and the United Nations Office in East Timor (UNOTIL) – remained behind to provide assistance to the country.

(b) *2006: To UNMIT*

The above story repeated itself in almost identical fashion in 2006 when internal strife inside the army and police of East Timor and conflicts between different members of the government led to a similar situation of insecurity and armed clashes as had prevailed in 1999, though on a lesser scale. Nevertheless, the Australian Prime Minister John Howard was again quick to react and again raised an intervention force largely consisting of Australian Army units, complemented by smaller contributions from Malaysia, New Zealand and Portugal. After deployment of this second multinational force under Australian stewardship, the Security Council adopted another resolution which established a follow-on mission in East Timor (or Timor-Leste or as it was now known), the United Nations Integrated Mission in Timor-Leste (UNMIT)[328]. This resolution expressed its appreciation and full support for the deployment of the international security forces from Australia and its partners. It was also noted that the deployment of these forces took place at the request of the government of the Democratic Republic of Timor-Leste[329]. However, this time there was no explicit reference to any legal basis at all for this resolution. That was perhaps not surprising since UNMIT was supposed primarily to be a civilian and policing mission, with a very small military liaison and staff component[330]. This accent on policing was agreed with the Timor-Leste government as best adapted to the needs of the country in the near future, and hence there was no absolute need for UNMIT to have a legal basis for enforcement action.

In these two cases it is pretty obvious that the invitations for an intervention by Australia and other nations from respectively the Indonesian government and the government of Timor-Leste came about under considerable pressure from neighboring States, the UN Secretariat and the United States and its allies. In these cases, it is clearer than in the Kosovo case that in a way the UN gave its *fiat* retroactively to a forcible intervention that, among other actors, it had itself helped to organize.

---

328. S/Res/1704 (2006), 26 August 2006.
329. *Ibid.*, at preambular para. 6.
330. *Ibid.*, at para. 2.

Therefore, these cases can be seen as delegating the task of maintaining peace and security in East Timor to non-UN forces until such time as the UN operations, UNTAET and UNMIT, would be up and running. That is not to say that the UN Security Council gave a blank check to these multinational forces led by Australia. The relevant resolutions are quite specific in circumscribing the tasks of these forces and how they have to interact with the UN peacekeeping forces that they will have to cooperate with (and may become part of). It is also possible to conclude that in the cases concerning East Timor there is a link between the authorization of a coalition of the willing (i.e. the Australian force combined with smaller contributions from other countries) and the establishment of the UN peacekeeping mission. This link is assured by the early inclusion of the UN Secretariat in the discussions on the formation of the coalition of the willing, of which the Security Council was naturally kept informed. This is an element that was clearly absent in the Kosovo case.

4. Coalitions of the willing

(a) Korea

Since the discussions on the implementation of Article 43 Charter on the formation of a permanent UN military force failed quite quickly after the foundation of the United Nations, it was inevitable that if the Security Council were to decide to fight an actual shooting war in order to safeguard peace and security in the world, it would have to rely on what later came to be called "coalitions of the willing". As we saw earlier, the Korean War resolutions represented the first example of the Security Council leaving the restoration of peace and security to such a coalition. As is well known, the Security Council soon lost control of this operation because of the persistent veto of the Soviet Union and due to the fact of life that the biggest contributor to the war effort in Korea, the United States, and in particular General MacArthur, called the operational shots. Moreover, it is impossible to say that the takeover by the General Assembly under the Uniting for Peace Resolution resulted in any real UN control over the conduct of the war. Hence it is impossible to maintain that there was a real delegation from the UN to some of its Member States in the Korean conflict of the 1950s.

(b) The Iraq-Kuwait war

A nearly ideal model of such a coalition of the willing is the group of States led by the United States that came to the aid of Kuwait after its invasion by Iraq. Initially the Security Council reacted to that invasion by adopting a number of resolutions, beginning with Resolution 660 (1990) which condemned Iraq, subjected it to a number of sanctions and other measures, and spelled out what it had to do to resume its place as a member in good standing with the United Nations [331]. When Iraq did not respond in any way to these successive resolutions, the Security Council on 29 November 1990 adopted Resolution 678 which reaffirmed the eleven resolutions that it had passed since early August of that year and noted that Iraq had refused to comply with any of these resolutions. Therefore, acting under Chapter VII Charter, the Member States cooperating with the Kuwaiti government were authorized, unless Iraq were to implement all these resolutions before 15 January 1991, "to use all necessary means to uphold these resolutions and to restore international peace and security to the area" [332]. This seemed to be a very sweeping delegation of powers to a certain number of cooperating Member States of the UN, again under leadership of the US, but it was clearly circumscribed by the earlier resolutions mentioned, and after the surrender of the Iraqi forces, other resolutions were still to follow on the question of the implementation of the earlier resolutions and on how Iraq would have to compensate for the damage that its invasion did to Kuwait and to natural and moral persons present in Kuwait.

There is certainly a lot to criticize in the aftermath of the Iraq-Kuwait war. The way in which continuing sanctions were imposed on Iraq and implemented has been subject to quite some soul-searching, not least in the countries that initially supported these measures, because of their negative effects on ordinary Iraqi citizens [333]. Nevertheless, the reversal of the occupation of Kuwait by Iraq and the subsequent restoration and

---

331. The most important of these resolutions were: S/Res/660, ordering the Iraqi withdrawal from Kuwait; S/Res/661, imposing economic sanctions against Iraq; S/Res/662, nonrecognition of the annexation of Kuwait; S/Res/664, nonclosure of diplomatic and consular missions and facilitating departure of third-country nationals; S/Res/665, implementing a maritime blockade of Iraqi and Kuwaiti ports; S/Res/666, controlled importation of foodstuffs into Iraq and Kuwait; S/Res/667, stopping aggressive actions against diplomatic and consular premises and the abduction of persons from these premises; S/Res/670, giving greater precision to transport sanctions, in particular in aviation; S/Res/674, stopping the maltreatment of persons, hostage taking, detention, etc., of Kuwaiti and third-country nationals and reminding Iraq of its liability under international law for such misdeeds. All these resolutions were adopted between early April and late November 1999.
332. S/Res/678 (1999), at para. 2.
333. See L. Oette, "A Decade of Sanctions against Iraq: Never Again! The End of Unlimited Sanctions in the Recent Practice of the UN Security Council", *EJIL*, Vol. 13 (2002), pp. 93-103, with many useful references. See also the Volcker report, *supra* footnote 293 and accompanying text.

delineation of the frontier between the two countries can be seen as a success for the coalition of the willing that was authorized by the UN Security Council to act against Iraq. The coalition, in using force, did not go beyond its mandate given by the Security Council and withdrew from the territories of Iraq and Kuwait broadly as planned. In the aftermath of the war, the compensation program indemnifying individuals and companies in Kuwait for the damage they suffered, delegated to and run by the UN Compensation Commission, was a considerable success [334]. In this case delegation broadly worked.

(c) *Other examples*

Three other examples of coalitions of the willing come to mind: (1) the acquisition of the use of air power for UNPROFOR, the United Nations Protection Force in Bosnia and Herzegovina; (2) the authorization of the International Security Assistance Force (ISAF) to ensure peace and security in Afghanistan in the wake of the US action in response to the attack on the Twin Towers on 11 September 2001; and (3) the authorization of the use of air power to prevent atrocities against civilians committed by the government of Libya in reaction to the popular movement during the so-called Arab Spring. In all these cases we see a similar authorization to use force by the Security Council to a particular group of States in order to reach a particular objective, either establishing a general prevalence of security and order, as in Afghanistan, or a more precise protection of civilians against war crimes, for instance in the safe areas of Bosnia-Herzegovina, or more broadly against atrocities, as were committed by the Gaddafi "government" in Libya. In all three cases the expression "use all necessary means", or some equivalent of it, were inscribed in the relevant Security Council resolutions and hence a lot depended on the description of the objectives and the potential limitation on the instances in which "all necessary means" could be used to achieve the actual result the authorization of the Security Council was intended to have.

(i) *Bosnia*

In the case of UNPROFOR, the Security Council authorized:

"Member States, acting nationally or through regional organizations or arrangements, may take, under the authority of the

---

334. For the activities of the UNCC, see its website https://uncc.ch/home.

Security Council and subject to close coordination with the Secretary-General and UNPROFOR, all necessary measures, through the use of air power in and around the safe areas in the Republic of Bosnia and Herzegovina, to support UNPROFOR in the performance of its mandate."[335]

In reality, airpower was requested by UNPROFOR mainly from NATO countries such as the US, the UK and France to give close combat protection to the troops of UNPROFOR guarding so-called safe areas. According to the terms of the relevant resolution, calling in close combat support from the air required close coordination between the Member States concerned, the Secretary-General and UNPROFOR [336]. The procedural requirements of consultation and coordination proved to be too time-consuming and, in the end, led to a lack of airpower intervention during the events leading up to the massacre at Srebreniča.

(ii) *Afghanistan*

The Security Council resolution concerning the International Security Assistance Force in Afghanistan went quite far in stimulating Member States of the UN to participate in and to contribute to ISAF [337]. The creation of this force was originally foreseen in the so-called Bonn Agreement that laid down provisional arrangements in Afghanistan pending the reestablishment of more permanent government institutions. This was essentially a State-building agreement [338], and as such it followed the model applied by the UN almost contemporaneously in East Timor and earlier in Western Africa. The mission of ISAF was laid down in Annex I of the Bonn Agreement and essentially amounted to training a new Afghan army and ensuring a secure and peaceful environment in which initially the new Afghan Interim Authority (later the elected government) and also the UN personnel in Afghanistan could do their work. ISAF was explicitly *not* a UN peacekeeping force; it was manned largely by NATO countries, directed by NATO and led

---
335. S/Res/836 (1993), at para. 10.
336. *Ibid.*, at paras. 10 and 11.
337. S/Res/1386 (2001), at paras. 2 and 7.
338. The Bonn Agreement, officially called the Agreement on Provisional Arrangements in Afghanistan Pending the Re-establishment of Permanent Government Institutions, was concluded on 5 December 1999 between a large number of Afghani leaders and co-signed by Lakhdar Brahimi, the Special Representative of the Secretary-General for Afghanistan. It was transmitted to the President of the Security Council the same day by UN doc. S/2001/1154.

by the US and other allies of these countries. On the other hand, it was of great importance for the UN and its personnel in Afghanistan. The Security Council, acting under Chapter VII Charter, called upon UN Member States to contribute personnel equipment and other resources to ISAF. Moreover, the Security Council authorized the Member States participating in ISAF "to take all necessary measures to fulfill its mandate"[339]. That mandate[340] was extremely broad since in Afghanistan maintaining a secure and peaceful environment could imply anything between patrolling specific areas, humdrum police work, basic engineering, social work and high-violence commando raids. Although ISAF succeeded in establishing itself step by step, beginning in Kabul, in nearly all provinces of Afghanistan its tasks proved too varied, Afghan society too tribal, the duration of presence too long and the motives for which the participating States had joined it too different to make it last successfully. From 2011 a gradual transfer of responsibility for internal security to the Afghan army began and in 2014 ISAF was terminated and replaced by a much more modest NATO training and support operation. Together with the remaining US troops, it was forced to withdraw completely in the summer of 2021.

(iii) *Libya*

When the Arab Spring reached Libya and the Gaddafi government started suppressing peaceful demonstrations by excessive violence, killing dozens if not hundreds of civilians, the Security Council, although it invoked Chapter VII Charter as the legal basis for this, originally reacted merely by imposing an arms embargo, a travel ban and an asset freeze against the Gaddafi family, as well as referring the matter to the International Criminal Court[341]. The Gaddafi clan was obviously not impressed by this and continued on a course of armed confrontation, thereby reaping what it sowed, namely civil war. This led once again to large-scale military operations essentially against civilians in cities that had not declared their fealty to Gaddafi. When the city of Benghazi came under threat of indiscriminate shelling and bombardments from the air, as well as the street-by-street liquidation of civilians who were assumed not to be in the Gaddafi camp, the Security Council had had

---

339. S/Res/1386 (2001), at para. 3.
340. ISAF's mandate was not in any UN document but in Annex I to the Bonn Agreement.
341. S/Res/1970 (2011).

enough. Slightly over two weeks after the first resolution, the Security Council, acting once again under Chapter VII Charter, decided to establish a no-fly zone, a ban on all flights (i.e. all Libyan military flights) in the airspace of Libya in the interest of protecting civilians. The Security Council authorized Member States acting nationally or through regional organizations or arrangements and acting in cooperation with the Secretary-General to take all necessary measures to protect civilians and civilian populated areas under the threat of attack in Libyan territory, including Benghazi, while excluding a foreign occupation force of any form on any part of the Libyan territory. The Secretary-General had to be informed of the measures that the States concerned had taken and had to pass that information on to the Security Council. A considerable number of preambular paragraphs lent a strong flavor of the protection of human rights, the reaffirmation of the basic norm of the law of war (namely the distinction between combatants and civilians) and even of the duty of the Libyan authorities to protect their own Libyan population (responsibility to protect) to the resolution [342]. The resolution did not have the desired effects and that is the least one can say. That did not have anything to do, however, with the resolution as such, but rather with the means that the Security Council was capable of marshaling to counteract the breaches of human rights law, the law of war and the responsibility to protect that were being committed in Libya at the time. All parties in the civil war were opposed to admitting foreign troops of whatever nature on Libyan soil and, in spite of having recourse to Chapter VII, the Security Council was not willing to go against this common wish. The no-fly zone thus remained the only forcible measure that the coalition of the willing could use to restrain the parties in the internal conflict. As is well known, some members of the Security Council, in particular Russia, have become convinced that surveilling the no-fly zone and other elements of the authorization were abused by the US and Western European countries for other purposes, notably a wish for regime change.

All the above examples of coalitions of the willing, over which the Security Council wanted to exercise some control under Chapter VII Charter, were or became serious shooting wars, many of which ended pretty badly. That should be no surprise. In a world where the UN does not dispose of Article 43 troops, planes and naval vessels, or a military staff steering them, delegating action to a coalition of the willing is

---

342. S/Res/1973 (2011), at paras. 6-12.

the only option the Security Council has when it wants to resort to enforcement action beyond economic sanctions, if, in such cases, it can agree on anything at all without one member exercising its veto. (Such coalitions may include international organizations, such as NATO, which have some coordination powers among the States that constitute the coalition of the willing.) One impression that one can take home from these five coalitions of the willing is that they do not work too badly *if* the conditions for the delegation to, and the tasks to be performed by, the "willing" are clear and well structured, as was the case in the Iraq-Kuwait war and with ISAF in Afghanistan. Then it does not matter whether they are based on an outside agreement (as in the latter case) or set out in one or more resolutions of the Security Council itself (as in the former). It also makes for better implementation and for less need for coordination and consultation during action (as in the Bosnian air support case). This conclusion is probably true for all delegations between UN organs and between these organs and their suborgans. But it is precisely in "coalitions of the willing", the cases of highest violence, that such conditions are least likely to be fulfilled.

G. *Conclusions on delegation by the Security Council*

Looking back at this chapter, it is clear that the Security Council, like the General Assembly, has the power to create organs and delegate tasks to them that lie beyond the nature of their own powers, as long as the delegation is conducive to reaching the objectives of the United Nations. Both the Security Council and the General Assembly created new suborgans with judicial tasks, whereas both organs have not been equipped with judicial powers in the UN Charter. The General Assembly created a judicial body that was necessary for a proper functioning of the Secretariat: UNAT, the United Nations Administrative Tribunal. The Security Council created the ICTY, which it found indispensable with a view to furthering a sustainable climate of peace and security in the former Yugoslavia after the many wartime atrocities that had been committed between the parties to that conflict. It is also clear that the creation of such new judicial organs has consequences for the balance between the institutions, and in particular for the budgetary powers of the General Assembly. The General Assembly was bound to obey the judgments of UNAT and its successor tribunals and bear the financial consequences of their judgments for the budget of the organization. Similarly, the General Assembly was held to create the necessary budgetary room for financing the ICTY once the Security Council had decided to create the tribunal.

It was disconcerting to discover that the General Assembly is less and less inclined to follow the letter and the spirit of the advisory opinions of the ICJ in respect of the functioning of the administrative tribunals of the UN, to which the Assembly has delegated judicial powers. Moreover, the General Assembly does not shy away from exerting disproportionate political pressure on the Courts of the new Internal Justice System of the UN by the repeated adoption of resolutions which deny these courts the right to determine their own jurisdiction as administrative law courts. There is nothing abnormal, in advanced systems of administrative law, about a system in which complaints by individual civil servants or even groups of civil servants can lead an administrative court incidentally to criticize a law that has had negative consequences as applied to that group of or individual civil servant(s), without annulling that law but at the same time awarding the civil servant(s) in question the necessary remedies. No magical formula, such as the meaningless assertion of being the "legislative sovereign" of the UN, can change that. As the ICJ has amply demonstrated, if the General Assembly or the Security Council decide to create a court or court system, it will have to bear the consequences of that by accepting its judicial character and the financial consequences that flow from it. If the General Assembly is not willing to do that, it should revoke the resolutions that have created this system. Trying to bludgeon the administrative tribunals of the UN into submission without ever changing their statutes, as the Assembly has done with the ICSC, is a travesty of good governance.

Less controversial but perhaps more important, this chapter has also showed that the Security Council, like the General Assembly, can create suborgans of its own and delegate tasks to them laying within them the core of its powers. In the case of the General Assembly, an example of such a suborgan was the ICSC, with its powers of advice and decision in the budgetary field, in particular with respect to the remuneration of the members of the Secretariat. Similarly, the Security Council, in constant collaboration with the Secretary-General and the Secretariat, over the years developed a comprehensive policy of creating peacekeeping forces as suborgans of the Security Council and delegating peacekeeping and peace-building tasks to these forces in specific conflict areas. It has been shown how the political aspects of a mandate for such peacekeeping forces were closely guarded by the Council itself, while the implementation – which involved such problems as selecting troop-contributing countries equipped with the right materiel, bringing the troops into the field, coordinating between troops from different countries, maintaining relations with the host country and concluding the relevant international instruments to that end, among many other tasks – rested mainly with the Secretariat. Over the years, the dialogue between the Security Council and the Secretary-General on appropriate methods of peacekeeping created a fairly clear doctrine in this field. On that basis, the Security Council was prepared to delegate responsibility for the implementation of peacekeeping forces largely to the Secretary-General and the Secretariat. This was illustrated above in particular by the broad leeway left to the Secretary-General by the Security Council in changing the composition of UNMIK in Kosovo. This reservation of the truly political aspects of peacekeeping to the Council itself and delegating its implementation to the Secretariat is also well known from a perusal of the national constitutional and administrative law practice in certain Member States of the United Nations.

This chapter has also demonstrated that peacekeeping missions, especially when they involve peace-building and even State-building in their remit, as well as the enforcement of economic sanctions directed at specific persons or groups of persons, organizations and companies, encounter serious legal problems when the rights of natural or moral persons are affected thereby. These problems have been extensively discussed in the literature and that is why this chapter has not touched on most of them at any length. For our purposes it was important to demonstrate that the delegation of powers has played a not unimportant role in these problems. The Security Council has done some violence to its own decision-making procedure by delegating the matter of placing persons, organizations and companies on, and subsequently taking them off, the sanctions lists to a subcommittee of itself (i.e. a sanctions committee), assisted by another of its suborgans (the Office of the Ombudsperson).

CHAPTER V

DELEGATION IN THE EUROPEAN UNION

A. Introduction: The Meroni *case* [343]

The development of a doctrine concerning the delegation of powers between the institutions of the European Union and from the institutions of the European Union to other bodies, inside or outside the European Union, started very early, during the period of the European Coal and Steel Community (ECSC). The founding Treaty of that organization did not contain any provision on matters of delegation. Nevertheless, the High Authority of the ECSC relied on outside bodies of experts, commonly called the Brussels agencies, to carry out certain arcane tasks of calculation concerning prices in the coal and steel markets, including the markets for ferrous scrap. One of these outside bodies was the Joint Bureau of Ferrous Scrap Consumers, which was charged with buying ferrous scrap on the international market on behalf of the European steel companies that used ferrous scrap in their production. Another outside body, the Imported Ferrous Scrap Equalization Fund then had the task of adjusting the price of this imported ferrous scrap in different parts of the Coal and Steel Community in such a way that steel producers throughout the ECSC could buy this input into their steel production on the basis of equal competitive opportunities. The Joint Bureau and the Equalization Fund both counted a representative of the High Authority among their board members, who could defer decisions that he considered erroneous to the High Authority for final decision. On the other hand there were many elements in the relevant decision that seemed to indicate that the High Authority had fully delegated the technical aspects of these decisions to the Brussels agencies and accepted the data advanced by them without any check on its part as the basis for its decisions, even if it was also explicitly stated that the way in which the Brussels agencies were to manage the equalization system remained under the responsibility of the High Authority [344].

---

343. Case 9/56, *Meroni* v. *High Authority*, ECLI:EU:C:1956:7, English Special Edition 1957-1958, at p. 133.
344. *Décision 14-55 instituant un mécanisme financier permettant d'assurer l'approvisionnement* régulier en *ferraille du marché commun*, OJ 1955, pp. 685-688 (no English text available). See Article 1 (responsibility of the High Authority);

This latter view of things was essentially confirmed by the statements included in the defense of the High Authority before the Court of Justice of the ECSC, when an Italian steel producer, Meroni, filed an action for annulment against a secondary decision of the High Authority imposing on Meroni its obligatory contribution to the Equalization Fund. The High Authority asserted that the expertise necessary for the calculations of the equalization rate throughout the Community was so specialized that the High Authority would not dream of taking these tasks upon itself, unless there was a clear misuse of powers by the Brussels agencies. As the Court pointed out, the High Authority could have argued that the power of its representative to demand that the decision should be subordinated to the approval of the High Authority signified that the latter remained responsible for any decision of the Brussels agencies, as Article 1 of the general decision clearly stated. Now that it had not done so and declared the opposite, the Court had to assume that the High Authority intended to create a true delegation of powers to the Brussels agencies [345].

Did the delegation comport with the requirements of the Treaty? The answer of the Court to that question was a resounding no. If the High Authority itself had taken the impugned decisions, it would have had to state reasons therefore and to refer to any opinions which were required to be obtained (Art. 15 ECSC); it would have had to include the decision in a general report on its activities and its administrative expenses (Art. 17 ECSC); and it would have been subject to the duty to publish such data as could be useful to governments or any other parties concerned (Art. 47 ECSC). Moreover, its decision or recommendation would have been subject to review by the Court of Justice on the conditions laid down by Article 33 ECSC. In its delegation of powers to the Brussels agencies, the High Authority did not make the exercise of such delegation subject to these requirements of the ECSC Treaty. Hence the delegation of powers resulting from Decision 14/55 infringed the Treaty. All the more so because in delegating certain powers to the Brussels agencies without imposing on them the same conditions that applied to its own decision-making, *the High Authority had granted these agencies more powers than it itself had under the Treaty*. In addition, the Brussels agencies had made certain assessments of the enterprises

---

Article 2 (obligatory contributions of the ferrous scrap consumers); Article 5 (operation of the equalization scheme); Articles 8 and 9 (decision-making and relation between the Brussels agencies and the High Authority).

345. See Case 9/56, *Meroni, supra* footnote 343, at pp. 148-149.

wanting to buy scrap on the European market and the criteria for such assessments were not explained in Decision 14/55. The Court ruled that any criteria used in such assessments had at least to be transparent and be presented in such a way as to be reviewable by a court of law [346].

The Court, however, did not stop there, but seemingly wanted to help the High Authority by giving some indications of when a delegation of powers could and would be legal. In passing, the Court rejected the argument that the absence of an explicit power of delegation in the ECSC Treaty was decisive. Having been attributed a power by the Treaty should be seen as sufficient basis for possibly delegating it. This is typical "implied power" reasoning. However, the Court recognized that the consequences that might flow from a delegation of powers are very different when it involves (1) clearly defined executive powers that can be subject to review in the light of objective criteria determined by the delegating authority, or (2) when it concerns a power that would imply a wide margin of discretion and lead to the delegate body making economic policy choices [347]. In the *Meroni* case this led to a transfer of the power to make these economic choices from the High Authority to the Brussels agencies and hence to "an actual transfer of responsibility". The Court added, and this is important, that "the balance of powers which is characteristic of the institutional structure of the Community" formed a guarantee for those private parties who were subject to the regime of the Treaty. To delegate discretionary powers and entrusting "the exercise of such powers to bodies other than those which the treaty has established to affect and supervise the exercise of such powers, each within the limits of its own authority, would render that guarantee ineffective". The Court ruled that Decision 14 (55), and in particular its Article 5, did exactly that [348].

In the light of these strictures the Court decided that the High Authority's reservation of the power to take back the decision from the Brussels agencies if and when its representative in these agencies so demanded was insufficient. Such a procedural limitation on delegated powers did not give a sufficient guarantee that the requirement that

---

346. *Ibid.*, at pp. 150-151.
347. *Ibid.*, at p 152. As shown in Chapter II, this distinction between executive powers and powers that imply a large measure of discretion derived from the national doctrine on delegation of powers of three founding Member States of the ECSC.
348. *Ibid.*, at pp. 152-153.

such delegation be detailed, precise and not leaving true discretion to the delegate body would always be respected [349].

The result of the *Meroni* case can be summarized as follows. Delegation of powers is possible even without a specific provision in the EEC/EU Treaty; it is an implied power derived from the explicit attribution of a power to one of the EU institutions. However, the case makes a clear distinction between two categories of powers that may be delegated.

1. What the Court calls "executive powers" are usually so detailed and precise that normally there should be no problem with their delegation to another body inside the structures of the ECSC. And if that is not the case, they can easily be made more precise and well circumscribed by the institution that grants the delegation in the delegating instrument that it adopts. It is not fully clear whether this could also apply to bodies outside the institutional structure of the ECSC, but in the *Meroni* case itself this was clearly considered impossible.
2. On the other hand, the Court makes it clear that discretionary powers and their delegation create specific problems. The Court is not fully clear that such powers cannot be delegated at all to other bodies than the institution to which the Treaty grants such powers. It is after all that specific institution that the Treaty has charged with making the policy choices that are inherent in the grant of a discretionary power, and that the Treaty has subjected to judicial scrutiny before the Court of Justice. In this connection the Court in *Meroni* uses the terms "the balance of powers between the institutions" and in later cases simply uses the words "the balance between institutions".
3. It is also not fully clear that it would in principle be impossible to circumscribe the exercise of discretionary powers in such detailed fashion that the Court's hesitations about delegating such powers could be fully laid to rest. However, the Court has been as clear as it could be in rejecting the mere possibility of the delegating institution "taking back" a specific case of the exercise of delegated powers of a discretionary nature and decide itself, as a valid mechanism for remedying a possibly illegal delegation of discretionary powers.

---

349. *Ibid.*, at p. 154. It is not entirely excluded that in certain circumstances the application of "taking back" the decision could be effective. We will encounter several examples of this technique – which has been persistent.

Harking back to the earlier chapters on the different national approaches to the delegation of powers in Member States' constitutional and administrative law and within another international organization like the UN, it is easy to recognize some of the restraints on the delegation of legislative powers that were present in some national systems of law of countries both inside and outside the Union. We recognize the distinction between executive and discretionary powers as being close to the distinction between regulatory and legislative powers in most States. Linked to that is a considerable aversion to allowing the delegation of (quasi-)legislative powers to nonlegislative bodies unless there is a clear constitutional authority to do so. However, in *Meroni* this is also directly connected to the balance (of power) between the institutions of the ECSC. Given that the High Authority was not obviously the legislative power of the ECSC – although it wielded great power over the fate of individual coal or steel companies while that industry was resurrected after the war and restructured at the same time – this was only natural. Another point on which the Court plausibly borrowed from the national systems was the necessity of circumscribing in all cases of delegation, whether (quasi-)legislative or executive in nature, very carefully, clearly and in detailed fashion, the actual powers that are delegated to another body, inside or outside the government, and how they should be used. This is also of great importance with a view to putting the Court of Justice in a position to exercise its judicial review of the legal instrument by which the delegation is made.

There is no direct reference, however, to any of the national law systems on delegation of France, Germany or Italy, as the Court was obviously unwilling to interpret Union law openly by reference to national law. Nevertheless Advocate-General (AG) Roemer in *Meroni* briefly referred to the fact that domestic economic law was not adverse from delegating power to non-State associations and mentioned

> "two points which, in a modern State founded on the rule of law [are] generally accepted as conditions governing the delegation of the administrative powers of public authorities to private associations: the delegation must be governed by a law which specifies the content of the delegation precisely and which must guarantee not only sufficient control by the State, but also complete legal protection against the measures adopted by these associations"[350].

---

350. *Ibid.*, at p. 190.

The AG made this reference to national approaches to delegation in vague and general terms, so as to make it palatable to the Court, but without success. On the other hand, there is no doubt that Roemer's reference to "complete legal protection" struck a chord with the Court and contributed to its rejection of the delegation of powers from the High Authority to the Brussels agencies since the agencies' decisions and recommendations were not exposed to an action for annulment under the terms of Article 33 ECSC like those issued by the High Authority.

Furthermore, in *Meroni* the notion that an institution cannot delegate more or different powers than those that have been attributed to it was explicitly mentioned. As mentioned earlier, in the UN the rule of *nemo plus iuris* did not play an important role except in administrative law delegation within a UN organ like the Secretariat. This can probably be explained by the fact that the powers conferred on the different organs/ institutions by the treaties establishing these organizations are much broader in the UN than in the ECSC, which was a *traité-loi*, in contrast to the UN Treaty and later even the EEC/EU Treaties, which are *traités-cadre*. This raises the question whether the *Meroni* case could still find application within the framework of the EEC Treaty, and even more so after the expiration of the ECSC Treaty in 2002 and its absorption into the EC/EU Treaty (now the TFEU). That is a question of some weight, but one that the Court of Justice has never confronted; after the entry into force of the Rome Treaty it simply went on invoking *Meroni* on a fairly regular basis. This is perhaps not surprising now that we have seen that a number of core concepts limiting delegation of powers contained in the *Meroni* case were probably derived from Member States' constitutional conceptions about the conditions under which the delegation of implementing and (quasi)-legislative powers could take place. Thus, they were presumably also of importance beyond the *traité-loi* of the ECSC [351]. All the more so since in the EC/EU it was crystal clear where the legislative power was and is concentrated: initially in the Council and later in the Council and Parliament together.

---

351. See also M. Chamon, *EU Agencies: Legal and Political Limits to the Transformation of the EU Administration*, Oxford, Oxford University Press, 2016, at p. 194. Chamon's approach is more intuitive: "In reality some of the limits in *Meroni* seem generally applicable in any modern state based on the rule of law." Moreover, this book gives a very interesting analysis of the doctrinal reception of *Meroni* by contemporaneous authors and in recent scholarship, mainly provoked by the agencification of the EC/EU (see pp. 183-192) within a broader section on the *Meroni* case and the notion of delegation(see pp. 175-249).

B. *The Rome Treaty and management committees*

The *Meroni* judgment was handed down in 1958, the year the Rome Treaty founding the European Economic Community entered into force. Article 155 of that Treaty, on the powers of the Commission, contained an explicit provision on a limited delegation of powers from the Council of Ministers, at that time the main legislative institution of the EEC, to the Commission. The article's fourth indent simply stated that the Commission was bound to "exercise the powers conferred on it by the Council for the implementation of the rules laid down by the latter"[352]. There was no corresponding provision in the article on the powers of the Council.

The first policy area of the Community where this new, explicit power of delegation between Council and Commission was regularly used was the common agricultural policy. In the framework of that common policy a number of so-called market organizations covering specific agricultural products were created. Each market organization had its own basic regulation. In order to apply that regulation to the actual economic conditions in that market required a steady stream of so-called implementing regulations. Special committees for each market regulation were created, consisting of representatives of the Member States; they were called management committees[353]. The Commission presented its drafts of implementing legislation to these management committees, which gave their advice on them. If their advice was positive or could be accommodated by the Commission, there was no problem: the Commission adopted the implementing measure. If the advice was and remained negative, even after Commission adjustments, the decision-making power could be taken back by the Council.

---

352. Note that at that time the Council was the sole legislator of the Community; the European Parliament merely gave its advice on the different proposals of the Commission, and the Council was free to take such advice or not. This changed only gradually through different treaty modifications until the Lisbon Treaty completed the road to elevating the Parliament to the status of full co-legislator with the Council, except in the field of the common foreign and defense policies.

353. Note how the terminology used ("implementing" and "management") is geared to emphasize the administrative and nonlegislative character of the regulations resulting from this process. This was all the more necessary because the EEC/EU to this day knows no terminologically expressed general hierarchy of norms (law, organic law, statutory instrument, decree, etc.), even though some *de facto* hierarchy has always existed. Lisbon changed very little, even if Articles 290 and 291 TFEU, with their distinction between "delegated" and "implementing" acts, which was confirmed by homonymous obligatory suffixes in the titles of such acts, confirmed that there was such a *de facto* hierarchy.

There are clear differences between the *Meroni* case and the 1970 *Köster* case about the management committee procedure [354]. The *Meroni* case was about the possibility to delegate certain aspects of a decision of the High Authority of primary law character – that is to say a decision directly based on the Treaty – to the Brussels agencies, which as creatures of the coal and steel industry were entirely outside the ECSC. The management committees, by contrast, were specifically set up as a new type of organ – half inside the EEC – in order to create a mechanism by which the Commission and the Member States' specialists could smoothly cooperate in the management of the agricultural product markets and transform them into one European market [355]. In effect it made a delegation, of which the possibility was foreseen in Article 155 of the Treaty, easier to apply in the eyes of the Member States and the Council, as they were involved by the Commission in the implementing measures it intended to take. The final decision was in principle taken by the Commission, and in exceptional cases by the Council and thus always fully justiciable by the Court [356].

This was different in the *Meroni* case, in which difficulties for proper judicial review of the actions of the delegate body (the Equalization Fund) arose since it was not a body whose actions could be reviewed by the Court – a problem that was wholly absent in the *Köster* case because the decisions of the Council and the Commission which resulted from the management committee procedure were fully subject to judicial control by the European Court of Justice. There is also a difference in the stringency and precision of the formulation of the delegated powers. In *Meroni*, where a power laid down in the Treaty and attributed to the High Authority, which it delegated to organisms outside the Treaty, powers that were not clearly of an executive character and left a large measure of discretion, could not be validly delegated. In *Köster*, where the delegation related to second order legislation, based on a market organization regulation, it was sufficient that "the Commission did not

---

354. Case 25/70, *Einfuhr- und Vorratstelle für Getreide und Futtermittel* v. *Köster, Berodt & Co.*, ECLI:EU:C:1970:115.
355. The management committees can be said to be half within the EC/EU structure because they were and remained, when called implementing committees under Article 291 TFEU, committees of the Member States and thus not part of the Council machinery. They were presided by Commission civil servants but not integrated into the Commission machinery either. On the other hand, they have been set up, initially by successive comitology decisions (see below) and later on the basis of Article 291 TFEU.
356. Pursuant to Article 173 EEC Treaty. See also Case 25/70, *supra* footnote 354, at para. 9.

go beyond the limits of the implementation of the principles" of the basic regulation [357].

The early development of the doctrine of delegation under Community law was completed by a case before the Court of Justice in which the authority of the Administrative Commission of the EEC in matters of the coordination of social security systems of the Member States to make recommendations or give interpretations that were considered binding on the social security organisms and the courts of the Member States was at issue, the so-called *Romano* case [358]. Although the Administrative Commission was an organ set up by the Council, it was not among the institutions and bodies whose decisions were subject to the jurisdiction of the Court according to the Treaty at that time. That led the Court to the simple conclusion that it followed "both from Article 155 of the Treaty and the judicial system created by the Treaty, and in particular Articles 173 and 177 thereof, that a body such as the Administrative Commission may not be empowered by the Council to adopt acts having the force of law" [359].

This demonstrates once again how important it is for the Court that the acts even of a body that is charged merely with the interpretation and explanation of a basic regulation, and therefore working at the level of secondary law, should be subject to judicial review of the Court of Justice, either through a direct action for annulment or by way of a preliminary question. This is a recurring theme, also in later case law. The reference the Court made to Article 155 also implies that it is *ultra vires* for the Council to delegate legislative powers, or in any case powers that pretend to have binding effects for the relevant authorities of the Member States, to an organ created by, and almost identical in composition to, the Council [360]. This we recognize as the prohibition of

---

357. Case 25/70, *supra* footnote 354, at para. 7.
358. Case 98/80, *Romano*, *supra* footnote 158.
359. *Ibid.*, at para. 20.
360. The acts of the Administrative Commission, which consisted of representatives of the Member States and a representative of the Commission in an advisory capacity, under Articles 80 and 81 of Reg. 1408/71 on "the application of social security schemes to employed persons and their families moving within the Community" were normally not considered binding. However, per Article 7 of Reg. 574/72 on "fixing the procedure for implementing", Reg. 1408 charged the Administrative Commission with fixing the rates of conversion of pensions and their date of applicability. This was obviously a binding decision and, although of a highly technical nature, it would have considerable practical consequences for the pensioners concerned. AG Warner in *Romano* was emphatic in his opinion that Article 7 was an unacceptable delegation of legislative power; see ECLI:EU:C:1980, at 1265-1266.

legislative self-delegation, which we know from the legal systems of some countries, such as the United States.

The *Meroni* and *Romano* cases have another aspect in common, namely that the bodies to which powers were delegated were arguably conceived as bodies that would merely "assist" the High Authority (as in *Meroni*) or the Commission and the Member States' bodies in the field of social security (as in *Romano*) to take certain decisions. The reality was different in both cases: from "helpers" these bodies became real delegate bodies because respectively the High Authority and the Member States' social security bodies saw their assistance as *binding*. One is tempted to conclude that these were almost cases of delegation by mistake. However, the European Court of Justice treated them as real delegations, which should be considered unlawful. This is testimony to the Court's wariness of the constitutional and administrative law risks involved in such cases in the young international organization that the EC still was at the time.

Nevertheless, as transpired from the *Rey Soda* case, primarily in the field of agricultural policy and within the framework of the system of management committees, and if the delegation was from the Council to the Commission, following the wording of the fourth indent of Article 155 EEC Treaty, the Court could be generous [361]. When these conditions were fulfilled, the Court considered that "it follow[ed] from the context of the Treaty . . . and also from practical requirements that the concept of implementation must be given a wide interpretation". The practical requirements mentioned by the Court boiled down to the Commission's extensive knowledge of, and capacity to follow, agricultural markets from day to day. This justified the Council's conferral on the Commission of "wide powers of discretion and action" [362]. However, as the Court saw it, Article 155 enabled the Council to subject these wide powers to strict conditions and the management committee procedures gave it, where necessary, "its own right to intervene". Under such conditions, the Court was free to interpret the power that had been conferred on the Commission "with regard to the basic general objectives of the organization of the market and less in terms of the literal meaning of the enabling decision" [363].

The Court, however, was less broad-minded when the Commission asserted that management committee procedures conflicted *ipso*

---

361. Case 23/75, *Rey Soda and Cassa Conguaglio Zucchero*, ECLI:EU:C:1975:142.
362. *Ibid.*, at paras. 10-11.
363. *Ibid.*, at paras. 12-14. 1.

facto with the Commission's treaty-based power to "implement the budget" (now Art. 317 TFEU). The Court reminded the Commission that the power to implement the budget was not a license to spend money "irrespective of any substantive decision"[364]. Such substantive decisions, in the case at hand on projects to be approved on the basis of a regulation on research in the fisheries sector, could legitimately contain a reference to the comitology decision and which procedure should be applied, also if they had repercussions on the implementation of the EEC budget by the Commission[365].

Over the years until the mid-1980s the system of committees developed and diversified itself depending on the area of economic activity in which it was being used, in particular how "sensitive" certain areas were for the Member States. Next to the management committees that continued to function in the framework of the different agricultural market organizations, so-called regulatory committees developed that fulfilled comparable functions in areas related to the internal market and trade policy, in particular in the field of application of safeguards, both initially inside the common market and later in relation to third countries. The push for completing the internal market provided an opportunity to limit the extreme diversity of such committees and to modify the treaty accordingly.

C. The Single European Act of 1987 and the codification of the implementing committees

The Single European Act introduced a provision in Article 145 (third indent) EEC on the powers of the Council, matching Article 155 (fourth indent) EEC on the powers of the Commission, but going further than that. It contained what was in principle an obligation of the Council to delegate to the Commission not only powers for the implementation of the rules that the Council laid down, but also to permit the Council to impose certain requirements in respect of the exercise of these powers. In specific cases, the Council could decide to implement certain provisions directly itself.

The obligation to delegate to the Commission was, therefore, heavily qualified by the possibility for the Council to reserve certain

---

364. Case C-16/88, *Commission* v. *Council*, ECLI:EU:C:1989:397, at para. 19.
365. *Ibid.*, at paras. 19 *in fine* and 20. For some excellent conclusions by AG Darmon relating to division of powers with respect to the budget, the system of management committees and the existential fears of both the Council and the Commission in respect of the constitutional allocation between them, see ECLI:EU:C:1989:280.

implementing powers to itself (but only in specific cases, not as a rule) and by the conditions that the Council could impose on the Commission when delegating implementing powers. It was important, however, that it was beyond doubt that such implementing powers could only be granted to the Commission, and not to any other institution or body of the Union.

Finally, the third indent of Article 145 EEC enjoined the Council to lay down the necessary principles and procedures that would govern this conferral of implementing powers on the Commission. To that end the Council was unanimously to adopt a decision based on a proposal from the Commission and after obtaining the opinion of the European Parliament.

This so-called comitology decision counted a mere five articles but was quite complicated in content [366]. Article 1 broadly repeated the wording of Article 145 EEC and added that the Council shall specify in the basic act delegating implementing powers the essential elements of these powers. If its objective was *inter alia* to streamline the existing practice of different committees, it failed. It turned out to be rather a sum of existing practices. Article 2 alone contained three different procedures – the advisory procedure, the management procedure and the regulatory procedure – of which the latter two each contained two variants. In the same way Article 3, which contains the so-called safeguard procedure, also contained two variants. There were thus seven different decision-making procedures that the Commission in its proposal and the Council in its decision could choose from. Four of these could result in the Council itself ultimately taking the decision, which showed that the Council was still wary of a broad delegation of powers to the Commission. The decision also failed to specify, apart from the two safeguard procedures where this was self-evident, which procedure was to go with what kind of delegation. It was fair to surmise that Procedure II, with its two variants, looked like the management procedure and thus was intended for the domain of agriculture and fisheries, but nothing was made explicit about this, or about Procedure III, the regulatory one, and its two variants. The choice of procedure would be decided by the substantive regulations governing different areas falling within various Community domains.

---

366. Council Decision 87/373/EEC, laying down the procedures for the exercise of implementing powers conferred on the Commission, OJ 1987, L197, at pp. 33-35.

It is clear from this summary of Decision 87/373, the first comitology decision, that the emphasis was mostly on procedure and that it contained very little of substance on the principles of delegation of powers from the Council to the Commission. In particular there was no clarity whatsoever on what was later called the distinction between delegation of implementing powers and delegation of legislative powers. This was a distinction that only the Treaty of Lisbon would bring, even though it would give no indication where to draw the boundary between the two kinds of delegated powers. Between the Single Act (July 1987) and the Treaty of Lisbon (December 2009), in a period of just over ten years, three treaty revisions entered into force (named after the three cities of Maastricht 1993, Amsterdam 1999 and Nice 2003) – but they changed nothing to the text of Articles 145 and 155 of the EC Treaty (except the numbering). This showed that the Member States were happy with the existing balance of powers between the Council and the Commission as far as delegation was concerned. Nevertheless, the comitology decision was revised several times.

Such changes were an indirect consequence of other changes in the EC Treaty. Existing policies of the Community, such as the social, environmental, trade and transport policies, expanded in these years and new policies, such as immigration and asylum, were largely brought under the Community method by the Treaty of Amsterdam. These were all areas of policy that required detailed secondary legislation and/or implementation in the field by national authorities under detailed implementing rules, preferably from the Commission.

This phenomenon did not merely increase the need for good and reliable procedures for delegating implementing legislation. In many of the policy areas mentioned above the necessity to create European agencies arose, as centers of expertise with an advisory character but also as centers that could produce decisions or rules that were primarily based on that expertise rather than on broad policy or political preferences. Others were centers of coordination; still others were even operational in nature. One may think of such agencies as the European Environmental Agency (1994), the European Intellectual Property Office, successor to the Office for Harmonization of the Internal Market (1999), the European Maritime and Aviation Safety Offices (2002 and 2003), the Fundamental Rights Agency (2005), the European Chemicals Agency (2007), Europol and Eurojust (1999 and 2002), the European Defence Agency (2004), the European Banking Authority and the European Securities and Markets Authority (2011), and Frontex (2005, refounded and expanded in 2016 and 2019)[367]. This limited selection merely illustrates their diversity. The one trait they have in common is their distance from EU political institutions, by which they had been created. Those that have a capacity to take independent decisions or even promulgate their own rules, outside the direct control of the EU political institutions, have special problems of (legislative) delegation and will receive special attention below.

These same treaties of Maastricht, Amsterdam and Nice also gave more and more powers to the European Parliament, not only by expanding its right to give opinions on more legislative proposals of the Commission being discussed for adoption in the Council than before, but later also by replacing parliamentary opinions by granting a cooperation power to Parliament on many subjects, finally culminating in its being recognized as a full-fledged co-legislator with the Council in the Treaty of Lisbon. This development made it increasingly unpalatable for the Parliament to accept that the implementation of legislation that had required its opinion, cooperation or approval should be granted to the Commission or reserved to itself by the Council without the Parliament having any say in it[368].

Another external pressure that militated in favor of restructuring and simplifying decision-making in the Council was the coming Eastern European and Mediterranean accession of ten, later twelve, Member States, which became more and more pressing over the period from 1989 to 2003. A well-organized system of delegation was seen as one (admittedly small) part of the solution to the problems that would be caused by such a radical enlargement of the Council of Ministers, which was destined to change overnight from a club into a small senate.

The tensions between the three institutions involved in the delegation of powers within the EC/EU found their expression in litigation before the European Court of Justice as well. It would be going too far to discuss the case law over the years leading up to the entry into force of the Lisbon Treaty in detail. Insofar as the case law may clarify trends on the road to the present post-Lisbon regime of delegation and illustrates remaining problems, however, it may be useful to sketch the

---

367. On agencies and on agencies and delegation in general, see M. Buiusoc, *The Accountability of European Agencies. Legal Provisions and Ongoing Practices*, Delft, Eburon, 2010; Chamon, *supra* footnote 351; M. Simoncini, *Administrative Regulation beyond the Non-Delegation Doctrine: A Study on EU Agencies*, Oxford, Hart, 2018.
368. See C. F. Bergström, *Comitology: Delegation of Powers in the European Union and the Committee System*, Oxford, Oxford University Press, 2005, at pp. 313-315.

development that the Court of Justice went through in respect of the problem of delegation.

The European Parliament regarded itself as the losing party after the adoption of the first comitology decision. It almost immediately brought an action for annulment against Decision 87/373. However, at that time the right of action of the Parliament against legal acts of Council and Commission was far from fully acquired. Since the Court was unable to conclude that the Parliament defended one of its own prerogatives in this particular case its action for annulment was declared inadmissible [369].

As was already mentioned earlier, the Commission also brought a case early after the adoption of the first comitology decision. Although it lost the battle on the relation with its power to implement the budget, that case also served to clarify two important points on the interpretation of Article 145, third indent. The choice of the Council to exercise a delegated power itself had to be duly reasoned. And the "powers of implementation" that were delegated could not only encompass general "rules of implementation" but also "acts of individual implementation" [370].

In the mid-1990s, the Parliament again brought two cases concerning the functioning of Comitology Decision 87/373. Again, the question of admissibility arose in both cases. Although the criteria for declaring the Parliament admissible in actions for annulment brought against the Council and the Commission were still the same, the Court – of which the composition had considerably changed since 1987 – was now more relaxed in applying these criteria and declared both cases admissible.

The first one [371], brought against the Council, alleged (1) that it had adopted its definitive decision on the Commission's proposal before the Parliament had adopted its opinion, (2) that the changes the Council

---

369. Case 302/87, *European Parliament* v. *Council*, ECLI:EU:C:1988:461, at paras. 22-28. The Court basically followed the Council in its argument to the effect that neither Case C-294/83, *Parti écologiste "Les Verts"* v. *European Parliament*, ECLI:EU:C:1986:66, nor Case 34/86, *Council* v. *European Parliament*, ECLI:EU:C: 1986:291, on the Parliament's power to increase noncompulsory expenditure were of a nature to support the Parliament's argument that it was defending one of its prerogatives.
370. Case C-16/88, *supra* footnote 364, at paras. 10-11. In particular the health and safety agencies needed to take individual decisions (of approval of medicines and pesticides, type approval of airplanes, etc.), but with general implications, namely admission to the EU market as a whole.
371. Case C-417/93, *European Parliament* v. *Council*, ECLI:EU:1995:127, which concerned the Regulation on the Technical Assistance to the Independent States of the former USSR and Mongolia, also known as the TACIS Regulation (Reg. No. 2157/91, OJ 1991, L 201, p. 2.

had made to a Commission proposal as to the choice of a management or regulatory committee procedure affected the division of powers between the two institutions, and finally (3) that the Council had crossed the line between implementation and legislation by creating a possibility of revision, in the light of experience gained, of the financial threshold fixed for awarding services contracts in the framework of the TACIS program by restricted invitations to tender. After the Court had rejected point (1) on the basis of its own reconstruction of the facts, it proceeded to discuss the other two points with the clear objective to let the committee procedures work. Point (2) was rejected by the Court with the argument that the difference between a management committee procedure and a regulatory procedure, both of which left room for the Council itself to intervene, did not "decisively affect" the "overall balance of the powers allocated to the Commission and the Council" [372]. Finally, point (3) was rejected by reminding the Parliament that the delegation of powers in spending TACIS money was entirely comparable to implementing basic regulations laying down agricultural market organizations. As a consequence, the more relaxed test for the permitted delegation of powers laid down in *Köster* was applicable, namely staying within the essential elements laid down in the basic regulation [373].

A similar attitude of the Court prevailed in the second case, against the Commission on the implementation of a regulation on organic production of agricultural foodstuffs and their labeling [374]. Again in that case, the *Köster* formula was used by the Court to decide that the criteria that the Commission and the Management Committee had to respect when deciding to add *inter alia* genetically modified microorganisms (GMMOs) to a list of permitted adjuvants in food processing, of which it had been shown that without using such substances it would be impossible to produce such processed foodstuffs, satisfied that formula. Hence there was no excess of powers on the part of the Commission. The Court also rejected the claim of misuse of powers, which the Parliament had based on the supposed hidden motive of the Commission to permit a generalized acceptance of GMOs (genetically modified organisms) in feed and food. The Commission and the Council (intervening) convinced the Court, fairly easily, that on the basis of one of the recitals of the basic regulation, the use of GMMOs in the

---

372. *Ibid.*, at paras. 25-26.
373. *Ibid.*, at paras. 30-33.
374. Case C-156/93, *European Parliament* v. *Commission*, ECLI:EU:C:1995:238.

production of certain foodstuffs with an organic production label was to be examined in detail when those products would be up for approval according to the relevant Community legislation. Consequently, there was no misuse of powers on the side of the Council in having recourse to the management committee procedure.

In conclusion: during the period between the codification of the management committees on the basis of the Single European Act and the conclusion of the Treaty of Amsterdam there was not much progress on the substantive problems of delegation, but the procedural rules were well established, developed and applied by the Court of Justice. For this the Court had to fall back on its existing case law, and in particular on the *Köster* case. If there was a situation in which the problem of delegation of quasi-legislative measures arose, it certainly did not reach the Court during these years. Hence, the problem of the relation between the *Köster* principles and the *Meroni* principles and to which category of delegation, legislative or executive, they had to be applied did not arise.

D. From the Treaty of Amsterdam and the second comitology decision to the Treaty of Nice

The Treaty of Amsterdam entered into force on 1 May 1999 and did not change anything to the articles relevant to the delegation of powers between the institutions and other bodies of the European Community. However, it did contribute to the increase in powers of the European Parliament, in particular because it brought the so-called third pillar into the Community treaty. Soon afterward the Council adopted a new decision on the procedures for the exercise of implementing powers delegated to the Commission, the so-called second comitology decision[375]. The Parliament obtained preciously little of its wishes. There were new provisions on information that the Commission should pass to the Parliament and on transparency of the procedures and on a register of all committees, which assisted the Commission in the exercise of implementing powers[376]. This enhanced information and transparency would then place the European Parliament in a position, if necessary, to adopt a resolution when it was of the opinion that a proposal of the Commission containing draft implementing measures

---

375. Council Decision 1999/468/EC, laying down the procedures of implementing powers conferred on the Commission, OJ 1999 L 184/23.
376. Article 7 of Decision 1999/468.

would exceed the implementing powers provided for in the basic instrument. The Commission had the duty to react to this resolution and inform the Parliament but retained considerable freedom whether or not to follow the Parliament's wishes as to the final resolution of the problem [377]. All this was perhaps not without importance but remained far removed from the old wish of the European Parliament to have a say in all the cases of proposed implementing powers in regulations that had received some kind of parliamentary approval, whether an opinion or real approval as co-legislator.

The more substantive change was the simplification of the different procedures: the different variants of each type of procedure were removed and only one management, one regulatory and one safeguard procedure remained. Article 2 also provided greater clarity about (or confirmation of) under which conditions the management procedure and the regulatory procedure should be resorted to. The first one was intended primarily for agricultural and fisheries implementation and important measures of budgetary implementation; the second for general measures applying essential elements of measures in the field of human, animal or plant health and safety [378]. However, each of these procedures left the possibility open that the Council, under certain conditions, would take its own decision and thus "take back" the delegation of powers or "delegate the decision to itself".

In such cases, according to the *Meroni* doctrine, the Council would have to follow the normal decision-making procedures laid down in the Treaty [379]. Actually, this aspect of *Meroni* was immediately confirmed by the Court, fairly soon after the second comitology decision was adopted. This was a case where the Council had painted itself into a corner by setting a legal deadline by which a provisional EC regime for beef labeling should be replaced. When incapable of agreeing on the new system in time, the Council saw no other way out than resorting to a provision for secondary legislation in the regulation on the provisional regime, with a view to prolonging the provisional regime beyond

---

377. Article 8 of Decision 1999/468.
378. A formal declaration from the Council and the Commission accompanied the new comitology decision, in which the Commission confirmed that it would continue its standing practice of seeking as much consensus as possible in the management procedure and to be particularly attentive in regulatory procedures relating to health and food safety. The Council and Commission declared that they would urgently adapt the relevant substantive regulations to the new procedures. See Declarations on Council Decision 1999/468, OJ C203/1.
379. See Case 9/56, *Meroni, supra* footnote 343, at p. 150.

its final date. Since the decision-making procedure for secondary legislation was lighter (without Parliament's participation) than the Treaty basis for the provisional regime, the European Parliament went to the Court, which needed only thirteen short paragraphs to annul the prolongation of the provisional regime. Obviously, the prolongation of the provisional regime could only be lawfully achieved by the same treaty-based procedures as its original adoption required and not by a procedure reserved for the promulgation of second order legislation [380].

Clearly, self-delegation by one-half of the legislature (the Council) is even more off the constitutional charts than self-delegation by the entire legislature following more flexible procedures than prescribed in the Treaty for a certain subject. However, there are certainly conditions under which a decision of the Council to reserve certain implementation measures to itself could be resorted to in a lawful manner. Such conditions were present in the view of the Court during the transitional period after the Amsterdam Treaty, when visa policy and the way of carrying out border checks were in an early stage of being transferred in their entirety from the Member States to the Union [381]. The Court harked back to its judgment in Case 16/88 [382] and reaffirmed that Article 145 (after Amsterdam Art. 202) meant that the Commission, in the normal course of events, is responsible for taking the measures necessary for implementing a basic instrument. Moreover, it is up to the Council to give detailed reasons why in a specific case it wishes to exercise implementing powers directly. However, the Court clarified that even if the reasons given seemed "general and laconic", they could still provide sufficient justification when assessed in their proper context. The Court was of the view that during the transitional period mentioned above there were many indications, also to be found in other legal texts, that the matters at hand were rightly considered to be very sensitive to the Member States as they closely touched on their relations with non-Member States. This could be a valid reason for the Council to take implementing decisions into its own hands; and it helped that in this case the Council had foreseen to reconsider this decision in three years, thus emphasizing the transitional nature of its decision [383].

---

380. Case 93/00, *European Parliament* v. *Council*, ECLI:EU:C:2001:689, at paras. 35-48.
381. Case C-257/01, *Commission* v. *Council*, ECLI:EU:C:2005:25.
382. Case 16/88, *supra* footnote 364, at paras. 10-11.
383. Case C-257/01, *supra* footnote 381, at para. 49 ff.

It is interesting to note that the Court solved the problem before it by having recourse to the relevant Treaty article and not by interpreting the comitology decision [384]. A few years later the Court got its opportunity to interpret the second comitology decision in a case concerning a directive harmonizing and ensuring free movement of food supplements in the single market, based on (then) Article 95 EC (now 114 TFEU) [385]. This directive referred to Article 5 of the second comitology decision, laying down the new regulatory procedure, for any amendment to the "positive lists" attached to the directive; that is, lists that contained a limitative number of approved supplements such as vitamins, minerals, and so forth, which were deemed – after advice from the European Food Safety Authority (EFSA) – to pose no threat to human health [386].

Two things turned out to be important for the Court: (1) that the list was indeed restricted to substances judged for their potential effects on human health and not for their nutritional value and (2) the nature of the implementing measures to be taken by recourse to the regulatory procedure and the need to take them within a reasonable time. The first point made clear that this was indeed a matter of harmonization for the internal market (and not a matter of public health, which is in principle left to the Member States by the Treaty) [387]. On the second point, the Court remarked that

> "'comitology' is intended to reconcile, on the one hand, the requirement of effectiveness and flexibility arising from the need regularly to amend and update aspects of Community legislation in the light of developments in scientific understanding in the area of human health or safety and, on the other hand, the need to take account of the respective powers of the Community institutions" [388].

---

384. It should be noted that although this reason sounds plausible, AG Léger, in his opinion (see ECLI:EU:C:2004:226, at para. 62 ff), had advised the Court that the requirements laid down in Articles 5 and 8 of the new comitology decision had not been followed by the Council and therefore the relevant provisions in the Council's regulation should be quashed. Perhaps that was the motive behind the Court's following the Treaty route of interpretation and leaving the new comitology decision to one side.
385. Joined cases C-154/04 and C-155/04, *Alliance for Natural Health* et al. *and Secretary of State for Health*, ECLI:EU:C:2005:449.
386. Directive 2002/46/EC on the approximation of the laws of the Member States relating to food supplements, OJ L 183/51-57.
387. Joined Cases C-154/04 and C-155/04, *supra* footnote 385, at paras. 34-42.
388. *Ibid.*, at para. 78.

In addition, the Court explained that the regulatory procedure, although opening the possibility that the Council would take the decision itself, also ensured that if such a Council decision were not forthcoming, the Commission would ultimately be obliged to step in and take the decision within a reasonable period of time [389]. The Court let shine through that thus the applicant for approval can be assured that he will have a timely decision that will be open to review by the Court [390]. Without doubt this was also an important element to approve the implementing measures as decided in this case. The Court still had some critical remarks to make [391] but nevertheless found that all the necessary elements were present in the implementing measure and that thus not only had the comitology decision been respected, but so too the criteria of its own case law, in particular *Meroni* and *Köster* [392].

One important demand that the Court implicitly made here was that the whole regulatory procedure, including the advice of the EFSA, should be made transparent in conformity with the principle of sound administration. This requirement should be laid down in the basic regulation and not merely observed during the procedure and mentioned in the implementing regulation. The same was true for the conditions imposed by the *Meroni* and *Köster* cases; according to the Court, these jurisprudential conditions should be part and parcel of the basic regulation, even when in this case the implementing regulation made sufficiently clear that these conditions had been respected. These critical remarks by the Court could also have been satisfied by rounding out the comitology decision by more procedural requirements and by the substantive elements formulated by the Court in *Meroni* and *Köster* and the cases that followed. But they were not [393].

---

389. *Ibid.*, at paras. 79-80 and 91-92.
390. *Ibid.*, at para. 83.
391. *Ibid.*, at paras. 81-82.
392. *Ibid.*, at paras. 90-93. Note the conflation between the two procedures.
393. This touches upon the problem of how the (constitutional) legislator adapts the text of the EU treaties or of basic legislation to the case law of the Court of Justice. Often the (constitutional) legislator does not succeed in doing justice to all aspects of the case law that it seeks to codify or even to constitutionalize, or to make clear that it wants to adjust the case law somewhat in the process of codification or constitutionalization. That is not surprising because Member States often have different views of the Court's case law in question. The result of this is that the Court just goes on with developing its own case law further, while giving limited attention to what the Member States intended to do in their attempt at codification or constitutionalization. A well-known example at the constitutional level of this dynamic is the attempt to constitutionalize the Court's *AETR* case law in Article 3 (2) TFEU. The attempt at codification of *Meroni*, *Romano* and *Köster* in successive comitology decisions and a regulation may count as an example at the legislative level. Note that AETR refers to the European Agreement

The approach set out by the Court in the above-mentioned case on the harmonization of food supplements was followed in a slightly later case on the harmonization of smoke flavorings on the basis of Article 95 [394]. The emphasis here was primarily on whether or not Article 95 was the right legal basis, but that such harmonization could be carried out, again with the help of EFSA's expertise, by the Commission implementing regulations approved through the regulatory procedure foreseen in the comitology decision was no longer much of a problem.

A case that followed hard on the heels of the smoke flavorings case, in which EFSA also played an important role, was the one in which the UK directly attacked the creation of a new agency, the European Network and Information Security Agency (ENISA), on the basis of Article 95. The UK sought the annulment of the regulation establishing the agency on the basis of a narrow interpretation of its tasks and of Article 95. Given that the objective of that article was the harmonization of national laws and the primary tasks of ENISA, as listed in Article 3 of its founding regulation [395], were among others the gathering of information, keeping abreast of technical developments, standards, and so on, as well as facilitating cooperation between the Union institutions and the Member States in the field of electronic communications, the UK reasoned that there was no direct link with the harmonization of legislation as mentioned in Article 95. Hence it concluded that the regulation founding ENISA had to be annulled. The Court, however, at the instigation of the Commission, but contrary to the advice of its Advocate-General [396], took a more holistic view of the matter. It pointed out that ENISA was embedded in a considerable package, consisting of a Framework Directive on a common regulatory framework for electronic communications networks and services and six substantive directives on access to, and authorization of, such networks, on the protection of privacy on such networks, the harmonization of electronic signatures, on electronic commerce, as well as the Universal Service Directive. ENISA was supposed to fulfill a role with respect to the functioning

---

Concerning the Work of Crews of Vehicles Engaged in International Road Transport, 1 July 1970.

394. Case C-66/04, *United Kingdom* v. *European Parliament and Council*, ECLI:EU:C:2005:743.

395. Regulation (EC) 460/2004 establishing the European Network and Information Security Agency (ENISA), OJ 2004, L 77/1. This regulation has been repealed in the meantime and ENISA has been refounded by Reg. (EC) 526/2013 establishing the European Union Agency for Network and Information Security (ENISA) and repealing Reg. (EC) 460/2004, OJ 2013, L 165/41-58.

396. Opinion of AG Kokott in Case 66/04, ECLI:EU:C:2005:520, *passim*.

of all these substantive directives, all of which were based on Article 95. Hence the legal basis of Article 95 for ENISA was fully justified in the eyes of the Court. For our purposes, it is important to point out here that all these substantive directives, and notably the Framework Directive, provided for implementation measures to be taken according to the different procedures laid down in the 1999 Comitology Decision. Depending on the importance of these measures the advisory or the regulatory procedure had to be followed in the "Communications Committee", which serves as the "comitology committee" in the field of electronic communications [397]. The examples of EFSA and ENISA, which are styled as independent Community/Union "bodies" with their own legal personality, show that such bodies can play an important role in implementing a body of technical regulations as long as their advisory character can remain just that – advisory. Thus the Commission or, in exceptional situations, the Council, informed by their advice, can exercise the role of proposer/ implementer in the Communications Committee and be responsible before the European Parliament or before the Court for any (legal) mishap in the process.

As these last two cases show, the process of *agencification* in the EC had progressed considerably by 2005. As such, soon the new issue was going to be whether a procedure comparable to comitology could be used by these agencies *themselves* to implement certain (nonessential) aspects of basic regulations in their field of action. We will return to that question later (Sec. I.3), when discussing the *ESMA* case.

E. After the Treaty of Nice and up until the Treaty of Lisbon

The Treaty of Nice, which entered into force in early 2003, was primarily intended to adapt the institutional structure of the Union to the accession on 1 May 2004 of a large number of Member States from Eastern Europe and the Mediterranean. It was considered unlikely that with so many new Member States the Union would be capable of maintaining a reasonably efficient way of decision-making. Unfortunately, the attempts to streamline the decision-making of the Union led to a rather disappointing compromise, as laid down in the Nice Treaty. The Parliament was especially unhappy with the outcome.

---

397. See Article 22 of Directive 2002/21/EC of the European Parliament and of the Council of 7 March 2002 on a common regulatory framework for electronic communications networks and services (Framework Directive), OJ 2002, L108/33-50, which has in the meantime be modified because the 1999 Comitology Decision has been modified after the entry into force of the Lisbon Treaty.

1. The amendment of the second comitology decision

All the more reason for the Parliament to continue its campaign of pressure in respect of the comitology decision, and now with success. In 2006 the Parliament finally obtained a special procedure within the framework of the comitology decision: a new article was added containing the so-called regulatory procedure with scrutiny [398]. Details of this procedure will be described when discussing the present-day comitology decision below. Let it suffice here to say that this procedure gave the Parliament, when the regulatory procedure concerned the implementation of a legal act that had passed through the process of co-legislation, an opportunity to stop the process at the moment that the Council was preparing to take its final decision, and to register an objection. This would trigger a new back and forth between the Parliament and the two other political institutions. Other articles of the decision were also adapted to this new procedure.

During the period of validity of the amended second comitology decision, it was not so much the new procedure that Parliament had obtained, which led to conflicts rising to the level of the Court of Justice. It was rather that the Parliament saw problems in new implementing procedures that the Council and the Commission attempted to introduce into the new fields of asylum, visa policy and border controls as a consequence of the integration of the third pillar and the Schengen *acquis* into the European Community Treaty after Amsterdam.

The first such case that the Parliament brought against the Council [399] concerned Directive 2005/85/EC on minimum standards on procedures in Member States for granting and withdrawing refugee status [400]. In that directive the Council had reserved to itself the power to change or complete the list of so-called safe third countries, annexed to the directive. The procedure for exercising this power was less demanding than the Treaty procedure by which the directive itself had been adopted. It was unclear whether this was done under the normal rules of the amended second comitology decision or whether this was a specific kind of delegation that had been specially decided by the Council for this directive. In the first hypothesis, the Court pointed out that, following

---

398. Council Decision 2006/512/EC amending Decision 1999/468/EC laying down the procedures for the exercise of implementing powers conferred on the Commission, OJ 2006 L 200/11-13, no longer in force.
399. Case C-133/06, *European Parliament & Commission v. Council & France*, ECLI:EU:C:2008:257.
400. OJ 2006, L 326/13-34.

earlier case law, the Council should have given grounds why, instead of letting the Commission take the implementing decisions as usual, it wanted to reserve these powers to itself, and had not done so [401]. Hence "reclassifying" the derived power that it claimed to have as having been inspired by the amended second comitology decision and Article 202, third indent, EC Treaty (formerly Article 145 EEC) was not feasible.

In the second hypothesis, as AG Poiares Maduro put it, "[t]he issue is none other than that of the permissibility, under the Community constitutional system, of delegations of legislative power" [402]. The Court, however, gave short shrift to this idea, noting that the contested provisions contained a procedure for adopting measures by qualified majority on a proposal from the Commission and after consulting Parliament, while the relevant Treaty article demanded either unanimity in the Council after consultation of the Parliament or a full co-decision procedure. The Court subsequently pointed out that, according to precedent, Treaty rules on decision-making were not at the disposal of the EU institutions or the Member States [403]. The Court gave one example where the Treaty had itself explicitly opened up this possibility during the transitional phase of the transition of asylum and border control to the Community model. Then came the clincher:

"To acknowledge that an institution can establish secondary legal bases, whether for the purpose of strengthening or easing the detailed rules for the adoption of an act, is tantamount to

---

401. Case C-133/06, *supra* footnote 399, at paras. 48-49, following AG Poiares Maduro, ECLI:EU:C:2007:551, at para. 21.
402. *Ibid.*, Opinion of Poiares Maduro, at para. 23. This view was based implicitly on the assumption that adding another country to, or removing it from, the list of safe third countries was a legislative act, which intuitively seems right. Nevertheless, comitology procedures are often used to remove products from or add them to lists of prohibited substances or of endangered species, when this is merely the consequence of a modification of the corresponding list decided by an international organization or a treaty body, by which the EU and/or all its Member States are bound in any case. See, for example, Article 7 of Council Reg. EC No. 881/2002 imposing certain specific restrictive measures directed against certain persons and entities associated with Usama Bin-Laden, the Al-Qaida network and the Taliban, at OJ 2002, L 1399-22. This article empowered the Commission to modify Annex I to the Regulation in function of the modifications in the corresponding Annex of the SC Resolution decided by the Security Council or its Sanctions Committee. However, the problem here was more serious, namely reserving the matter to the Council, but then modifying the strictness of its decision-making procedure foreseen in the EC Treaty.
403. See Case 68/86, *United Kingdom v. Council (Hormones)*, ECLI:EU:C:2008:85, at para. 38

according that institution a legislative power which exceeds that provided by the Treaty."[404]

Moreover, according to the Court, it would enable the institution concerned to disturb the balance between the institutions, which demands "that each institution exercises its powers with due regard for the powers of the other institutions"[405]. This was contrary to the principle of Community loyalty or sincere cooperation (now Art. 4 (3) TFEU). Thus the Court reached the conclusion that the Council had infringed the relevant Treaty article (then Art. 67 EC).

It could be argued that the Court had not condemned (self-)delegation of legislative power as such. However, since the aim of most, if not all, delegation of powers is (next to other considerations such as bringing in expertise), subject to certain conditions, to simplify decision-making procedures as laid down in the Treaty, in reality Case C-133/06 amounts to a *de facto* prohibition of the delegation of legislative power.

The second case that the Parliament brought against the Council[406] concerned the question of whether in looking for a way to implement the Schengen Borders Code (SBC) the Council had not lost sight of the crucial difference between essential elements involving political choices – which ought to remain reserved to the Community legislature – and nonessential elements that could be freely delegated to the Commission. During the procedure before the Court, the Council and the Commission took the radical view that the question of which elements of a matter must be categorized as essential or not was a matter to be decided exclusively by the Community legislature. The Court, as might have been expected, rejected this position out of hand. It simply stated that such a decision by the Union legislature must be based on objective factors amenable to judicial review[407]. Furthermore, when reading the implementing decision, the Court found that it conferred enforcement powers on border guards, which entailed political choices falling within the responsibilities of the European Union legislature since it would require the weighing up of the conflicting interests at stake for different categories of persons who wanted to cross the EU external borders. The same was true, according to the Court, for the conferral of powers of public authority on border guards, such as the powers of stopping

---

404. Case C-133/06, *supra* footnote 399, at para. 56. This language comes almost directly from the *Meroni* case, *supra* footnote 344 and accompanying text.
405. *Ibid.*, at para. 58.
406. Case C-355/10 *European Parliament* v. *Council*, ECLI:EU:C:2012:516.
407. *Ibid.*, at para. 65 ff.

persons, seizing vessels and cars, and conducting persons apprehended to a specific location, all of which affect the fundamental rights of the persons concerned to such an extent as to require the involvement of the Community legislature itself. On that basis the Court quashed the implementing provisions of the SBC [408]. In this connection it is useful to recall the Dutch example, where an organic law directly attributed powers of public authority on border guards, customs officers and police officers, without intermediate implementing legislation [409].

2. Some interim conclusions

When looking at the legislative and jurisprudential developments since the adoption of the second comitology decision, the obvious point that stands out is the growing importance of the European Parliament. The second comitology decision gives the Parliament a toehold in the regulatory procedure and the amendment of 2006 gives it a full foot in the door. As to the Court, simply by deciding one case after another, it becomes more and more stringent in the requirements that it imposes on the application of the comitology decision and the Treaty articles on which it is based. And it becomes more restrictive as well in respect of the delegation of powers in other contexts.

Initially the Court shows some flexibility in accepting that the delegated decision itself contains some of the reasoning relating to the essential elements that are not delegated but can be implemented as far as the nonessential aspects are concerned. Later it demands with increasing insistence that such elements are set out in the basic regulation itself. Initially the Court allows limited reasoning justifying the delegation, as long as the context further supports and clarifies it, but later it is less forgiving, especially in cases of self-delegation by the Council. Initially it treats such self-delegation as in principle possible, although the Council should apply the same decision-making procedure as was necessary for the basic regulation. Later the Court further clarifies that any deviation from the decision-making procedure of the basic regulation, whether it be lighter or more demanding, is excluded. This puts an end to any realistic possibility of self-delegation by the legislature, even of implementation of an executive nature. However, the problem of the acceptability of delegation of legislative powers

---

408. *Ibid.*, at para. 76 ff., following AG Mengozzi, ECLI:EU:C:2012:207, at paras. 80-85.
409. See *supra* Chap. II.E.

or, as the Court intimates, powers requiring choices between different societal interests and/or groups, remains unresolved. This problem is linked to that of legislative self-delegation because the Court from the very beginning *(Meroni)* has insisted that all delegated legal acts should be adopted by an institution or other organ of the Community/Union that has standing before the Court.

F. The Treaty of Lisbon, delegation of legislative powers and the third comitology decision

The Treaty of Lisbon, which entered into force on 1 December 2009, brought a number of improvements in the field of delegation of implementing acts and, for the first time, explicitly created the possibility of the delegation of legislative acts.

1. Jurisdiction of the Court of Justice

First of all, however, it is important to mention here a very simple improvement of the Treaty that was apt to put to rest an important recurring preoccupation of the Court. Namely its impossibility to review the legally binding acts of many bodies, offices or agencies of the Union to which powers had been delegated, since they were not mentioned in the Treaty among the institutions whose acts could be reviewed – and, if necessary, annulled – by the Court of Justice. Article 263 TFEU (previously Article 230 TEC and 173 (E)EC) was complemented by a phrase that exposed acts intended to produce legal effects of such EU bodies, offices or agencies to the action for annulment under the conditions mentioned elsewhere in the article. This made delegation of powers to them in principle easier and more acceptable to the Court. Moreover, in principle the political institutions, in particular the Council and the Commission, had no absolute need any longer to concoct complicated procedures in which either of them remained the final decision-maker, whereas the decision had been prepared in reality by an expert body that in some cases went beyond a mere advisory role.

2. Delegated acts

To return to the matter of delegation itself, the new Article 289 TFEU describes the ordinary legislative procedure, which is basically identical to the co-legislation procedure between Council and Parliament in earlier EC/EU treaties. The article defines any other legislative procedure foreseen in the Treaty in which Council and Parliament participate together as a special legislative procedure. Legislative acts are defined as any acts adopted by either of these procedures.

Article 290 TFEU then lays down the conditions under which such legislative acts may be the basis for delegating powers to the Commission. The conditions of such delegation are strongly reminiscent (1) of the case law in *Meroni* and the cases following it, as discussed above, and (2) of the regulatory procedure with scrutiny, as laid down in the 2006 amendment to the 1999 Comitology Decision. Such delegation shall empower the Commission only "to adopt nonlegislative acts of general application to supplement or amend certain nonessential elements of the legislative act". These delegated acts shall be clearly identified by the word "delegated" in the title and they cannot contain themselves any of the essential elements of the area regulated by the legislative act. These are reserved to the legislative act itself.

Article 290 also foresees two possible "brakes" that may be included in the legislative act. (1) The delegation may be revoked by either of the two arms of the EU legislative power: the European Parliament or the Council; or (2) the delegated act may only enter into force if no objection has been expressed by either of the two institutions within a period defined in the legislative act (tacit approval). The Council will take any decisions on revoking, or objecting to, the delegated act by qualified majority and the Parliament by a majority of its members.

Less than a year and a half after the entry into force of the Lisbon Treaty, the three political institutions agreed on a Common Understanding on Delegated Acts. Presumably it was not a full-fledged interinstitutional agreement under the new Article 295 TFEU since it did not refer to this legal basis [410]. The timing of the understanding was in sync with the adoption of the new comitology regulation, which was to deal only with implementing acts under Article 291 TFEU. That stands to reason since the content of both texts had to be in harmony as the regulatory procedure with scrutiny was no longer seen as being part of the implementing powers, now defined in Article 291 TFEU and hence, in principle, should not figure in the new comitology regulation

---

410. In the Lisbon Treaty, interinstitutional agreements were canonized in Article 295 TFEU, thus codifying preexistent practice. Such agreements can be concluded only between the three political institutions: Parliament, Council and Commission. Whether that means that all three of them always *have* to be parties too such agreements is controversial. This is the view of the Council, but not of the Commission.

(or better perhaps "implementing regulation"). Henceforth what once was the amalgam of comitology, was now divided over two Treaty articles, 290 and 291, each with their own rules of application.

Let it suffice to say here that the original Common Understanding on Delegated Powers of 2011 was not a success. In particular the paragraph on the consultations that the Commission was to carry out in the course of the preparation of delegated acts was rather brief and quite vague in comparison to the provisions on the regulatory procedure with scrutiny, as laid down in the amended second comitology decision of 1999. This gave the Council and the Member States less opportunity to be involved in the preparation of delegated acts by the Commission than they previously had in that second comitology decision. It remains a bit of a mystery how they ever had agreed to that short paragraph at all since in the years that followed, the Council and the Member States did not stop complaining about it [411].

In the end the three political institutions of the Union used the European Parliamentary elections of May 2015 and the investiture of the new Juncker Commission later that year as an opportunity to draft and agree on a new Interinstitutional Agreement on Better Law-Making in April 2016, which contained a Chapter V on delegated and implementing acts [412]. The first clause of this chapter states that delegated and implementing acts play an important role in Union law and that, if used in an efficient and transparent manner, they contribute to keeping legislation up to date and to its swift implementation.

The discussions on this new Better Law-Making initiative also provided an occasion for the three institutions to develop its Chapter V and draft a broader Common Understanding on Delegated Acts; it was annexed to the Interinstitutional Agreement and thus acquired treaty-based status [413]. It is still in force today and has a new and expanded section on "Consultations in the preparation and drawing-up of delegated acts" at the center of it. This section clearly puts the consultation of experts of the Member States at the forefront when the Commission starts its work on a proposal for a new delegated act. When the proposal is ready, the Member State experts have to be consulted again. Consultation of stakeholders is also possible. If the

---

411. Based on the author's personal experience.
412. Interinstitutional Agreement between the European Parliament, the Council of the European Union and the European Commission on Better Law-Making, OJ 2016, L 123/1-9.
413. Common Understanding between the European Parliament, the Council of the European Union and the Commission on Delegated Acts, OJ 2016, L 123 10-14.

Commission changes the material content of the draft in any way there must be a last opportunity for the Member States' experts to react once again [414]. The Common Understanding also contains further rules on the early transmission of the delegated acts to the Council and the Parliament, so as to put them in a position to take a timely decision on a possible revocation or objection pursuant to Article 290 (2) TFEU [415]. There are rules on the duration of delegations and, if they are time-limited, their tacit renewal. The right of objection of Parliament and the Council has to be fixed at no less than two months in the delegated act and may be extended at the request of either institution with no more than two months [416]. An urgency procedure is foreseen in many of the basic regulations, especially those relating to security and safety matters, the protection of health and safety, and external relations, including humanitarian crises, and is further developed in the Common Understanding [417].

3. Implementing measures

Where implementing measures are concerned, the Treaty of Lisbon supplied some clarifications in Article 291 TFEU. First of all, it clarifies that a form of cooperative federalism prevails in the Union: Member States are bound to implement legally binding Union acts and adopt all the necessary measures of national law to do so [418]. Thus far this fundamental truth had not been so clearly expressed in the Treaty. Paragraph 2 of the article states that when uniform conditions for implementing legally binding Union acts are necessary, such basic acts shall confer implementing powers on the Commission. Only in duly justified specific cases under the TFEU and, presumably without such justification, in the field of the Common Foreign and Security Policy (CFSP), implementing powers may be kept by the Council to itself. Furthermore, the new so-called comitology rules for the Commission will be laid down in a regulation adopted according to the ordinary legislative procedure by the Council and the European Parliament,

---

414. *Ibid.*, at Section II.
415. *Ibid.*, at Section III.
416. *Ibid.*, at Section IV.
417. *Ibid.*, at Section VI.
418. Robert Schütze is an excellent and prolific guide on cooperative federalism and the EU. See his works on the European Constitution, in particular *From Dual to Cooperative Federalism: The Changing Structure of European Law*, Oxford, Oxford University Press, 2009.

instead of by a decision by the Council alone. Moreover, implementing acts will be clearly distinguished as such by the word "implementing" in their title.

The new (third) comitology regulation was adopted in February 2011, two months before the first version of the Common Understanding on Delegated Acts. It remains unamended to this day [419]. The title and the first article make clear that the regulation applies when a basic act states that there is a need for the uniform implementation by Member States and for submitting the adoption of implementing acts by the Commission to the control of Member States. There is thus greater formal emphasis on the control by Member States over the measures that are going to restrict their freedom in implementing their Union obligations in the manner they see fit – a freedom that is normal in nearly all other international organizations. The role of the Union legislature (Council alone or Council and Parliament) is less important than it was in the older versions of the comitology decision. The European Parliament and the Council only have a right of scrutiny when either of them believes that the Commission has exceeded its implementing powers as laid down in the basic act [420].

There are only two procedures left, the advisory procedure and the examination procedure. The latter procedure is applied in an explicitly limited number of cases: implementing acts of general scope and other implementing acts in five fields. These are: programs with substantive implications; the common agricultural and fisheries policies; the environment, security and safety, and the health and safety of humans, animals or plants; the common commercial policy; and finally, taxation. The advisory procedure applies to all other implementing acts. In case that procedure is followed, the opinion of the Committee is expressed by a simple majority of its component members. The Commission can go ahead regardless of a majority advice that is negative or the absence of any advice but should take "utmost account of . . . the discussions within the Committee and of the opinion delivered" [421].

The implementing committees remain as they were: composed of experts from the Member States with a Commission civil servant as Chair. When following the examination procedure, the Committee

---

419. Regulation (EU) No 182/2011, laying down the rules and general principles concerning mechanisms for control by Member States of the Commission's exercise of implementing powers, OJ 2011 L 55/13–18.
420. *Ibid.*, at Article 11, n. 77.
421. *Ibid.*, at Article 4.

gives its opinion about the Commission draft of an implementing measure by qualified majority, and even then, the Chair is under the obligation to endeavor to find a solution which commands the widest support possible. If the Committee cannot muster a qualified majority, the Commission can still adopt the implementing act, unless (1) the basic act states otherwise, (2) there is a simple majority opposed to the Commission draft, and (3) the proposed implementing act falls in the fields of taxation, financial services, the protection of the health and safety of humans, animals or plants, or definitive multilateral safeguard measures [422]. These are all obviously sensitive subjects.

Even more sensitive are countervailing duties and definitive antidumping duties, both for external and internal reasons. (Until some years ago such duties were still adopted by the Council). Hence, if there is no qualified majority in favor and there is a simple majority opposed to the Commission draft (i.e. (2) above applies), the Commission, after a further discussion with the Committee, may activate a special referral of the proposed or an adapted draft implementing act on antidumping and countervailing duties to the so-called Appeal Committee. In the case of a positive opinion or the absence of an opinion, the Commission shall, respectively may, adopt the implementing act. In the case of a rejection, no countervailing or antidumping duty may be imposed [423]. The Appeal Committee also has to deal with direct appeals by the Commission in case the implementing committee rejects a draft implementing act in a situation where such rejection would contribute to a significant disruption of agricultural markets or enhance a risk for the financial interests of the Union within the meaning of Article 325 TFEU [424]. Finally, there is an urgency procedure that entitles the Commission to take immediately applicable implementing measures with a limited validity of six months in cases where the basic act provides that the Commission can do so, without consulting the implementing committee for "duly justified imperative grounds of urgency". This procedure applies also to the adoption of provisional antidumping or countervailing measures, which may have a longer duration according to the relevant basic acts and the relevant WTO instruments. (check) As was already mentioned above, the Council and the European Parliament have a right of scrutiny in cases where they are of the view that the

---

422. *Ibid.*, at Article 5 (1)-(4).
423. *Ibid.*, at Articles 5 (5) and 6.
424. *Ibid.*, at Article 7.

Commission has exceeded its powers of implementation granted by the Treaty and the comitology decision [425].

As mentioned above, the 2016 Agreement on Better Law-Making paid most attention to delegated acts and the annex relating to such instruments. Chapter V of that Agreement, however, also mentioned implementing acts, albeit principally to insist on the integrity of the new 2011 Comitology Regulation. That is to say that the Union legislator (Council and Parliament) should refrain from adding new procedural requirements that would alter the mechanisms for control set out in that regulation. Moreover, implementing committees set up under the comitology regulation should not be called upon to perform additional tasks to those they had been set up for [426].

Finally, it is important to point out that Chapter VI of the Agreement on Better Law-Making sets great store on transparency throughout the legislative procedure. This also true for the implementing and delegated procedures [427]. The new comitology regulation contains a long Article 10 that requires transparency in many respects for the implementing procedures. This includes an obligation for the Commission to keep a full register of all proposed implementing acts and how they move through the procedure [428]. A similar obligation to keep a register, resting on the three institutions together, is now also applicable to delegated acts [429]. This has resulted in an impressive combined online Register of Delegated and Implementing Acts that is also accessible to the general public [430]. Similarly, an obligation to pass all information going to and from experts who are consulted (Member State experts, of course, but also often agencies like EFSA and ENISA, as mentioned above) to the other two institutions is now applicable. It is justified to conclude that the transparency that the Court of Justice put so much emphasis on in the beginning of its case law on implementing acts is by now fully assured by law, also for delegated acts.

4. Some preliminary questions and conclusions

This final stage of the codification separates the former regulatory procedure with scrutiny from the former management committees

---

425. *Ibid.*, at Article 8.
426. Agreement on Better Law-Making, *supra* footnote 412, at para. 30.
427. *Ibid.*, at Chapter VI.
428. Reg. No. 182/2011, *supra* footnote 419, at Article 10 (Information on committee proceedings), n. 77.
429. Agreement on Better Law-Making, *supra* footnote 412, at para. 29.
430. See https://webgate.ec.europa.eu/regdel/#/home.

approach, as laid down in the amended second comitology decision. The first approach now produces delegated acts and the second implementing acts. Delegated acts refine existing legislation, based on the Union treaties, and would constitute a true delegation to the Commission (or possibly to other EU bodies) of legislative powers held by the Union were they not hemmed in by very strong conditions such as the affirmation that they are nonlegislative acts, that they can pertain only to nonessential elements of the basic regulation and that they are subject to the possible exercise of the rights of revocation and objection available to both arms of the Union legislature. Implementing acts, on the other hand, are an instrument by which the Commission gets to control the duty of Member States to ensure the fulfillment of their obligations under the Treaty and to implement legally binding Union acts [431]. It thus disciplines the (remaining) freedom of action of the Member States. Hence the exercise of this power is subject to the control of a Committee of the Member States, whereas the Council and the European Parliament can only step in with a right of scrutiny if the Commission exceeds the implementing power granted in the basic legislative instrument [432].

After the new provisions of the Lisbon Treaty and the two instruments that were based thereon, the Common Understanding on Delegated Acts between the three institutions, and the new, third, comitology regulation, a provisional end had been reached of a legal development that started with the *Meroni* judgment. After the entry into force of the Lisbon Treaty in late 2009, between 2011, when the new comitology regulation was fashioned, and 2016, when the Interinstitutional Agreement on Better Law-Making was finalized and this resulted in the second version of the Common Understanding on Delegated Powers between the three institutions, a sort of final stage in the development of the codified law of delegation within the Union was reached. This was the result of the accumulation of case law syncopated by attempts to codify this case law, which in the end was lifted to a different level by the modifications introduced by the Lisbon Treaty. Nevertheless, it is striking that the institutions never went much beyond the case law in their attempts at codification. Even after more than sixty years of jurisprudence and codification it is remarkable how much of what is

---

431. This obligation flows from the combined effect of Articles 4 (3) TFEU and 291 (1) TFEU.
432. See also the conclusions of AG Cruz Villalion in Case C-427/12, *Commission v. Parliament and Council (Biocidal Products)*, ECLI:EU:C:2013:871, at paras. 57-58.

codified can be directly traced back to the very first case on the matter, namely *Meroni*, even when it concerns delegation within an institution of the Union.

The following crucial elements, which can easily be recognized in the present-day legal instruments on delegated and implementing powers, were already present in that case. The preliminary point is of course that if an organ, institution, agency or body of the Union has been allocated a power by the Treaty this implies the possibility of delegating that power. However, such delegation has to satisfy certain criteria. First of all, a true delegation that changes the decision-making procedure from those that had been laid down in the Treaty for the exercise of that power was not acceptable. Second, a delegation to an organ or body of which the decisions were not subject to judicial review was equally unacceptable. Third, a basic regulation that failed to explain fully the factual basis of the delegation and the criteria to which a delegation of powers had to respond, would give rise to an illegal delegation of power. Fourth, any delegation is exposed to the risk of disturbing the balance between the institutions if the delegated power is one that requires the weighing up of different interests and values involved and the delegated organ or body is one that is not equipped for performing such a weighing up. This is where the essential and nonessential elements of Article 290 (1) find their origin. Fifth, and finally, a mere *possibility* to take back or to stop the delegation is not enough to make the delegation legal. It is then no longer a true delegation, or it has to conform to the criteria set out in the third point above.

What are the questions that arise at first sight from this codification of delegated powers and implementing powers in the Treaty itself and in the two instruments that have been created on the basis of Articles 290 and 291 of the Lisbon Treaty? Are legislative acts indeed only those acts that, according to Article 289 TFEU, have passed through one of the legislative procedures? Is a purely formal criterion enough to decide that? What precisely is the difference in Article 290 between essential and nonessential elements? Is any matter that poses political questions essential? Or does it also include any matter that poses policy questions, though policy questions often are questions of technical expertise [433]? Can one truly differentiate between "supplementing" a legislative

---

433. As the *New York Times* columnist Jamelle Bouie felicitously put it, but in an entirely different context: "Policy is rational. Politics is not." See J. Bouise, "Why We Have to Wave the 'Bloody Shirt' of 6 January", New York Times, 5 November 2021, https://www.nytimes.com/2021/11/05/opinion/democrats-bloody-shirt-jan-6.html.

act and "amending" such an act? Do not the powers of objection and revocation at the disposal of the two branches of the EU legislature put into question whether one can still speak of truly delegated powers as conceived (but deemed unacceptable in the then prevailing institutional balance) in the *Meroni* case?

The coexistence between the article on delegated powers on the one hand and the article on implementing powers on the other raises the question of where exactly to draw the line between the two. Article 291 is well-known territory to the reader by now; its second paragraph is still very close in drafting, if not identical, to the former Articles 145 and 155 of the EC Treaty. Its third paragraph is still the basis for the new, third comitology instrument, which, though thoroughly overhauled, in its major aspects is not that much different from the previous comitology instrument (without the regulatory procedure with scrutiny, of course). Inevitably the question arises whether there is really anything new to be expected in the field of implementing powers.

Below we will look at how the new treaty articles and the new derived instruments on implementing powers and on delegated powers have fared before the European Court of Justice in order to find some answers to these questions. We will first look at a few cases that are concerned with the dividing line between delegated powers and implementing powers. That will set the scene for the further discussion of cases dealing with the details of the delegation of implementing powers (Art. 291 TFEU) and the transfer of delegated powers (Art. 290 TFEU).

G. The post-Lisbon cases and the present state of the law of delegation in the EU

1. The borderline between delegated acts and implementing acts

The first and most important case concerning the borderline between Articles 290 and 291 TFEU was concerned with the harmonization of the rules on marketing and use of so-called biocidal products. These rules were to be fixed with the help of the European Chemicals Agency (ECA), which for this purpose provided services to private parties such as producers and traders in these biocidal products. The Union legislature (the Council and the Parliament) charged the Commission with adopting measures setting the fees that the ECA could ask for its services rendered in the framework of various steps in the process of approving an active substance and of obtaining EU authorization for biocidal products. It did so by granting implementing powers to the Commission under Article 291 TFEU. It is interesting to note that it was the Commission that attacked this aspect of the regulation adopted by the Council and the European Parliament, arguing that devising rules for the fees charged by the ECA could only be delegated to it by way of a delegated act and not an implementing act.

The core arguments of the Commission were: (1) that Articles 290 and 291 are mutually exclusive and that hence no overlap between the two is possible, and (2) that the regulation contains too little detail to enable the Commission to take mere implementing measures, from which it inexorably followed that (3) the EU legislature ought to have provided delegated powers for the Commission and that the article on implementing powers of the regulation had to be annulled. The Grand Chamber of the Court, by contrast, after having recalled the history behind Articles 290 (1) and 291 (2), when so-called implementing powers included what are now called in the Lisbon Treaty delegated powers *and* implementing powers, begins to explain its own views on the matter with the laconic sentence: "[I]t must be noted that the EU legislature has discretion when it decides to confer a delegated power on the Commission pursuant to Article 290 (1) TFEU or an implementing power pursuant to Article 291(2)." [434]

The Court gave no arguments for this statement beyond its earlier remarks on how implementing powers and delegated powers in the past had been treated in one comitology decision, while it had been the obvious intention of the constitutional legislator, the Intergovernmental Conference of the Member States at Lisbon, to make a distinction between these two kinds of powers that could be granted to the Commission by the EU legislature. By deciding that overlap between delegated powers and implementing powers was possible the Court made its own task in cases concerning delegation quite a bit lighter. The obvious result of this move was to bring judicial review in these cases back on the terrain of manifest errors of assessment made by the EU legislator when deciding for one or the other form of delegated power, instead of requiring of the Court to apply a precise criterion of delimitation each time that the choice for one of these powers was contested. Needless to say, after this opening of its reasoning the Court

---

434. Case C-427/12, *Commission v. Parliament and Council (Biocidal Products)*, ECLI:EU:C:2014:170, at para. 40.

managed to find enough elements in the text of the regulation to come to the conclusion that indeed

> "the EU legislature could reasonably have taken the view that the article attacked by the Commission conferred on the latter the power not to supplement certain nonessential elements of that legislative act but to provide further detail in relation to the normative content of that act, in accordance with Article 291 (2) TFEU"[435].

The Court's new doctrine granting discretion to the EU legislature when choosing between implementing powers or delegated powers in order to let the Commission handle second order legislation was soon put to the test in a new case brought by the Commission relating to the procedure by which the EU would exercise its reciprocity rights in cases where EU citizens' rights to visa-free travel to a third country are suspended or terminated by that country[436]. This procedure was divided into three steps[437]. The first step was to be taken by the Commission under implementing powers and consisted of a suspension of visa-free travel for certain categories of citizens of the third country concerned for a maximum of six months; the second step, in case the third country concerned did not react positively to the Union's exercise of reciprocity rights, involved the suspension of visa-free travel of the third country's citizens for a period of twelve months, to be imposed by the Commission under delegated powers. In case even this had no success, the final stage of the procedure was a decision by the Council, on a proposal of the Commission, to transfer the country in question from the list of visa-free countries to the list of countries whose citizens required a visa for travel to the EU. The three escalating steps of the Union's response to visa restrictions imposed by a third State on EU citizens were thus taken successively by recourse to implementing powers, to delegated

---

435. *Ibid.*, at para. 52. AG Cruz Villalon's opinion, at para. 77, advised differently. He was of the view that in principle "once the legislature concludes its regulation of the essential elements, it is completely free to choose a delegated act or an implementing act". On the other hand, he found, at para. 96, that the principles laid down in Article 80 (3) on the setting of fees and charges of the ECA ended the "regulatory process" of fixing such fees and that what was left for the Commission to do was mere implementation with a view to securing uniform implementation.
436. Case C-88/14, *European Commission v. European Parliament & Council*, ECLI:EU:C:2015:499.
437. See Article 1 (1) *(a)* of Reg. No. 1289/2013 amending Article 1 (4) of Reg. No. 539/2001 (the "Visa Regulation"), quoted in full at para. 5 of Case C-88/14, *supra* footnote 436.

powers and, finally, by a full-fledged legislative amendment procedure.

Obviously the Commission directed its arguments at the seeming inconsistency between the recourse to implementing acts for the first suspension of visa-free travel and the recourse to delegated powers for the second stage, which seemed only to be a longer version of the first stage. Hence the provision on this second stage should be annulled. The Court saw this differently. It referred to the first principles of the judgment discussed above and added to that the finding of a case which had been decided in the meantime to the effect that "in exercising an implementing power, the Commission may neither amend or supplement the legislative act, even as to its non-essential elements" [438].

Furthermore, it rejected some of the Commission's arguments to the effect that the discretion allowed the Commission, and its breadth should be an important aspect of the decision whether a delegated power (much discretion) or an implementing power (little discretion) should be inscribed in the basic instrument. For an answer to this question the Court had recourse to the wording of Article 290 (1) TFEU: the lawfulness of conferring a delegated power on the Commission depends entirely on whether the acts the Commission is to adopt are of general application and whether they supplement or amend nonessential elements of the legislative act [439]. The parties were in agreement that the acts mentioned were indeed of a general nature and that they were supposed to amend the basic regulation.

From there, the Court could once more return to its well-known pattern of controlling whether the EU legislature had exceeded the bounds of its discretion in opting for delegated powers for the Commission when it was called upon to proceed to the second stage in the "escalation ladder" when exercising the EU's reciprocity rights in a conflict with a third State about visa policy. Precisely because this was an escalation ladder, the Court was of the view that the second stage was not exactly the same as the suspension in the first phase, but only twice as long. Moreover, the Court pointed to the fact that application of the second stage was confirmed by a footnote to the name of the country in question in Annex II of the Regulation, listing the countries whose citizens did not need visas for entry into the Union for stays shorter than ninety days, thus confirming that that country was, as it

---

438. Case C-65/13, *European Parliament* v. *European Commission*, ECLI:EU:C: 2289, in particular para. 45, quoted at para. 31 of Case C-88/14, *supra* footnote 436.
439. Case C-88/14, *supra* footnote 436, at para. 32.

were, in transition to Annex I listing the countries whose nationals are required always to obtain a visa for entry into the Union. It followed that the EU legislature had indeed conferred power on the Commission to amend the normative content of a legislative act within the meaning of Article 290 (1) on delegated acts and that the Commission's action had to be dismissed [440].

2. Delegated powers

Articles 290 and 291 TFEU mention only two ways in which the EU legislature may delegate powers to the Commission. Even if there is no rigid boundary between delegated powers and implementing powers, the question arises whether they are indeed the only two flavors in the field of delegation within the Union. When discussing agencies and other bodies in the banking and insurance field and such agencies in the field of economic and monetary policy as ESMA, we will return to this question once more. Obviously, it is not made explicit in the Treaty that only these two ways of delegating powers exist within the constitutional order of the Union. It is not excluded, however, that the two ways of delegating mentioned in these Treaty articles can go together in one basic regulation as a way in which the EU legislature may delegate powers to the Commission.

This was the case for instance in a regulation establishing the so-called Connecting Europe Facility [441] which was part of the legislative package concerning the Trans-European Network. Moreover, the EU legislature seemed to create a third way of delegating powers to the Commission by authorizing it to "detail" funding priorities to be reflected in the work programs referred to elsewhere in the regulation. The Commission took this at face value and used this authorization by including an additional Part VI containing such funding priorities, in Annex I of the Regulation in question. This was too much for the European Parliament (supported by the Council). It started an action for annulment, and it argued before the Court that the Commission thus had exceeded the scope of its empowerment, also because it had not adopted a separate act to do so but had simply directly inserted the new Part VI into Annex I to the Regulation [442].

---

440. *Ibid.*, at para. 40 ff.
441. Regulation No. 1316/2013, establishing the Connecting Europe Facility, OJ 2013 L 348/129-171.
442. Case C-286/14, *European Parliament and Council v. Commission*, ECLI:EU:C:2016:183.

The Court looked in some depth at the overall structure of the regulation in question and noted that the provision authorizing the Commission to "detail funding priorities" referred directly, or was closely linked to, a number of other provisions which in turn were linked to Article 290 TFEU. This was a point that the Commission had to concede at the hearing of the case [443]. The Court also deduced from the history of Article 290 and from the Commission's Guidelines on Delegated Acts [444] that the function of supplementing a legislative act within the meaning of Article 290 is essentially to flesh out the details of the legislative scheme (the essential elements) that were not fully worked out but already present in the basic regulation. Therefore, according to the Court, "by empowering the Commission to adopt delegated acts 'detailing' funding priorities, that provision authorizes the Commission to 'supplement' that regulation within the meaning of Article 290 TFEU" [445]. In the end, in reaction to the additional plea of the European Parliament, the Court also arrived at the conclusion that to "supplement" a legislative act with further detail implied that a separate document was necessary for such a supplement, as it did not constitute an amendment [446].

Other recent cases on the interpretation of Article 290 mainly reconfirm earlier case law, for instance on the issue of essential and nonessential elements in that article. In a case concerning "supplementing" the rules on energy labels for vacuum cleaners, the Court recalled that essential elements are "those which, in order to be adopted, require political choices falling within the responsibility of the EU legislature" and "identifying the elements of a matter which must be categorized as essential must be based on objective factors amenable to judicial review. These are standard phrases well known from many areas of EU Law" [447].

Similar affirmations were expressed also in an appeal case brought by the Czech Republic. The Court recalled that recent case law on Article 290 TFEU required that "not only the objectives but also the content, scope, and duration of the delegation of power must be explicitly defined in the legislative act" [448]. It also mentioned again that the scope

---

443. *Ibid.*, at para. 38.
444. Attached to document SEC/2011/855.
445. Case C-286/14, *supra* footnote 442, at para. 47.
446. *Ibid.*, at paras. 52-58.
447. Case C-44/16 P, *Dyson v. Commission*, ECLI:EU:C:2017:357, at paras. 58-63.
448. Case C-696/15 P, *Czech Republic v. Commission*, ECLI:EU:C:2017:595, at para. 48.

of the delegated power had to be precisely defined in such a way that the Commission's use of that power could be reviewed by reference to objective criteria. If such use of a delegated power involved any discretion, the measure of discretion must also be delimited by criteria laid down in the basic act [449].

This case also dealt with the question of whether a supervisory body could be created by the delegated act of the Commission. The appellant, the Czech Republic, saw this body as an essential element that ought to have been included in the basic regulation (on the deployment of intelligent transport systems in road transport) and hence was not amenable to be delegated. The Court, however, was not in agreement with that assessment since that particular supervisory body was composed of independent and impartial experts who were charged with collecting information and writing assessment reports. The obligations of operators to provide information to the supervisory body were strictly limited. In the final analysis the establishment of this body did not rise to the level where political choices had to be made about interference with the fundamental rights of operators so as to require the involvement of the EU legislature [450].

3. *Implementing powers*

New developments in respect of implementing powers have not been dramatic since the entry into force of the Lisbon Treaty and its Article 291 TFEU and the new 2011 version of the third comitology instrument. New case law is in part a repetition and affirmation of existing case law on delegation of implementing powers, but in some respects also a further development of old case law.

A good example of a case in which such affirmation of standing case law goes together with a new step forward is the one concerning the restructuring of EURES [451]. Originally called the European Coordination Office, this was a bureau within the Commission that was charged with vacancy clearance at Union level so as to define more clearly the areas of the labor market in which each Member State had a surplus or a shortage of labor and how the offer of and demand for labor could be brought together in a better way across national frontiers within the Union. This should facilitate cross-border mobility of workers within

---

449. *Ibid.*, at paras. 49-52.
450. *Ibid.*, at paras. 59-64 and 86-87.
451. Case C-65/13, *European Parliament* v. *Commission*, ECLI:EU:C:2014:2289.

the Union. The basic regulation charged the Commission with adopting measures pursuant to that regulation for its implementation. To that end the Commission was to cooperate closely with the relevant public authorities of the Member States [452, 453].

The Court recalled a number of principles known from earlier case law. First, the resort to implementing measures means that the Commission is called upon to provide further detail in order to implement the content of the legislative act so that it will be enforced by Member States under uniform conditions in all of them. Second, the limits of the Commission's implementing power must be determined by reference to the essential general aims of the legislative act in question, but the Commission has considerable freedom to adopt *all the measures* that are necessary for that purpose, provided they are not contrary to it. Third, in exercising implementing powers the Commission may neither command nor supplement the legislative act, even in respect of its nonessential elements, in order not to come into conflict with Article 290 on delegated powers [454]. In the light of those principles, the Court discusses the Parliament's objections to the Commission's implementing decision in two steps. First, do the contested provisions of the delegated act comply with the essential general aims pursued by the basic regulation? Second, are the contested provisions necessary or appropriate for the implementation of the basic regulation without amending or supplementing them?

As to the first question, the Court refers to numerous elements that are present in the basic regulation in order to demonstrate that the contested provisions of the delegated act are in conformity with it. Even the creation of the new EURES Management Board and conferring a consultative role on it in the delegated act, as well as the adoption by the Commission of the EURES Charter, were considered by the Court to improve the operation of EURES so as better to support the clearance of vacancies and applications for employment within the European Union [455]. With respect to the second question, the Parliament

---

452. Article 31 of Reg. 492/2011 of the European Parliament and the Council on freedom of movement for workers within the EU, OJ 2011 L141/1-12, Article 38.

453. In the meantime, EURES has been integrated into the European Labour Authority (ELA); see Reg. No. 2019/1149 establishing a European Labour Authority, amending Regulations (EC) No. 883/2004, (EU) No. 492/2011 and (EU) 2016/589 and repealing Decision (EU) 2016/344, OJ L 186/21-56, in particular Articles 4 and 6.

454. Case C-65/13, *supra* footnote 451, at paras. 43-46.

455. *Ibid.*, at para. 48 ff.

had raised four points that all actually amount to actions for exceeding or abusing the Commission's implementing powers. The Court rejected them all on the basis of what it deemed to be the correct interpretation of the basic regulation in relation to the implementing regulation [456]. It is not necessary here to rehash the Court's arguments in detail; this part of the judgment clearly shows that in the case of implementing powers of the Commission, supported by a body like EURES, the Court is willing to be reasonably generous in accepting implementation with the help of a new body like the EURES Management Board and the proposed creation of a new EURES Charter [457].

In two judgments involving economic sanctions against Iran, both rendered in the spring of 2016, the Court had no problem in accepting that the implementation of such sanctions, imposed on specific companies or persons, could be done by way of delegation to the Commission under Article 291 (2) TFEU. Such sanctions are normally based on Article 215 TFEU but require a preceding decision of the Council under the CFSP, requiring unanimity. However, since there is no indication that Article 215 TFEU or the specific title of the Treaty of which it is part are not subject to the application of Article 291 TFEU, there is no reason why in particular the lists of States, natural or legal persons, and groups or non-State entities, which are subject to regular modification and amendment, should not be delegated to the Commission or to the Council under Article 291 (2). The Court recognized that it was often necessary to take such action in strict coordination with the preceding political decision in the Council under the CFSP and as quickly as possible after, for instance, a decision of the UN Security Council. These were circumstances that would justify the Council in keeping the delegation to itself, that is, within the same institution, which was in the best position to guarantee complete correspondence, consistency and speedy adoption as between the CFSP decision and the TFEU regulation imposing the sanctions [458]. This case is a nice example of how the Court uses contextually salient particularities, such as the CFSP decision-making procedures, in its appreciation of the limits to delegation by implementing measures. As will be shown below, the Court proceeds in the same way when general principles such as the precautionary

---

456. *Ibid.*, at para. 58 ff.
457. *Ibid.*, at paras. 85-87 and 91-92.
458. Case C-440/14 P, *NIOC* v. *Council & Commission*, ECLI:EU:C:216:128, at para. 41 and preceding paragraphs; C-358/15 P, *Bank of Industry and Mine* v. *Council*, ECLI:EU:C:2016:338, at paras. 35-42.

principle in the field of agricultural policy and its sanitary measures are in play, when ruling on the legality of implementing measures [459].

It is interesting to note that in contrast to external sanctions imposed on third States under Article 215 TFEU, the Court ruled that implementing powers could not be relied on by the Commission when imposing a sanction on a Member State in the context of the monetary and budgetary surveillance of the Euro area. As the Court pointed out, Article 291 (2) TFEU relates solely to legally binding acts of the Union that lend themselves in principle to implementation by Member States but that, for particular reasons, have to be implemented not by measures of each individual Member State but by the Commission or the Council in order to ensure that they are applied uniformly within the Member States of the Union. In the view of the Court, that was not the case when the act consisted in the imposition of a fine on a Member State:

> "Such an act does not lend itself in the slightest to implementation by the Member States themselves, as implementation of that kind involves the adoption of an enforcement measure in respect of one of them." [460]

When it concerns the recourse to implementing powers, even after so many years after they had first started to function in the area of agricultural policy, it is important to realize that management committees in this field and the neighboring fields of animal and plant pests have been granted over the years a large freedom of appreciation, justified by their long experience and high expertise, when giving their advice or decisions to the Commission. Recently the Court has given a new twist to the deference that agricultural management committees have been granted, but on the other hand it has also moved against the Commission and these committees deciding implementing measures in a too informal way.

In a case involving a very noxious and infectious foreign plant pest, the *Xylella fastidiosa* bacterium, the Commission, bolstered by advice from EFSA, had moved with very strong implementing measures in order to prevent *Xylella*'s introduction into the Union and to achieve its eradication in so far as it had already entered the territory of the Union. It is in the context of this case that the Court remarked that in taking its implementing measures, the Commission should take into

---

459. See, in relation to the *Xylella* case, *infra* footnote 461 and accompanying text.
460. Case C-521/15, *Spain* v. *Council & Commission*, ECLI:EU:C:2017:982, at paras. 48-49.

account, next to the essential elements of the basic regulation, the precautionary principle and the principle of proportionality. Moreover, it should also be granted a wide measure of discretion when adopting risk management measures. Finally, the Court recalled that the validity of any measure cannot depend on any retrospective assessment of its efficacy but only on the state of the problem as it was known at the moment the measure was taken. On the basis of these principles the Court decided that the Commission's implementing decisions against the introduction and spread of *Xylella* did not reveal any elements capable of affecting their validity [461].

It is important to point out here that actually the old world of a separate, specialized management committee for virtually every agricultural product that had its own common market organization had disappeared after the reform of the EU agricultural market policy in 2007. There now was a single regulation on the organization of the agricultural markets and a single management committee for the Common Organization of the Agricultural Markets. In the old management committees, a practice had taken hold that in exceptional cases the Commission could present a draft implementing act to the Committee on the eve or the morning of the meeting and have it discussed and adopted (or modified) before the end of that meeting. Even under the old comitology instruments this practice was probably not in conformity with the rules on presenting draft implementing acts and discussing them in the Committee. Nevertheless, it was tolerated most of the time. In another case devoted to the *Xylella* infestation the Court finally put an end to this practice [462].

A painstaking comparison of the old procedural rules when taking decisions on implementing acts and the new rules laid down in the regulation on the subject [463] put the Court in a position to show that the procedures had fundamentally changed and that the old practice was obviously contrary to Articles 3 (3) and (4) of the 2011 Implementing Regulation. Moreover, it was also contrary to the overall scheme of that regulation, which gave the Commission the power as per Article 8 to take immediate implementing measures without prior consultation of a management committee in cases of "duly justified grounds of imperative urgency" [464]. In its subsequent discussion of the justifications

---

461. Case C-78/16 and C-79/16 *Pesce & others and Serinelli & others* v. *Presidenza del Consiglio dei Ministri & others*, ECLI:EU:C2016:428, at para. 44 ff.
462. Case C-183/16 P, *Tilly-Sabco SAS* v. *Commissie & Doux*, ECLI:EU:C:2017:704.
463. Reg. No. 182/2011, *supra* footnote 419, at n. 77.
464. Case C-183/16, *supra* footnote 462, at paras. 95-108.

that the Commission had advanced for its avoidance of Article 3 (3) of the Implementing Regulation – which it all rejected – the Court shows that the constitutional change in the scheme of the different systems of delegation of powers and the principle of transparency, as mentioned in the relevant interinstitutional instruments relating to this change, are so important that they cannot be ignored. Thus Article 3 (3) must be considered an essential procedural requirement of which the nonobservance entails the nullity of the legal act in question [465]. In other words, the Court indeed takes the need for transparency of the adoption of the different delegation instruments seriously.

4. Some conclusions on the post-Lisbon state of the law of delegation

If one takes the view that delegated acts and implementing acts are of a fundamentally different nature, it would not be strange to demand a bit more clarity from the Court than the "you can choose what you want" approach advanced by the Court in the *Biocides* case discussed above. There is, in spite of the Court's seeming lightheartedness, a serious difference for the EU legislature to consider. When it chooses delegated acts, it decides about the level at which within the EU legislative machinery further or more precise rules will be determined on the basis of its EU "law" – whether it is a regulation, a directive or a decision. Will it indulge in self-delegation; will it delegate to the Commission as Article 290 requires and will it leave room for subdelegation, or will it delegate directly to an agency [466]? When it opts for implementing acts, however, the legislature will activate the role of the Commission as guardian of the Treaty, which is responsible for maintaining a "level playing field" between the Member States. These two radically different functions of delegation (Art. 290 TFEU) and implementation (Art. 291 TFEU) should play a role in the choice of the legislature and in the review by the Court of this choice. As yet there is no indication in recent case law that the Court does take account of the elements mentioned above, which also ought to have consequences for the leeway that should be accorded to the Commission in particular when charged with implementation under Article 291. It is clear that the Commission's discretion and room for maneuver in respect of implementation should be much larger if implementation is indeed seen

---

465. *Ibid.*, at paras. 110-117.
466. On delegation to agencies, see *infra* Sec. I.

as part and parcel of the Commission's role as guardian of the Treaty, in which role the Court has always recognized that the Commission's discretion should be particularly large [467].

If the development of the Court's case law since the entry into force of the Lisbon Treaty on the distinction between delegated acts and implementing acts is somewhat unsatisfactory, the evolution of its views on delegating acts under Article 290 continue along the lines set out before. The delegating acts should be as complete as possible, both with respect to the powers to be delegated and as to the way in which they should be applied. Even if the Commission is given a certain leeway, the extent of it should be clearly defined so as to give the Court the possibility to review the Commission's use of the delegated power. In this respect the Court seems to follow the German case law, which also emphasizes the completeness of the delegating act, rather than the approach of the Italian CCost., which is ready to give more room to the delegated act in filling gaps and developing the delegating act further. On the other hand, in the same case the EUCJ turned out to be ready to accept that the Commission created a supervisory body consisting of experts by way of the delegated act, since its activities would not rise to the level of making political choices.

In respect of implementing acts, the Commission's practice and the Court's case law follow perhaps a bit more the Italian approach by leaving the Commission more flexibility in the execution of the implementing instrument than in the case of delegating and delegated acts. There is also greater readiness on the part of the Court to admit contextual elements to influence the implementation of the implementing decision. One example was letting the decision-making rules of the CFSP influence decision-making on the implementation of unilateral so-called "smart sanctions"; another was the inclusion of the precautionary principle among the elements fashioning its judgment on an implementing act in a health and safety case. Finally, the Court has become more strict over the years on the procedural rules surrounding delegating and implementing measures, especially with a view of making them as transparent as possible.

---

467. On the Commission's discretion or freedom of policy in infringement cases, see L. Prete, *Infringement Proceedings in EU Law*, Alphen aan den Rijn, Kluwer, 2017, at pp. 49-51; L. Prete and B. Smulders, "The Age of Maturity of Infringement Proceedings", *CMLRev.*, Vol. 58 (2021), at p. 296.

H. Administrative delegation within the Commission and other institutions

1. The rules on administrative delegation

The question of delegation within the Commission as one of the institutions of the Union is almost an entirely administrative law question; there is hardly a constitutional aspect to it, except at the outset. That is to say that from a constitutional perspective the Commission has been conceived as a college. The Commission, as a body, according to Article 7 (8) TEU, shall be responsible to the European Parliament, and Article 1 of the Commission's Rules of Procedure states that the Commission shall act collectively[468]. Accordingly, the title of Article 1 is "The Principle of Collective Responsibility". As a consequence, large parts of the Commission's Rules of Procedure are devoted to reconciling this principle of collective responsibility with (1) the increased powers of the President of the Commission after the Treaty of Lisbon[469] and (2) the need of efficient decision-making within the Commission as a political decision-making institution and within the Commission as a bureaucratic machinery. For purposes of this course we will concentrate on point (2) and leave point (1) largely to one side.

The latter point can be summarized as follows. In spite of the principle of collective responsibility, the Commission President has the authority to allocate certain "portfolios" to each Commissioner. What is more, next to the High Representative of the Union for Foreign Affairs and Security Policy, who, by definition, carries the title of Vice-President, the President can create other vice presidents and set up groups of members of the Commission, which will be presided by these vice presidents[470]. This has become common practice under the last two Commissions. As far as decision-making is concerned, the "normal" way of taking decisions is by oral procedure during one of the weekly meetings of the Commission. In such meetings different members of the Commission will advance their proposals, which will be adopted by the Commission, if necessary, after a vote proposed by one of the members. The proposal will be adopted if a majority of

---

468. Rules of Procedure of the Commission, Doc. C(2000) 3614, OJ 2000, L308/26, consolidated version after 22 April 2020, https://eur-lex.europa.eu/legal-content/EN/TXT/?uri=CELEX%3A02000Q3614-20200423.
469. *Ibid.*, at Article 3.
470. *Ibid.*, at Article 3 (2-4).

the number of members specified in the treaty vote in favor of it[471]. Given the huge number of proposals that the Commission has to act upon at every weekly meeting, there are three other ways of taking Commission decisions: decisions taken by written procedure; decisions taken by empowerment; and decisions taken by delegation[472]. All three procedures try to reconcile the requirements of a collegial decision with the need of efficient decision-making within the Commission.

The written procedure is exactly what it says it is, namely a decision approved purely in the form of written documents. A precondition for such a decision is that all the Directorates-General (DGs) involved and the Legal Service of the Commission have approved the draft of such a decision. This draft will be circulated to all members of the Commission with a time limit attached to it, within which the members must make known any reservations that they may have or any amendments they want to be made. This will lead to a discussion between the Commissioners and the Commission DGs concerned, including the Legal Service. Ideally the Commissioners and the DGs concerned will reach an agreement and such a generally accepted proposal will then be laid before the Commission with a time limit attached to it again, after the expiry of which the written procedure shall stand as adopted by the Commission. If there is no agreement or a member of the Commission directly requests that the draft text be discussed, accompanied by a reasoned request to that effect to the President, the draft will follow the oral procedure[473]. It is clear that the written procedure is not a true delegation. It is at most a delegation to the lower level of the Commission as a political decision-maker or a nonobjection procedure (also called a "silence procedure" in some international organizations) and there is always a possibility, open to any Commissioner, to bring the decision back up to the level of the Commission itself and have it decided there, by oral procedure[474].

By contrast, the other two decision-making procedures, empowerment and delegation, are clearly forms of delegation. Tongue in cheek, one might say that this is confirmed by the fact that the two relevant

---

471. *Ibid.*, at Article 8.
472. *Ibid.*, at Article 4.
473. See *ibid.*, at Articles 12 and 23.
474. It is useful to recall that such a return to the competent institution/organ itself and its "normal" rules of decision-making was also available in the special procedures for delisting persons or companies that were subjected to so-called smart sanctions of the UN Security Council. See *supra* Chap. IV.C.

articles [475] in the Commission Rules of Procedure, namely the provisions on empowerment and delegation, begin with the incantation "provided the principle of collective responsibility is fully respected" before continuing to set out what decisions by empowerment and decisions by delegation really are; a magic formula for which the provisions on the written procedure had no need. There are two kinds of empowerment, or *habilitation*, as it is called in French. One by which certain members of the Commission are empowered to take management or administrative measures on behalf of the Commission and subject to such restrictions and conditions as the Commission shall impose [476]. The other is the so-called *finalization* empowerment: one or more members of the Commission may be empowered, with the agreement of the President, to finalize the text of an instrument or a proposal that has to be submitted (urgently) to another institution and of which the substance has already been determined in discussion [477]. Both kinds of empowerments may be subdelegated to Directors-General or Heads of Department unless the relevant empowering decisions forbid this [478].

Further, the Commission may *delegate* the adoption of measures of a management or administrative nature to the Directors-General and Heads of Department, subject to such restrictions and conditions as the Commission shall impose. In the case of such delegation, Directors-General and Heads of Department shall act in name of the Commission [479].

These provisions on empowerment and delegation are complemented by a relatively recent chapter in the Rules of Procedure on "deputizing", which is indebted to the idea of the "continuity of service" that, as was shown earlier, takes an important place in French administrative law [480]. Its provisions on automatic deputizing, especially for hierarchical superiors, have a stabilizing effect on empowerment and delegation within the administrative machinery as they guarantee that

---

475. Rules of Procedure, *supra* footnote 468. These are Article 13 on decisions taken by the empowerment procedure and Article 14 on decisions taken by the delegation procedure. Article 13 was only introduced in the text of the Rules of Procedure after the merger of the executives of EC, ECSC and Euratom into one Commission in 1975.
476. *Ibid.*, at Article 13 (1).
477. *Ibid.*, at Article 13 (2).
478. *Ibid.*, at Article 13 (3).
479. *Ibid.*, at Article 14. In addition, Article 15 of the Rules of Procedure mentions the possibility of further subdelegation by the Directors-General and Heads of Department, who have received subdelegations under Articles 13 and 14, to civil servants lower down the hierarchical ladder subject to restrictions and conditions.
480. See *supra* Chap. II.B.

empowerment and delegation will always result in an actual person being present to perform the tasks and duties that flow with the empowerment or delegation [481].

In the fields of personnel policy, the execution of the budget and the management tasks linked to those activities, internal administrative delegation within the Commission and other institutions of the EU takes place in the framework of rules set out in the Staff and Financial Regulations of the Union. This delegation is organized more or less along similar lines and thus meshes well with the provisions of the Rules of Procedure of the Commission discussed above, although, where necessary, it is exempted from the effect of these rules [482]. Within each institution a person is appointed who shall exercise the powers of the appointing authority [483] or shall perform the duties of authorizing officer [484] or of the accounting officer [485]. The staff exercising these powers may be appointed at an appropriate level of the institution. Moreover, the powers of these officers may be delegated and subdelegated further down the line. All this could be described in considerably greater detail but is only of limited interest. This kind of rather straightforward delegation down the hierarchical ladder must be meticulously executed so that there can be no doubt that the person finally taking a decision of personnel management or evaluation, of expenditure authorization, or relating to accounting controls is fully empowered to take such decisions. Such delegation, which is of a purely administrative law character, has at first sight very little to do with the *Meroni* case and its progeny, where constitutional rules and the balance between the institutions are always present, at least in the background [486].

Since the agencification of the European Union has set in, matters have become more complicated in the fields of personnel and financial management because the agencies and other bodies have been construed in such a way that they are bound to a great extent by the EU Staff

---

481. Rules of Procedure, *supra* footnote 468, at Articles 24-27.
482. *Ibid.*, at See Article 13 (4).
483. Article 2 of the Staff Regulations of Officials of the European Union, consolidated version, retrieved at https://eur-lex.europa.eu/legal-content/EN/TXT/?uri=CELEX%3A01962R0031-20210101.
484. Article 73 of the Financial Regulation applicable to the General Budget of the Union, consolidated version, retrieved at https://op.europa.eu/en/publication-detail/-/publication/25153ebc-2b06-11ec-bd8e-01aa75ed71a1.
485. *Ibid.*, at Article 77.
486. This is a question of pure agency or public law *mandate*, or even mere *délégation de signature* as discussed at *infra* footnote 488 and accompanying text.

and Financial Regulations, which their officers have to apply broadly in the same way as the officers of the Commission itself. Within the agencies in principle the same delegation (of signature) can be applied down the hierarchical ladder as within the Commission. What is more, many of these agencies have decided, in particular in the field of personnel management and payments of salary and pensions, to rely on the services of the Personnel Management Office, which is a semi-independent executive agency of the Commission.

2. Case law on administrative delegation within the Commission

It is important for conceptual reasons at the outset to make a differentiation between disputes arising about delegation within the Commission as a decision-making machinery and delegation down the administrative line. The first court cases relating to administrative delegation arose in the field of competition policy. In this field the Commission had used its power of internal delegation relatively early, both inside the Commission and down the line, to the Director-General of what was then DG IV (now DG for Competition). This was before the present Article 13 on empowerment had been included in the Rules of Procedure of the Commission in 1975. The Commissioner had authorized the Director-General of DG IV to sign the letter by which the notice of objections, setting out the facts which, in the view of the Commissioner, constituted *prima facie* infringements of the competition rules, were transmitted to the company or companies concerned.

The first companies that had an opportunity to attack competition decisions of the Commission after this delegation had been introduced were particularly shocked by the fact that it was signed by a mere Director-General, perhaps because they interpreted this as a direct delegation from the Commission to the Director-General in question. In *ICI* v. *Commission* the Court clarified that the Director-General for competition

> "did no more than sign the notice of objections which the member of the Commission responsible for problems of competition had previously approved in the exercise of the powers which the Commission had delegated to him".

Therefore, in this case there was not a true delegation of powers, but the Director-General of DG IV had "simply signed as a proxy on authority received from the Commissioner responsible". The French text of the judgment here makes the contrast much clearer by stating that this was not a *délégation de pouvoir* but rather a mere *délégation de signature*[487]. This was repeated more or less in the same language in two later cases[488]. It was clear that administrative delegation down the line was not a particularly serious problem for the Court, subject always to the condition that there was proof that it had been properly decided and made known to the relevant group of persons or to the general public.

It was only in the *AKZO Chemie* case[489] that the Court was forced to look in greater detail into the type of delegation described above. This was ten years after the Rules of Procedure had been augmented by what is now Article 13, which covers both the Commission's empowerment of one of its members and the subdelegation from that member to a Director-General. In this case the two-stage empowerment of the Director-General related to a decision authorizing a so-called dawn raid on a company suspected of anticompetitive practices. The Court launched a number of arguments. The first argument was that the delegation did not authorize the Commissioner concerned to act in his own right. The decision, according to the text of Article 13, was taken *in the name of* the Commission, which implies that the Commission retains responsibility for it and hence the decision can be attacked before the Court under the same conditions as any other legal act of the Commission. The second argument was that the delegation was restricted to specific acts of management and administration, thus excluding decisions of principle. This was necessary given the continuing increase in the number of decisions that the Commission took on a weekly basis. Moreover, the authorization to carry out a dawn raid is precisely such an act of management, even if the companies concerned are opposed to it. Dawn raids are authorized when the Commission has reason to assume that the company in question will oppose an investigation or if there is a risk that the company will destroy possibly incriminating documents. The only point on which the Court was critical was the failure to publish the general authorization of delegation of authority. The Commission should do so in future, the

---

487. Case 48/69, *ICI* v. *Commission*, ECLI:EU:C:1972:70, at paras. 11-15.
488. Case 8/72, *Cementhandelaren* v. *Commission*, ECLI:EU:C:1972:84, at paras. 10-14; Joined Cases 43 and 63/82, *VBBB & VBVB* v. *Commission*, ECLI:EU:C:1984:9, at paras. 12-14. In the latter case the Court states that it has recognized that "the delegation of power to sign . . . is the normal method by which the Commission exercises its powers".
489. Case 5/85, *AKZO Chemie* v. *Commission*, ECLI:EU:C:1986:328.

Court held, but by its omission it has not deprived the company of the opportunity to seek the annulment of the delegation [490].

It is useful to recall that the elements that the Court adduced as new reasons for accepting delegation from the plenary Commission to individual members were inspired to a large extent by the *Meroni* and *Romano* cases, even if the Court did not explicitly say so in *AKZO Chemie*. The fact that the delegated decision will be open to judicial review, that it will be limited to questions of management and administration, and the need to have transparency about delegation decisions, are all elements from this line of case law. In this way *AKZO Chemie* emphasizes the constitutional underpinnings of delegation at the "political" level of the Commission, whereas delegation at the administrative level is implicitly of a different order.

It is interesting to follow the further development in the case law on the two stages of delegation as discussed above as they were applied to personnel cases within the agencies of the EU. In such cases another layer of administrative delegation may be added. The most interesting of these cases is *Tralli* v. *European Central Bank* of May 2005, in which the European Court of Justice, on appeal from the Court of First Instance, had to rule on the lawfulness of Mr Tralli's dismissal during his probationary period as a civil servant of the European Central Bank (ECB) [491].

As the Court put it, an important question was whether the rules governing delegation of powers to staff within the ECB and the exercise of those powers by the latter's organs were lawful. The Court analyzed this question in three steps. First, the original grant of competence in the field of personnel matters was laid down at the constitutional level in the Protocol on the ESCB (European System of Central Banks) Statute, of which Articles 12 (3) and 36 (1) determined that the Governing Council, the organ in which the Member States are represented, was invested with legislative powers to adopt Rules of Procedure to determine the internal organization of the ECB and its decision-making bodies, as well as to fix the conditions of employment of ECB staff on a proposal of the Executive Board [492]. The Court immediately pointed out that the powers of organization and management thus granted to the ECB were entirely comparable to those conferred

---

490. *Ibid.*, at paras. 35-39.
491. Case 301/02 P, *Tralli* v. *European Central Bank*, ECLI:EU:C:2005:306.
492. Protocol (No. 4) on the Statute of the European System of Central Banks and of the European Central Bank, OJ 2016, OJ 202/230-250.

on other institutions and bodies established under primary legislation in the Union. Based on the conferral granted in the above-mentioned articles of the ESCB Protocol, the Governing Council began the second step in the delegation chain and adopted the conditions of employment of the ECB. These, as the Court pointed out, in turn authorized the Executive Board of the ECB to specify further, by means of the Staff Rules, the general rules for applying those conditions of employment of the Bank [493]. The Court then went on to invoke the inherent right of self-organization and internal management of such institutions, invoking the *Meroni* case as a precedent. The same case is used as a yardstick by the Court where it concerns the rule that a delegating authority cannot confer upon the authority to which the powers are delegated powers different from those which it has itself received. Moreover, with respect to the requirement that the decisions of the Executive Board should be subject to the same conditions as those to which it would be subject if the delegating authority had exercised these powers directly, particularly as regards the requirements to state reasons and to publish. On both counts the Court gave a pass to the ECB institutions [494].

With all due respect to the Court, one wonders whether the *Meroni* case is not invoked too much in this case, forty-six years after the judgment. If there is an inherent right of self-organization and management for the executive organs of international organizations, such as the Executive Board of the ECB, that is simply a question of implied powers for which *Meroni* does not need to be invoked once again. Moreover, if the Executive Board, in the course of managing the ECB's personnel, were to take decisions that affected the staff as a whole, groups of employees or individual functionaries, the Executive Board would be duty-bound by rules of proper administration and the right of defense to give reasons for its decisions and to make them known to personnel in a suitable fashion. Moreover, the model by which the "legislative" organ of an international organization decides and promulgates its staff regulations but leaves the further implementation of these to the "executive" organ of that organization by issuing staff rules is universally followed by international organizations, both in the UN family and elsewhere. The EU Council of Ministers and Parliament, as the legislature, have acted according to this same model when the EU legislature in Article 110 of the Staff Regulations granted a general power to the Commission to

---

493. *Tralli, supra* footnote 491, at paras. 38-40.
494. *Ibid.*, at paras. 41-46.

further implement these through Staff Rules, as well as a specific power to do so in areas where this is seen as particularly necessary [495].

As far as the third step in the delegation chain was concerned – that is, the delegation by the Executive Board of the ECB to the Vice-President of the ECB of the power to adopt decisions extending the probationary periods of newly recruited staff – the Court found itself on firmer ground. Following its Advocate-General, Philippe Léger, the Court recalled once again the broad powers of internal organization by which the Commission may delegate to one or more of its members the power to adopt staff management decisions of an individual nature in a context which has already been the subject of general rules adopted by the Commission itself. This model could be readily applied to the agencies of the Union, while referring back to the *AKZO Chemie* case discussed earlier. On that basis and having examined the delegation of authority to the Vice-President of the ECB, the Court concluded that the VP was duly empowered to adopt the decision extending the applicant's probationary period [496].

3. Some concluding remarks

It may be argued that, on closer inspection, what has been dubbed "administrative law type delegation" thus far in this study is not really of an exclusively administrative law nature as far as the European Union is concerned. At the level of delegation within the Commission there are undertones of a constitutional law character. But once it has been decided that in spite of the collective nature of decision-making within the Commission, it is acceptable that certain decisions are delegated to individual members and from them to the highest level of the Commission civil service, the administrative law nature takes over and one is reduced to the verification of whether the transfer has been duly effectuated according to the rules. It is at the Commission level that what one might call a slight *Meroni* infection has taken place, expressed in the limitation of delegation to individual members of the Commission mostly to procedural steps toward a final decision of the Commission that would need to be taken by the full college.

---

495. ConsolidatedtextofReg.31layingdownStaffRegulationsofOfficialsetc.,https://eurlex.europa.eu/legalcontent/EN/TXT/?uri=CELEX%3A01962R0031-20140501. Article 45*a* (5) of the Staff Regulations is an example of Commission receiving a specific empowerment to promulgate further rules to implement the special transition from category AD civil servants (administrators) to category AST (assistants).

496. *Tralli, supra* footnote 491, at paras. 56-61.

Nevertheless, this section and the preceding one have given rise to the increasingly urgent question why, after nearly seventy years of development of Community/Union law, it is still necessary to fall back on a case like *Meroni* and its "eternal companion" *Romano*. This is a question that will only grow in urgency as we move to discuss delegation and EU agencies in the next section.

I. Delegation to EU agencies

1. Introduction

In several sections above we have already mentioned European agencies in passing, especially where they were involved in comitology procedures. Below we will continue in some depth on the question of delegation of regulatory powers to such agencies. But first we will discuss the agencies themselves in slightly more detail.

In the early 2000s, the European Commission launched its wide-ranging white paper on the governance of the European Community [497]. Part of the paper was devoted to the question of agencies and evinced a wish on the part of the Commission to better structure the role and the power of such agencies. At that time the Commission made a distinction between so-called executive agencies and regulatory agencies. It succeeded in bringing forward a draft regulation laying down a statute for executive agencies that were to be entrusted with certain tasks in the management of Community programs. The draft regulation was subsequently adopted by the Council [498]. This new category of agencies will be left to one side since they are essentially restricted to the management of certain Community programs, with a strong emphasis on financial management and disbursement, in conformity with the Financial Regulations. Their lifespan is dependent on that of the program. They have their own personality, distinct from the Commission, but remain closely linked to it.

As to the classic regulatory agencies, the Commission first launched a communication on the operating framework for regulatory agencies in late 2002 [499], and in early 2005 it followed up with a draft

---

497. European Governance: A White Paper, Doc. COM(2001) 428, https://ec.europa.eu/commission/presscorner/detail/en/DOC_01_10.
498. Reg (EC) No. 58/2003, laying down the Statute for Executive Agencies to be entrusted with certain tasks in the management of Community programs, OJ 2003, L 11/1-8.
499. Communication from the Commission, The Operating Framework for the European Regulatory Agencies, COM/2002/0718 final.

interinstitutional agreement on this operating framework [500]. However, soon afterward the Council lost interest in this proposal; among other elements, doubts about the appropriateness of an interinstitutional agreement for this purpose played a role. It would take another six years before the Commission, after having launched another discussion paper, titled "European Agencies: The Way Forward" [501], in the course of 2008, finally succeeded in convincing the European Parliament and the Council in July of 2012 to sign a Joint Statement on decentralized agencies. Attached to the Joint Statement was the so-called Common Approach that these institutions would pursue with respect to the role and position of these agencies, their structure and governance and their operation, programming and funding [502]. The accountability and transparency and relations with stakeholders of these agencies also played a major role in this document. In the years that followed, the three institutions collaborated on recurring reports on the progress made with the implementation of a common approach [503].

From the preparatory work for this Joint Statement it may be concluded that the tasks of these decentralized agencies, as they are now called, vary a great deal, but a common definition of them is nevertheless possible. There are also common traits in their organizational structure, although there will always be agencies that are unique in their structure. The three institutions nevertheless wanted to strive toward a greater uniformity in structure and functioning of the different agencies. The following elements broadly define all European regulatory agencies. They are bodies governed by EU law. They are set up by an act of secondary legislation (a regulation, a decision or a joint action) [504]. They have their own legal personality, independently

---

500. Draft Interinstitutional Agreement on the Operating Framework for the European Regulatory Agencies, COM/2005/59 final.

501. Doc. COM(2008) 135 final.

502. Joint Statement of the European Parliament, the Council of the EU and the European Commission on Decentralised Agencies of 19 July 2012, with an Annex on the Common Approach, https://europa.eu/european-union/sites/default/files/docs/body/joint_statement_and_common_approach_2012_en.pdf.

503. The Common Approach was intended, *inter alia*, to bring greater uniformity in the structure of decentralized agencies, the selection of their directors and in their financial management. Indeed, various founding documents of these agencies have been adapted to the Common Approach, but sometimes only partially. This is illustrated by the statement of Commissioner Avramopoulos on the restructuring of CEPOL (the EU Agency for Law Enforcement Training) to the European Parliament on 28 October 2015, in which he points out that precisely the financial management aspects of the Common Approach have not been respected.

504. Whether the founding acts must be based on Article 352, the so-called flexibility clause, requiring unanimity in the Council, in combination with a clause like

from other European institutions. They are charged with a great number of different tasks and some of them may even take legally binding individual decisions directed at third parties. They normally receive financial contributions from the Union budget but have financial and administrative autonomy and are independent in the execution of their assigned tasks in relation to other European institutions. And, finally, they are normally permanent bodies that have their seat in one of the Member States of the EU.

2. Classification of agencies

In an attempt at classification, the Commission has divided the agencies in groups according to their primary mission. First, there are the agencies that are responsible for gathering, analyzing and forwarding objective, real and reliable information, and for performing networking in their sector; among the agencies already mentioned in this study, examples include EFSA and ENISA. A second category of agencies is mainly in charge of operational activities: well-known examples are Frontex (the European Border and Coast Guard Agency), Eurojust (the European Union Agency for Criminal Justice Cooperation) and Europol (the European Union Agency for Law Enforcement Cooperation). Another important category consists of agencies providing direct assistance to the Commission and, where necessary, to Member States, mainly in the form of technical or scientific advice. Of these agencies we have already encountered EFSA and EMA. The final group of agencies distinguished by the Commission consists of agencies that may adopt individual decisions that are legally binding on third parties. Of those ECA, also called ECHA (the European Chemicals Agency), has already been mentioned. Other well-known examples include the Community Plant Variety Office (CPVO); the OHIM (Office for Harmonization of the Internal Market), which became EUIPO (European Union Intellectual Property Office) in 2016; the European Aviation Safety Agency (EASA); the European Maritime Safety Agency (EMSA); and, again, EMA. As this last example shows, an agency can fall into more than one category and thus be involved in comitology procedures leading up to regulatory decisions by the Commission, and in exceptional circumstances by the Council, and also in taking decisions binding on individuals.

Article 114 on harmonization of the internal market, or whether they may be based on Article 114 alone, requiring merely a qualified majority, has been a major issue in political and legal discussions. For a discussion of the *ESMA* case, see *infra* Sec. I.3 and footnote 509.

As to the structure of the agencies, most of the more recent ones have as their main organ a management board, consisting of representatives of both Member States and the Commission, and a director. Many of them also have a scientific committee and, if that committee is empowered to take decisions that may affect individuals and organizations in the Union, also a board of appeal. The appeals to such boards are so-called administrative appeals; judicial appeal from decisions of these boards is open to the General Court of the Union and subsequently to the Court of Justice [505]. Some older agencies have a different structure, but it is the intention of the three institutions that adopted the Common Approach to gradually reform agencies so that they broadly conform to this model. However, agencies that have a strong network aspect to their activities and thus also need to have close contact with the national authorities in their field have additional organs to fulfill this function. Next to a management board and a director they also have a board of supervisors and a chairperson of that board. This is the case, for instance, for ACER and BEREC, which need to keep in close contact with the national energy authorities and the authorities in the field of approval of electrical machinery respectively [506].

A group of agencies that stands a bit apart from the others is formed by the agencies of the European System of Financial Supervision (ESFS) [507], consisting of the European Banking Authority (EBA), the European Security and Markets Authority (ESMA), the European Insurance and Occupational Pensions Authority (EIOPA) and the European Systemic Risk Board (ESRB), all of which were successively created after the financial crisis of 2008/2009. The EBA has a Board of Supervisors consisting of representatives from the national banking authorities, which fulfills the network function of the EBA. The Chair of the Board of Supervisors also represents the EBA in the outside world. The Management Board, consisting of representatives of the Member States, oversees the Executive Director, who runs the day-to-day work of the EBA. The EBA's tasks are various. The staff prepares

---

505. For an example see Case T-102/13, *Heli-Flight* v. *EASA*, ECLI:EU:T:2014:1064, appealed as C-61/15, *Heli-Flight* v. *EASA*, Dismissal of the Appeal in OJ 2015 C 155 without published judgment.

506. This also exposes such network agencies to greater risk of "capture" by the national agencies and the national industries in such sectors that have traditionally close links with "their" national regulators. See *supra* footnote 151 and accompanying text.

507. For a brief overview of the ESFS, see T. Papadopoulos, "European System of Financial Supervision", in R. Wolfrum (ed.), *Max Planck Encyclopedia of Public International Law*, Oxford, Oxford University Press, 2014, https://opil.ouplaw.com/view/10.1093/law:epil/9780199231690/law-9780199231690-e2127.

expert opinions for the Commission, which may use them in preparing legislation. Other duties include preparing informal regulatory instruments to be followed by the national banking authorities and codifying "best practices" [508]. Finally, the EBA may even prepare fullfledged drafts for legislation to be proposed by the Commission to the Council and the Parliament. An exceptional feature of these preproposals is that the Commission, if and when it believes it should deviate from such drafts, must follow a special procedure in which it has to lay down detailed reasoning explaining why it does not want to follow the EBA draft. This special duty of justification on the part of the Commission is testimony to the importance attached to technical financial expertise in the sector. The other ESFS agencies have a comparable structure; in addition, ESMA has the power to take individual decisions binding on private parties. These so-called Article 28 powers have been the subject of intense litigation, during which the question of the obligatory recourse to Article 352 TFEU, next to a substantive legal basis (Art. 114 TFEU), was broached again.

3. The ESMA *case*

The *ESMA* case is the most exemplary case concerning delegation to European agencies and, as already mentioned above, concerned an agency that had an actual power to address binding rules to individuals and banks [509]. The case concerning ESMA was brought by the United Kingdom in particular with respect to this specific power of the agency. The UK had been outvoted in the Council of Ministers and therefore addressed the Court with a number of complaints, in particular concentrating on ESMA's power, laid down in Article 28 of the regulation on short selling and certain aspects of credit default swaps [510], granting this body – that had already been established at an earlier date [511] – the power of prohibiting certain short selling activities by individuals, banks and other actors on EU financial markets, during

---

508. The justiciability of these informal instruments, which have always been common in the financial and banking sector, is controversial at the European level, see Case C-911/19 *Fédération bancaire française* v. *Autorité de controle prudentiel et de résolution*, ECLI:EU:C:2021:599.
509. Case C-270/12, *United Kingdom* v. *Council*, ECLI:EU:C:2014:18.
510. Reg. No. 236/2012 of the European Parliament and of the Council on short selling and certain aspects of credit default swaps, OJ 2012 L 86/1 ff.
511. Reg. No. 1095/2010 of the European Parliament and of the Council establishing the European Securities and Markets Authority, OJ 2012 L 331/84 ff.

periods of particular turbulence in those markets. The United Kingdom raised four complaints in law against the creation of ESMA and giving it this power: (1) the lack of a valid legal basis for the creation of the agency, (2) the applicability of the *Meroni* criteria to the power of ESMA to prohibit short selling, (3) the same question with respect to the applicability of the *Romano* case, and finally (4) the assertion that a delegation of powers in question was contrary to Articles 290 and 291 TFEU on delegated and implementing powers.

The first complaint was possibly the weakest and was dealt with last by the Court, but it is nevertheless interesting to discuss it first, as it demonstrates the Court's willingness to empower the European legislature (Council and Parliament) to continue the creation and development of agencies with a view to delegating specialized tasks of regulation to them, especially in relation to "the harmonization of legislation, regulations and administrative action in Member States, which have as their object the establishment and functioning of the internal market"[512]. The UK based itself on a long-standing practice, according to which the establishment of Union bodies that were intended to play a role in the achievement of objectives of the Union, such as the internal market, without an explicit provision having been made in the treaty to create such bodies, needed to be based on Article 352 TFEU, next to Article 114 (1) for the substantive legal basis. Hence the establishment of ESMA and charging it with tasks, which aimed to perfect the internal market, would have required unanimity in the Council, and the UK would have been able to block the relevant regulation. However, when deciding the case concerning ENISA mentioned earlier, in which the UK was also the complaining party, the Court had already clarified that if the establishment of an agency was closely connected to the objective of perfecting the internal market through harmonization, such an agency could be established on the basis of Article 114 (1) TFEU alone[513].

Moreover, the Court had also decided in the same case, contrary to the somewhat old-fashioned position of the United Kingdom, that nothing in the wording of Article 114 implied that only Member States could be the addressees of measures of harmonization. Finally, and

---

512. See Article 114 (1) TFEU. A qualified majority was enough to adopt legal acts under that article as long as they did not contain fiscal provisions or touch upon the free movement of persons and the rights and interests of employed persons; see Article 114 (2).
513. See Case C-217/04, *United Kingdom v. Parliament*, ECLI:EU:C:2006:279, at paras. 43-47 and 58 ff.

once again referring to its judgment in the *ENISA* case, the Court also decided on the basis of an analysis of the preambular paragraphs of the contested regulation that the purpose of the legislation was to improve the conditions for the establishment and functioning of the internal market. Hence the specific provision enabling ESMA in exceptional circumstances to restrict or even prohibit short selling and credit default swaps by banks and other financial operators in the Member States could be lawfully based on Article 114 TFEU [514]. This meant that the ESMA and short selling regulations were lawfully adopted by a qualified majority in the Council in conformity with Article 114 TFEU and the UK had not been denied a possibility to stop the adoption of both regulations.

The real problems concerning delegation in the EU were the subject of the three other complaints of the United Kingdom. The first concerned the applicability of the conditions for lawful delegations as laid down in the *Meroni* judgment. The Court recalled the two types of delegation, which it had distinguished in that case. The first was the delegation of clearly defined executive powers, which can be subject to strict review in the light of objective criteria that are determined by the delegating authority. The second involved "discretionary power implying a wide margin of discretion which may, according to the use which is made of it, make possible the execution of actual economic policy". The second kind of delegation was essentially of a political nature and replaced the choices of the delegator by the choices of the delegate and brought about an actual transfer of responsibility to the latter. On the other hand, the Court made the rather enigmatic remark that *Meroni*'s "Brussels authorities" involved in the second kind of delegation were entities governed by private law, whereas ESMA was "a European Union entity, created by the EU legislature" [515].

---

514. In the *ENISA* case the Court had already gone against AG Kokott on this point and it was not going to change now. See the opinion of AG Kokott in *ENISA*, ECLI:EU:2005:574, at paras. 50-53. In his opinion in *ESMA*, AG Jääskinen took the view that the powers that ESMA potentially wielded went well beyond those of ENISA and simply replaced national decision-making with EU-level decision-making, see ECLI:EU:C:2013:562, at paras. 48-53. However, once again the Court ignored its AG since it saw this, not as going *beyond* harmonization, as the AG did, but as part and parcel of permitted harmonization with a view to further improvement of the internal market. See Case C-270/12, *supra* footnote 509, at paras. 41-43.

515. See Case C-270/12, *supra* footnote 509, at para. 43. At the time when the *Meroni* case was handed down, this aspect seemed to be merely an additional consideration, but the crucial reason why the High Authority's decision was annulled.

Furthermore, the Court remarked that, again unlike the situation in *Meroni*, the exercise of the powers limiting or forbidding credit default swaps or short selling techniques were circumscribed by strong conditions and criteria which limited ESMA's discretion, according to the regulations establishing ESMA and laying down its powers with respect to credit default swaps and short sales. ESMA could act only if there is a serious threat to the orderly functioning and integrity of financial markets, or if the financial stability of part or the whole of the financial system in the Union was at risk. Moreover, there had to be cross-border implications while no national authority had taken measures already, or their measures had been proven to be inadequate. Even when taking measures, ESMA had to be careful to avoid specifically mentioned negative effects. Finally, ESMA was duty-bound to consult the ESRB about the intended measures and to notify them in advance, together with their underlying reasons, to the national authorities of the Member States. Combined with a number of less important restraints on the actions of ESMA, such as their temporary nature, this brought the Court to the conclusion that the powers available to ESMA were precisely delineated and amenable to judicial review in the light of the objectives established by the delegating authority. The margin of discretion of ESMA is thus considerably restricted. This is also borne out, in the Court's view, by the combined effect of certain specific provisions of the two regulations concerned, the one establishing ESMA itself and the one on short selling and credit default swaps [516]. And since these powers, after the Lisbon Treaty, were wielded by an agency created by a new EU legislature, of which the Parliament was equipped with almost full co-legislative powers and was therefore democratically legitimized in the eyes of the Court, the exercise of these powers by ESMA complied with the requirements laid down in the *Meroni* case. This must be the meaning of the Court's brief phrase that ESMA "was a European entity, created by a European legislature". Perhaps it is better to say that the new EU democratic structure after Lisbon justified going beyond *Meroni*, rather than that it complied with the case.

The second additional complaint of the United Kingdom concerned the conformity of ESMA's powers to adopt quasi-legislative measures of general application with the principles established in the *Romano* case, in particular the Court's holding to the effect that the system of the Treaty was at odds with the way in which the Council had pretended to

---

516. See Case C-270/12, *supra* footnote 509, at paras. 45-58.

confer a power of final interpretation of Community rules in the field of social security on an administrative commission. At most, such a commission could be empowered *to advise* institutions of the Union and of the Member States that were called upon to interpret such rules, but no more than that [517]. In addition, the UK fixed the attention in its pleadings on another element of the *Romano* case, namely that the delegation was too wide, and a prohibition on short sales was actually "a measure of general application, having the force of law", such as the Court had also censured in the *Romano* case.

Both these holdings in the *Romano* case were easy to dismiss, after the Lisbon Treaty, on the basis of the additions in Articles 263 (action for annulment) and 277 TFEU (plea of illegality) opening up the Court's jurisdiction to actions brought by natural or legal persons against acts of Union bodies, offices or *agencies* in respect of their acts which were intended to have legal effects on such natural or legal persons. It was obvious from both provisions that they permitted acts of general application to be taken by agencies such as ESMA and that the Court, contrary to the situation at the time of the *Romano* case, was now empowered by the TFEU to sit in judgment of such acts [518]. Such acts of general application were then restricted by the *Meroni* criteria and notably the applicable discretion was circumscribed by the strict conditions that were required according to that line of case law. However, the Court had already accepted that this requirement was satisfied in this case, when discussing and rejecting the UK's complaint on the conformity of ESMA's powers with *Meroni*.

The United Kingdom argued in its third additional complaint that ESMA's delegated power to prohibit short selling was incompatible with Articles 290 and 291 TFEU. These articles authorized the Union legislature to delegate certain powers only to the Commission. Since ESMA was not the Commission and there was no other authorization to be found in the Treaty that would allow such delegation from the legislature to ESMA or a comparable agency, the delegation was unlawful. The Court was therefore called upon to decide whether or not there was a third way, next to the Articles 290 and 291, by which the EU legislature could delegate certain rulemaking or executive tasks that could affect the position of legal and natural persons to a body other than the Commission. The Commission was of the view that ESMA's

---

517. On the *Romano* case at the time it was handed down, see *supra* footnote 358 and accompanying text.
518. See Case C-270/12, *supra* footnote 509, at paras. 64-68.

powers were of an executive nature and remarked that Article 291 did not exclude a delegation of such powers to a body other than any of the institutions of the EU, in particular the Commission [519].

The Court admitted that the treaties after Lisbon did not contain an explicit provision to this effect, but nevertheless a number of provisions in the TFEU presupposed that such a possibility existed. And again, the Court made reference to the various provisions on judicial protection, namely Articles 263, 265, 267 and 277 TFEU. It noted that these provisions were intended to apply to bodies, offices and agencies that already existed at the time of the entry into force of the Treaty of Lisbon and that had been given powers to adopt measures legally binding on natural or legal persons. In this connection it made reference to ECA, EMA, OHIM, CPVO and EASA. Although the Court did not say so explicitly, like ESMA all these agencies are active in specific areas relating to the functioning of the internal market [520]. The Court did note, however, that ESMA needed "specific technical and professional expertise" for the exercise of its decision-making powers. This was obviously equally important for the other agencies that the Court mentioned. And it was also obvious, as the Court stated, that the particular conferral of powers on ESMA did not correspond to any of the situations defined in Articles 290 and 291 TFEU [521]. With that the Court returned to the way in which ESMA was embedded, with a number of other financial and market authorities, including EBA, ESRB and EIOPA, within the European System of Financial Supervision (ESFS), which was geared to prevent or counteract any major disturbances or crises in the European financial system [522]. This system was dedicated to pursuing the objective of financial stability within the Union. Thus the Court arrived at the somewhat odd conclusion that Article 28 of Regulation 236/2012, read in conjunction with the other regulatory instruments in the financial and banking field, could not "be regarded as undermining the rules governing the delegation of powers laid down in Articles 290 and 291 TFEU" [523].

Why is this an odd qualification of the legal situation? Because the Court had already said that Articles 290 and 291 TFEU were not applicable to ESMA and that hence the kind of delegation that was

---

519. *Ibid.*, at para. 76.
520. *Ibid.*, at paras. 78-81.
521. *Ibid.*, at paras. 80-83.
522. See *supra* footnotes 507 and 508 and accompanying text on the ESFS and its components.
523. Case C-270/12, *supra* footnote 509, at paras. 84-87.

granted to ESMA in respect of short sales in the financial markets could not breach these Treaty articles anyway. Presumably this is a conclusion that applies to all the financial agencies that are part of the EFSF. Moreover, the third way of delegation that the Court accepted, next to the forms of delegation laid down in Articles 290 and 291 TFEU, found its origin in the enlarged scope given in the Lisbon Treaty to the different actions that the Court was competent to rule on (the action for annulment, the action for failure to act and the plea of illegality) by adding the acts of the ECB and of all bodies, offices and agencies of the Union. This new formulation eliminated one of the major reasons for the Court to reject certain forms of delegation in EU law, namely the lack of judicial protection against acts that were taken pursuant to such delegation. Henceforth such acts could be attacked in the Union Courts and, by way of the plea of illegality, natural and legal persons could also demand the annulment of the relevant provisions of the regulation or decision that granted the delegation in the first place. By mentioning the risk of undermining Articles 290 and 291 does the Court seek to open a way to apply the conditions of these articles indirectly to cases of delegation which in law fall outside the terms of these articles?

After the *ESMA* case, the only element that remains of the edifice of case law that ruled the question of delegation in the European Community/Union in cases that are not covered by Articles 290 and 291 TFEU is the *Meroni* case. Why should this be so? Why should a case of more than sixty years old, after numerous constitutional changes and after numerous institutional evolutions, still set particular conditions for the creation of an agency, office or body of the Union on which delegated powers are bestowed that fall outside Articles 290 and 291? The core of *Meroni* is concerned with the balance between the institutions, and in particular the democratic legitimacy as well as the judicial control of delegated acts. However, all these agencies are nowadays created by the Union legislature, which includes a directly elected European Parliament, on a proposal of the Commission, and they are fully part of the institutional landscape of the Union, unlike "the Brussels agencies" to which the High Authority had delegated certain tasks. They are all supposed to perform tasks that require highly specialized knowledge and expertise in the relevant area that they are charged with covering. Their delegated "legislation" or "execution" can always be controlled by the Court in the light not only of the delegating acts by which they were created but also of the principles of Union law and the treaties themselves. Moreover, the delegating act itself can be challenged before the Court of Justice either directly by the privileged parties or indirectly through the plea of illegality in case the delegated act is subject to an action for annulment. Moreover, there is no doubt that at the national level, the preliminary question is always available, as the case of the Fédération bancaire française (FBF) discussed below demonstrates. Why indeed is the *Meroni* case still standing, even after the Court, as was shown above, has moved beyond it?

Indeed, it is striking, when one reads the recent – and so far only – post-*ESMA* case, the *FBF* case, that the passages that contain echoes of the *Meroni* case [524] have a completely ritualistic flavor. That is not only because the case is about formally nonbinding guidelines, a technique of "steering" banks and other financial establishments charactcristic of bodies overseeing the actors in the financial sector in Europe. Why must the EU legislature delineate this power of the EBA with particular precision, based on the objective criteria? Why must the Court exercise particularly stringent judicial review in the light of these objective criteria? There is after all the Commission with a proposal and a serious bicameral legislature consisting of the Council and Parliament – each in its own, direct or indirect, manner fully democratically legitimized – that have decided that certain powers should be delegated to the EBA. Why should the second order legislation resulting from this process be approached with special circumspection by the Court because there is delegation involved? The legislature should be considered fully capable of modeling the delegation that in its eyes best serves the economic sector and the activities that it wants to be ruled by second order regulations. That is quite proper if the delegation does not fall within the terms of Articles 290 or 291, as is the case in the financial sector, and as long as the legislature can do so on the basis of an applicable legal basis in the TFEU.

It is also obvious that the EBA will then be bound by the delegating legislation and cannot issue a regulatory act that would go beyond the terms of the delegating regulation. The Court would be there to see to it that that would not happen, even if the guidelines are only that, and not legally binding. There is nothing special about that, but one would

---

524. See Case C-911/19, *FBF*, *supra* footnote 508, at paras. 67 and 75. The *Meroni* case is not explicitly referred to and present only through the intermediary of the *ESMA* case, which seems to have become the new standard with which future delegation cases will have to comply if they do not come under TFEU Articles 290 or 291.

think otherwise since the Court needed six paragraphs to belabor this point [525].

Given the present structure of the treaties (TEU and TFEU), and the relation between the institutions and the scope of the jurisdiction of the Court after Lisbon, there is no reason to return to the stringent *Meroni* criteria. This leads to *ex ante* restraints on the EU legislature shaping the delegating legislation that it considers adapted to specific sectors and activities and a heightened level of judicial control, which are no longer justified after Lisbon. It should be clear that this applies only to "second order legislation"; that is, regulatory acts of individual or general application that are based on a delegating act. Any first order legislation directly based on the treaties will obviously need the full involvement of the Commission with a proposal that may be based on advice from EU agencies.

It has often been suggested that the Commission should also stay involved in deciding on second order legislation in this way. Above the example has been mentioned of the EBA, which prepares complete proposals for second order legislation for the Commission, from which the latter may only deviate in the final text of the second order legal act after giving duly reasoned arguments. It has been argued that maintaining the Commission's role guarantees a secondary legal act that will be more coherent with other aspects of the EU's policy at any time. However, such coherence can also be ensured by letting the EBA and the Commission change places and grant the Commission an important *droit de regard* on the final text of the legal act that the EBA will promulgate. This can be bolstered by putting this requirement of coherence (for instance between secondary banking regulations and climate change policy) in the delegating act charging the EBA with the power to make delegated legislation.

J. Some final remarks on delegation in the EU

Since the preceding sections of this chapter all end with a short summary, it is not necessary to summarize these once again. What bears repeating at the end is the sheer longevity of the *Meroni* and *Romano*

---

525. See Case C-911/19, *FBF*, *supra* footnote 508, at paras. 72-77. This overkill of explanation, it is fair to say, may have been triggered by nightmares of the French banking sector imagining that if the EBA's "guidelines" did not constitute delegation or implementation within the terms of Articles 290 and 291 TFEU, the EBA would be free to issue guidelines left, right and center, presumably unrestrained by the terms of the delegating regulation. Para. 72 of the judgment seems to hint at this.

cases, while the organizational landscape around them changed fundamentally. The founding treaties moved from *traité-loi* to *traité-cadre*. They went from sectoral integration in coal and steel alone to covering nearly all economic life, including its external aspects, and then beyond, to other areas of the law necessary for full integration in the field of movement of persons, civil, commercial and criminal law and, finally, also including fundamental rights, insofar as they applied to the laws and the action of the Union. How was this possible? Do we have to assume that both cases, and in particular *Meroni*, contained eternal truths that ought to be applied in any (quasi-)constitutional environment?

As argued earlier, it is plausible that the Court was influenced in the *Meroni* case in 1958 and later by the constitutional provisions of Germany and Italy (and to a lesser extent also by the drafts for the French Constitution of 1958) and the early interpretations of these provisions by their constitutional courts. These constitutional provisions were inspired by the negative historical experience of the legislatures in Germany and Italy delegating too many powers of a legislative nature to the executive too easily, voluntarily or under pressure from the Nazi and Fascist representatives in Parliament [526]. Hence the strong aversion from any delegation of legislative powers or anything resembling legislative powers in the case law of the EUCJ subsequent to the *Meroni* case. This is closely linked, as we saw, to maintaining the balance between the institutions and the powers allocated to them by the Treaty and, due to the slow evolution of the EC/EU in the direction of an international organization that is also founded on a form of representative democracy, to the notion of democratic legitimacy.

On the other hand, delegation in the form of *implementation* of legislative acts did not run into many of the obstacles mentioned above as long it was the Commission that was responsible for such implementation. This was due to the fact that the Court in *Romano* had required that the delegation of the power of promulgating acts with legal effect in any form could only be granted to bodies whose acts were reviewable by the EUCJ. This was also due to the fact that implementation was then, and remained later, much more closely associated with the Commission's function as a guardian of the Treaty

---

526. The French Constitution's strict separation between the legislative domain and the regulatory domain was rather inspired by the largely negative experiences in that country with excessive use of so-called *décrets-lois* under the Third and Fourth Republic. See *supra* footnote 70 and accompanying text.

and the application of its legislation by the Member States. Moreover, as was pointed out earlier (Chap. II.F), the comparative study of national systems of delegation in countries like France, Italy and Germany also left ample room for what was regarded as straightforward implementation.

As was demonstrated above, the evolution of the question of delegation and implementation of Union law moved along with the institutional development of the EC/EU over the years. As the number of Member States grew and the terrain covered by powers of the EC/EU expanded and its institutional edifice became more democratic, more diversified and more segmented, with many specialized committees, bodies and agencies, the case law of the Court on implementation and regulatory delegation became more and more refined, even convoluted. It was the Lisbon Treaty, with its new provisions on implementing powers and regulatory powers (Arts. 290 and 291 TFEU) and with a broader jurisdiction of the Court over "the legality of the acts of bodies, offices or agencies of the Union intended to have legal effects vis-à-vis third parties" (Art. 263 TEU) that created the possibility for the Court to found its future jurisprudence on delegation in the EU on a new and strong basis. In the *ESMA* case the Court has taken a first step. It is clear that the Court to a certain extent is "liberated" because it can review the acts of numerous bodies and agencies which the EU legislature may empower to adopt second order legislation under specific, well-defined conditions, and as long as no weighing up between truly political choices is involved. It is no longer necessary for the Court to be always watchful and to annul delegations in first order legislation to such bodies and agencies, because it was excluded by the Treaty to review their acts.

As a matter of fact, the EU has changed so much since its beginnings in the ECSC, that *Meroni* should be considered effectively dead. Even if, as AG Bobek, citing *Game of Thrones,* reminded the Court that "what is dead may never die" [527], it would seem that the time has come to drive a stake through *Meroni*'s heart. The Court should create a new approach to delegation that takes full account of the new democratic

---

527. Opinion AG Bobek in Case C-911/19, *FBF*, *supra* footnote 508, at para. 1. His point, however, related to the question of how legally nonbinding guidelines from the EBA could be annulled by the Court, as they were already "dead" as a matter of law. The Court found the solution by arguing that even nonbinding guidelines, which had always been considered as legally nonexistent by the EUCJ and not worthy of its attention, could go beyond the legal powers of EBA, as laid down in its founding regulation, and, if so, should be annulled.

structure of the Union, which in turn brings with it a new balance between the institutions and a broadened access to justice. In this new constitutional environment the *Meroni* case is no longer good law and the Court should fully acknowledge this and openly complete what it began in the *ESMA* case and move beyond it.

CHAPTER VI

CONCLUDING REMARKS

These final remarks will concentrate on some core points in order to show what are the most important differences between the UN system and the EU as far as delegation within international organizations is concerned. They complement the concluding remarks that can be found at the end of each chapter and section, which will not be summarized here a second time.

It is beyond doubt that the UN and the EU have borrowed concepts and attitudes from national principles of delegation in countries such as France, Germany, Italy and the US when shaping their own systems of delegation of power. Core concepts underlying delegation in these national systems turned out to be, in the first place, the separation of powers or the system of attribution of powers within the State. In the second place, great importance was attached in these national systems to reserve the truly legislative powers to the legislature and to maintain the proper legislative procedure in the process. Finally, on a factual level and responding to the increased technical detail involved in modern government and the need to deal with that in an expert way, delegation by way of secondary rulemaking or quasi-legislation by expert bodies was seen as necessary, and even desirable. Democratically legitimized State organs, such as the parliament and the government, lacked such expertise, as did the independent judiciary. In some instances, it was even considered desirable that certain decisions be taken by experts and not be exposed to political pressures at all. However, this is only indicated if the relevant decisions can truly be taken by experts only and do not need a further political weighing up against other social and economic interests [528].

---

[528]. This has been amply demonstrated during the Covid-19 pandemic since late 2019. The approval of vaccines and medicines combating Covid as such was best left entirely in the hands of national and supranational medicines agencies. Before that approval came down, governments relied very strongly on experts in the field of public health and epidemics when deciding on the measures to be taken, such as quarantines, lockdowns, etc. Once vaccines and medicines were approved; measures on the distribution of vaccines, combined with the continuation of lockdowns and quarantines, required additional expertise on social and economic interests and mental health so that other factors could receive a certain weight in the equation.

It is remarkable that both the UN and the ECSC/EC/EU, and respectively the ICJ and the ECSC Court of Justice, borrowed notions on the delegation of legislative powers from national legal systems, whereas the organs that took the impugned decisions could scarcely be regarded as legislative organs giving away their powers. The UN General Assembly, in spite of what has been said about this later, is not a legislative organ in the first place, and the High Authority was an executive organ rather than a legislature [529].

Where the General Assembly was concerned, the decision of the ICJ in the *Effect of Awards* case was primarily founded on the competence question. The ICJ reacted to that question by relying on the implied powers doctrine and the need for any organization to lay down its internal functioning in an orderly fashion. A well-organized administrative court (or internal justice system, as it is now called) was key to that natural objective and there was no Charter norm which directly or indirectly could stand in the way of that. The remedies offered by such a court, namely the UNAT-old, were integral to its status as a true court and had to be respected by the General Assembly and any award of damages had to be defrayed from the normal UN budget.

In contrast, the *Meroni* case led to a blockage of the High Authority's decision, which implied a delegation, on the basis of the competence question. A narrow interpretation of the powers granted to the High Authority (later: the Commission) in the ECSC Treaty led to the conclusion that even an individual decision setting the level of the assessment of Meroni's share in the ECSC common scrap buying scheme could not be decided by the Commission with the help of outside expert organs as long as the Commission did not shoulder full responsibility for it. A very important reason for this was that otherwise the steel companies would have no access to the Court in order to have the lawfulness of the measure that affected them reviewed. Hence, the Commission's delegation of certain technical decisions to outside bodies was unlawful.

It was only in the *obiter dicta* of the *Meroni* case that the ECSC Court was ready to show the way, under which stringent restrictions the High Authority/Commission (but also the other major institutions

---

529. It will be recalled that in the *Meroni* case, the High Authority took a number of individual decisions, deciding on the contributions different steel companies, among which the Meroni company, were obliged to make to the cost of the companies' ECSC-supported common buying-up program of steel scrap outside the Community. At best, it might be argued that the sum of these contributions constituted a general measure.

of the ECSC/EEC/EU) could delegate powers to other bodies and committees, whether existing, or created for this purpose. Remarkably, the ECSC Court, just like the ICJ in the *Effect of Awards* case, for the power of delegation itself relied on the notion of implied powers. Having been granted a power in the Treaty, the Court found that the Commission (and presumably any other ECSC/EU institution) could rely on the need for a well-organized decision-making procedure and/ or the input of the necessary specialized knowledge in order to create the desired delegation. How this delegation was to be granted and circumscribed was prescribed by the ECSC Court in a way redolent of the restrictions and conditions imposed on the delegation of (quasi-) legislative powers by the national constitutions of the most important Member States. In the subsequent development of the case law of the European Court of Justice, these *obiter dicta* became more important than the narrow basis, on which the Court actually decided the case.

It is interesting to note that the initial decisions governing delegation in each organization, in the final analysis, served to protect the interests of non-State actors: in the UN system, the civil servants of the organization; in the ECSC/EU, the economic operators in the coal and steel market. Because of the *obiter dicta* of the European Court of Justice, in the end the point of departure of the further development of the delegation of powers in both organizations was comparable. The actual development, however, in each organization was very different. In the UN, the General Assembly over time developed a view of delegation to an expert body like the ICSC, as well as to judicial bodies like the UN administrative tribunals, and even to a principal organ of the organization, the Secretary-General and his Secretariat, which became increasingly restrictive and almost intolerant of any sliver of autonomy that these institutions tried to maintain in the exercise of the powers delegated to them. The attitude of the General Assembly, especially in budgetary matters, is hardly compatible with the status of the Secretary-General as a coequal organ of the organization and with the judicial independence of the administrative tribunals and the consideration that judgments of these courts are due.

As has been demonstrated, the Security Council has succeeded in developing a policy of delegation in the field of international peacekeeping to the Secretary-General and the Secretariat, which has become quite stable. The political issues remain with the Council itself, while the practical aspects of the composition of the force, the various agreements with the host countries and the troop-providing countries, the lines of command, the rules of engagement, and so on, are all in the hands of the Secretariat and approved by the Security Council when necessary. On the other hand, the Security Council has been somewhat less successful in delegating tasks to specially created committees of its members in connection with the implementation and enforcement of economic sanctions by States, but more importantly by companies and individuals. It has been shown that there are problems with delegation in these areas of implementation, but they are arguably less problematic from a legal point of view than the backpedaling from the principles of delegation by the General Assembly.

The evolution has been wholly different within the ECSC/EEC/EU. As we have seen, the ECSC and subsequently the EEC and EU approaches to delegation started from a quite restrictive approach under the influence of the Court of Justice. But room was made early on for what was called "implementation", usually through the executive organs of the Member States, and along the lines of administrative execution of the laws accepted in the Member States. This was considered fundamentally innocuous also in the constitutional systems of these Member States themselves. When secondary lawmaking of necessity had to go beyond self-evident implementation, step by step the Court adjusted its doctrine. In response the Council of Ministers (in the early days the single legislature) adopted secondary legislation. Later on, the three major institutions, the Commission, the European Parliament and the Council, agreed interinstitutional agreements on legislation, including delegation, which often was not much more than a codification of the Court's case law. However, even such mere codification was often taken by the Court as an encouragement to continue on the road taken and develop its case law a bit more. Member States changed the founding treaty. In a few instances, the Member States, acting as the constitutional legislature, were brought to the point where they had to accept that constitutional change was necessary. This happened early on (1) when delegation from the Council to the Commission was put in the EEC Treaty, and later, (2) when the Lisbon Treaty fundamentally overhauled the TFEU on two kinds of delegation (harmonizing the normal delegation of implementation to Member States' authorities and regulatory delegation to EU agencies and bodies) and, perhaps more importantly, (3) by creating justiciability of the decisions of EU agencies and bodies. The Court then picked up these treaty modifications in the well-known *ESMA* case and began to run with them. And there is hope that it will advance a new delegation doctrine that will probably still contain some core ideas underlying *Meroni*, but will no longer need many of its now stultifying restrictions.

What was at the core of these diverging developments in the UN and the EU where delegation was concerned? Why did delegation in the UN, in particular as practiced by the General Assembly, develop into what, with all due forbearance, can be qualified only as a rather chaotic situation that does not do justice to certain underlying principles of delegation, such as the balance between the institutions? Why does the General Assembly regard itself as the UN's "sovereign lawgiver" and its decisions, in particular on budgetary and employment matters, as superior to those of other major organs? Why, on the other hand, has delegation in the ECSC/EEC/EU, after starting out as a very restrictively interpreted notion, slowly but fairly surely developed, through interaction between all major institutions, into a much broader concept that fulfills a very useful role in the EU decision-making machinery?

These were basically the questions that originally inspired this lecture series and the answer, in the end, is not very difficult. "It is the Court, stupid!"[530] The fact that the UN does not dispose of a court that is authorized and willing to function as an arbiter of quasi-constitutional questions makes it very difficult to solve recurring problems, such as those relating to delegation. Even if in certain instances the ICJ and later the ICTY have been able to advance and repeat certain fundamental legal principles relating to delegation, notably relating to the creation of courts, such principles can fall victim very quickly to political infighting. In the UN setting it is clear that such judicial decisions are one-off occasions and that there is no chance – the ICJ having decided that it is not, and does not aspire to be, the constitutional court of the UN – that the institutions or the Member States can go back to that Court in order to test how its enunciated principles would apply in another situation. There is also no incentive to follow the Court, or to try to adjust the Court's approach through legislation and see what happens in the next case.

As the description and analysis of the evolution of the questions inherent in delegation in the ECSC/EEC/EU clarifies, the EUCJ (an administrative court that is also, if necessary, and over time, more and more willing to function as a constitutional court) has been highly

---

530. A variation of the motto used in President Clinton's reelection campaign in 1996.

conducive to making a sensible development of delegation in decision-making and even in legislation possible. The EU Court was also a "repeat player" in cases on delegation and, unlike the ICJ and the UN administrative tribunals, could hone its decisions over time. But this also presupposes that the other actors within the organization, the institutions and the Member States, individually and collectively, are willing to play their part too, and react at least loyally to the Court's decisions, precisely when they try to make it change or adjust its position. This proved to be the case in the ECSC/EEC/EU, but not in the UN.

BIBLIOGRAPHY

Delegation (General)

Abbott, K.W., "Why States Act through Formal International Organizations", *Journal of Conflict Resolution*, Vol. 42, No. 1, 1998, pp. 3-32.
Alter, K., "Delegating to International Courts: Self-Binding v. Other-Binding Delegation", *The Law of Politics and International Delegation – Law and Contemporary Problems*, Vol.71/1, 2008, pp. 37-76.
Bogdandy, A., R. Wolfrum, J. von Bernstorff, P. Dann and M. Goldmann, M. (eds.), *The Exercise of Public Authority by International Organizations, Advancing International Institutional Law*, A Research Project of the Max Planck Institute for International Law, Springer, 2010.
Elsig, M., "Principal-agent theory and the World Trade Organization: Complex agency and 'missing delegation'", *European Journal of International Relations*, Vol. 17/3, 2011, pp. 495-517.
Epstein, D., and S. O'Halloran, "Sovereignty & Delegation in International Organizations", in *The Law of Politics and International Delegation – Law and Contemporary Problems*, Vol. 71/1, 2008, pp. 77-92.
Göttelmann, W., *Die Delegation hoheitlicher Befugnisse internationaler Organisationen und ihrer Organe: ein Vergleich mit dem deutschen Recht*, München, Druck Schön, 1968.
Guzman, A., "International organizations and the Frankenstein problem", *European Journal of International Law*, Vol. 24/4, 2013, pp. 999-1025.
Hawkins, D. G., D. A. Lake, D. L. Neilson and M. J. Tierney, *Delegation and Agency in International Organizations*, Cambridge University Press, 2006.
Klabbers, J., "The changing image of international organizations", in J. M. Coicaud and V. Heiskanen (eds.), *The Legitimacy of International Organizations*, Tokyo, United Nations University Press, 2001.
Lucian, B., "The presumption against delegation in public law. Was the impact from private law really justified?", *Romanian Journal of Comparative Law (Revista Româna de Drept Comparat)*, Issue 2, 2012, pp. 304-320.
Meier, G., "Das Recht internationaler Organisationen zur Schaffung und Bevollmächtigung eigener Organe", *Archiv des Völkerrechts*, Vol. 12/1, 1964, pp. 14-33.
Pollack, M. A., "Principal-Agent Analysis and International Delegation: Red Herrings, Theoretical Clarifications, and Empirical Disputes", *Bruges Political Research Paper No. 2*, Europa College, Brugge (2007).
Sarooshi, D., "Conferrals by States of Powers on International Organizations: The Case of Agency", *The British Yearbook of International Law*, Vol. 74, 2003, pp. 291-332.
–, *International Organizations and their Exercise of Sovereign Powers*, Oxford University Press, 2005.
–, "The Essentially Contested Nature of the Concept of Sovereignty: Implications for the Exercise by International Organizations of Delegated Powers of Government", *Michigan Journal of International Law*, Vol. 25, 2003-2004, p. 1107.
–, "The Role of Domestic Public Law Analogies in the Law of International Organizations", *International Organizations Law Review*, Vol. 5/2, 2008, pp. 237-239.
Voermans, W., *Toedeling van bevoegdheid*, Den Haag, Boom Juridische Uitgevers, 2004.

Delegation of powers in National Legal Systems

Ackermann, S. R., and T. Perroud, "Policymaking and Public Law in France: Public

Participation, Agency Independence, and Impact Assessment", *Columbia Journal of European Law*, Vol. 19, Spring 2013, pp. 225-312.
Garoupa, N., and J. Mathews, "Strategic Delegation, Discretion & Deference: Explaining the Comparative Law of Administrative Review", *American Journal of Comparative Law*, Vol. 62/1, Winter 2014.
Garry, P. M., "Accomodating the administrative state: the interrelationship between the Chevron and nondelegation doctrines", *Arizona State Law Journal*, Vol. 28, Winter 2006, p. 921.
Kelley, W. K., "Justice Scalia, the Nondelegation Doctrine, and Constitutional Argument", *Notre Dame Law Review*, Vol. 92/5, 2017, pp. 2107-2127.
Lawson, G., "Delegation and Original Meaning", *Virginia Law Review*, Vol. 88/2, 2002, p. 327.
Lepsius, O., "Gesetzesstruktur im Wandel, Teil 2: Strukturmerkmale delegierter Rechtserzeugung", *Juristische Studien*, JuS. 2, 2019, pp, 123-128.
Lindseth, P. L., "The Paradox of Parliamentary Supremacy: Delegation, Democracy & Dictatorship in Germany and France", *Yale Law Journal*, Vol. 113, May 2004, p. 1341.
Nevola, R., and D. Diaco, "La delega della funzione legislativa nella giurisprudenza della Corte Costituzionale", Premessa, *Servizio Studi*, Corte Costituzionale, 2018.
Nolte, G., "Ermächtigung der Exekutive Zur Rechtsetzung: Lehren Aus Der Deutschen Und Der Amerikanischen Erfahrung", *Archiv des Öffentlichen Rechts*, Vol. 118, No. 3, 1993, pp. 378-413.
"Nondelegation's Unprincipled Foreign Affairs Exceptionalism", *Harvard Law Review*, Vol. 134, 2021, pp. 1132-1161.
Pünder, H., "Democratic legitimation of delegated legislation – a comparative view on the American, British and German law", *International & Comparative Law Quarterly*, Vol. 58/2, 2009, pp. 353-378.
"The Legislative Process: The Delegation of Powers", *Select Committee on the Constitution, 16th Report of Session 2017-2019*, Authority of the House of Lords, 2018.
Verpeaux, M., "Les ordonnances de l'article 38 ou les fluctuations contrôlées de la répartition des compétences entre la loi et le règlement", *Cahiers du Conseil Constitutionnel No. 19*, Dossier: Loi et Règlements, 2006.
Wischmeyer, T., "Grundwissen – Öffentliches Recht: Die Rechtsverordnung", *Juristische Studien*, JuS. 4, 2015, pp. 311-314.

Delegation in the UN

Aldrich, G. H., "Jurisdiction of the International Criminal Tribunal for the Former Yugoslavia", *American Journal of International Law*, Vol. 90/1, 1996, pp. 64-69.
Arato, J., "Constitutionality and constitutionalism beyond the state: Two perspectives on the material constitution of the United Nations", *International Journal of Constitutional Law*, Vol. 10/3, 2012, pp. 627-659.
De Hoogh, A. J. J., "Attribution or Delegation of (Legislative Power by the Security Council? – The Case of the United Nations Transitional Administration in East Timor (UNTAET)", in M. Bothe and B. Kondoch (eds.), *International Peacekeeping. The Yearbook of International Peace Operations 2001*, The Hague etc., 2002, pp. 1-41.
De Wet, E., "The Relationship between the Security Council and Regional Organisations during Enforcement Action under Chapter VII of the United Nations Charter", *Nordic Journal of International Law*, Vol. 71/1, 2002, pp. 89-121.
Dijkstra, H., "Efficiency v. Sovereignty: Delegation to the UN Secretariat in Peacekeeping", *International Peacekeeping*, Vol. 19/5, 2012, pp. 581-596.
Elberling, B., "The Ultra Vires Character of Legislative Action by the Security Council", *International Organizations Law Review 2/2*, Leiden, 2005, pp. 337-360.

Geslin, A., "Le Pouvoir d'Habilitation du Conseil de Sécurité: la Délégation des Pouvoirs du Conseil aux Organisations Internationales", *Revue Belge de Droit International 2004/2*, pp. 484-497.
Gulati, R., "The International Dispute Resolution Regime of the United Nations – Has the Creation of the United Nations Dispute Tribunal and United Nations Appeals Tribunal Remedied the Flaws of the United National Administrative Tribunal?", in A. Von Bogdandy and R. Wolfrum, (eds.), *Max Planck Yearbook of United Nations Law*, Vol. 15, 2011, pp. 489-538.
Klabbers, J., "Global Governance before the ICJ: Re-reading the WHO Opinion", *Max Planck Yearbook of United Nations Law*, Vol. 13, 2009, pp. 1-28.
Marchi-Uhel, C., "From adjudicating international crimes to reviewing delisting requests by individuals and entities on the 1267 Sanctions List: a comparative approach", Presentation by the Ombudsperson, Security Council ISIL (Da'esh) and Al-Qaida Sanctions Committee, 2016.
Oette, L., "A Decade of Sanctions against Iraq: Never Again! The End of Unlimited Sanctions in the Recent Practice of the UN Security Council", *European Journal of International Law*, Vol. 13, No. 1, 2002, pp. 93-103.
Prost, K., "Remarks" by the Ombudsperson, Security Council Al-Qaida Sanctions Committee, to the 49th meeting of the Committee of Legal Advisors on Public International Law (CAHDI) of the Council of Europe, delivered in Strasbourg on 20 March 2015.
Sarooshi, D., "The Powers of the United Nations International Criminal Tribunals", *Max Planck Yearbook of UN Law*, 1998, p. 141.
–, *The United Nations and the development of collective security: the Delegation by the UN Security Council of its Chapter VII powers*, Oxford University Press, 1999.
Talmon, S. A. G, "Delegation of Powers by the UN", in P. Shiner and A. Williams (eds.), *The Iraq War and International Law*, Hart Publishing, 2008.
"The Prosecutor v. *Tadic* – The Appellate Decision of the ICTY and Internal Violations of Humanitarian Law as International Crimes", Case Analysis, *Leiden Journal of International Law*, Vol. 9/1 (1996), pp. 219-231.
Von Sternberg, M. R., "Yugoslavian War Crimes and the Search for a New Humanitarian Order: The Case of Dusko Tadic", *12 John's Journal Legal Comment*, (1996-1997), p. 351.
Wilson, G., "The Legal, Military and Political Consequences of the 'Coalition of the Willing' Approach to UN Military Enforcement Action", *Journal of Conflict & Security Law*, Vol. 12, No. 2, 2007, pp. 295-330.

Delegation in the EU

Adamski, D., "The ESMA Doctrine: A Constitutional Revolution and the Economics of Delegation", *European Law Review*, Vol. 39/6, 2014, pp. 812-834.
Bergström, C. F., *Comitology: Delegation of Powers in the European Union and the Committee System*, Oxford University Press, Oxford, 2005.
Bergström, C. F., and D. Ritleng (eds.), *Rulemaking by the European Commission, The New System for Delegation of Powers*, Oxford University Press, Oxford 2016.
Bianchi, D., "La Comitologie est morte! Vive la comitologie!: premières réflexions sur l'exécution du droit de l'Union après le Traité de Lisbonne: l'exemple de la Politique agricole commune", *Revue trimestrielle de droit européen*, Vol. 48/1, 2012, pp. 75-116.
Blumann, C., "Un nouveau départ pour la comitologie: le règlement n° 182/2011 du 16 février 2011", *Cahiers de droit européen*, vol. 47/1, 2011, pp. 23-52.
Bourgeois, J., et M. Chamon, "The Integration of EU Trade Defence in the Horizontal Comitology Regime", in M. Hahn and G. Van der Loo (eds.), *Law and Practice of the Common Commercial Policy. The first ten years after the Treaty of Lisbon*, Leiden, Brill, Nijhoff, 2021, pp. 512-530.

Busuioc, E. M., "The Accountability of European Agencies: Legal Provisions and Ongoing Practices", Delft, Eburon, 2010.
Chamon, M., "Comitologie onder het Verdrag van Lissabon", *Sociaal-economische Wetgeving: Tijdschrift voor Europees en economisch recht*, Vol. 61/2, 2013, pp. 63-75.
–, "EU Agencies: between Meroni and Romano or the devil and the deep blue sea", *Common Market Law Review*, Vol. 48/4, 2011, pp. 1055-1075.
–, *EU Agencies. Legal and Political Limits to the Transformation of the EU Administration*, Oxford University Press, Oxford 2016.
–, "How the concept of essential elements of a legislative act continues to elude the Court", *Common Market Law Review*, Vol. 50/3, 2013, pp. 849-860.
–, "Institutional balance and community method in the implementation of EU legislation following the Lisbon treaty", *Common Market Law Review*, Vol. 53/5, 2016, pp. 1501-1544.
–, "The Empowerment of Agencies under the Meroni Doctrine and Article 114 TFEU: Comment on United Kingdom v. Parliament and Council (Short-selling) and the Proposed Single Resolution Mechanism", *European Law Review*, Vol. 39/3, 2014, pp. 380-403.
–, "The legal framework for delegated and implementing powers ten years after the entry into force of the Lisbon Treaty", *ERA Forum*, https://doi.org/10.1007/s12027-020-00646-2, Springer, 2021.
Christiansen, T., and M. Dobbels, "Comitology and delegated acts after Lisbon: How the European Parliament lost the implementation game", *European Integration online Papers (EIoP)*, Vol. 16, Article 13, 2012.
Dehousse, R., "Delegation of Powers in the European Union: The Need for a Multi-principal Model", *West European Politics*, Vol. 31/4, 2008, pp. 789-805.
DeSomer, S., "International and European impulse with regard to the creation of autonomous public bodies: and emerging trend", *UCL Journal of Law & Jurisprudence*, Vol. 13/1, 2014, pp. 58-86.
Di Noia, C., and M. Gargantini, "Unleashing the European Securities and Markets Authority: governance and accountability after the ECJ decision on the Short Selling Regulation (Case C-270/12)", *European Business Law Review*, Vol. 15/1, 2014, pp. 1-57.
Falke, J., "Comitology after Lisbon: what is left of Comitology as we have praised it?", in C. Joerges and C. Glinski (eds.), *The European crisis and the transformation of transnational governance*, Oxford and Portland, Oregon, Hart Publishing, 2014, pp. 271-291.
Franchino, F., *The Powers of the Union: Delegation in the EU*, Cambridge University Press, 2007.
Griller, S., and A. Orator, "Everything Under Control?: The 'way forward' for European agencies in the footsteps of the Meroni doctrine", *European Law Review*, Vol. 35/1, 2010, pp. 3-35.
Groenleer, M. L. P., *The Autonomy of European Agencies: A Comparative Study of Institutional Development*, Leiden University Press, 2009.
Hofmann, H. Ch., and A. Morini, "Case Note: Constitutional aspects of the pluralization of the EU executive through 'agencification'", *European Law Review*, Vol. 37/4, 2012, pp. 419-443.
Jorda, J., "L'art d'exécuter le droit Communautaire : une lecture de la comitologie", in *L'Union européenne: union de droit, union des droits: mélanges en l'honneur du professeur Philippe Manin*, ed. A. Pedone, 2010, pp. 271-282.
Kollmeyer, D., "Delegierte Rechtssetzung in der EU – Eine Analyse der Art. 290 und 291 AEUV", Nomos, Baden-Baden, 2015.
Majone, G., "Delegation of Regulatory Powers in a Mixed Polity", *European Law Journal*, Vol. 8/3, 2002, pp. 319-339.
Marjosola, H., "Bridging the constitutional gap in EU executive rule-making: the Court of Justice approves legislative conferral of intervention powers to European Securities and Markets Authority", *European Constitutional Law Review*, Vol. 10/3, 2014, pp. 500-527.

Papadopoulos, T., "European System of Financial Supervision", in R. Wolfrum (ed.), *Max Planck Encyclopedia of Public International Law*, Oxford University Press, 2015.
Piris, J.-C., "La comitologie: vers l'épilogue d'une longue saga?", in *Chemins d'Europe: mélanges en l'honneur de Jean Paul Jacqué*, Paris, Dalloz, 2010, pp. 547-558.
Pollack, M. A., "Delegation, agency, and agenda setting in the European Community", *International Organization*, Vol. 51/1, 1997, pp. 99-134.
–, *The Engines of European Integration: Delegation, Agency, and Agenda Setting in the EU*, Oxford University Press, Oxford 2003.
Ponzano, P., "Comitologie : un point de vue de la Commission", *Revue trimestrielle de droit européen*, Vol. 44/4, 2008, pp. 713-728.
Ritleng, D. (ed.), *Independence and Legitimacy in the Institutional System of the EU*. Collected Courses of the Academy of European Law, Oxford University Press, Oxford, 2016.
–, "La délégation du pouvoir législatif de l'Union européenne", in *Chemins d'Europe: mélanges en l'honneur de Jean Paul Jacqué*, Paris, Dalloz, 2010, pp. 559-576.
Scholten, M., "The Political Accountability of EU and US Independent Regulatory Agencies", *Nijhoff Studies in European Union Law*, Vol. 6, Leiden, Brill, Nijhoff, 2014.
Scholten, M., and A. Brenninkmeijer (eds.), *Controlling EU Agencies – The Rule of Law in a Multi-jurisdictional Legal Order*, Edward Elgar Publishing, 2020.
Simoncini, M., "Administrative Regulation Beyond the Non-Delegation Doctrine – A Study on EU Agencies", Hart Publishing, 2018.
Skowron, M., "Die Zukunft europäischer Agenturen auf dem Prüfstand", *Europarecht*, Vol. 49/2, 2014, pp. 250-261.
Yataganas, X., *Delegation of Regulatory Authority in the European Union: the relevance of the American model of independent agencies*, Occasional Paper, Harvard Law School, 2001.

International Delegations

Bradley, C. A., and J. G. Kelley, "The Concept of International Delegation", *Law and Contemporary Problems*, Vol. 71, 2008, pp. 1-36.
Daugirdas, K., "International Delegations and Administrative Law", *Maryland Law Review*, Vol. 66, 2007, pp. 707-749.
Guzman, A. T., and J. Landsidle, "The Myth of International Delegation", *California Law Review*, Vol. 96, 2008, pp. 1693-1723.
Hathaway, O. A., "International Delegation and State Sovereignty", *Law and Contemporary Problems*, Vol. 71, Winter 2008, pp. 115-149.
"International Delegation as Ordinary Delegation", *Harvard Law Review*, Vol. 125, 2011-2012, p. 1042.
Ku, J. G., "The Delegation of Federal Power to International Organizations: New Problems with Old Solutions", *Minnesota Law Review*, Vol. 85 (2000), pp. 71-146.
Swaine, E. T., "The Constitutionality of International Delegations", *Columbia Law Review*, Vol. 104, 2004, pp. 1492-1614.
Wiersema, A., "The New International Law-Makers? Conferences of the Parties to Multilateral Environmental Agreements", *Michigan Journal of International Law*, Vol. 31, Fall 2009, pp. 231-287.

THE EVOLUTION OF THE LAW
OF INTERNATIONAL WATERCOURSES

by

STEPHEN C. McCAFFREY

S. C. McCAFFREY

TABLE OF CONTENTS

Chapter 1. Introduction and Overview. 257
  I. Overview of the Course. 259
    1. The Umma-Lagash Treaty (ca. 3100 BC). 259
    2. Grant to a monastery by Charlemagne (805 AD) 260
    3. The Peace of Westphalia (1648) 261
    4. The Congress of Vienna (1815) 261
    5. The First Assertion of a Rule concerning the Non-navigational Uses of International Watercourses (1856) 262
    6. The "Harmon Doctrine" (1895) 262
    7. The 1906 Convention between Mexico and the United States. . 263
    8. The US Supreme Court decision in *Kansas* v. *Colorado* (1907) 263
    9. The 1909 Boundary Waters Treaty, Canada-United States . . . 264
    10. The Madrid Resolution of the Institute of International Law (1911). 264
    11. The *Donauversinkung* Case (1927) 264
    12. The *River Oder* Case (1929) 265
    13. The Trail Smelter Arbitration (1941) 266
    14. The Salzburg Resolution of the Institute of International Law (1961). 266
    15. The Helsinki Rules on the Uses of the Waters of International Rivers of the International Law Association (1966) 266
    16. The Athens Resolution of the Institute of international law (1979). 267
    17. International Law Commission's draft articles on the Law of International Watercourses (1994) 267
    18. Convention on the law of the non-navigational uses of international watercourses (1997) 267
    19. Illustrative case law 268
  II. Definitions. 281

Chapter 2. Fresh water and its use by humans 283
  I. Introduction 283
  II. The impact of climate change on shared freshwater resources . . . 290
  III. Uneven distribution 293
  IV. Water transfers 294
  V. Groundwater: out of sight, out of mind?. 300
    1. The general characteristics of groundwater. 301
    2. The international legal regulation of groundwater 304
    3. Groundwater in the two multilateral treaties concerning international watercourses 304
    4. Groundwater in case law. 305
    5. The ILC's resolution on "Confined Transboundary Groundwater" 308
    6. The ILC's draft articles on the Law of Transboundary Aquifers 309
  VI. Conclusion. 311

Chapter 3. Beyond the Hobbesean state of nature: The perceived need for reliability of access to shared freshwater resources and early evidence of a quest for stability 313
  I. Introduction. 313

II. "Nasty, brutish and short" 313
III. Further evidence from treaty practice 315
IV. The quest for stability in fluvial relations 315
V. Lessons from the fate of the "Harmon Doctrine" 318

    1. Background 318
    2. Harmon's Opinion 322
    3. The events following the issuance of Harmon's opinion 325

VI. The 1906 Treaty 329
VII. Conclusion 330

Chapter 4. Navigation: nature's highways in a forested land 331

I. Introduction 331
II. Early practice 331
III. Development of the law of navigational uses of international watercourses in Western Europe 333
IV. Influential cases and the law as it stands today 338
V. The *River Oder* case 339
VI. The *Oscar Chinn* case 341
VII. The *Navigational and Related Rights* case 343
VIII. The Contributions of Learned Societies 346
IX. Conclusions 349

Chapter 5. Evolution of the law governing the non-navigational uses of international watercourses 351

I. Introduction 351
II. Ancient times 351
III. The Institute of International Law 360
IV. The International Law Association 363
V. Indicia of the evolution of the law 366

    1. From preeminence of navigation to the absence of inherent priorities 366
    2. From the surface water channel to the system of waters 368
    3. From piecemeal problem-solving to integrated management and development 372
    4. From protection of fisheries to protection of fish 374
    5. From "no harm" to equitable utilization 376

Chapter 6. Conclusions and outlook 381

I. Some conclusions 381
II. Outlook 384

BIOGRAPHICAL NOTE

Stephen C. McCaffrey, born 21 January 1945, in San Mateo, California, USA. Carol Olson Endowed Professor of International Law at the University of the Pacific, McGeorge School of Law in Sacramento, California. BA degree from the University of Colorado (1967), JD degree from the University of California, Berkeley (1971), Dr. iur. degree from the University of Cologne (1974). 2017 Laureate of the Stockholm Water Prize, presented by the King of Sweden. Two terms on the UN International Law Commission (ILC), chair of the ILC for its 1987 session, and Commission's special rapporteur on international watercourses. The ILC's work on that topic formed the basis of the negotiation of the 1997 UN Convention on the Law of the Non-Navigational Uses of International Watercourses.

2018 recipient of the Elisabeth Haub Award for Environmental Law and Diplomacy and the recipient, in 2007, of the Order of the Dual White Cross, Republic of Slovakia (the highest distinction awarded by Slovakia to foreign nationals). Elected twice by the parties to the UNECE Water Convention as a member of that agreement's Implementation Committee. Served as counsel to States in cases before the International Court of Justice and the Permanent Court of Arbitration and extensive publications in the fields of public international law, the law of international watercourses and international environmental law.

PRINCIPAL PUBLICATIONS

*Selected Books,
Monographs and Reports*

Private Remedies for Transfrontier Environmental Disturbances, IUCN Environmental Policy and Law Paper No. 8, International Union for the Conservation of Nature and Natural Resources, Morges, Switzerland (1975).

Pollution Suits Between Citizens Of The Republic Of Mexico And The United States: A Study In Private International Law (Ansprüche Aus Immissionen Über Die Grenze Zwischen Mexico Und Den USA im Internationalen Privatrecht), published as Volume 14 Berkeley-Kölner Rechtsstudien (Berkeley-Cologne Legal Studies) (C. F. Müller, Karlsruhe, 1976) (doctoral dissertation, University of Cologne, Cologne, Federal Republic of Germany (1974)).

Seven Reports to the International Law Commission on the Law of the Non-Navigational Uses of International Watercourses, 1985 YB Int'l L. Comm'n (Vol. 2, pt. 1), p. 87 (1987).

1986 *YB Int'l L. Comm'n*, Vol. 2, pt. 1, p. 87 (1988).
1987 *YB Int'l L. Comm'n*, Vol. 2, pt. 1, p. 15 (1989).
1988 *YB Int'l L. Comm'n*, Vol. 2, pt. 1, p. 205 (1992).
1989 *YB Int'l L. Comm'n*, Vol. 2, pt. 1, p. 91 (1992).
1990 *YB Int'l L. Comm'n*, Vol. 2, pt. 1, p. 41 (1993); and 1991 *YB Int'l L. Comm'n*, Vol. 2, pt. 1, p. 45 (1994).

International Environmental Law and Policy, with E. Brown Weiss, D. Magraw and A. D. Tarlock, 2nd ed., Aspen (2007).

International Law for the Environment, with E. Brown Weiss, D. B. Magraw, S. Tai and A. Dan Tarlock (West, 2016), with Documents Supplement.

The Law of International Watercourses: Non-Navigational Uses, Oxford University Press (2001) (awarded Certificate of Merit for High Technical Craftsmanship, 2002, by the American Society of International Law); 2nd ed., *The Law of International Watercourses*, Oxford University Press (2007); 3rd ed., OUP (2019).

Guidebook for Policy and Legislative Development on Conservation and Sustainable Use of Freshwater Resources, with G. S. Weber, United Nations Environment Programme (2004).

Negotiator's Handbook on International Freshwater Agreements, United Nations Environment Programme (2005).

Understanding International Law, Carolina Academic Press, 3rd ed. (2021).

Trans-boundary Water Cooperation as a Tool for Conflict Prevention and for Broader Benefit-Sharing, with D. Phillips, M. Daoudy, J. Öjendal and A. Turton, Swedish Ministry for Foreign Affairs (2006).

Bridges Over Water: Understanding Transboundary Water Conflict, Negotiation and Cooperation, with A. Dinar, S. Dinar and D. McKinney, World Scientific Publishing (2007).

Global Issues in Environmental Law, with R. Salcido, West (2009).

Transnational Litigation in Comparative Perspective: Theory and Application, with T. O. Main, Oxford University Press (2010).

Public International Law: Cases, Problems, and Texts, with D. Shelton and J. Cerone, Lexis Nexis (2010).

Promoting Equity, Cooperation and Innovation in the Fields of Transboundary Waters and Natural Resources Management: The Legacy of Dr. David J. H. Phillips, S. C. McCaffrey, J. S. Murray and M. Woodhouse (eds.), Brill Nijhoff (2017).

T. O. Main and S. C. McCaffrey, Learning Conflict of Laws, West (2019).

Research Handbook on International Water Law, S. C. McCaffrey, C. Leb and R. T. Denoon (eds.), Edward Elgar (2019).

The Evolution of the Law of International Watercourses 249

Selected Articles and Papers

Standing on the Side of the Environment: A Statutory Prescription for Citizen Participation, 1 Ecology LQ 561 (1971) (co-authored with R. E. Lutz, II).

Trans-Boundary Pollution Injuries: Jurisdictional Considerations in Private Litigation Between Canada and the United States, 3 Cal. West. Int'l LJ 191 (1973) (cited and quoted from in Prefatory Note to Uniform Transboundary Pollution Reciprocal Access Act (1982)).

The Use of Law in Environmental Conservation: A Survey of Legal Responses to Selected Problems, in *Organization and Administration of Environmental Programmes*, UN Doc. ST/ESA/16, at 109 (1974) (co-authored with F. Burhenne-Guilmin).

The OECD Principles Concerning Transfrontier Pollution: A Commentary, 1 Environmental Policy and Law, p. 2, Lausanne, Switzerland (1975).

Assessment of Environmental Impact – Some Reflections on the American Experience, in *British Institute of International Law and Comparative Law, Environmental Law, International and Comparative Aspects, A Symposium*, J. Nowak (ed.) (1976).

Private Remedies for Transfrontier Pollution Injuries, in *British Institute of International and Comparative Law, Environmental Law, International And Comparative Aspects, A Symposium*, J. Nowak (ed.) (1976).

Pollution of Shared Natural Resources: Legal and Trade Implications in [1977], Proceedings of The American Society of International Law, p. 56 (1977).

The Swiss Draft Conflicts Law, 28 American Journal of Comparative Law p. 235 (1980).

Private Remedies for Transfrontier Pollution Damage in Canada and the United States: A Comparative Survey, 19 University of Western Ontario L. Rev., p. 35 (1981).

The 34th Session of the International Law Commission, 77 Am. J. Int'l L. 323 (1983).

International Environmental Law and the Work of the International Law Commission, in [1983], Proceedings of The American Society of International Law, p. 414 (1983).

The Work of the International Law Commission Relating to the Environment, 11 Ecology LQ 189 (1983).

The 35th Session of the International Law Commission, 78 Am. J. Int'l L. 457 (1984).

Judicial Control of Administrative Authorities: A New Development in Eastern Europe, 18 Int'l Law, 645 (1984) (with M. Wiersbowski) (reprinted in 8 K. Redden, Modern Legal Systems Cyclopedia 157 (1985)).

Current Work of the International Law Commission, 13 (2) Int'l L. News 9 (1984).

Codification and Progressive Development: Law and the World Environment, 7 Harv. Int'l Rev. 8 (1984).

The 36th Session of the International Law Commission, 79 Am. J. Int'l L. 755 (1985).

The Contributions of the International Law Commission to International Environmental Law: An Update, 15 Env'l L. 667 (1985).

The 37th Session of the International Law Commission, 80 Am. J. Int'l L. 185 (1986).

The 38th Session of the International Law Commission, 81 Am. J. Int'l L. 668 (1987).

Introductory Note, International Law Commission, Draft Articles on Jurisdictional Immunities of States and Their Property, 26 ILM 625 (1987).

Accidents Do Happen: Hazardous Technology and International Tort Litigation, 1 Transnat'l Law 41 (1988) (excerpted in T. Schoenbaum and R. Rosenberg, *Environmental Policy Law* 1257 (1991)).

The 39th Session of the International Law Commission, 82 Am. J. Int'l L. 144 (1988).

Environment-Related Work of the International Law Commission at its 1988 Session, 18 Environmental Policy and Law, December 1988.

The 40th Session of the International Law Commission, 83 Am. J. Int'l L. 153 (1989).

Recent Work of the International Law Commission on the Draft Code, paper presented at panel on the Draft Code of Offenses Against the Peace and Security of Mankind, in *Proceedings, Eightieth Annual Meeting, American Society of International Law*, 9-12 April 1986, p. 120 (1988).

The Relevance of the ILC's Work on International Watercourses, paper presented at panel on Water Resources in the Middle East: Impact on Economics and Politics, in *Proceedings, Eightieth Annual Meeting, American Society of International Law*, 9-12 April 1986, p. 261 (1988.)
The Work of the International Law Commission Relating to Transfrontier Environmental Harm, 20 *Nyu J. Int'l L. & Pol.* 715 (1988) (excerpted in T. Schoenbaum and R. Rosenberg, *Environmental Policy Law* 1249 (1991)).
The Law of International Watercourses: Some Recent Developments and Unanswered Questions, 17 *Denver J. Int'l L. & Pol'y* 505 (1989).
The Forty-First Session of the International Law Commission, 83 *Am. J. Int'l L.* 937 (1989).
Environment-Related Work of the International Law Commission at its 1988 Session, 19 *Environmental Policy & Law*, December 1989.
Remarks on panel, *International Responsibility for Manmade Disasters*, in *Proceedings, 81St Annual Meeting, American Society of International Law*, 8-11 April 1987, p. 325 (1990).
The Forty-Second Session of the International Law Commission, 84 *Am. J. Int'l L.* 930 (1990).
«International Lawmaking and Its Relevance,» paper presented at panel on *Environment, Economic Development and Human Rights: A Triangular Relationship?*, in *Proceedings, 82Nd Annual Meeting, American Society of International Law*, 20-23 April 1988, p. 55 (1990).
The International Law Commission: Its Documents and Their Relevance to International Legal Practice, 1 (No. 2) *The California International Practitioner* 20 (1989-90).
The 1990 Session of the International Law Commission, 3 (No. 3), *California International Law Section Newsletter* 1 (1990).
International Law and the Gulf War, 4 (No. 1) *California International Law Section Newsletter* 1 (1990).
Paul Reuter (1911-1990), 85 *Am. J. Int'l L.* 150 (1991).
Environment-Related Work of the International Law Commission at its 1988 Session, *Environmental Policy & Law*, December 1990.
International Organizations and the Holistic Approach to Water Problems, 31 *Nat. Res. J.* 139 (1991).
The Law of International Watercourses: Ecocide or Ecomanagement?, 59 *Revista Juridica de la Universidad De Puerto Rico* 1003 (1990).
The International Law Commission and its Efforts to Codify the International Law of Waterways, in [1990] *Swiss Yearbook of International Law*, vol. XLVII, p. 32 (1991).
The Restatement's Treatment of Sources and Evidence of International Law, 25 *Int'l Law* 311 (1991), republished in *Commentaries on the Restatement (Third) of the Foreign Relations Law of the United States* (1992), at p. 1.
The Law of International Watercourses: Theoretical and Practical Issues, Remarks as Chair of Seminar, "International Watercourses", in *Proceedings, 84Th Annual Meeting, American Society of International Law*, 28-31 March 1990, p. 228 (1991).
International Law: The Year in Review, remarks on panel, in *Proceedings, 84Th Annual Meeting, American Society of International Law*, 28-31 March 1990, p. 142 (1991).
Fresh Water, entry in [1990], *Yearbook of International Environmental Law*, Vol. 1, p. 105 (1991).
International Law Commission, entry in [1990], *Yearbook of International Environmental Law*, Vol. 1, p. 298 (1991).
The Forty-third Session of the International Law Commission, 85 *Am. J. Int'l L.* 703 (1991).
Introductory Note, United Nations: International Law Commission Report on the Draft Articles Adopted at its Forty-Third Session, 30 *ILM* 1554 (1991).
The Law of International Watercourses: The International Law Commission Completes Its Draft Articles, 22 *Environmental Policy and Law* 66 (1992).

Fresh Water, entry in [1991], 2 *Yearbook of International Environmental Law*, Vol. 2, p. 117 (1992).
International Law Commission, entry in [1991], 2 *Yearbook of International Environmental Law*, Vol. 2, p. 357 (1992).
Water, Human Rights and Sustainable Development, in *Human Rights, Sustainable Development and the Environment* 99, A. Cancado Trindade (ed.) (1992), Proceedings of the First Inter-American Seminar on Human Rights and the Environment, (1992).
A Human Right to Water: Domestic and International Implications, 5 Geo. Int'l Envtl. L. Rev. 1 (1992).
The Evolution of the Law of International Watercourses, 45 Austrian J. Pub. & Int'l L. 87 (1993).
The Work of the International Law Commission on the Law of the Non-Navigational Uses of International Watercourses, American Society Of International Law & Nederlandse Vereniging Voor Internationaal Recht, Proceedings Of The Second Joint Conference Held In The Hague, The Netherlands, 22-24 July 1993, p. 378 (1994).
The International Law Commission Adopts Draft Articles on International Watercourses, 89 American Journal of International Law 395 (1995). Translated into Chinese in the Journal of Postgraduate Studies of Zhongshan University (1996).
The International Law Commission's Draft Articles on International Watercourses: An Overview and Commentary, with R. Rosenstock, 4 Rev. Eur. Comm. & Int'l Envtl. L. 89 (1996).
Developments in Public International Law, 30 Int'l Law 287 (1996).
An Assessment of the Work of the International Law Commission, 36 Nat. Res. J. 297 (1996.)
The Harmon Doctrine One Hundred Years Later: Buried, Not Praised, 36 Nat. Res. J. 965 (1996).
Is Codification in Decline?, 20 Hastings Int'l & Comp. L.Rev. 639, *Festschrift* for S. A. Riesenfeld (1997).
The United Nations Starts Work on a Watercourses Convention, 91 Am. J. Int'l L. 374 (1997) (with J. R. Crook).
The Coming Fresh Water Crisis: International Legal and Institutional Responses, 21 Vermont L. Rev. 803 (1997).
The 1997 United Nations Convention on International Watercourses, 92 Am. J. Int'l L. 97 (1998) (with M. Sinjela).
An Overview of the U.N. Convention on the Law of the Non-Navigational Uses of International Watercourses, 20 J. Land, Resources & Envtl. L. 57 (2000).
International Water Law for the 21st Century: The Contribution of the UN Convention, 118 Water Resources Update 11 (January 2001).
Biotechnology: Some Issues of General International Law, 14 Transnat'l Law 91 (2001).
The contribution of the UN Convention on the law of the non-navigational uses of international watercourses, 1 Int'l J. Global Envtl. Issues 250 (2001) (special issue on International Water Law).
The Need for Flexibility in Freshwater Treaty Regimes, 27 Natural Resources Forum 156 (2003).
The Rule of Law Among Countries, 18 Transnat'l Law 175 (2004).
The Shrinking Dead Sea and the Red-Dead Canal: A Sisyphean Tale?, 19 Pac. McGeorge Global Bus. & Dev. LJ 259 (2006).
The Jordan River Basin: 1. Clarification of the Allocations in the Johnston Plan, 32 (1) Water Int'l 16 (2007) (with D. J.H. Phillips, S. Attili and J. S. Murray).
The Jordan River Basin: 2. Potential Future Allocations to the Co-Riparians, 32 Water Int'l 39 (2007) (with D. J.H. Phillips, S. Attili and J. S. Murray), awarded Best Paper Published in *Water International* in 2007 (shared with paper authored by M. Zeitoun).
Federal Court: The "Roadless Rule" Reinstated, 37 Envtl. Pol'y & L. 54 (2007) (with A. E. J. Frostic).

The 1997 UN Watercourses Convention: Retrospect and Prospect, 21 *Pac. McGeorge Global Bus. & Dev. LJ* 165 (2008).
The International Law Commission Adopts Draft Articles on Transboundary Aquifers, 103 *Am. J. Int'l L.* 272 (2009).
Introduction: Politics and Sovereignty over Transboundary Groundwater, 102 *ASIL Proc.* 353 (2008).
Small Capacity and Big Responsibilities: Financial and Legal Implications of a Human Right to Water for Developing Countries, 21 *Geo. Int'l Envtl. L. Rev.* 679 (2009) (with K. J. Neville).
Beyond International Water Law: Successfully Negotiating Mutual Gains Agreements for International Watercourses, 22 *Pac. McGeorge Global Bus. & Dev. LJ* 139 (2010) (with A. Grzybowski and R. K. Paisley).
Foreword, Nahid Islam, The Law of Non-Navigational Uses of International Watercourses: Options for Regional Regime-Building in Asia, p. xxv, Wolters Kluwer (2010).
Sovereignty and Cooperative Management of Shared Water Resources In a Time of Shrinking Availability: The Role of International Law, UNESCO, ISARM 2010, Conference Materials (2010).
California and Climate Change, 40 *Envtl. Pol'y & L.* 352 (2010) (with A. Frostic).
The International Law Commission's Flawed Draft Articles on the Law of Transboundary Aquifers: The Way Forward, 36 *Water International* 566 (2011).
International Commission of the Oder, Jurisdiction of, Case, in *Max Planck Encyclopedia of Public International Law*, R. Wolfrum (ed.), Oxford (2012), available at http://www.mpepil.com/.
International Watercourses, in Max Planck Encyclopedia of Public International Law, R. Wolfrum (ed.), Oxford (2012), available at http://www.mpepil.com/.
The Role of International Tribunals in Managing Coherence and Diversity in International Law, remarks on panel, *American Society of International Law*, Proceedings of the 105th Annual Meeting, 23-26 March 2011, 105 *ASIL Proc.* 167, at pp. 170, 172, 176, 178, 179, 182, 188, 189 (2012).
There's a Whole World Out There: Justice Kennedy's Use of International Sources, 44 *McGeorge L. Rev.* 201 (2013).
International Water Cooperation in the 21st Century: Recent Developments in the Law of International Watercourses, 23 *Review of European, Comparative & International Environmental Law* 4 (2014).
Dr Stephen McCaffrey on the entry into force of the 1997 Watercourses Convention, in G. Eckstein (ed.), Specially invited opinions and research report of the International Water Law Project: global perspectives on the entry into force of the UN Watercourses Convention 2014: part one, 16 *Water Policy* 1202 (2014).
UN Watercourses Convention: Implementation and Relationship to the UNECE Water Convention, 46 *Envtl. Pol'y & L.* 35 (2016).
The Human Right to Water: A False Promise?, 47 *The U. of Pac. L. Rev.* 221 (2016).
Laureate's Lecture, Elisabeth Haub Prize for Environmental Law and Diplomacy, *International Water Law in the Anthropocene*, 48 *Envtl. Pol'y & L.* 154 (2018).

On-Line Papers and Articles

Comments on the International Law Commission's Draft Articles on.
The Law of Transboundary Aquifers (2006), SSRN, included in SSRN's Top Ten download list for PIL: Treaties & Other Sources of International Law (Topic) and its Top Ten download list for Environmental Law & Policy.
The entry into force of the 1997 Watercourses Convention, blog of the International Water Law Project (www.internationalwaterlaw.org)

Translation

Kegel, *Obligation and Disposition: Should Dispositions be* Abstrakt *or* Kausal? (*Verpflichtung und Verfügung: Solen Verfüguengen abstrakt order kausal sein?*), in 81 *Beiträge zum Deutschen und Israelischen Privatrecht* 103 (1977).

Chapters

Conflict of Laws, in The US Legal System, A Practice Handbook, ch. VI at p. 119, D. Campbell and W. Hepperle (eds.) (1983).
Crimes Against the Environment, in 1 International Criminal Law 541, M. C. Bassiouni (ed.) (1986).
Expediting the Provision of Compensation to Accident Victims, in Transferring Hazardous Technologies and Substances: the International Legal Challenge, G. Handl and R. Lutz (eds.) (1989).
Transboundary Environmental Relations between Mexico and the United States, in Cross-Border Relations: European and North American Perspectives, p. 192, S. Ercmann (ed.) (1987).
Lex Lata or the Continuum of State Responsibility, and *The Objectives of a New Regime and the Means for Accomplishment*, in International Crimes Of State: a Critical Analysis of the Ilc's Draft Article 19 on State Responsibility, pp. 242 and 249, J. Weiler, A. Cassese and M. Spinedi (eds.) (1989).
International Liability and International Watercourses: The Work of the International Law Commission Relating to International Pollution, in International Law and Pollution 90-119, D. Magraw (ed.) (1991).
Water, Politics, and International Law, in Water In Crisis: A Guide to The World's Fresh Water Resources, p. 92, Peter H. Gleick (ed.), Oxford University Press (1993).
The Management of Water Resources, in The Environment after Rio: Law and Economics, p. 149, L. Campiglio et al. (eds.) (1994).
Article 5: Responsibility of States, in Commentaries on the International Law Commission's 1991 Draft Code of Crimes against the Peace and Security of Mankind 129 (1993).
The Law of International Watercourses: Present Problems, Future Trends, in Festschrift for Wolfgang Burhenne, p. 113 (1994).
International Cooperative Mechanisms Related to Transboundary Watercourses, in United Nations, Freshwater Consultative Forum, Report of The Meeting, p. 59 (1994).
Liability for Transfrontier Environmental Harm: The Relationship between Public and Private International Law, in INternationales Umwelthaftungsrecht I (International Environmental Liability Law I), pp. 81-104 (1995).
Transboundary Water Resources, in Transboundary Water Resources, Report of the Ad Hoc Expert Group Meeting on Strategic Issues concerning Transboundary Water Resources, New York, 14 May 1996, p. 7, UN Doc. WA/SEM.97/1 (1997).
Water Scarcity: Institutional and Legal Responses, in The Scarcity of Water: Emerging Legal and Policy Responses, E. H. P. Brans, E. J. de Haan, A. Nollkaemper and J. Rinzema (eds.), p. 43 (1997).
Middle East Water Problems: The Jordan River, in The Scarcity of Water: Emerging Legal and Policy Responses, E. H. P. Brans, E. J. de Haan, A. Nollkaemper and J. Rinzema (eds.), p. 158 (1997).
The UN Convention on the Law of the Non-Navigational Uses of International Watercourses: Prospects and Pitfalls, in S. M. A. Salman and L. Boisson de Chazournes (Eds.), International Watercourses: Enhancing Cooperation and Managing Conflict, Proceedings of a World Bank Seminar, World Bank Technical Paper No. 414, pp. 17-28 (1998). Reprinted in Conflict Prevention and Resolution in Water Systems, A. T. Wolf (ed.).
International Watercourses, in Hague Academy of International Law, A Handbook on International Organizations, p. 725, R-J Dupuy (ed.) (1998).
Crimes Against the Environment, in 1 International Criminal Law 983, M. C. Bassiouni (ed.), 2d ed. (1999).
International Groundwater Law: Evolution and Context, in S. M. A. Salman (ed.), Groundwater, Legal and Policy Perspectives, Proceedings of a World Bank Seminar, World Bank Technical Paper No. 456, pp. 139-162 (1999).

International Watercourses in the Jurisprudence of the World Court, in 1 *Liber Amicorum Judge Shigeru Oda*, p. 1055, Ando, McWhinney and Wolfrum (eds.) (2002).
Water Disputes Defined: Characteristics and Trends for Resolving Them, in *Resolution of International Water Disputes*, p. 49, International Bureau of the Permanent Court of Arbitration (ed.) (2003).
The Danube River Basin, in *The Multi-Governance of Water: Four Case-Studies* 79, Matthias Finger et al. (eds.), SUNY Press (2006).
The Human Right to Water, in *Water and International Economic Law* 93, E. Brown Weiss, L. Boisson DeChazournes and N. Bernasconi-Osterwalder (eds.), Oxford University Press (2005).
Water Conflict and International Law, in *Water: Values and Rights* 659, I. Khatib et al. (eds.) (2005).
Of Paradoxes, Precedents, and Progeny: The Trail Smelter *Arbitration 65 Years Later*, in *Transboundary Harm In International Law: Lessons from the* Trail Smelter *Arbitration*, p. 34, R. M. Bratspies and R. A. Miller (eds.) (2006).
Sharing Water, Sharing Benefits: Working Towards Effective Transboundary Water Resources Management, A Graduate/Professional Skills-Building Workbook, Compiled and edited by Prof. A. T. Wolf (contributor) (forthcoming 2006).
General Introduction to International and Comparative Law, in *Teacher's Manuals accompanying books in the Global Issues series*, e.g., in F. A. Gevurtz, *Teacher's Manual to accompany Global Issues in Corporate Law*, p. 3, Thomson West (2006).
Liability and compensation regimes related to environmental damage, and *Freshwater resources*, both with M. C. Zucca, Chapters 5, at p. 51 and 18, at p. 253, respectively, in *United Nations Environment Programme, Training Manual on International Environmental Law* (UNEP 2006).
Some Developments in the Law of International Watercourses, Chapter 44, in *Promoting Justice, Human Rights and Conflict Resolution through International Law*, Liber Amicorum Lucius Caflisch, p. 781, M. G. Kohen (ed.), Koninklijke Brill NV, Leiden (2007).
Doctrinal Divisions and Issues in Environmental Law, in *Encyclopedia of Law and Society: American and Global Perspectives*, D. Clark (ed.) Sage (2008) (with R. Salcido).
International Organization and the Environment, in R. Miller and R. Bratspies (eds.), *Progress in International Law* 709, Martinus Nijhoff (2008).
International Waterways and Watercourses, in P. Cane and J. Conaghan (eds.), *Oxford Companion to Law* 626 (2008).
Criminalization of Environmental Protection, in *International Criminal Law*, Vol. I, p. 1013, C. Bassiouni (ed.), 3rd ed. (2008).
The Politics of Sharing Water: International Law, Sovereignty and Transboundary Rivers and Aquifers, in K. Wegerich and J. Warner (eds.), *The Politics of Water* 18 (2010) (with K. J. Neville).
The Progressive Development of International Water Law, in F. Rocha Loures and A. Rieu-Clarke (eds.), *The UN Watercourses Convention in Force: Strengthening International Law for Transboundary Water Management*, p. 10, Routledge (2013).
The Codification of Universal Norms: A Means to Promote Cooperation and Equity?, in *International Law and Freshwater: the Multiple Challenges*, L. Boisson de Chazournes, C. Leb and M. Tignino (eds.), p. 125, Edward Elgar (2013).
Legal Protection of the Environment, with R. E. Salcido, *Comparative Law and Society*, D. S. Clark (ed.), Edward Elgar Series, Research Handbooks in Comparative Law (2012).
International Water Cooperation in the 21st Century: Recent Developments in the Law of International Watercourses, 23 RECIEL 4 (2013).
The Codification of Universal Norms: A Means to Promote Cooperation and Equity?, in *International Law and Freshwater: The Multiple Challenges*, L. Boisson de Chazournes, C. Leb and M. Tignino (eds.), p. 125, Edward Elgar (2013).

The 1997 UN Convention: Compatibility and Complementarity, in *The UNECE Convention on the Protection and Use of Transboundary Watercourses and International Lakes: Its Contribution to International Water Cooperation*, A. Tanzi, O. McIntyre, A. Kolliopoulos, A. Rieu-Clarke and R. Kinna (eds.), p. 51, Brill Nijhoff (2015).

Pollution of Shared Freshwater Resources in International Law, in *Transboundary Pollution: Evolving Issues of International Law and Policy*, p. 81, S. Jayakumar, T. Koh, R. Beckman and Hao Duy Phan (eds.), Edward Elgar (2015).

The Siren Song of Sovereignty in International Water Relations, Chapter 3 in *A History of Water*, Series III, Vol. 2, Sovereignty and International Water Law, p. 47, T. Tvedt, O. McIntyre and T. Kassa Woldetsadik (eds.), I. B. Tauris (2015).

The Evolution of International Law relating to Transboundary Waters, in *Routledge Handbook of Water Law and Policy*, p. 205, Rieu-Clarke *et al.* (eds.), Routledge (2017).

The Customary Law of International Watercourses, in *Research Handbook on Freshwater Law and International Relations*, p. 147, M. Tignino, C. Bréthaut and L. Turley (eds.), Edward Elgar (2018).

Introduction: The Path to the UN Watercourses Convention and Beyond, in L. Boisson de Chazournes, M. Moïse Mbengue, M. Tignino and K. Sangbana (eds.), *The UN Convention on the Law of the Non-Navigational Uses of International Watercourses: A Commentary*, p. 1, Oxford University Press (2018).

Intertwined General Principles, in *Research Handbook on International Water Law*, p. 83, McCaffrey, Leb and Denoon (eds.), Edward Elgar (2019).

CHAPTER 1

INTRODUCTION AND OVERVIEW

There can be no life without water. But Earth's water is distributed unevenly around the globe. While ancient human civilizations tended to arise near rivers, there are significant examples today of populations that are concentrated where water is scarce and must be imported by colossal engineering projects. In addition, much of Earth's fresh water is internationally shared, which can complicate its management. Nearly half of Earth's land surface is covered by the world's 263 international river basins; these basins generate about 60 percent of global freshwater flows; and some 40 percent of the world's population lives in them [1]. In addition, a portion of the territory of 145 countries lies in an international river basin. These facts alone hold the seeds of potential conflict [2] over this most precious resource [3]. The question to be addressed here is whether an international normative system for the regulation of human uses of fresh water has evolved, and if so, how and to what extent has it done so.

We will see that such a normative system has indeed evolved, over millennia. This development reached what may be regarded, thus far at least, as its apogee with the conclusion in 1997 of the Convention on the Law of the Non-Navigational Uses of International Watercourses [4]. The 1997 Watercourses Convention was at the time the only agreement on this subject that was open to universal participation [5], and lays down

---

1. United Nations Environment Programme, *Atlas of International Freshwater Agreements*, United Nations, 2002, p. 2.
2. See e.g. P. Gleick, "Water and Conflict", in *Occasional Paper No. 1 of the Am. Acad. Of Arts and Sci. & U. of Toronto* (Sept. 1992), and see P. Gleick, *Water in Crisis: A Guide to the World's Fresh Water Resources*, New York, Oxford Univ. Press, 1993.
3. The term "resource" will be used here to refer to fresh water, though it is anthropocentric in its implication that it refers to something that can be exploited profitably by humans. That it should not be understood in an anthropocentric sense is obvious from the fact that all living things depend on it.
4. UN Doc. A/RES/51/869, 21 May 1997, 36 *ILM* 700 (1997) (hereafter "UN Watercourses Convention").
5. The 1992 ECE Convention on the Protection and Use of Transboundary Watercourses and International Lakes, 1936 UNTS 269, 31 *ILM* 1312 (1992), has since been opened to universal participation (i.e. to UN member states outside the ECE region), by amendment adopted in 2003, which became effective in 2014. Due to a decision adopted by the parties, states outside the ECE region were permitted to accede to the Convention beginning 1 March 2016.

the basic principles of law in the field. Its provenance, including work of the International Law Commission, suggests the Convention reflects rules of general international law on the subject.

Yet, in evaluating the normative system that has developed, we must bear constantly in mind the overriding reality of our time, global climate change. The disruptions climate change has already begun to bring will present challenges to the applicability of a normative order that was developed on the basis of a different set of facts. These facts include such things as the timing and quantity of precipitation, the size of snow pack in mountains, the status of glaciers and other such natural phenomena. Both countries sharing a watercourse may need more water than it provides. If volumetric allocations are set forth in treaties that were based on pre-climate change conditions, and the quantities allocated are no longer available, the riparian States will have to make adjustments accordingly. If both agree to the adjustments, they could amend the treaty or perhaps agree to interpret it flexibly. If it is not possible to reach such an agreement, the countries will be presented with a situation that at best is a diplomatic irritant. Therefore, another question we must ask is whether the legal system that has evolved to govern the relationships between countries sharing freshwater resources – along with air, the quintessential "natural" resource – is up to the task of adapting to a world whose natural conditions are dominated by climate change. This question will be addressed in Chapter 6.

The topic of the evolution of the law of international watercourses is of interest for a number of reasons. These include the fact that water is essential to life, and everyone on Earth shares water through the hydrologic cycle; and that while the origins of the law of international watercourses can be traced considerably further back in time, as we will see, that body of law has developed largely in parallel with public international law itself, at least since the Peace of Westphalia in 1648 [6]. As complex as it is, both scientifically and legally, the topic could be summarized in a single sentence: the law of international watercourses has evolved in tandem with the uses, needs and values of human society with respect to fresh water generally, and shared freshwater resources, in particular.

The evolution of law is generally not linear or one-dimensional. It occurs in historical context and is influenced by other factors outside the field of law in question. Therefore, the effort here will be to examine

---

6. 1 CTS, p. 119 (Osnabrück) and 271 (Münster).

the evolution of the law of international watercourses from a number of different perspectives, beginning with the milestones discussed below. It is hoped that this will enrich our understanding of how and why the law in this field has evolved in the way that it has.

I. Overview of the course

This overview will begin with a review of highlights over time of the evolution of the law of international watercourses, both to provide a foretaste of what is to come and to demonstrate ways in which the law in this field has evolved. I have called these highlights "selected milestones" in the evolution of the law of international watercourses.

1. The Umma-Lagash Treaty (ca. 3100 BC)

We can begin at the beginning, with the "rock star" of all milestones: this is the treaty between the ancient Mesopotamian city-states of Umma and Lagash, preserved on the so-called "Stele of the Vultures". The stele is a stone monument with a cuneiform inscription that archaeologists and scholars agree is the oldest extant document of any kind of which we have knowledge [7]. The document is actually a treaty, which makes it also the oldest known international agreement. Its vintage is difficult to pinpoint, but is probably around 3100 BC. In any event, it is quite venerable! The treaty is between the Mesopotamian city-states of Umma, the upstream State, and its downstream neighbor, Lagash (today the city of Telloh, in southern Iraq). "Mesopotamia" is the Ancient Greek name for the region, meaning the land between the two rivers – those rivers being, of course, the Tigris and the Euphrates. Given the aridity of the area, it was entirely dependent on irrigation from Tigris and Euphrates waters, which were brought through what has been called "an elaborate system of canals and levees that inevitably require close inter-community cooperation" [8]. Customary practices were therefore developed concerning "the use of shared water resources and irrigation works . . ." [9].

---

7. On the Umma-Lagash dispute, see generally P. H. Sand, *Environmental Dispute Resolution 4,500 Years Ago: The Case of* Lagash v. Umma, YB Int'l Envtl. L., 2000, pp. 1-6. See also S. C. McCaffrey, *The Law of International Watercourses*, 3rd ed., Oxford University Press, 2019, pp. 66-67.
8. Sand (*above* footnote 7), p. 4.
9. *Ibid.*

The Umma-Lagash Treaty resolved a dispute that had resulted in hostilities between the two city-states, which continued on and off for some forty years. But what was the dispute about? Water resources, of course, but also the boundary between the two city-states. The water was drawn by Umma from a branch of the Tigris, the Shatt al-Gharraf, through a lengthy canal, or ditch, to irrigate barley crops. Umma farmed land along the canal under a lease from Lagash but repeatedly refused to pay rent that was due and owing, in the form of a portion of its barley. Lagash was the victor in the resulting hostilities and as per the then-prevailing idea of good-neighborliness, slayed the leader of Umma. In addition to setting forth the terms of the treaty, the stele depicts vultures devouring slain warriors of Umma, hence its name. A boundary stone was laid by Mesilim, the ruler of a kingdom in the region called Kish that held traditional hegemonial status among the small Sumerian States located between the Tigris and Euphrates Rivers. Mesilim served as arbitrator in the Umma-Lagash dispute and issued an award that is memorialized on the Stele of the Vultures. Also recorded there are the promises of the parties to uphold the arbitral award, which took the form of oaths sworn to the most powerful Sumerian gods, who thereby became guarantors of the treaty [10].

The Umma-Lagash dispute has been described as the first war over water [11], and the document inscribed on the stele as the first treaty [12], which contained what is viewed as the first arbitral clause. In all, a fitting place to begin our tour of significant milestones.

2. Grant to a monastery by Charlemagne (805 AD)

The second milestone came several millennia after the Umma-Lagash Treaty. This gap most probably does not mean that there were no agreements or other arrangements concerning the use of shared watercourses during that time period, but may be taken as an indication that evidence of such agreements has not yet been discovered [13]. It was

---

10. See generally Sand (*above* footnote 7); and Arthur Nussbaum, *A Concise History of the Law of Nations*, Macmillan, rev. ed. 1954, pp. 1-2.
11. H. Elver, *Peaceful Uses of International Rivers: The Euphrates and Tigris Rivers Dispute*, New York, Transnational Publishers, 2002, p. 8.
12. C. F. J. Doebbler, *Dictionary of Public International Law*, Rowman and Littlefield Publishers, Inc., 2018, p. 374 ("the oldest international treaty of which there is a reliable record").
13. Nussbaum notes that more than a millennium passed after the Umma-Lagash Treaty before the next treaty of which we have evidence was concluded. He states that "a goodly number" of treaties, whose texts are preserved on clay tablets or monuments,

a grant to a monastery of freedom of navigation on the Rhine in the year 805 by Charlemagne, then Emperor of the Romans. This grant illustrates the early importance of navigation on what we would today consider an international watercourse. It was particularly important because, as we will see in Chapter 4, the Rhine having been a boundary of the Roman Empire, it was not governed by the principle of freedom of navigation as were rivers within the empire, but was strictly controlled.

3. The Peace of Westphalia (1648)

The third milestone in the evolution of the law of international watercourses is the celebrated Peace of Westphalia of 1648, which consisted of two treaties [14] containing, among others, important provisions concerning navigation on shared waterways. For example, the Treaty of Münster opened the Lower Rhine to free navigation. More generally, the Peace of Westphalia, which ended the Thirty Years' War of religion in Europe, is also considered to be a watershed in the development of both the system of sovereign States – which also owes much to the Reformation's freeing states from the controlling influence of the Church – and the international legal system we know today, which may be thought of as taking the place of the unifying influence of the Church [15].

4. The Congress of Vienna (1815)

The fourth milestone is the Congress of Vienna of 1815 [16], which laid down a model for the regulation of navigation on international waterways that was followed by numerous agreements for at least a century. The Central Commission for the Navigation of the Rhine, which the great scholar Paul Reuter called the *doyen* of international

---

were concluded by Egyptian or Hittite rulers, and also involve Babylon and Assur. The treaties, Nussbaum reports, concern peace, alliances and boundary lines. Nussbaum (*above* footnote 10), p. 2.

14. 1 CTS, p. 119 (Osnabrück) and 271 (Münster).
15. See generally J. L. Brierly, *The Law of Nations*, 6th ed., Sir H. Waldock, Oxford, Clarendon Press, 1963, pp. 4-7. Speaking of the Reformation, Brierly states that "in one of its most important aspects [it] was a rebellion of the states against the Church", and "resulted in the decisive defeat of the last rival to the emerging unified national state". *Ibid.*, at p. 5.
16. Congress of Vienna, 9 June 1815, 1 MPT, pp. 519, 567; French text in 64 CTS p. 453.

organizations [17], and which is indeed the oldest one still in operation, was established pursuant to Article 108 of the Congress's Final Act.

5. *The first assertion of a rule concerning the non-navigational uses of international watercourses (1856)*

The fifth milestone in the evolution of the law of international watercourses is what Professor Herbert Smith found to be "the first diplomatic assertion of any rule of international law upon the question" of non-navigational uses of international watercourses [18]. This was a protest by Holland in 1856 concerning a Belgian diversion of water from the Meuse to serve the Campine Canal. The Dutch statement reads in part as follows:

> "The Meuse being a river common both to Holland and to Belgium, it goes without saying that both parties are entitled to make the natural use of the stream, but at the same time, following general principles of law, each is bound to abstain from any action which might cause damage to the other. In other words, they cannot be allowed to make themselves masters of the water by diverting it to serve their own needs, whether for purposes of navigation or of irrigation." [19]

Holland claimed that Belgium had caused damage of three kinds: diminished navigability of the Meuse, increased velocity of the current in the Zuid-Willemsvaart and flooding of land in Noord-Brabant, caused by the discharge of irrigation water [20]. Smith reports that "[t]he dispute was ultimately settled by the treaties of 1863 and 1873" [21].

6. *The "Harmon Doctrine" (1895)*

The sixth milestone is the infamous "Harmon Doctrine", articulated in 1895 by Judson Harmon, then the Attorney General of the United States, in the context of a dispute with Mexico over use of the waters of

---

17. P. Reuter, *International Institutions*, J. M. Chapman transl., New York, Praeger, 1961, p. 207. On the Central Commission, *see* G. Kaeckenbeeck, *International Rivers*, Grotius Society Publications, No. 1, London, Sweet & Maxwell, 1918, pp. 52, *et seq.*
18. H. A. Smith, *The Economic Uses of International Rivers*, London, King & Son Ltd., 1931, p. 137.
19. *Ibid.*, Appendix II, at p. 217.
20. *Ibid.*
21. *Ibid.* These treaties are excerpted by Smith at *ibid.*, pp. 162 and 165. The second treaty revises the first.

The Evolution of the Law of International Watercourses 263

the Rio Grande. This river rises in the US State of Colorado and later forms the border between the United States and Mexico for 1,240 miles before emptying into the Gulf of Mexico. In the late nineteenth century, diversions in the United States resulted in reduced flows downstream, prompting protests by Mexico. The US Government requested a legal opinion from its Attorney General, Mr Harmon, who responded in essence that the absolute territorial sovereignty the United States enjoyed over everything within its borders, including the portions of international watercourses located there, allowed it complete freedom of action with regard to the use of those waters, regardless of the effects in Mexico. Mexico, of course, disagreed. Following negotiations, the two countries concluded a treaty that resolved the dispute. The Harmon Doctrine will be discussed further in Chapter 3.

7. The 1906 Convention between Mexico and the United States

The seventh milestone is the treaty between Mexico and the United States that resolved the dispute during the course of which the Harmon Doctrine was articulated. The treaty, concluded in 1906, is entitled the "Convention concerning the *Equitable Distribution* of the Waters of the Rio Grande for Irrigation Purposes"[22]. That the object of the treaty was the equitable allocation of Rio Grande waters demonstrates how countries actually resolve disputes over shared freshwater resources and offers insight into the understanding of the two countries of what the basic, governing principle of law in the field was, even as early as 1906.

8. The US Supreme Court decision in Kansas v. Colorado *(1907)*

The eighth milestone is the 1907 United States Supreme Court decision in the case of *Kansas* v. *Colorado* [23], in which the Court required that in order to obtain relief, Kansas, the downstream State, would have to show that depletion by Colorado of the waters of the Arkansas River shared by the two States "destroy[ed] the equitable apportionment of benefits between the two States resulting from the flow of the river"[24]. Whether the Court's emphasis on equitable apportionment as the basic,

---

22. 21 May 1906, USTS No. 455, available at http://www.ibwc.gov/Files/1906 Conv.pdf.
23. *Kansas* v. *Colorado*, 206 US 46 (1907).
24. *Ibid.*, pp. 117-118.

guiding principle was influenced by the 1906 treaty between the United States and Mexico providing for the "equitable distribution" of Rio Grande waters is unknown, but it is at least a good possibility.

9. The 1909 Boundary Waters Treaty, Canada-United States

The ninth milestone is the 1909 Boundary Waters Treaty between Canada and the United States [25]. This far-sighted agreement established the International Joint Commission [26], which continues to function today and is one of the most successful joint management institutions in the field of international watercourses. The 1909 Boundary Waters Treaty was also an early agreement prohibiting "boundary waters and waters flowing across the boundary" from being polluted "on either side to the injury of health or property on the other" [27].

10. The Madrid Resolution of the Institute of International Law (1911)

The tenth milestone is a resolution of a non-governmental organization, the *Institut de Droit International* or Institute of International Law. In 1911, the Institute adopted its Madrid Resolution on International Regulations regarding the Use of International Watercourses. This pathbreaking resolution was perhaps a half-century ahead of its time in its formulation of what it referred to as

> "the rules of law resulting from the interdependence which undoubtedly exists between riparian States with a common stream [what we would today call a contiguous watercourse] and between States whose territories are crossed by a common stream".

These rules included a prohibition of utilization of a contiguous watercourse that would interfere seriously with the other State's utilization thereof; a prohibition of alterations injurious to the water; and a prohibition of withdrawing so much water that the "utilizable character" of the stream in the downstream state is seriously modified.

11. The Donauversinkung case (1927)

The eleventh milestone is a case decided by a national court. In 1927, the German *Staatsgerichtshof* decided the so-called *Donauversinkung*,

---

25. Treaty between Great Britain and the United States relating to Boundary Waters, and Questions Arising between the United States and Canada, 11 January 1909, 12 Bevans 319, USTS No. 548.
26. *Ibid.*, Article VII.
27. *Ibid.*, Article IV, para. 2, 12 Bevans 319, TS 548.

or "Sinking of the Danube" case, between the German States of Württemberg and Prussia, the plaintiffs and the State of Baden, in which the plaintiff States sought relief from this eponymous phenomenon. In a remarkable decision, the Court stated several general principles of law, including the following:

"The exercise of sovereign rights by every State in regard to international rivers traversing its territory is limited by the duty not to injure the interests of other members of the international community... The application of this principle is governed by the circumstances of each particular case. The interests of the States in question must be weighed in an equitable manner against one another. One must consider not only the absolute injury caused to the neighboring State, but also the relation of the advantage gained by one to the injury caused to the other."

This was thus another early recognition by a national court of the principle that an equitable balance of interests of the States concerned should be the objective in the governance of the relations between them.

12. The River Oder case (1929)

The twelfth milestone is the 1929 decision of the Permanent Court of International Justice (PCIJ) in the *River Oder* case [28], in which the Court articulated the doctrine of the "community of interest of riparian States". According to the Court, this community of interest

"becomes the basis of a common legal right, the essential features of which are the perfect equality of all riparian States in the user of the whole course of the river and the exclusion of any preferential privilege of any one riparian State in relation to the others".

This concept is thus the absolute opposite of a Hobbesean state of nature, where every individual actor takes whatever and as much as it can, and looks out only for itself. It is instead a fraternal doctrine of being bound together, of sharing, almost of generosity and altruism. The community of interest doctrine made clear that freedom of navigation is a two-way street: not only can upstream States navigate freely through downstream States to the sea, but downstream States are permitted to navigate freely through the territories of upstream States.

---

28. Territorial Jurisdiction of the International Commission of the River Oder (Czechoslovakia, Denmark, France, Germany, Great Britain, and Sweden/Poland), 1929 *PCIJ (Ser. A)*, No. 23, pp. 5-46 (10 September 1929).

While the *Oder* case concerned navigation rights, the International Court of Justice (ICJ) later made clear, in the *Gabčíkovo-Nagymaros Project* case, that the community of interest principle applies to non-navigational uses, as well.

13. The Trail Smelter Arbitration (1941)

The thirteenth milestone is the 1941 arbitral award in the Trail Smelter dispute between the United States and Canada [29]. While an air pollution case, the arbitration tribunal relied on US Supreme Court cases in inter-state air and water pollution cases, as permitted by the *compromis* by which the two countries submitted the dispute to arbitration. The arbitral tribunal in that case found that

"no State has the right to use or permit the use of its territory in such a manner as to cause injury by fumes in or to the territory of another or the properties or persons therein, when the case is of serious consequence and the injury is established by clear and convincing evidence".

The tribunal's holding, based in part as it was on inter-state water pollution decisions, may be applied in cases involving international watercourses, as it was, in effect, in the *Indus Waters Kishenganga Arbitration* [30] between Pakistan and India in 2013, as we shall see presently.

14. The Salzburg Resolution of the Institute of International Law (1961)

The *fourteenth* milestone is another resolution of the Institute of International Law, the 1961 Salzburg Resolution on the Use of International Non-Maritime Waters. This document provides in part that any dispute between States sharing a watercourse "shall be settled on the basis of equity, taking into consideration the respective needs of the States, as well as any other circumstances relevant to any particular case".

15. The Helsinki Rules on the Uses of the Waters of International Rivers of the International Law Association (1966)

The fifteenth milestone is the 1966 Helsinki Rules on the Uses of the Waters of International Rivers, adopted by the International

---

29. *Trail Smelter Arbitration (United States v. Canada)*, 3 RIAA 1911, 1938 (1941).
30. *Indus Waters Kishenganga Arbitration (Pakistan v. India), Record of Proceedings (2010-2013)* (hereafter *"Kishenganga Arbitration Record"*), Permanent Court of Arbitration Award Series, Case No. 2011-01 (2014).

Law Association (ILA). This was a major exercise in codification of the rules of international law relating to both navigational and non-navigational uses of international watercourses. Despite the title of the Helsinki Rules, which refers to "international rivers", they take a drainage basin approach to the subject, which was quite progressive for the time and the most science-based approach that had theretofore been adopted. Reflecting the attitude of States toward the Helsinki Rules, they have been cited by governments in diplomatic exchanges as support for States' positions in disputes concerning international watercourses.

16. The Athens Resolution of the Institute of International Law (1979)

The sixteenth milestone is the 1979 Athens Resolution of the Institute of International Law on Pollution of Rivers and Lakes and International Law. This resolution recognizes the "common interest" of States sharing international rivers and lakes "in a rational and equitable utilization of such resources through the achievement of a reasonable balance between the various interests . . .".

17. International Law Commission's draft articles on the Law of International Watercourses (1994)

The seventeenth milestone is the adoption by the International Law Commission (ILC) in 1994 of draft articles on the Law of the Non-Navigational Uses of International Watercourses after twenty-years' work on the topic. Like all ILC work, the articles reflect an effort to codify and progressively develop the law in the field.

18. Convention on the Law of the Non-Navigational Uses of International Watercourses (1997)

The eighteenth milestone in the development of the law of international watercourses is the conclusion in 1997 of the United Nations Convention on the Law of the Non-Navigational Uses of International Watercourses, which was negotiated on the basis of the ILC's articles. That the Convention is generally regarded as largely reflecting rules of general international law in the field was indicated by the International Court's reference to it several times in its 1997 judgment in the *Gabčíkovo-Nagymaros Project* case, decided only four months after the conclusion of the UN Watercourses Convention.

19. Illustrative case law

As a nineteenth and final milestone in the evolution of the law of international watercourses, I would like to refer briefly to some leading examples of the body of case law that has helped to shape it.
- An early case to which Herbert Smith has called to our attention is what he calls the "Zwillikon Dam Case"[31]. This was a decision of the Swiss Federal Court in 1878 in a dispute between private parties in which the Cantons of Aargau and Zurich intervened, giving it what Smith calls a "quasi-international character"[32]. A private firm, Biedermann Brothers, constructed a dam on the Jonabach, a stream in the village of Zwillikon, in the Canton of Zurich, to produce power for its factory. Mill owners downstream on the Jonabach, in the Canton of Aargau, complained that the Zwillikon Dam deprived them of sufficient water flow to operate their mill, arguing that they had a right to have the water of the Jonabach continue to flow as it had flowed prior to the construction of the Zwillikon Dam. The Swiss Federal Court declined to uphold the Aargau mill owners' contention. It reasoned as follows:

> "Especially where the relations among component units of a federal State are at stake, a rule of international law derived from the law of good neighborliness applies. According to that rule, the exercise of a right may not affect the right of a neighbor. The two rights are equal, and, in the event of a conflict, a reasonable arrangement has to be found on the basis of the relevant circumstances."[33]

According to Smith, the decision "essentially rests upon the principle of the 'equitable apportionment of benefits', which was later adopted by the Supreme Court of the United States"[34]. Although Smith does not name it, this decision of the US Supreme Court was almost certainly *Kansas* v. *Colorado*, the eighth milestone discussed above. But the Swiss Federal Court's holding reflects the importance of the

---
31. *Aargau* v. *Zurich*, Entsch. des Schweizerischen Bundesgerichts (1878), Vol. IV, p. 34. See Smith (*above* footnote 18), p. 39.
32. Smith, *ibid.*
33. *Aargau* v. *Zurich* (*above* footnote 31), as translated and quoted in L. Caflisch, "The Law of International Waterways and Its Sources", in *Essays in Honor of Wang Tieya*, R. St. J. Macdonald (ed.), p. 115, at p. 123, footote 42 (Martinus Nijhoff, The Hague, 1993).
34. Smith (*above* footnote 18), p. 40.

The Evolution of the Law of International Watercourses 269

fundamental principle of equality of right, which is the cornerstone of the principle of equitable and reasonable utilization.

- I have already referred to the 1929 *River Oder* case and the judgment's articulation of the community of interest principle, applied by the Court in *Gabčíkovo* to non-navigational uses. This is a fascinating and powerful concept, whose potential in cases involving international watercourses is still largely untapped. In *Gabčíkovo*, the Court cited what it called the "principle" of the community of interest in international watercourses as having been strengthened by the "[m]odern development of international law, . . . as evidenced by the adoption of the Convention of 21 May 1997 on the Law of the Non-Navigational Uses of International Watercourses by the United Nations General Assembly"[35]. The Court thus linked the 1997 Watercourses Convention with the principle of community of interest, using the Convention as evidence of the strengthening of the principle for non-navigational uses through the modern development of international law. I will have more to say about *Gabčíkovo* presently, but the Court's finding that the community of interest principle has been strengthened by the modern development of international law makes it clear that the principle, despite the Court's not having had occasion to rely on it in the interim, did not somehow perish over the period of time that had elapsed since the *Oder* case was decided. All riparian States, and perhaps others – especially with regard to navigation – therefore have an interest in common with respect to the watercourse that constitutes a "community". The idea of "community" in this context connotes a shared interest, to be sure, but also may imply an interdependence, an attitude of cooperation and even perhaps an attitude of fellowship with other relevant states due to the common interest they share with respect to the river.
- The 1957 arbitral award in the *Lake Lanoux* arbitration between France and Spain[36] was for long the leading decisional authority in the field. I will give it more detailed attention than the other

---

35. *Gabčíkovo-Nagymaros Project (Hungary/Slovakia), ICJ Reports 1997*, p. 7, at p. 56, para. 85.
36. *Lake Lanoux Arbitration (Fr. v. Spain)*, award of 16 November 1957, 12 RIAA, p. 281 (French). English translations in 24 ILR 1957 p. 101 (1961); 53 AJIL p. 156 (1959); and 1974 *YB Int'l L. Comm'n*, Vol. 2, pt. 2, p. 194 (1976). The *Lake Lanoux* case is discussed in L. Caflisch, "Règles générales du droit des cours d'eau internationaux", *Recueil des cours*, Vol. 219 (1989), p. 13, at p. 39.

cases because of its status as the *locus classicus* in the field of non-navigational uses of international watercourses.

The case involved a French hydroelectric project affecting a river, the Carol, on which France was upstream and Spain downstream. The project was complex, but is not unusual as engineers strive to move water from its natural course to locations where there is a sufficiently significant drop in elevation to produce the maximum hydroelectric power possible. In the natural state of the basin, water flowed out of Lake Lanoux, in the Eastern Pyrenees within France, via the Font Vivre stream, one of the headwaters of the Carol River, and thence into the Carol, which after flowing in a southerly direction for some twenty-five kilometers from Lake Lanoux in France, crosses the border into Spain at Puigcerda [37]. The project called for diverting water as it emerged from Lake Lanoux through a tunnel down a steep incline [38] and through a power plant on the Ariège River. After emerging from the plant the water would join the Ariège and flow north into the Garonne River and thence into the Atlantic, away from Spain. Carol waters were used by important irrigation interests in Spain; return flows and unused Carol water ultimately flowed via other rivers in a southerly direction into the Mediterranean. But France's initial version of the project involved no return of water to the Carol River despite the reliance on Carol waters by the irrigators in Spain.

Negotiations between the two countries ultimately led France to modify its project and offer to return to the Carol, from the Ariège upstream of the power plant via a tunnel, an amount of water equivalent to that which had been diverted from Lake Lanoux into the Ariège for power production. But Spain opposed any diversion at all of Lake Lanoux waters without prior agreement between the parties, arguing that the project would alter the natural conditions of the hydrographic basin of Lake Lanoux and thus make restitution of the waters to the Carol physically dependent upon human will. This would, in turn, according to Spain, result in the *de facto* preponderance of one party only, rather than in the preservation of the equality of the two parties as required by the Treaty of Bayonne and the Additional Act.

---

37. 24 *ILR*, *ibid.*, at p. 102.
38. The ILR report of the case states that according to the French Memorial, "[t]he water would be channeled through a tunnel toward the Atlantic watershed and directed to a power station where it would be run through a turbine after dropping straight from a height of 780 metres", 24 *ILR* (*above* footnote 36), p. 101.

Negotiations between the two States not having yielded a solution, the parties entered into a *compromis* providing for the submission of the dispute to arbitration. While the formulation of the question submitted to the arbitral tribunal in the *compromis* focused on whether the French project would violate the provisions of the Treaty of Bayonne and its Additional Act, the tribunal found that any interpretation of the instruments would have to be done according to international law, in light of what the tribunal called "the spirit which governed the Pyrenees treaties and the generally accepted rules of international law".

The tribunal found that the issue posed in the *compromis* gave rise to two basic questions: first, whether the French project would in and of itself constitute a violation of the 1866 Treaty and Additional Act; and second, if not, whether the implementation of the project without a prior agreement between the two countries would constitute a violation of the Treaty and Additional Act.

The tribunal ultimately concluded that the French project violated neither the Treaty of Bayonne nor the Additional Act, and that implementing the project without a prior agreement likewise violated neither instrument, interpreted in light of the applicable principles of international law.

Article 8 of the Additional Act provided that

"[a]ll still and running water, whether in the public or the private domain, shall be subject to the sovereignty of the country in which it is situated and, consequently, to that country's laws, except for such amendments as are agreed to by both Governments".

In addressing the contention that "these amendments should be interpreted restrictively, because they derogated from sovereignty", the tribunal declared that it

"could not accept so absolute a statement. Territorial sovereignty acts as a presumption. It must yield to all international obligations, whatever their origin, but only to them.

The question is, therefore, to determine what the obligations of the French Government are in this matter" [39].

Spain was, perhaps understandably, concerned that the French project made restitution of the waters to the Carol physically dependent

---

39. 1974 *YB Int'l L. Comm'n*, Vol. 2, pt. 2, p. 195, para. 1063.

upon human will [40], namely, the will of France to continue the process of restoring the same amount of water as was taken from the Carol back into that river and thence to Spain. For Spain, "the physical superiority acquired by one of the parties [was] contrary to the system of community which is sanctioned by the Act" [41]. Spain therefore argued that transfers by one riparian State of water to another basin without the consent of the other riparian were prohibited, even if an equivalent amount were returned to the basin of origin [42].

The tribunal found, however, that "withdrawal with return, as provided in the French project and proposals, is not in conflict with the Treaty and Additional Act of 1866" [43]. As to Spain's fear that France had the "physical possibility of stopping the flow of the Lanoux water or the return of an equivalent quantity of water" [44], the tribunal pointed to the French "'assurance that it will not, in any case, interfere with the regime thus established' . . ." [45]. According to the tribunal, Spain could not contend that, despite this assurance it did not have a sufficient guarantee, "for it is a well-established general principle of law that bad faith is not presumed" [46]. The tribunal summed up on this point as follows:

> "In any case, there is not, in the Treaty and Additional Act of 26 May 1866 or in the generally accepted principles of international law, a rule which forbids a State, acting to protect its legitimate interests, from placing itself in a situation which enables it in fact, in violation of its international obligations, to do even serious injury to a neighbouring State." [47]

---

40. 24 *ILR* (*above* footnote 36), p. 113. Spain argued that "the water flows today according to physical [natural] laws, whereas after the scheme has been completed its eventual equivalent will be restored solely by the work of the human will which abstracted it", *ibid.* (brackets in original).
41. *Ibid.* A similar argument was made in the *Kishenganga* case, where Pakistan argued that it was unfair that India's project allowed India to have its hand on the tap of the Kishenganga River, figuratively speaking.
42. The tribunal observed: "In reality, it seems that the Spanish thesis is twofold and covers, on the one hand, the prohibition, without the consent of the other Party, of compensation between two basins . . . and, on the other hand, the prohibition, without the consent of the other Party, of all actions that may create along with a *de facto* inequality, the physical possibility of a violation of law", 1974 *YB Int'l L. Comm'n*, Vol. 2, pt. 2, p. 196, para. 1064.
43. 1974 *YB Int'l L. Comm'n*, Vol. 2, pt. 2, p. 196, para. 1064. Today, there could be fears of biota transfer from the Ariège which were not found in Lake Lanoux water and which could affect farming operations in Spain.
44. *Ibid.*
45. *Ibid.*
46. *Ibid.*
47. *Ibid.*

The Evolution of the Law of International Watercourses 273

On the question of whether a "preliminary agreement" was required before France could execute its project, the tribunal made the following general observation on the nature of the obligations Spain alleged to be incumbent on France.

"[T]o evaluate in its essence the need for a preliminary agreement, it is necessary to adopt the hypothesis that the States concerned cannot arrive at an agreement. In that case, it would have to be admitted that a State which ordinarily is competent has lost the right to act alone as a consequence of the unconditional and discretionary opposition of another State. This is to admit a 'right of consent', a 'right of veto', which at the discretion of one State paralyzes another State's exercise of its territorial competence." [48]

Having made clear why a requirement of a prior agreement would be contrary to the right of a State to exercise its competence within its territory, the tribunal proceeded to explain the requirements of international law in such a case:

"[I]nternational practice prefers to resort to less extreme solutions, limiting itself to requiring States to seek the terms of an agreement by preliminary negotiations without making the exercise of their competence conditional on the conclusion of this agreement." [49]

The tribunal made clear that this was an obligation to engage in good-faith negotiations, not to reach an agreement through negotiations [50].

The tribunal then made some observations concerning the case before it that are of general applicability in the relations between States sharing watercourses:

"[W]hile admittedly there is a rule prohibiting the upper riparian State from altering the waters of a river in circumstances calculated to do serious injury to the lower riparian State, such a principle has no application to the present case . . . In fact, States today are well aware of the importance of the conflicting interests involved in the industrial use of international rivers and of the necessity of reconciling some of these interests with others through mutual concessions. The only way to achieve

---
48. *Ibid.*, p. 197, para. 1065.
49. *Ibid.*
50. *Ibid.*

these adjustments of interest is the conclusion of agreements on a more and more comprehensive basis . . . [T]he rule that States may use the hydraulic power of international waterways only if a *preliminary* agreement between the States concerned has been concluded cannot be established as a customary rule or, still less, as a general principle of law." [51]

The importance of this decision derives largely from the fact that it was the first case that addressed fully issues concerning non-navigational uses of international watercourses, and remained the only one for forty years, until the *Gabčíkovo-Nagymaros Project* case, discussed next, was decided by the International Court in 1997. But the case is also important because of the careful and nuanced way the tribunal treated it, dealing for the first time with fundamental issues such as the effect of territorial sovereignty and the degree to which a downstream State can influence, or even stop, a project proposed by an upstream State on a shared watercourse.

– The next case, to which I have just referred, is the *Gabčíkovo-Nagymaros Project* case between Hungary and Slovakia, decided in 1997 by the International Court of Justice [52]. This case also involved a hydroelectric power scheme, this time on the Danube, largely where it forms the border between the two parties, Hungary and Slovakia. The project was provided for in a 1977 treaty between the two countries. For various reasons, including popular protests against the project in Hungary as the influence of the Soviet Union in Eastern Europe plummeted in the late 1980s and ultimately vanished with the USSR itself, Hungary attempted to terminate the 1977 Treaty to free itself from the project.

To pick out only one interesting feature of a case that is full of them, the Court, in addressing the effect of Hungary's attempted suspension and withdrawal of its consent to the project, stated that this "constituted a violation of Hungary's legal obligations", and continued, "but that cannot mean that Hungary forfeited its *basic right* to an equitable and reasonable sharing of the resources of an international watercourse" [53]. The Court found that Slovakia's having unilaterally implemented the upstream portion of the project by constructing

---

51. *Ibid.*, para. 1066 (emphasis in original).
52. *Gabčíkovo-Nagymaros Project (Hungary/Slovakia), ICJ Reports 1997*, p. 7, reprinted in 37 *ILM* 162 (1998).
53. *Ibid.*, at p. 54, para. 78 (emphasis added).

its own dam on the river where it is wholly within Slovak territory constituted a breach of Slovakia's obligations. Thus, even assuming Hungary had successfully terminated its treaty obligations – which the Court found that it had not – this would not affect what the Court called its "basic right" to an equitable and reasonable sharing of the resources of an international watercourse – there, the Danube River.

- The *San Juan River* cases [54] are a series of three cases between the same parties, Costa Rica and Nicaragua, and concerning the same watercourse, the San Juan River. They are the *Navigational and Related Rights* case; the *Case concerning Certain Activities Carried Out by Nicaragua in the Border Area*; and the *Case concerning Construction of a Road in Costa Rica Along the San Juan River* [55]. The latter two cases were joined by the Court and decided together, though the Court discussed and analyzed each case separately in its judgment. In *Navigational and related Rights*, the Court used evolutionary interpretation to determine the meaning in 2009 of the phrase *"con objetos de comercio"* in the 1858 Treaty between the two countries. In *Certain Activities*, the Court found that Nicaragua had unlawfully entered the territory of Costa Rica in the delta area of the San Juan and granted relief for certain alterations made there that had impacts on environmental services. And in the *Road* case the Court declined to grant Nicaragua relief for Costa Rica's having caused additional sediment to enter the river by the construction of a road along the river's right (Costa Rican) bank. The situation was somewhat unusual, as the border between the countries follows the right bank of the river rather than either of the more usual features for demarcating a border, the median line, or the *Thalweg* (the deepest navigable channel). The three cases demonstrate the Court's willingness to consider detailed scientific testimony by experts, interpret treaties in an evolutionary way – giving the terms a meaning that makes sense in the present rather than one that may have been more likely over a century ago – and compensate parties for such

---

54. *Dispute regarding Navigational and Related Rights (Costa Rica v. Nicaragua)*, *ICJ Reports 2009*, p. 213 (hereinafter *Navigational and Related Rights*); *Certain Activities Carried Out by Nicaragua in the Border Area (Costa Rica v. Nicaragua)*, and *Construction of a Road in Costa Rica Along the San Juan River (Nicaragua v. Costa Rica)*, judgment of 16 December 2015, *ICJ Reports 2015*, p. 665. See also *Certain Activities Carried Out by Nicaragua in the Border Area (Costa Rica v. Nicaragua), Compensation Owed by the Republic of Nicaragua to the Republic of Costa Rica*, judgment of 2 February 2018, available at http://www.icj-cij.org/files/case-related/150/150-20180202-JUD-01-00-EN.pdf.
55. *Ibid.*

things as the loss or degrading of environmental services, something that would have been unheard of in the past. In addition, the importance of wetlands and their protection was strongly endorsed by the Court, something that would have been unthinkable a century ago, when these features were considered malarial swamps that had to be drained and filled.

– *Pulp Mills on the River Uruguay* [56], a suit by Argentina against Uruguay, was the first major environmental case to come before the International Court. In the end it involved only one pulp mill, situated in Uruguay on the left bank of the river. Pulp mills, which require large quantities of water and whose effluent is noxious if untreated, are notorious for being sources of river pollution. Today, however, pulp mill technology has advanced to the point that it is possible to treat and render largely unharmful a plant's effluent before it is released back into the river. In this case the Court found that, while Uruguay had breached its procedural obligations under the 1975 treaty between the parties (the Statute of the River Uruguay), it had not been breached its substantive obligations under that agreement. Importantly, the Court observed that "the principle of prevention [of transboundary harm], as a customary rule, has its origins in the due diligence that is required of a State in its territory". Perhaps most notably, the Court found that the obligation to protect and preserve under the 1975 treaty

> "ha[d] to be interpreted in accordance with a practice, which in recent years has gained so much acceptance among States that it may now be considered a requirement under general international law to undertake an environmental impact assessment where there is a risk that the proposed industrial activity may have a significant adverse impact in a transboundary context, in particular, on a shared resource" [57].

(The Court clarified later, in the *Road* case, that the obligation to conduct an environmental impact assessment applied generally, not only to "industrial" activities [58].)

---

56. *Pulp Mills on the River Uruguay (Argentina v. Uruguay), ICJ Reports 2010*, p. 14.
57. *Ibid.*, at p. 83, para. 204.
58. *Construction of a Road in Costa Rica Along the San Juan River (Nicaragua v. Costa Rica)* (*above* footnote 54), para. 104.

The Evolution of the Law of International Watercourses 277

- The *Indus Waters Kishenganga Arbitration*[59] is a final case that illustrates factors influencing the evolution of the law. It is the most important arbitration in the field of international watercourses since *Lake Lanoux*. The case was brought by Pakistan against India before an arbitral tribunal set up under the 1960 Indus Waters Treaty[60]. The Court of Arbitration was a star-studded seven-member panel[61] that included then-present and former members of the International Court of Justice. It was presided over by a former President of the International Court who, before his ascension to that body, had served as special rapporteur for the work of the International Law Commission on International Watercourses[62]. Interestingly, as required by the treaty, the panel also included an Engineer Arbitrator as one of the three neutral arbitrators. This provision was presumably put in place due to the highly technical provisions in the many annexes to the treaty, which itself was negotiated largely by engineers[63]. Pakistan contended that the Kishenganga Dam and hydropower plant project being built by India violated the treaty. Pakistan was developing a hydropower project downstream on the same river and was also concerned that India's project − which, as in *Lake Lanoux*, diverted Kishenganga River water to a power plant in another basin − would take water away from its plant. The tribunal ruled in 2013 that India's dam was consistent with the 1960 treaty but that a sediment control technique India had planned to use to cope with the heavy sediment load carried by rivers such as the Kishenganga that originate in the Himalayas, was inconsistent with the treaty. Pakistan made environmental arguments to justify its position that more water should be released through the Kishenganga Dam even though the 1960 treaty said nothing about environmental protection, having been concluded before the advent of environmental consciousness in many countries. But the Court of Arbitration, noting the treaty's provision for the use by the Court of customary international law in interpreting the treaty, observed that the duty to

---

59. *Indus Waters Kishenganga Arbitration (Pakistan v. India), Kishenganga Arbitration Record* (above footnote 30), p. 292, para. 452.
60. Indus Waters Treaty, 19 September 1960, 419 *UNTS* 290.
61. This was the first time in the 115-year history of the Permanent Court of Arbitration, which acted as Registry for the case, that a seven-member tribunal was constituted. *Kishenganga Arbitration Record, ibid.*, p. xi.
62. This was S. M. Schwebel, appointed President of the Court of Arbitration by the UN Secretary-General.
63. See e.g. N. D. Gulhati, *Indus Waters Treaty*, Bombay, Allied Press, 1973, p. 11.

avoid transboundary environmental harm had been recognized in the *Trail Smelter* arbitration [64] in 1941, "[w]ell before the [Indus Waters] Treaty was negotiated" [65]. The Court of Arbitration also referred to the International Court of Justice's statement in the *Gabčíkovo -Nagymaros Project* case that "new norms have to be taken into consideration, and . . . new standards given proper weight" [66] in cases involving "interfere[nce] with nature" "[o]wing to new scientific insights and to a growing awareness of the risks for mankind – for present and future generations – of pursuit of such interventions at an unconsidered and unabated pace . . ." [67]. The Kishenganga Court of Arbitration concluded: "It is therefore incumbent upon this Court to interpret and apply this 1960 Treaty in light of the customary international principles for the protection of the environment in force today" [68]. This determination supported the Court's finding that India was required to release a certain environmental flow through the dam [69] even though, due to the design of India's project, that flow would be unavailable to the project's power plant. For present purposes, it is striking to note how the Court of Arbitration in effect breathed new life into the 1960 Treaty by interpreting it to reflect "new scientific insights" and an "awareness of the risks for mankind – for present and future generations – of pursuit of such interventions at an unconsidered and unabated pace . . ." [70].

This concludes the review of what may be considered milestones in the evolution of the law of international watercourses. It is hoped that this overview has illuminated some of the many ways in which the law of international watercourses has evolved.

The present examination of the evolution of the law of international watercourses will be presented in six parts, or chapters. After this Introduction and Overview, which forms Chapter 1, Chapter 2 will provide information on the subject matter that is regulated by the law of international watercourses: fresh water. There is an intimate

---

64. 13 RIAA 1905 (1941).
65. *Kishenganga Arbitration Record* (*above* footnote 30), p. 290, para. 448.
66. *Ibid.*, p. 292, para. 452, citing *Gabčíkovo-Nagymaros Project*, 1997 ICJ, 7, at p. 78.
67. *Gabčíkovo-Nagymaros Project*, 1997 ICJ, p. 7, at p. 78.
68. *Kishenganga Arbitration Record* (*above* footnote 30), p. 292, para. 452.
69. The Court of Arbitration in its Final Award "fixe[d] the minimum flow to be released downstream from the [Kishenganga Dam] at 9 cumecs", *ibid.*, p. 458, para. 116.
70. *Ibid.*, p. 292, para. 452, quoting from *Gabčíkovo-Nagymaros Project* (*above* footnote 66), at p. 78.

The Evolution of the Law of International Watercourses 279

connection between science and law in this field, similar perhaps to that prevailing in the law of the sea. One of the inevitable consequences of the physical nature of water and its distribution globally through the hydrologic cycle is interdependence between the nations of the world, all of which rely on it. But it is not only the hydrologic cycle that binds nations together as a physical phenomenon. Global climate change is also working enormous and sometimes very harmful changes to the climate and water systems our civilizations have been built on and whose stability and predictability they rely upon – characteristics that are now a thing of the past. These challenges, which will require accelerated evolution, or development, of international water law to meet new threats and conditions, will also be noted in Chapter 2.

Chapter 3 of the course will review briefly the history of human uses of fresh water. It is well known that ancient civilizations, often located in arid regions, were frequently built around the fresh water they used to irrigate their crops, leading them to be known as the fluvial civilizations [71]. This was true of ancient Mesopotamia – the "Land between the Rivers" – and ancient Babylon, which was built along both banks of the Euphrates, and it was also true, of course, of ancient Egypt and the Nile. In addition, these waters were often shared with other political entities. Fresh water supported not only the lives of these populations, but also the economies of the city-states in which they lived. It has been argued with some force that the ancient political structures of which we have evidence seem to have grown up, and actually to have been designed, chiefly to make the most efficient use of water for purposes of irrigated agriculture [72]. Many lay people are aware of this through the popularization, in books and films, of the Egypt of the Pharaohs and the reliance of that civilization on the Nile for everything from drinking water and other domestic uses to transportation and, predominantly, agriculture. It was the great, and perhaps the original, historian Herodotus who called Egypt the "gift of the Nile" because Egypt could not have existed in the desert without the nourishment provided by that iconic river – which we call today an international watercourse. And the "international" element meant that principalities and even kingdoms sought stability *vis-à-vis* one another. The alternative was a Hobbesean state of nature, characterized by no accepted rules governing the behavior of political entities and a

---
71. L. Teclaff, *Water Law in Historical Perspective*, Buffalo, W. S. Hein, 1985, p. 15.
72. *Ibid.*

resulting *bellum omnium contra omnes* – a war of all against all. This quest for stability based upon a consistent normative order proceeded in fits and starts but was to be given a strong boost by the establishment of the modern system of nation-states around the time of the Peace of Westphalia in 1648 [73]. Chapter 3 will trace this development into the twentieth century.

Chapter 4 will explore the evolution of the legal regulation governing navigation on international watercourses. Water as a fluvial highway was also tremendously important historically. We will see that there was what might be considered an "international" aspect of navigation even in ancient times, as vessels passed through stretches of rivers that were controlled by other rulers or were banned altogether in an important reach of a river governed by a kingdom that did not wish foreign vessels to intrude into territory it controlled. Like irrigation and the use of water for drinking and other domestic uses, navigation was a primordial use of rivers, the best known of which – such as the Nile, the Tigris and the Euphrates – may be viewed as having been "international" in the sense that they were shared by different political entities, whether city-states, principalities, tribes or others. Navigation attracted attention and may have cried out for regulation earlier than non-navigational uses because unlike the latter it can entail a physical entry by an alien craft into the territory of another political unit. This forced societies to confront the problem of whether, and if so, under what conditions, a foreign vessel would be permitted to enter a given ruler's territory. Navigation has thus long been regulated by normative orders. Chapter 2 will trace the development of these systems, from fragmented rules – sometimes even on the same river – to more uniform regimes. Navigation was a particularly important use in Europe when transportation on land was difficult, and even thereafter, prior to the construction of good roads and the development of motorized transportation on land. It remains an important use today, even in such highly developed regions as Western Europe and North America, where constant shipping traffic can be observed on the Rhine, the Danube, the Great Lakes, the Mississippi and other international watercourses [74].

---

73. The two treaties comprising the Peace of Westphalia were those of Osnabrück, 1 CTS, p. 119, and Münster, *ibid.*, p. 271.

74. Regarding the Mississippi's status as an international watercourse, *see, e.g.*, University of Iowa Libraries, "Mississippi River: The Life and Landscape of The Father of Water", stating that the river "drains three-fifths of the continent, including thirty-one states and two Canadian provinces", available at https://www.lib.uiowa.edu/exhibits/previous/mississippi/.

The Evolution of the Law of International Watercourses   281

Chapter 5 will discuss the evolution of today's legal regime governing non-navigational uses of international watercourses. It has already been seen, in the form of the Stele of the Vultures, that the most ancient evidence we have of what we may call inter-state water relations concerned not navigation but non-navigational uses – the particular non-navigational use in the case of the dispute between Umma and Lagash having been irrigation. Beginning with the great "fluvial civilizations"[75] of ancient Mesopotamia, Egypt and China, Chapter 5 will examine why the legal regime of non-navigational uses of international watercourses was somewhat slower to develop than that of navigational uses. It will look at six indicia of the evolution of the law governing non-navigational uses beginning with how the subject matter of legal regulation is conceived, and including the way shared water resources are managed, the way in which nations assign priorities to different uses of international watercourses, from the river as a means of waste disposal to the river as an essential part of nature's life support systems, and the shift among the basic, governing principles of the law of international watercourses.

Finally, Chapter 6 will draw some conclusions from the foregoing surveys and venture a brief look into the future. Will the law of international watercourses be capable of responding to the overriding challenge of climate change? Is the treaty, relied on for millennia to stabilize water relations, obsolete in this time of climate change, which disrupts many factors treaties are meant to stabilize? Chapter 6 will consider these questions in a preliminary way.

The following definitions are offered of terms that will be used throughout the course.

II. Definitions

- *Watercourse*: A system of surface waters and groundwaters constituting by virtue of their physical relationship a unitary whole [76].
- *International watercourse*: A watercourse, parts of which are situated in different States [77].
- *Successive international watercourse*: A watercourse which flows from one State, across an international boundary, into another State,

---
75. See Teclaff (*above* footnote 71).
76. This definition is taken from Article 2 *(a)* of the Convention on the Law of the Non-Navigational Uses of International Watercourses, 21 May 1997, UN Doc. A/RES/51/869, 21 May 1997, 36 *ILM* 700 (1997).
77. *Ibid.*, Article 2 *(b)*.

i.e., a watercourse that traverses a boundary between States and thus flows successively from one State into another.
– *Contiguous international watercourse*: A watercourse that forms a boundary between States and is thus contiguous to the States on either side of the boundary [78].
– *Aquifer*: A water-bearing geological formation. The water contained in the formation is commonly referred to as "groundwater".
– *Transboundary aquifer*: An aquifer, parts of which are situated in different States [79].
– *Riparian State* or *riparian*: A State that shares freshwater resources, whether in the form of, e.g. a river, lake, aquifer, or glacier, with another State or States. The term is thus broader than the strict meaning of the word "riparian", which refers to a legal entity whose territory extends to the banks of a watercourse, or, e.g. in the expression, "riparian vegetation", vegetation on the bank of a watercourse.

---

78. The relatively rare situation of a river like the San Juan, which runs along the boundary between Costa Rica and Nicaragua, the boundary being located on the right (Costa Rican) bank of the river, would be covered by the definition of "contiguous international watercourse".
79. This definition is adapted from Article 2 *(c)* of the draft articles on the law of transboundary aquifers adopted by the International Law Commission in 2008. 2008 *YB Int'l L. Comm'n*, Vol. 2, pt. 2, p. 19, at p. 20, UN General Assembly resolution 63/124, 11 December 2008, Annex.

CHAPTER 2

FRESH WATER AND ITS USE BY HUMANS

I. Introduction

Earth has been called the "blue planet" because some 70 percent of it is covered by water. It thus appears blue when seen from space. And this does not count the fresh water that is the main subject of these lectures: some 97.5 percent of the water on Earth is salt water. Only 2.5 percent is fresh water; and of that 2.5 percent, just three-tenths of 1 percent is held in lakes and rivers. So, what these lectures address is the efforts of human societies over time to regulate legally the use of only a tiny fraction of the water on Earth.

Most of the water on Earth is in constant motion within the hydrologic cycle, binding together all living things, because all of them rely on it. A drop of water that falls into the sea as rain today may evaporate into the atmosphere tomorrow and shortly thereafter fall onto land as rain or snow. It may make its way from there into a stream, then a river and then ultimately flow back into the sea. This verbal and much simplified snapshot of the hydrologic cycle makes clear that water is perhaps the quintessential shared natural resource.

Life as we know it would be impossible without water. Scientists search for signs of water on other planets as indications that there may be life there. Speaking of its efforts to find life on Mars, the United States National Aeronautics and Space Administration (NASA) observed: "Water is key because almost everywhere we find water on Earth, we find life."[80] Humans are composed mostly of water[81], and while we can live without food for three weeks or more, we can only survive for some three days without water[82].

In addition to its existential importance to all life on Earth, water is also essential in terms of its many uses by humans. We in fact use it

---

80. NASA, "Mars Exploration: Programs & Missions", available at http://mars.nasa.gov/programmissions/overview/.
81. Institute of Medicine, *Dietary Reference Intakes For Water, Potassium, Sodium, Chloride, and Sulfate*, Washington, DC: The National Academies Press, 2005, available at www.nap.edu/read/10925/chapter/1.
82. *Water in diet*, National Institute of Health (last updated 2 July 2021), available at https://medlineplus.gov/ency/article/002471.htm#.

for practically everything imaginable, as well as some things that may not be imaginable, at least to most laypeople [83]. Domestic uses, such as drinking, cooking, bathing, washing and sanitation, are the most obvious ones, but agricultural and industrial uses, power production, recreation and navigation are also quite important in the lives of humans today. The "water content" of various common items can be quite surprising. For example, it takes about 2,498 liters of water (about 660 gallons) to produce the humble hamburger, and around 2,494 liters (or some 659 gallons) for a cotton shirt – which can be taken as establishing that cotton plants are "thirstier" than cows, in terms of their relative water consumption [84]. And speaking of thirsty crops, it takes about one gallon of water (almost four liters) to produce a single almond and some five gallons (about nineteen liters) to produce a walnut [85]. Given the acreage of almond orchards in my home state of California, it is said that almonds grown there use as much water annually as Los Angeles, a city of some four million people, does in three years [86].

If we were to imagine that the almonds were grown in an upstream country and were irrigated with water from a river that flowed to Los Angeles, which was in another country, the conditions for a possible conflict between the upstream and downstream uses would be present.

---

83. For example, an average dairy cow can drink up to fifty gallons of water per day and it takes 683 gallons of water to produce just one gallon of milk. *See Meat and the Environment*, People for the Ethical Treatment of Animals (PETA), available at https://www.peta.org/issues/animals-used-for-food/meat-environment/ (last visited 23 July 2021). For more statistics and sources of information, *see* Marcelo Gleiser, "Take A Shorter Shower – It's World Water Day", NPR (22 March 2015, 12:37 PM ET), https://www.npr.org/sections/13.7/2015/03/22/394652422/take-a-shorter-shower-its-world-water-day. See also *20 Amazing Water Facts*, Able Skills, available at https://www.ableskills.co.uk/infographics/water-facts/ (last visited 23 July 2021).

84. *What is the Water Footprint of. . .?*, Water Footprint Calculator (20 December 2019), https://www.watercalculator.org/footprint/what-is-the-water-footprint-of/. And see generally Water Footprint Network, https://www.waterfootprint.org/en/ (last visited 23 July 2021). See also Peter H. Gleick *et al.*, *The World's Water 2008-2009: The Biennial Report on Freshwater Resources*, Washington, Covelo, London, Island Press, 2008, p. 337, available at https://worldwater.org/wp-content/uploads/2013/07/Table19.pdf.

85. Specifically, "to grow one almond requires 1.1 gallons of water, and to grow a pound takes 1,900 gal/ lb". See PAESTA, *How much water does it really take to grow almonds?*, Apple Podcasts: Episode 43, 6 August 2017, available at https://podcasts.apple.com/us/podcast/what-are-impacts-climate-change-on-water-resources/id1017828453?i=1000390744535.

86. J. Lurie, "California's Almonds Suck as Much Water Annually as Los Angeles Uses in Three Years", *Mother Jones* (12 January 2015), available at www.motherjones.com/environment/2015/01/almonds-nuts-crazy-stats-charts/. See also EcoMotion, https://ecomotion.us/almond-farming-and-california-water/ (last visited 26 July 2021).

The Evolution of the Law of International Watercourses 285

Of course, whether such a conflict existed would depend to a large extent upon whether the flow of the river could support all uses, in both the upstream and the downstream country. This hypothetical fact situation is actually not too far removed from reality, except that the two "countries" are Northern and Southern California and the "stream" is made up of two enormous projects that convey water from north to south in hundreds of miles of cement-lined canals. We will revisit these projects momentarily. The point here is that land uses, especially in upstream states [87], that require water but use excessive quantities, can give rise to disputes between riparian states.

The transfer of water from Northern to Southern California is an obvious recipe for conflict between the two parts of the state, and seemingly interminable conflict there has in fact been. We will be examining later whether international law has evolved to deal with a situation in which the two parts of the state were separate countries.

Water itself has become industrialized and commercialized. When I was growing up I do not recall that there was any such thing as commercially bottled water for personal use. I was fortunate to live in a place where water treated to drinking quality was piped into every home. So, one just turned on the tap and drank the water that flowed from it. But today, and for quite some time now, a feature of life has been the ubiquitous little plastic bottles filled with drinking water, the source of which is often obscure and may be simply a tap, drawing water from the public supply. Whatever the source, the value of the bottled water industry is slated to reach 334 billion US dollars by the year 2023 [88]. There are already conflicts within countries over the right of bottled water companies to withdraw sometimes unlimited quantities of "spring water", or groundwater, for their bottled water enterprises [89]. If the source were in a border area, it is quite possible that withdrawals in one country would draw down an aquifer that straddled the border, affecting the neighboring country.

---

87. "Especially" in upstream states because as we will soon see, "harm", in the form of foreclosure of future uses, can also travel upstream. See note 100 *below* and accompanying text. See generally McCaffrey (*above* footnote 7), pp. 471-477.
88. "Global Bottled Water Market 2018-2023: A $334 Billion Opportunity, Driven by Heath & Wellness Concerns", *Business Wire* (13 August 2018, 10:14 AM EDT), available at https://www.businesswire.com/news/home/20180813005378/en/Global-Bottled-Water-Market-2018-2023-334-Billion.
89. T. Perkins, "The fight to stop Nestlé from taking America's water to sell in plastic bottles", *The Guardian* (29 October 2019), available at https://www.theguardian.com/environment/2019/oct/29/the-fight-over-water-how-nestle-dries-up-us-creeks-to-sell-water-in-plastic-bottles.

A critical characteristic of water that is important to bear in mind in this time of change is that its quantity is finite, and does not change. The quantity of water on Earth has been the same for billions of years, and there is nothing to indicate that the overall supply will expand or contract, in either the near or the distant future [90]. Water is endlessly recycled, both naturally through the hydrologic cycle and by humans, through treatment and reuse. It has thus been observed, rather startlingly, that "Last night's potatoes may have boiled in what was, ages ago, the bath water of Archimedes" [91].

When this fixed supply is juxtaposed against steadily increasing demand due to, among other things, population growth, the seriousness of the problem and urgent need for solutions come into sharp focus. Development of a State's water resources may, of course, occur even without population growth, but growth in demand due to greater numbers of people can be an important driver of increased water use and expanded efforts to enhance supply. According to the United Nations World Water Development Report for 2019, "Water use has been increasing worldwide by about 1% per year since the 1980s, driven by a combination of population growth, socio-economic development and changing consumption patterns" [92]. But the most highly developed countries have actually seen a decline in their water consumption, due in part to technological advances [93].

While birth rates tend to decrease as a country's standard of living improves [94], population growth continues its seemingly inexorable march upward. According to the UN Population Division, "The world's population is expected to increase by 2 billion persons in the next 30 years, from 7.7 billion currently to 9.7 billion in 2050 and could peak at

---

90. L. B. Leopold and K. S. Davis, *Water*, New York, Time Inc., 1966, p. 33. This fact is consistent with the law of the indestructability of matter, or conservation of mass.
91. *Ibid*.
92. United Nations, World Water Development Report 2019, available at www.unwater.org.
93. W. K. Stevens, "Expectations Aside, Water Use in the US Is Showing Decline", *New York Times* (10 November 1998), available at https://www.nytimes.com/1998/11/10/us/expectation-aside-water-use-in-us-is-showing-decline.html. See also "Per Capita Water Use in the US Drops", *Pacific Institute* (28 October 2009), available at https://www.watereducation.org/aquafornia-news/pacific-institute-capita-water-use-u-s-drops-analysis-new-national-water-use-data. See also K. Donnelly and H. Cooley, "Water Use Trends in the United States", *Pacific Institute* (April 2015), available at https://pacinst.org/wp-content/uploads/2015/04/Water-Use-Trends-Report.pdf.
94. A. Kaps and H. Dembowski, "Lives are now 20 years longer", *D+C* (August 29, 2018), available at https://www.dandc.eu/en/article/birth-rates-go-down-standards-living-improve.

The Evolution of the Law of International Watercourses 287

nearly 11 billion around 2100"[95]. Experts have forecast that very soon, by the year 2025, population growth alone will prevent more than thirty countries from providing their populations with at least 1,000 cubic meters of water per person per year[96]. While a minimum per capita water requirement is dependent upon a number of factors, including climate and the availability of technology to increase efficiency, 1,000 cubic meters per capita per year may actually be below the quantity required to maintain an adequate standard of living[97]. A country would generally be considered to be water scarce that had available less than 1,000 cubic meters of renewable freshwater per person per year[98]. It has been estimated that, again, by 2025, "one out of every three people – almost three and a quarter billion people – will live in as many as 52 countries plagued by water stress or chronic water scarcity"[99]. The expression "water stress" is a broader concept than water scarcity. It

---

95. "World Population Prospects 2019", *United Nations*, available at https://population.un.org/wpp/Graphs/DemographicProfiles/Line/900 (last visited 21 August).
96. See P. Gleick, "Water in the twenty-first Century", in *Water in Crisis* (*above* footnote 2), at pp. 105-106.
97. Falkenmark and Lindh give a figure of 1,205 cubic meters per year as the minimum per capita availability requirement. M. Falkenmark and G. Lindh, "Water and Economic Development", in *Water in Crisis* (*above* footnote 2), at p. 84. This quantity includes water to produce food, using best irrigation practices, and that for domestic needs. Other sources put the minimum quantity higher. According to the World Bank's Vice President for Environmentally Sustainable Development in 1995, "Generally, a country will experience periodic water stress when supplies fall below 1,700 cubic meters per person". I. Serageldin, "Water Resources Management: A New Policy for a Sustainable Future", 20 *Water International* 15, at 15 (1995). A 2003 report from the World Water Assessment Programme indicated that several developing countries have a hard time supplying the minimum annual per capita water requirement of 1,700 cubic meters of drinking water for their people. WWAP. 2003. *The United Nations World Water Development Report: Water for People, Water for Life*. United Nations World Water Assessment Programme, Paris, UNESCO (2003).
98. M. Falkenmark and C. Widstrand, "Population and Water Resources: a Delicate Balance", *Population Bulletin* (47) 3: 1-36 (1992).
99. Serageldin (*above* footnote 97), p. 15. See also United Nations Development Programme, *Human Development Report 2006, Beyond scarcity: Power, poverty, and the global water crisis* (2006); and Food and Agriculture Organization of the United Nations, *Coping with water scarcity: Challenge of the twenty-first century*, UN Water (2007). The respected Pacific Institute has defined the terms "water scarcity" and "water stress" as follows:

> "Water scarcity" refers to the volumetric abundance, or lack thereof, of water supply. This is typically calculated as a ratio of human water consumption to available water supply in a given area. Water scarcity is a physical, objective reality that can be measured consistently across regions and over time.
>
> "Water stress" refers to the ability, or lack thereof, to meet human and ecological demand for water. Compared to scarcity, "water stress" is a more inclusive and broader concept. It considers several physical aspects related to water resources, including water scarcity, but also water quality, environmental flows and the accessibility of water.

includes not only water scarcity but also such factors as water quality, environmental flows and the accessibility of water.

These figures portend possible conflicts over access to water on all levels – local, regional, national and international. The focus here is, of course, on internationally shared freshwater resources, and those will inevitably be impacted. Upstream increases in water demand due to population growth and economic development may reduce both the quantity and the quality of water available downstream. The same is true of water infrastructure development upstream, such as the construction of dams for, e.g. hydropower production. Conversely, increases in freshwater resource use downstream, whether driven by population growth or development decisions, may reduce the scope of permissible water development upstream [100]. We see this phenomenon played out in most regions of the world, and I would like to spend just a moment on it here.

The question is, can downstream uses cause upstream harm (other than to navigation, fish migration and the like)? The answer is an emphatic "yes". We begin with the fact that downstream areas, which may be States, generally develop their water resources intensively before upstream areas or States, because they are generally flatter and warmer than more mountainous upstream regions. Egypt (downstream on the Nile) and Ethiopia (upstream on the Blue Nile) are classic examples, but others abound, such as mountainous states in the Western United States upstream and Mexico downstream, with respect to both the Rio Grande and the Colorado River; and China and the Lower Mekong countries, with respect to that river. In all of these cases, later upstream development, often taking the form of dams, triggered disputes with downstream co-riparians that had long-since developed and had come to rely on shared water resources, including seasonal floods and timing of supply, often for irrigated agriculture.

The concept of foreclosure of future uses within this context is simply this: Assume that downstream State X develops the portion

---

Pacific Institute, "Defining Water Scarcity, Water Stress, and Water Risk", available at https://pacinst.org/water-definitions/.

100. This latter phenomenon, that harm conveyed through international watercourses can be a two-way street, is important to recognize. The basic idea is that future uses upstream may be legally foreclosed by development projects downstream where the latter leave no room for development upstream without breaching obligations of equitable and reasonable utilization and prevention of significant harm owed to the downstream State. See S. M. A. Salman, "Downstream Riparians Can Also Harm Upstream Riparians: The Concept of Foreclosure of Future Uses", 35 *Water International* 350, p. 350 (2010); and McCaffrey (*above* footnote 7), pp. 471-477.

The Evolution of the Law of International Watercourses 289

of an international watercourse within its territory to the point that it would be significantly harmed by any lessening of quantity or change in timing of flow due to new projects in upstream State Y. State X might then maintain that a planned use in State Y affecting the watercourse is foreclosed by State X's legal right to continue to receive the same quantity of water (and perhaps at the same time) as it had in the past and, we may assume, on the basis of which State X had developed significant infrastructure. Whether State X actually has such a right is highly debatable, but this would not prevent it from asserting that it does, and bringing to bear whatever pressure it could on State Y to stop its planned project. In this sense, harm – *legal* rather than factual harm – can travel upstream through the possible foreclosure of future upstream uses in State Y.

The controversy between Egypt, in particular [101], and Ethiopia over the "Grand Ethiopian Renaissance Dam" (GERD) is a case in point [102]. The dam, some twenty kilometers upstream on the Blue Nile from Ethiopia's border with Sudan, will be the largest dam in Africa in terms of hydropower production potential (6,000 megawatt hours, according to Ethiopia) [103]. Egypt has developed Nile waters over millennia, and has asserted it has a historic right to continue to receive the same quantity of Nile water from upstream countries on the Blue and White Niles that it has in the past. Ethiopia, on the other hand, may assert that the construction and putting into operation of the GERD is within its rights of equitable and reasonable utilization of Blue Nile waters.

The dispute has thus far focused primarily on the filling of the GERD reservoir [104]: Egypt would like it halted until further scientific studies are

---

101. The position of Sudan with respect to the dam has varied. In April 2021, BBC reported on Sudan's latest shift in attitude with respect to the GERD: "Sudan wants Ethiopia to commit to a legally binding agreement, rather than guidelines, on the amount of water retained and the timetable for filling the reservoir. It also wants clarity on how disputes will be resolved in the future." An advisor to the head of Sudan's sovereign council warned of a "water war 'that would be more horrible than one could imagine' unless the international community helped find a solution [to the GERD conflict]". "Gerd: Sudan talks tough with Ethiopia over River Nile dam", *BBC*, 22 April 2021, available at https://www.bbc.com/news/world-africa-56799672.
102. See generally Z. Yihdego, A. Rieu-Clarke and A. E. Cascão, *The Grand Ethiopian Renaissance Dam and the Nile Basin: Implications for Transboundary Water Cooperation* (Routledge, London & New York 2018); and McCaffrey (*above* footnote 7), pp. 321-322.
103. S. M. A. Salman, "The Grand Ethiopian Renaissance Dam: The Road to the Declaration of Principles and the Khartoum Document", 41 *Water International* 512, 512 (2016), available at http://dx.doi.org/10.1080/02508060.2016.1170374.
104. See generally K. G. Wheeler *et al.*, "Cooperative filling approaches for the Grand Ethiopian Renaissance Dam", 41 *Water International* 611, 611-634 (2016).

completed, and when (and if) begun, wishes it to proceed slowly, with large releases that would benefit Egypt. Ethiopia, on the other hand, would prefer a more rapid filling, so that production of hydropower could commence at an early date. The first and second filling of the reservoir have reportedly already been completed [105]. This controversy is continuing to play out at this writing.

The World Economic Forum in its Global Risk Report for 2016 identified water crises as the greatest risk facing the world over the decade lasting until 2026 [106]. While the focus more recently has been on global climate change, and properly so as we will see presently, a critical impact of climate change is that it is resulting, as predicted, in too much water in some areas (flooding [107]) and too little in others (drought [108]).

II. The impact of climate change on shared freshwater resources

The Intergovernmental Panel on Climate Change (IPCC) is the most authoritative international scientific body studying and reporting on global climate change. Its most recent full report, the Fifth Assessment

---

105. See "Ethiopia says second filling of Renaissance Dam Complete", *Al Jazeera* (19 July 2021), available at https://www.aljazeera.com/news/2021/7/19/ethiopia-says-second-filling-of-renaissance-dam-complete.
106. The Global Risks Report 2016 (World Economic Forum, 11th ed. 2016) available at https://www.weforum.org/reports/the-global-risks-report-2016. The World Economic Forum in its Global Risks Report for 2019 identified water crises as the fourth greatest risk in terms of societal impact. The Global Risks Report 2019 (World Economic Forum, 14th ed. 2019), available at http://www3.weforum.org/docs/WEF_Global_Risks_Report_2019.pdf. By the 2020 Global Risks Report, water crises had fallen to the eighth most likely risk, but the fifth greatest impact. The Global Risks Report 2020 (World Economic Forum, 15th ed., 2020), available at https://www.weforum.org/agenda/2020/01/top-global-risks-report-climate-change-cyberattacks-economic-political/. However, since water is necessary to all living things, treating it in isolation for almost any purpose can be misleading. A summary of the 2020 Report states: "for the first time the Global Risks Report is dominated by the environment." More specifically, the Report highlights "failure to mitigate and adapt to climate change as the key concern for the Forum's network of business leaders, NGOs, academics and others". *Ibid.* Water is intimately interwoven with the causes and impacts of climate change.
107. See e.g. Melissa Eddy, "Hundreds Missing and Scores Dead as Raging Floods Strike Western Europe", *New York Times* (15 July 2021), available at https://www.nytimes.com/2021/07/15/world/europe/flooding-germany-belgium-switzerland-netherlands.html; *and see* Steven Lee Myers, "A Somber Toll as Record Rain Swamps China", *New York Times*, 22 July 2021, at p. 1.
108. See Alejandra Borunda, "'Megadrought' persists in western US, as another extremely dry year develops; The long-running dry stretch rivals anything in the last 1200 years, a sign of climate-change induced 'aridification'", *National Geographic* (7 May 2021), available at https://www.nationalgeographic.com/environment/article/megadrought-persists-in-western-us-as-another-extremely-dry-year-develops.

Report (AR5), was published in 2014[109]. The Assessment Reports consist of three working group reports and a Synthesis Report[110]. Impacts, adaptation and vulnerability are dealt with by Working Group II. Chapter 3 of the report of Working Group II forming part of AR5 concerns Freshwater Resources[111]. Some of the key findings identified in that chapter are the following:

- First, "Climate change is projected to reduce renewable surface water and groundwater resources significantly in most dry subtropical regions... This will intensify competition for water among agriculture, ecosystems, settlements, industry, and energy production, affecting regional water, energy, and food security ...".
- Second, "Climate change is likely to increase the frequency of meteorological droughts (less rainfall) and agricultural droughts (less soil moisture) in presently dry regions by the end of the 21st century ... This is likely to increase the frequency of short hydrological droughts (less surface water and groundwater) in these regions ...".
- Third, "Climate change negatively impacts freshwater ecosystems by changing streamflow and water quality ...".
- Fourth, "Climate change is projected to reduce raw [untreated] water quality, posing risks to drinking water quality even with conventional treatment ... The sources of the risks are increased temperature, increases in sediment, nutrient and pollutant loadings due to heavy rainfall, reduced dilution of pollutants during droughts, and disruption of treatment facilities during floods".
- Fifth, "In regions with snowfall, climate change has altered observed streamflow seasonality, and increasing alterations due to climate change are projected ...".
- And sixth, "Because nearly all glaciers are too large for equilibrium with the present climate, there is a committed water resources change during much of the 21st century, and changes beyond the committed change are expected due to continued warming; in glacier-fed rivers,

---

109. See IPCC, 2014: Climate Change 2014: Synthesis Report. Contribution of Working Groups I, II, and III to the Fifth Assessment Report of the Intergovernmental Panel on Climate Change (AR5), available at https://www.ipcc.ch/report/ar5/. The Sixth Assessment Report (AR6) will be released in installments, like its predecessors, in 2021 and 2022.
110. The working group (WG) reports deal with the physical science basis (WG I), impacts, adaptation and vulnerability (WG II), and mitigation of climate change (WG III).
111. See *above* footnote 109, at https://archive.ipcc.ch/pdf/assessment-report/ar5/wg2/WGIIAR5-Chap3_FINAL.pdf.

total meltwater yields from stored glacier ice will increase in many regions during the next decades but decrease thereafter..."[112].

These findings and predictions provide stark evidence of the kinds of water-related challenges that countries will increasingly confront due to climate change. The challenges will, of course, also affect countries' relations with each other concerning internationally shared freshwater resources. The IPCC's findings show that already arid regions are likely to become more arid and suffer increasingly frequent droughts (this is happening to us in California and several other Western States at this writing[113]). This increased aridity will intensify competition for diminishing water supplies among countries sharing freshwater resources. The health of freshwater ecosystems will also be impacted, with ripple effects on human uses of the watercourses concerned and very possibly on relations between countries sharing the affected freshwater resources. Climate change will also likely have negative effects on water *quality* in shared freshwater systems and is already changing the seasonal timing of water availability in regions with snowfall. *Glaciers*, critical water sources in a number of regions of the world including Europe and Asia, will continue to shrink and streamflow from their meltwater yields will first increase (with glacial meltwater) and later decrease (as glaciers diminish in size). These effects will be of particular significance for countries dependent on Himalayan glaciers, including Bhutan, China, India, Nepal, and Pakistan[114], where the bulk of the world's population is located and where there are already tensions over shared watercourses[115].

---

112. *Ibid.*, pp. 232-233.
113. See e.g. J. Healy and S. Kasakove, "A Utah Town Halts Growth. It Lacks the Water", *New York Times*, 21 July 2021, at p. 1.
114. See *ibid.*, Box 3-1, Case Study: Himalayan Glaciers, p. 242. See also D. Filkins, "The End of Ice: Exploring a Himalayan Glacier", *New Yorker*, 4 April 2016, at p. 58.
115. Fortunately, the two South Asian countries between which relations are perhaps the most delicate, India and Pakistan, are parties to a treaty governing the principal watercourse system they share, the Indus, which has continued to function for over a half-century despite armed conflicts between them. Indus Waters Treaty 1960, 419 *UNTS* 125. The arbitration provisions of the treaty were invoked by Pakistan in the *Indus Waters Kishenganga Arbitration*, discussed earlier and available at http://archive.pca-cpa.org/showpageb106.html?pag_id=1392. Climate change has been said to be a "contributing factor" in the conflict in Syria due to its likely role in the failure of five consecutive rainy seasons beginning in 2005. See C. P. Kelley *et al.*, "Climate change in the Fertile Crescent and implications of the recent Syrian drought", *Proceedings of the National Academy of Sciences of the United States of America*, Vol. 112, No. 11 (17 March 2015), available at http://www.pnas.org/content/112/11/3241; summarized in http://www.climatecentral.org/news/climate-change-contributing-factor-syrian-conflict-18718. See also T. L. Friedman, "Without Water, Revolution: The Syrian

The Evolution of the Law of International Watercourses 293

Thus, climate change portends heightened possibilities for conflict among states sharing freshwater resources. Management of freshwater resources is often based on historical records relating to such matters as precipitation, temperature and river flows, but the usefulness of those records will decline the more climate change takes hold due to the disruptions it entails.

III. Uneven distribution

While the quantity of the world's water has remained constant for billions of years, as noted earlier, it is not evenly distributed around the planet. In terms of global per capita average, fresh water is plentiful. But much of it is in effect locked in polar ice caps (Greenland and Antarctica) and glaciers [116]. Thus humankind is faced with the challenge of meeting society's needs when populations are far removed from reliable sources of water supply.

Although ancient civilizations, in particular those of Mesopotamia and Egypt, owed their existence to rivers where they were located [117], one of the paradoxes of modern societies' relationships to watercourses and other sources of supply is that populations are sometimes concentrated where water is relatively scarce, while water can be plentiful where people are scarce.

This misalignment has to do in part with hydrogeography. Generally, rivers rise in mountainous areas that are not well suited to agriculture on any significant scale or the accommodation of large numbers of people. Conversely, downstream areas such as alluvial plains are typically more hospitable to human populations and large-scale agriculture. Both of these characteristics are found in Egypt and the Mesopotamian area that is located in what is now Iraq. They are responsible in part for the fact that downstream areas generally develop their water resources before upstream areas, and do so more intensively. This was especially true historically, before the development of materials permitting the construction of large dams and the invention of the turbine for use

---

Regime Ignored a Devastating Drought, Radicalizing Its Citizens", *New York Times*, 19 May 2013, Sunday Review, at p. 1.
   116. Though these are melting due to climate change, that is of little help to humans since most of the meltwater will flow into the sea. This will contribute to sea-level rise, which will contaminate some land-based water supplies, further reducing quantities available to human populations.
   117. These were, of course, the Tigris and the Euphrates in the case of Mesopotamia (meaning, in Greek, the land between the rivers) and the Nile in that of Egypt.

in generating hydroelectricity – both of which permit mountainous upstream areas to develop their water resources by means other than the extensive planting of crops. But more often than not, it remains the case that a downstream area will have developed its water resources, and often its economy in general, far earlier than its upstream neighbor. If we posit that the downstream area is a country, such as Egypt, and the one upstream is also a country, such as Ethiopia, it becomes obvious that this natural lack of synchronization of the development of the countries' respective uses can give rise to conflict: the downstream country may well believe that its entrenched uses are threatened by the construction of a dam in the upstream country [118]. We will return to this problem in Chapter 5 when considering the evolution of the law of the non-navigational uses of international watercourses.

IV. Water transfers

Humans have been bringing water from areas of surplus to areas of deficit for thousands of years. It is well known that in ancient times the Romans developed advanced water supply systems [119], and the Chinese did, as well [120]. The Mesopotamians brought water to the city of Babylon through a system of canals they constructed, and ceramic pipes discovered in the Indus River valley are thought to have supplied water to cities there ca. 3,000 BC [121].

The US State of California provides a more contemporary, and quite striking, illustration of how societies can respond to the misalignment of people and water. California's water situation has been described as follows: "three-fourths of the water *supply* lies within the northern one-third of the state; three-fourths of the water *demand* rests in the southern two-thirds" [122]. California measures some 800 miles (some

---

118. This is true of the Grand Ethiopian Renaissance Dam (GERD) in Ethiopia, discussed above, and Egypt's reaction to it. See e.g. Yihdego *et al.* (*above* footnote 102); S. M. A. Salman, "The Grand Ethiopian Renaissance Dam: The Road to the Declaration of Principles and the Khartoum Document" (*above* footnote 103); and McCaffrey (*above* footnote 7), pp. 321-322.

119. The first Roman aqueducts were completed ca. 312 BC. When the empire reached its zenith nine major aqueducts supplied Rome. Peter Gleick, "Water and Energy", in *Water in Crisis* (*above* footnote 2), at p. 67.

120. Over 2,000 years ago the first stage of the Grand Canal, 150 km long, was completed. Today it is over 1,700 km long. *Ibid.*

121. *Ibid.*

122. M. Arax, *The Dreamt Land: Chasing Water and Dust Across California*, New York, A. A. Knopf, New York, 2019, p. 244 (describing language in the preamble to legislation concerning the preparation of a state water plan to move water from the north to the south in the state) (emphasis added). See generally M. Reisner, *Cadillac Desert*, New York, Viking, 1986.

1,287 kilometers) from its northern to its southern border. The State has effectively extended the length of rivers that rise in the north and stop well short, not only of Los Angeles in the south, but also of vast tracts of semi-arid desert in the State's Central Valley that are suitable for farming but for the lack of water [123]. Since there is limited surface water in the San Joaquin Valley, a prime agricultural area located in the southern portion of the Central Valley, massive agricultural operations there are irrigated largely [124] with surface water imported from the northern part of the State. This is accomplished by means of two systems of dams, reservoirs, canals and aqueducts: the California State Water Project [125] and the federal Central Valley Project [126]. The former system takes water from a reservoir formed by Oroville Dam on a tributary of the upper Sacramento River, some 150 miles upstream of the river's mouth in the Sacramento–San Joaquin River Delta and San Francisco Bay. At 770 feet (230 meters), Oroville Dam is the tallest dam in the United States. The project includes twenty-one dams and over 700 miles (1,100 kilometers) of canals, pipelines and tunnels and brings water from the mountains of Northern California 700 miles south to greater Los Angeles and beyond, as far south as the Mexican border [127]. It is one of the largest public water and power projects in the world [128]. The effect of this movement of water has been characterized as "stealing" a river from the northern part of the state to serve the southern portion [129].

Some 70 percent of the water in the State Water Project is delivered to urban areas and industry in the San Francisco Bay Area and Southern California. Bringing water to Southern California requires that it be pumped over the Tehachapi Mountains, which form the southern end of the Central Valley. One of the pumping plants alone lifts the water

---

123. Arax, *ibid.*
124. Some land is irrigated with increasingly limited supplies of local groundwater.
125. Information on the State Water Project is available on the California Department of Water Resources website, at https://water.ca.gov/Programs/State-Water-Project.
126. Information on the Central Valley Project is available on the US Bureau of Reclamation website, at https://www.usbr.gov/mp/cvp/.
127. "SWP contractor service areas extend from Plumas County in the north to San Diego County adjacent to the Mexican border." More information on the State Water Project is available on the California Department of Water Resources website, at https://water.ca.gov/Programs/State-Water-Project/Management.
128. Information on the State Water Project is available on the Water Education Foundation website, available at https://www.watereducation.org/topic-state-water-project.
129. Arax (*above* footnote 122), at p. 244. The river referred to is the Sacramento River.

1,926 feet (587 meters), which is said to be the highest single water lift in the world [130]. The remaining 30 percent of the State Project's water is dedicated to irrigated agriculture in the Central Valley. The older federal Central Valley Project, on which construction began in the late 1930s, primarily serves agriculture in the Valley [131], unlike the State Project.

Each of these projects is breathtaking by itself. The combination of the two almost defies comprehension. If California were a sovereign nation, its economy would be the fifth largest in the world. Thanks to the projects, the State is the source of most of the fruits, vegetables, meat and other agricultural products consumed in the rest of the country [132], and the State Water Project is probably responsible in significant part for the mushrooming of the population of Los Angeles and surrounding areas. But neither project would in all likelihood have been built if California were a developing country, unless it received massive and unprecedented financial assistance from multilateral development banks and bilateral donor countries. As it is, California's unique and extravagant water infrastructure demonstrates the capacity of humans to move water from where it is plentiful to where it is not, but is regarded as being needed (although it could be argued that bringing water to Southern California for domestic use was an important factor in stimulating population growth there [133]). It also demonstrates that given enough money, water can be pumped over, through, or around virtually any obstacle. The tunnels for the conveyance of water involved in the *Lake Lanoux* and *Kishenganga* cases are also illustrative. In

---

130. Amy Quinton, "California's Water Supply, A 700 Mile Journey", *Capital Public Radio* (7 October 2013), available at https://www.capradio.org/articles/2013/10/07/californias-water-supply-a-700-mile-journey/. See also Management of the California State Water Project, State of California: The Resources Agency – Department of Water Resources, Bulletin 132-84 (September 1984), available from the Department of Water Resources at request; and J. E. McMahon and S. K. Price, "Water and Energy Interactions", 36 *Annual Review of Environment and Resources* 163, 179 (2011), available at https://www.annualreviews.org/doi/pdf/10.1146/annurev-environ-061110-103 827.

131. See generally the US Bureau of Reclamation website, http://www.usbr.gov/projects/Project.jsp?proj_Name=Central%20Valley%20Project.

132. In 2018, the California Department of Food & Agriculture reported that over a third of the country's vegetables and two-thirds of the country's fruits and nuts are grown in California. "California Agricultural Production Statistics", *California Dep't of Food & Agriculture*, https://www.cdfa.ca.gov/statistics/ (last visited August 2021).

133. The Colorado River, after running a veritable gantlet of diversions and dams, including the immense G. Canyon and H. Dams, "then goes to California, where some of it irrigates the Imperial Valley and the rest allows Los Angeles and San Diego to exist". Reisner (*above* footnote 122), at p. 7. Reisner adds that by that point in its course, "the water is so salty that restaurants often serve it with a slice of lemon. If you pour it on certain plants, they will die", *ibid*.

The Evolution of the Law of International Watercourses 297

Kishenganga, for example, India's tunnel is some twenty-three and a half kilometers long and Pakistan's thirty kilometers [134]. And these are *tunnels*, not surface canals.

A project that rivals those of California in its grandiosity is Libya's "Great Man-Made River" (GMMR). The GMMR has been characterized as "the world's largest engineering venture" [135]. This is another effort to redress what has been called water's "grossly uneven spatial and temporal distribution" [136], though the project was also a showpiece of the revolution in that country led by the late Colonel Muammar Gaddafi [137]. In this case, it was groundwater that was tapped, from deep wells in the Sahara desert of southern Libya, and pumped north to population centers and agricultural operations along the Mediterranean coast. The groundwater reserves were, in effect, discovered by accident in 1953 while a search was being conducted for new oilfields. The search led to the discovery of not only significant oil reserves, but also vast quantities of fresh water [138].

The groundwater that supplies the project was later found to be held in a part of the Nubian Sandstone Aquifer System, "the world's largest 'fossil' water aquifer system" [139]. This system underlies parts of Chad, Egypt, Libya and Sudan, and the groundwater it contains is thus a shared resource. It is also non-renewable. The basins of the

---

134. Permanent Court of Arbitration, Record of Proceedings (2010-2013), Case No. 2011-01 (2014), available at http://www.pca-cpa.org.
135. "GMR (Great Man-Made River) Water Supply Project", *Water Technology*, available at https://www.water-technology.net/projects/gmr (last visited August 2021) (hereafter "Water Technology").
136. The quotation is from the *Kishenganga* award, Permanent Court of Arbitration, Record of Proceedings (2010-2013), Case No. 2011-01 (2014), available at http://www.pca-cpa.org.
137. Water Technology (*above* footnote 135).
138. *Ibid.*
139. IAEA, Transboundary Aquifers and River Basins, "Nubian Sandstone Aquifer System", available at http://www-naweb.iaea.org/napc/ih/documents/factsheetsPosters/Nubian%20-%20Transboundary%20Aquifers%20and%20Rivers%20Basins.pdf. "The joint Nubian Aquifer Project, undertaken by the IAEA [International Atomic Energy Agency], the Global Environment Facility (GEF) and the United Nations Development Programme (UNDP), is groundbreaking and challenging. The goal is to establish equitable management of the NSAS for sustainable socioeconomic development and the protection of biodiversity and land resources." *Ibid.* "Fossil" water, also referred to as paleowater, has been defined as "water that infiltrated thousands of years ago under geological conditions different from the present". It is stored in aquifers that are "confined" geologically by impermeable rock at their upper and lower limits. John Misachi, "What is Fossil Water?" *WorldAtlas: World Facts* (17 August 2018), available at https://www.worldatlas.com/articles/what-is-fossil-water.html. Most of the water drawn by the GMMR "was collected between 38,000 and 14,000 years ago, though some pockets are only 7,000 years old". Water Technology (*above* footnote 135).

aquifer from which the GMMR draws are estimated to hold between 4,800 and 20,000 cubic kilometers of water [140]. For comparison, the entire geographic region of Asia has about 12,000 cubic kilometers of water available per year [141]. Like most fossil water, these reserves that supply the GMMR can be very deep, as much as 2,000 meters below the surface, requiring powerful pumps and considerable energy to bring water to the surface. And then the water must be pumped from the southern parts of the country to the coast through thousands of kilometers of pipeline, which is four meters in diameter and is buried seven meters below ground level [142].

The GMMR introduces the additional element that the water that is being moved is shared with other countries. So far as is known, there was no prior notification to, or consultation with, the other States sharing the Nubian Sandstone Aquifer (Chad, Egypt and Sudan) of Libya's plans to pump vast quantities of water from the aquifer and transport it north, to the coast. After use there, it would drain into the sea or otherwise rejoin the hydrologic cycle, ultimately falling back onto land or the oceans, though not necessarily in North Africa. In any event, virtually none of it would recharge the Nubian Aquifer, and would thus be lost to the other States sharing the formation and the water it contains. As in the case of shared petroleum resources, determining what would constitute an equitable and reasonable share would be challenging since the resource is finite and non-recharging. A decision would also have to be made on whether some water (or oil) should be left for future generations. Questions relating to allocation of shared freshwater resources will be examined in Chapter 5.

But Libya's reach may have exceeded its grasp. The project has been plagued by financial difficulties throughout its life. More than 80 percent of Libya's development spending was devoted to the project over a period of eight years [143], forcing the country to seek financing from the African Development Bank for the project's second phase [144]. The

---

140. Water Technology (*above* footnote 135).
141. R. Osborn, "Which continent has more than 12,000 cubic kilometers of water available per year?", *Lifeder.com*, https://en.lifeder.com/continent-more-12000-cubic-kilometers-water-available-per-year (last visited August 2021).
142. Britannica, The Editors of Encyclopaedia, "Great Man-Made River", *Encyclopedia Britannica* (26 March 2021), available at www.britannica.com/topic/Great-Man-Made-River.
143. Britannica, The Editors of Encyclopaedia, *1991 Britannica Book of the Year*, Chicago, 1991.
144. McCaffrey (*above* footnote 7), p. 15. Evidently funding from this source was not forthcoming as all reports indicate that the GMMR was funded by the Libyan government. Water Technology (*above* footnote 135).

first phase alone reportedly cost over nine billion US dollars in today's dollars [145]. Of a total of five planned phases, three had been completed by 2009. It is not known whether the entire project, as originally envisioned, will ultimately be completed.

But be this as it may, the GMMR testifies again to the willingness of humans to move water across vast distances from where it is plentiful to where it is scarce but humans need it. As in California, however, this can obviously become a self-fulfilling prophesy. The Southern California experience demonstrates that water brought to previously dry areas can be an important factor in encouraging people to move there [146], irrigated agriculture to be established there and industry to locate there. Thus, bringing water to a water-short area may well create a demand for more.

Other water-transfer schemes that at first glance may seem to border on the bizarre also demonstrate that the ways in which water can be provided are restricted only by the limits of human imagination. Thus, plans that have been floated include Turkey's proposal to export water to the Middle East and Persian Gulf through a "Peace Pipeline" [147]; the RAND Corporation plan to tow icebergs in twelve-mile-long trains from the seas off of Antarctica to water-short areas, with power supplied by, among other things, a floating nuclear power plant [148]; and a private plan to ship water in tankers and in 600-meter-long "Medusa Bags", each able to hold as much as five supertankers, from Turkey to Haifa and Gaza [149]. Recently, India has given renewed consideration to a nineteenth century British proposal to divert water from the Brahmaputra and Ganges Rivers to arid regions in the south

---

145. F. Pearce, *The Dammed*, London, The Bodley head, 1992, p. 3, reporting, on the date of that publication, that the first phase of the project cost five billion US dollars. Since its completion, the first and largest phase, providing two million cubic meters of water a day along a 1,200km pipeline, had a finished cost of fourteen billion US dollars. See Water Technology (*above* footnote 135).
146. To take but one indicator, housing would not be constructed without water for municipal water systems.
147. For a general description *see* Stephen McCaffrey, "Water, Politics and International Law", in *Water in Crisis* (*above* footnote 2) at p. 94.
148. S. Braun, "A Deluge of Drought Solutions, *Los Angeles Times*, June 21, 1990, at p. 1. See generally A. A. Husseiny (ed.), *Iceberg Utilization: Proceedings of the First International Conference and Workshops on Iceberg Utilization for Fresh Water Production, Weather Modification, and Other Applications*, Iowa State University, Ames, Iowa, 2-6 October 1977 (Pergamon Press, New York, 1978).
149. J. Cran, "The Supply of Water to Jordan, Israel, Gaza, Israel, Gaza and Egypt from Turkey by Medusa Bag", 15 October 1993 (on file with author). See generally, G. E. Gruen, "Contribution of Water Imports to Israeli-Palestinian-Jordanian Peace", 58 *Studies in Environmental Science*, p. 273 (1994), available at https://doi.org/10.1016/S0166-1116(08)71416-X.

of the country [150]. Some of these plans seem far-fetched, all are well-intentioned and all demonstrate the existential importance of water and the resulting lengths to which humans will go to secure it [151].

V. Groundwater: out of sight, out of mind? [152]

The legal regulation of the use of internationally-shared groundwater lagged considerably behind that of surface water. This was due in part to the fact that groundwater, and the aquifers that often hold it, were at best only dimly understood historically. Surface manifestations of groundwater, usually taking the form of springs, have been recognized for millennia. The same is true of the fact that if one dug down far enough into the ground, one might encounter water, which could be accessed by reinforcing the opening and transforming it into a well. Wells are often relied upon to this day, even in highly-developed countries, in more remote areas, or in places not served by municipal water-supply systems. The chances are relatively good that well water will be more pure than surface water from a stream, for example. Unlike flowing water in a stream, however, once contaminated, it is difficult to decontaminate groundwater [153]. But again, until relatively recently the behavior of groundwater and the kinds of geologic formations that hold it were often not well understood. This meant that the legal regime for its regulation had only a slim scientific basis, and that until recently, internationally shared groundwater was hardly regulated at all by international law. This brief discussion will focus on the latter form of groundwater, that which is internationally shared, after outlining some of the chief characteristics of groundwater generally.

---

150. "India set to start massive project to divert Ganges and Brahmaputra rivers", *The Guardian* (19 May 2016), available at https://www.theguardian.com/global-development/2016/may/18/india-set-to-start-massive-project-to-divert-ganges-and-brahmaputra-rivers. This project would also have international implications, as Bangladesh is downstream on both rivers and some 100 million people there could be affected.

151. P. Gleick describes a number of other "massive" and "grandiose" water transfer projects in "Water and Energy" (*above* footnote 96), p. 68.

152. The present discussion of the international legal regulation of shared groundwater will of necessity be brief. For a more extended treatment, see McCaffrey (*above* footnote 7), Chapter 13, "The Special Case of Groundwater", at pp. 544 *et seq.*

153. A discussion of the most common methods of groundwater remediation may be found at "The Most Common Methods of Groundwater Remediation", *Industrial Environmental Contracting*, https://www.iec-nj.com/common-methods-groundwater-remediation/ (last visited September 2021). These for the most part rely upon technologies that are not available in much of the world, or are too expensive to be practical.

1. The general characteristics of groundwater

The general characteristics of groundwater that are perhaps most striking are the following:

– First, its sheer quantity in relation to surface water. Groundwater constitutes some 96 percent of the available supply of fresh water, excluding ice caps and glaciers [154]; "there is over a thousand times more water in the ground than is in all the world's rivers and lakes" [155].
– Second, its relative purity, due to the fact that subsoils in many recharge areas have the capacity to mitigate a number of water pollutants [156].
– And third, its vulnerability to both depletion – through overexploitation – and contamination, which may reside in groundwater for long periods of time and, once present, can be very difficult and costly to remove or attenuate [157].

It goes without saying that these characteristics apply equally to groundwater that is internationally shared. In fact, groundwater that is shared by two or more States is, if anything, even more vulnerable than that which is not so shared. The reasons for this have to do with the negative synergies produced by several factors: the lack in many instances of full understanding or awareness of the characteristics, extent and location of aquifers; the rather embryonic nature of the law in this area, which is in part a consequence of the first factor; the very fact that the groundwater is internationally shared, meaning that without some form of cooperative arrangement, it is subject to two or more different domestic regulatory regimes or no such regime at all in one or

---

154. See United States Geological Survey (USGS), "Where is Earth's Water", available at https://www.usgs.gov/special-topic/water-science-school/science/where-earths-water. This site explains that: "Only a little more than 1.2 percent of all freshwater is surface water, which serves most of life's needs." And: "Rivers make up 0.49 percent of surface freshwater. Although rivers account for only a small amount of freshwater, this is where humans get a large portion of their water." *See also* Igor A. Shiklomanov, "World Fresh Water Resources", in P. Gleick (ed.), *Water in Crisis* (*above* footnote 2), p. 13.
155. United States Geological Survey (USGS), "What is Groundwater?", available at https://www.usgs.gov/special-topic/water-science-school/science/groundwater-what-groundwater.
156. See generally the extensive discussion of groundwater at "Groundwater Quality in Eastern US", USGS, available at https://www.usgs.gov/news/groundwater-quality-eastern-us.
157. See generally "Getting Up to Speed: Groundwater Contamination", *Environmental Protection Agency*, available at https://www.epa.gov/sites/default/files/2015-08/documents/mgwc-gwc1.pdf.

both States; and the phenomenon of the "tragedy of the commons"[158], according to which a common resource whose use is unregulated will tend to encourage users to exploit it to the maximum of their abilities, which if not stopped or controlled can lead to effective exhaustion or destruction of the resource. Professor Hardin illustrates this principle in the following way:

> "Picture a pasture open to all. It is to be expected that each herdsman will try to keep as many cattle as possible on the commons . . . [When the] long-desired goal of social stability becomes a reality[,] the inherent logic of the commons remorselessly generates tragedy . . . [T]he rational herdsman concludes that the only sensible course for him to pursue is to add another animal to his herd. And another; and another . . . But this is the conclusion reached by each and every rational herdsman sharing a commons. Therein is the tragedy. Each man is locked into a system that compels him to increase his herd without limit – in a world that is limited. Ruin is the destination toward which all men rush, each pursuing his own best interest in a society that believes in the freedom of the commons. Freedom in a commons brings ruin to all."[159]

The "pasture", in our case, is a shared aquifer. If left to their own devices, the countries sharing the aquifer would in all probability act as the rational herder would act in Professor Hardin's illustration. Each would maximize its use of the resource, despite the fact that it is shared with another country, just as Hardin's rational herder would do in respect of other herders sharing the pasture open to all. Thus, "[r]uin is the destination toward which all [countries sharing a common aquifer] rush, each pursuing [its] own best interest in a society [such as the international community] that believes in the freedom of the commons. Freedom in a commons [here an unregulated shared aquifer] brings ruin to all"[160]. This is what is so dangerous about the notion of "sovereignty of aquifer states" proposed in the International Law Commission's 2008 draft articles on the Law of Transboundary Aquifers[161], as discussed

---

158. See G. Hardin, "The Tragedy of the Commons", 162 *Science* 1243, 1243 (1968).
159. *Ibid.*, at p. 1244.
160. This logic can of course be applied to the world's oceans, with observable results that Hardin predicted, despite the international community's efforts to regulate these common spaces (see *below* footnote 161).
161. The UN General Assembly adopted a resolution taking note of the ILC's draft articles, which are annexed to the resolution. UNGA Res. 63/124, 11 December 2008

further below and in Chapter 5. First, how can one nation be "sovereign" over something that is shared? And second, does the notion that a State is "sovereign" over shared groundwater not lead it, as a rational entity like Hardin's herder, to maximize its use of that resource? And would all States sharing the aquifer not have the same incentives? If so, this would "brings ruin to all", not to mention the aquifer. Fortunately, as will be shown in Chapter 5, the international community does not believe in the "freedom of the commons". The international community "believes in", or accepts as binding, rules governing the use of shared resources, such as groundwater [162]. It is the translation of this position to individual cases of use of shared groundwater that is the principal challenge.

Returning to the general characteristics of groundwater, most of the groundwater that is used by humans is related to – that is, it interacts with – surface water. Water in a stream can infiltrate into the ground and reemerge later to rejoin the stream [163]. It perhaps goes without saying, however, that the water moves more slowly underground than on the surface. But move it does, unless it is held in a non-recharging aquifer [164]. The interrelationship of groundwater and surface water means that pollution of one can affect the other. Thus depletion or pollution of groundwater in one State may affect not only groundwater, but also surface water, in another. The UN Watercourses Convention takes this interrelationship into account by defining the term "watercourse" to include groundwater that is related to surface water [165].

(hereafter ILC Transboundary Aquifers Articles). The ILC's articles are discussed below. See S. C. McCaffrey, "The International Law Commission Adopts Draft Articles on Transboundary Aquifers", 103 *AJIL* 272 (2009).

162. Only a few examples, among many, will be given here. Articles 5-7 of the UN Watercourses Convention (*above* footnote 4), set forth rules regulating the use of shared freshwater resources. Article 192 of the 1982 United Nations Convention on the Law of the Sea provides simply: "States have the obligation to protect and preserve the marine environment". UN Doc. A/CONF.62/122, 10 December 1982, 21 *ILM* 1261 (1982). And Article 3, "Principles", of the United Nations Framework Convention on Climate Change provides in part: "The Parties should protect the climate system for the benefit of present and future generations of humankind . . .". New York, 9 May 1992, 1771 *UNTS* 107. With regard to the stratospheric ozone layer, *see* the Vienna Convention for the Protection of the Ozone Layer, 22 March 1985, 1513 *UNTS* 323.

163. "Water moves underground downward and sideways, in great quantities, due to gravity and pressure. Eventually it emerges back to the land surface, into rivers, and into the oceans to keep the water cycle going". United States Geological Survey (USGS), "Groundwater Flow and the Water Cycle", available at https://www.usgs.gov/special-topic/water-science-school/science/groundwater-flow-and-water-cycle (last visited September 2021).

164. *Ibid.* "[W]ater below your feet is moving all the time . . .".

165. "'Watercourse' means a system of surface waters and groundwaters constituting by virtue of their physical relationship a unitary whole and normally flowing

2. The international legal regulation of groundwater

In contrast with surface water, internationally shared groundwater has often been ignored or inadequately regulated by States that share it [166]. There are, however, international agreements that address transboundary groundwater, either directly or indirectly, some of which date back to the early twentieth century [167]. There are also several cases dealing with the subject of shared groundwater. The treatment of shared groundwater in the two major multilateral agreements on shared freshwater and its treatment in past and current cases will be considered in turn.

3. Groundwater in the two multilateral treaties concerning international watercourses

The two multilateral treaties open to universal participation, the 1997 UN Watercourses Convention [168], and now the 1992 ECE Helsinki Convention on the Protection and Use of Transboundary Watercourses and International Lakes [169], both include forms of groundwater in their coverage. The UN Convention includes only groundwater that is related to the surface waters of an international watercourse system, although this is the most common form of groundwater in many areas. The ECE Convention, on the other hand, applies to "any surface or ground waters which mark, cross or are located on boundaries between two or more States . . .". Thus the ECE Convention, unlike the UN Watercourses Convention, would apply to an aquifer that is intersected by a boundary

---

into a common terminus; . . .", UN Watercourses Convention, *above* footnote 4, Article 2 *(a)*.

166. See generally McCaffrey (*above* footnote 7), Chapter 13, "The Special Case of Groundwater", p. 544 *et seq.*

167. See L. Teclaff and A. Utton (eds.), *International Groundwater Law*, New York, Oceana, 1981. This study contains a compilation of treaties concerning international groundwater, arranged in the following categories: International Agreements concerning the Use of Wells and Springs in Frontier Areas; Frontier Waters Agreements Indirectly Protecting Ground Waters; Comprehensive Agreements Specifically Including Ground Waters within their Scope; and Agreements Recognizing the Effects of Surface Water Development on Ground Waters, and of Ground Water Development upon Surface Waters.

168. UN Watercourses Convention (*above* footnote 4).

169. Helsinki, 17 March 1992, 31 *ILM* 1312 (1992). While originally a treaty applicable within the UN Economic Commission for Europe, a regional organization, the Water Convention has now been opened to universal participation. See "UNECE Water Convention Goes Global", *United Nations Economic Commission for Europe* (5 February 2013), available at http://www.unece.org/index.php?id=32154.

but which is not related to surface water, such as the Nubian Sandstone Aquifer discussed previously.

4. *Groundwater in case law*

The well-known *Donauversinkung* case [170], the eleventh milestone in the evolution of the law of international watercourses, involved the extraordinary phenomenon of the sinking of the level of the Danube River during certain parts of the year. The loss of water, or sinking, was due to the geological composition of the banks and bed of the river. While passing through the State of Baden, the Danube lost considerable water, which passed through the banks and the bed of the river into an aquifer, emerging as the source of the River Aach in Baden. The Aach terminates in Lake Constance, which feeds the Rhine River. This resulted in "a complete drying up of the river" downstream, in the State of Württemberg, for ten to twelve kilometers.

Württemberg and Prussia sued Baden seeking relief from the sinking of the Danube. Württemberg and Baden each requested that the court grant injunctive relief. The court held that:

"Baden must refrain from causing such increase in the natural sinking of the waters of the Danube as is due *(a)* to the artificially erected . . . works [Baden had constructed] . . . and *(b)* to the accumulation of sand and gravel in the bed of the Danube . . ., but that it is not bound to undertake the responsibility for the permanent improvement of the bed of the river."

The court further held that Württemberg was required to refrain from causing such decrease in the natural sinking of Danube waters as was due to certain works and artificial damming of avenues of sinking. The court found that:

"The sinking of the Danube is a natural, though rare, phenomenon, and Württemberg and Prussia must submit to it. They cannot demand from Baden that it should close the cracks which suck away the water of the Danube." [171]

---

170. *Württemberg and Prussia v. Baden.* (the *Donauversinkung* case), German *Staatsgerichtshof*, 18 June 1927, *Entscheidungen des Reichsgerichts in Zivilsacen*, Vol. 116, appendix, pp. 18-45; *Annual Digest of Public International Law Cases: Years 1927 and 1928*, Vol. 4, A. D. McNair and H. Lauterpacht (eds.), Cambridge, Grotius Publications Ltd., 1981, p. 128. Today *Württemberg* and Baden are combined, forming the *Land* of Baden-*Württemberg*.
171. *Annual Digest of Public International Law Cases: Years 1927 and 1928* (*above* footnote 170), pp. 131-132.

As seen earlier, the court held that the exercise of sovereign rights by a State in regard to an international river traversing its territory "is limited by the duty not to injure the interests of other members of the international community." The court continued:

> "The application of this principle is governed by the circumstances of each particular case. The interests of the Sates in question must be weighed in an equitable manner against one another. One must consider not only the absolute injury caused to the neighboring State, but also the relation of the advantage gained by one to the injury caused to the other." [172]

The court also held that riparian States had a limited duty to perform positive acts in relation to a shared watercourse. This duty was said to be "grounded in the modern practice of States in regard to rivers." Thus a State

> "must not fail to do what civilized States nowadays do in regard to their rivers . . . This duty to perform positive acts has been clearly recognized in regard to the requirements of navigation on international rivers. There is no reason why it should not apply to questions relating to the utilization of the flow of rivers for industrial purposes" [173].

A second case involving groundwater is the *Gabčíkovo-Nagymaros Project* case [174], decided by the International Court of Justice in 1997 and discussed earlier as part of the nineteenth and final milestone in the development of the law in this area. As noted earlier, that case also involved the Danube and, in particular, a project on that river largely where it forms the border between Hungary and Czechoslovakia that was to be constructed pursuant to a 1977 treaty between the two countries. The case is of present interest because of the allegations concerning the effect on groundwater of the project.

Hungary contended that, *inter alia*, as a result of a reduction of the flow in the old bed of the Danube by diversion of water into a bypass canal that was part of the project, the groundwater level would fall in most of the Szigetköz, an area of Hungary opposite the bypass canal. Hungary alleged that

---

172. *Ibid.*
173. *Ibid.*
174. *ICJ Reports 1997*, p. 7.

"the groundwater would then no longer [be] supplied by the Danube . . . but by the reservoir of stagnant water at Dunakiliti [the site of the dam that would divert water into the bypass canal] . . . In the long term, the quality of the water would have been seriously impaired . . ."[175].

There was also to have been, as part of the project, a dam further downstream, at Nagymaros, in Hungarian territory. (While Hungary started to construct this dam, it ultimately demolished the works.) Hungary argued that had the Nagymaros dam been built it would have caused the bed of the Danube upstream of the dam to silt up and, consequently, the quality of the water collected in Hungary's bank-filtered wells would have deteriorated.

"Furthermore, [according to Hungary], the construction and operation of the Nagymaros dam would have caused the erosion of the riverbed downstream, along Szentendre Island [a major island in the Danube between Nagymaros and Budapest]. The water level of the river would therefore have fallen in this section and the yield of the band-filtered wells providing two-thirds of the water supply of the city of Budapest would have appreciably diminished. The filter layer would also have shrunk or perhaps even disappeared, and fine sediments would have been deposited in certain pockets in the river. For this twofold reason, the quality of the infiltrating water would have been severely jeopardized."

These arguments demonstrate emphatically the relationship between surface water and groundwater, and how alterations in surface water flows could have significant effects on groundwater. Of course, the foregoing were Hungary's contentions in a case that was being closely watched by the public at home, a public that had turned against the project for reasons explained earlier. But the contentions were backed up by detailed scientific studies and were plausible effects that could conceivably occur.

A final case is one that was filed with the International Court of Justice on 6 June 2016, by Chile against Bolivia, the *Dispute over the Status and Use of the Waters of the Silala (Chile v. Bolivia)*. The case concerns water emerging from springs in Bolivia and flowing downhill across the border into Chile a few kilometers from its source. The

---

175. *Ibid.*, p. 35, para. 40.

Silala's flow at the border is about 160 liters per second. The aquifer from which the springs emanate seems to straddle the border between the two countries. Until 1999, they treated the Silala as an international watercourse. In that year Bolivia for the first time claimed that the waters of the Silala were exclusively Bolivian and that it had a right to one hundred percent of its waters [176]. Chile requests a declaration from the Court that the Silala is an international watercourse, with the resulting rights and obligations for the two States [177]. Hearings in the case are not yet scheduled, but will probably occur in 2022.

The Silala is located at high altitude, some 4,400 meters (over 14,400 feet) above sea level [178], in the Atacama Desert, one of the driest places on Earth. Any water at all would therefore be highly valuable there, providing there were uses for it. There are no settlements or other human activities in Bolivia that have used Silala waters but in Chile the river's waters, augmented by springs within Chile, have been used for more than a century for different purposes, including supplying the city of Antofagasta and two towns with water, and supplying water to the Antofagasta (Chile) and Bolivia Railway Company Ltd., and to various mining companies, including the State-owned Corporación Nacional del Cobre (CODELCO) [179].

The case illustrates vividly how groundwater and surface water can interrelate, how the purity of some groundwater can enhance its usefulness to humans, and how groundwater can occur even in extremely arid areas, increasing its value for ecosystems and any human users.

5. The ILC's resolution on "Confined Transboundary Groundwater"

After debating the issue during the last session of its work on international watercourses in 1994, the ILC decided not to include so-called "confined transboundary groundwater" within the scope of its draft articles, despite the recommendation of the special rapporteur to the contrary [180]. The Commission did, however, adopt a resolution on "Confined Transboundary Groundwater" [181] that accompanied its articles on international watercourses and thus was submitted to the

---

176. See Chile's Application Instituting Proceedings, 6 June 2016, para. 7, available at http://www.icj-cij.org/files/case-related/162/162-20160606-APP-01-00-EN.pdf.
177. *Ibid.*
178. *Ibid.*, para. 2.
179. *Ibid.*, para. 11.
180. 1994 *YB Int'l L. Comm'n*, Vol. 2, Part. 2, p. 88, para. 216.
181. *Ibid.*, p. 135.

The Evolution of the Law of International Watercourses 309

General Assembly along with those articles. "Confined groundwater" is defined in the preamble to the resolution simply as "groundwater not related to an international watercourse" [182]. The resolution "Commends States to be guided by the principles contained in the draft articles on the law of the non-navigational uses of international watercourses, where appropriate, in regulating transboundary groundwater; . . ." [183]. Furthermore, the resolution's preamble records the Commission's "view that the principles contained in its draft articles on the law of the non-navigational uses of international watercourses may be applied to transboundary confined groundwater, ..." [184]. Having gone this far, one would think that the Commission could have taken the next step and included "confined transboundary groundwater" within the scope of the draft articles. But some members of the ILC may have been uneasy about applying the principles and rules contained in the draft articles to a form of shared fresh water they had not had in mind when formulating the texts containing those principles and rules. Some members may even have felt that including groundwater that was related to surface water was more than they were comfortable with, despite the extensive state practice on the question laid before the Commission over twenty years (1974-1994) by the succession of five special rapporteurs on the topic.

6. The ILC's Draft Articles on the Law of Transboundary Aquifers

The ILC decided in 2002 to include the topic, "Shared Natural Resources", in its program of work. The topic was understood to include groundwater, oil and natural gas, and perhaps other shared natural resources such as migratory birds and animals [185]. The Commission began its work by focusing on transboundary groundwater. It must be said that the ILC unfortunately got off to a rather confused start in its work on this topic in deciding to focus on transboundary groundwater "as the follow-up to the Commission's previous work on the codification of the law of surface waters" [186], citing the UN Watercourses Convention. The latter agreement, and the ILC's work leading to it, did not, of course, deal only with "surface waters", but as we have

---

182. *Ibid.*, 3rd preambular para.
183. *Ibid.*, para. 1.
184. *Ibid.*, last preambular para.
185. Report of the International Law Commission on the Work of Its Fifty-fourth Session, 2002 *YB Int'l L. Comm'n*, Vol. 2, Part. 2, pp. 100-101, paras. 518-519; and ILC Report on the Work of Its Sixtieth Session (2008), 2008 *YB Int'l L. Comm'n*, Vol. 2, Part. 2, p. 22, "General commentary", para. 1.
186. 2008 *YB Int'l L. Comm'n*, Vol. 2, Part. 2, p. 22, "General commentary", para. 1.

seen, defined "watercourse" as a "system of surface waters and groundwaters . . ."[187]. The ILC's watercourses articles, and the UN Watercourses Convention which is based on them, therefore cover a common form of groundwater, that which is related to surface water. And here there is an overlap between the ILC's work on international watercourses and that on transboundary groundwater, something the Commission would ordinarily do its best to avoid. But fortunately, with the exception of Article 3, "Sovereignty of Aquifer States", the transboundary aquifers draft builds on, and is not inconsistent with, the watercourses articles or the UN Watercourses Convention.

In 2003, the Commission received the first report from its special rapporteur on transboundary aquifers. In 2008, the ILC adopted a final set of draft articles on the Law of Transboundary Aquifers and transmitted the articles to the General Assembly[188]. The Assembly took note of the articles, annexing the text to its resolution[189]. The resolution commends the articles to the attention of governments. At this writing in 2021, the Assembly has yet to reach a decision on the final form to be given to the articles, that is, whether they should be left standing as a set of articles adopted by the ILC – which the Assembly has done with respect to a number of important ILC drafts, such as its articles on State Responsibility and on Reservations to Treaties – or whether a diplomatic conference should be convened at which a convention on the topic could be negotiated.

The Transboundary Aquifers draft generally applies the principles set forth in the UN Watercourses Convention to transboundary aquifers. Indeed, the commentary to the Transboundary Aquifers articles states that: "The draft articles rely to a large extent on the 1997 Watercourses Convention."[190] This indicates that on closer examination, the Commission found that the principles set forth in the Convention are indeed largely applicable to transboundary groundwater.

The 2008 draft itself is largely helpful, but mostly in a didactic way, in the sense of being instructive. For example, the draft teaches that groundwater recharge zones – that is, areas of land surface through which water can infiltrate into the ground – should be protected to avoid contamination of the groundwater. It also applies the funda-

---

187. UN Watercourses Convention (*above* footnote 4), Article 2 *(a)*.
188. *Ibid.*
189. UNGA Res. 63/124 of 11 December 2008.
190. 2006 ILC Rep., 2006 *YB Int'l L. Comm'n*, Vol. 2, Part. 2, p. 94, para. 5 of commentary.

mental principle of equitable and reasonable utilization to transboundary aquifers (Art. 4), although more specific attention could have been given in the article to how the principle applies to non-recharging aquifers since a finite quantity of water is involved in those cases.

The one aspect of the draft that is clearly not helpful is the article entitled "Sovereignty of aquifer states" that I have already mentioned. That article risks encouraging States sharing groundwater with other States to engage in a pseudo-tragedy-of-the-commons race to the bottom under the banner of "sovereignty". It is a misguided provision that should have had no place in the draft. The Aquifers articles define the term "aquifer" as "a permeable water-bearing geological formation underlain by a less permeable layer and the water contained in the saturated zone of the formation; . . ."[191]. Thus the term includes both the geological formation and the water contained therein. Article 3's establishment of "sovereignty of aquifer states", giving those States "sovereignty over the portion of a transboundary aquifer . . . located within its territory", therefore confers sovereignty over both the geologic formation – which the situs State would have in any event – and the water contained therein, water that it shares with the other State or States in which a portion the aquifer is located. As already indicated, this sets up a clash of sovereignties between the States sharing an aquifer and encourages each State to exploit "its" water (which is actually water shared with other States in which a portion of the aquifer is located) to the maximum.

VI. Conclusion

In conclusion, this chapter has emphasized that water is necessary to all life and underpins human societies in a variety of ways. We have also seen that most of Earth's water is in constant motion through the hydrologic cycle and to a lesser extent in other ways, as well. In addition, we have seen that for one reason or another, human populations are often concentrated in places that are lacking in adequate supplies of water. This has resulted in the construction of massive water transfer schemes to move water from where it originates, but is not needed, to other places where it is, in fact, needed. These schemes may or may not have international implications, but their portent in this time of

---

191. ILC Transboundary Aquifers Articles (*above* footnote 161), Article 2 *(a)*.

climate change indicates that there will be many more such projects in the future. These will test the limits of a legal regime designed chiefly to regulate the use of natural watercourses.

All of the foregoing considerations demonstrate why human societies need some form of normative system to govern their relations with regard to shared freshwater resources. And, in the ancient case involving the Mesopotamian city-states of Umma and Lagash, we have seen that political units, for as far back as history extends, have sought to stabilize their water relations through precisely such normative systems. In the next Chapter, we will note some of the indications we have of the search for a measure of stability in water relations between political units and, later, modern nation-states.

CHAPTER 3

BEYOND THE HOBBESEAN STATE OF NATURE:
THE PERCEIVED NEED FOR RELIABILITY OF ACCESS
TO SHARED FRESHWATER RESOURCES AND EARLY
EVIDENCE OF A QUEST FOR STABILITY

I. Introduction

The history to be traced in this chapter is also the history of law in human society and indeed of human social organization in general. As noted in Chapter 1, the evolution of the law of international watercourses cannot be viewed in isolation, separate and apart from the historical forces that helped shape it. The purpose of this chapter is to demonstrate that as in other fields, human societies have sought stability in their fluvial relations since the earliest times of which we have evidence. We will therefore begin at the beginning, with our old friend, the Stele of the Vultures.

II. "Nasty, brutish and short"

I have included a reference to the English lawyer and philosopher of the sixteenth and seventeenth centuries, Thomas Hobbes, in the title of this chapter because of Hobbes' justification for some degree of regulation of society. Hobbes is well known for his argument that without government – a situation he called a "state of nature" – there would be *bellum omnium contra omnes* – war of all against all – and human life would be "solitary, poor, nasty, brutish and short". This is clearly not a pleasant prospect.

So, as we know, from what Arthur Nussbaum has called "the dawn of documentary history"[192], there is evidence of law in the form of the so-called Stele of the Vultures of the fourth millennium BC, circa 3100 BC, which recorded the conditions under which the conflict over water and a boundary between the Mesopotamian city-states of Umma and Lagash would be resolved. As we have seen, the agreement between the two States was mediated, or perhaps arbitrated, by Mesilim, the

---

192. A. Nussbaum (*above* footnote 10), at p. 1.

ruler of Kish, a regional hegemon in Mesopotamia at the time. The ideas of third-party dispute resolution, of writing down the terms of an agreement between the parties, and of appealing to respected guarantors of the agreement – in this case, the most powerful Sumerian gods – are consistent with treaty practice today.

In all probability, the fact that this is the oldest documentary evidence of inter-jurisdictional law and dispute resolution that has been discovered does not mean that these practices were new in 3100 BC. It is far more likely that they represent refinements of a practice that had developed over time, probably a considerable period of time. But we simply lack tangible evidence of other contemporaneous agreements, let alone still earlier ones that must have paved the way for the Umma-Lagash Treaty. Perhaps such evidence will come to light as archaeological efforts continue. But as things stand, more than a millennium passed before the next treaties of which evidence is available were concluded [193].

The documentary history of the Umma-Lagash dispute is important because it confirms that human social organization as early as the fourth millennium BC had moved beyond a Hobbesean state of nature, to the extent one ever existed among groups of humans. Assurance that the treaty between the two city-states would be observed was provided by the deities invoked by Umma, and no doubt also by Mesilim in his capacities as both an arbitrator and the representative of a regional hegemon. Umma could not continue to grow barley without the assurance that it could rely on the water in the boundary ditch. And since Umma paid rent for use of the strip of agricultural land to Lagash in the form of the barley grown there, it was in Lagash's interest for there to be stability in its relations with Umma. Whether viewed as a mundane commercial transaction (which, in view of the consequences for Umma of violating the lease agreement that are depicted on the stele, it evidently was not) or as a matter implicating the most vital interests in the affairs of the city-states, the agreement, as reinforced contextually by the stele's graphic description of the war leading up to it, offers clear evidence of the desire to achieve and maintain stability in the relations between the parties in respect of such vital matters as boundaries, water and food. While civilization has moved beyond putting to death the leader of the losing party in a war, this value of stability in international relations has only strengthened over time.

---

193. *Ibid.*, p. 2, referring to a series of agreements to which Egyptian or Hittite rulers were parties.

III. Further evidence from treaty practice

My friend and colleague Professor Edith Brown Weiss, for her 2007 Hague Academy lectures on the topic of "The Evolution of International Water Law" [194], compiled a database of international water treaties including more than 2,000 international agreements having to do with fresh water. Rather than beginning with the Umma-Lagash agreement of 3100 BC, Professor Brown Weiss chose a different historical inflection point: the Peace of Westphalia of 1648 [195]. This is an equally appropriate place to begin, especially because the pivotal agreements comprising the Peace mark the emergence of modern international law and the system of sovereign States that we know today [196]. Professor Brown Weiss also reached back to include sixteen pre-1648 agreements and other instruments that are included in the *Systematic Index of International Water Resources Treaties* prepared by the UN Food and Agriculture Organization and published in 1978 [197]. Professor Brown Weiss's work offers valuable lessons for our own inquiry.

IV. The quest for stability in fluvial relations

Professor Brown Weiss hypothesized that "the purpose and content of international water agreements have changed over time to reflect changes in the primary uses for water" [198], a perfectly reasonable assumption. For example, when we come to consider priorities among different uses of water, we will see that while navigation was for long given priority over other uses, that prioritization has now changed with the increased importance of water for those other uses.

Professor Brown Weiss identified five major purposes of international water treaties: "[first,] to demarcate a boundary; [second,] to facilitate navigation; [third,] to allocate the use of water or to develop [or] control it for certain purposes; [fourth,] to protect the ecosystem; and [fifth,] to control pollution" [199].

---

194. E. Brown Weiss, "The Evolution of International Water Law", *Recueil des Cours*, Vol. 331 (2007), pp. 165 *et seq*. See also J. L. Wescoat, Jr., "Main Currents in Early Multilateral Water Treaties: A Historical-Geographic Perspective, 1648-1948", 7 *Colo. J. Int'l L. & Pol'y* 39, 39 (1996).
195. The Peace of Westphalia consisted of two treaties, those of Osnabrück, 1 CTS p. 119, and Münster, *ibid*., p. 271.
196. Brown Weiss (*above* footnote 194), p. 231.
197. Food and Agriculture Organization of the United Nations, *Systematic Index of International Water Resources Treaties, Declarations, Acts and Cases by Basin*, FAO, Rome, 1978.
198. Brown Weiss (*above* footnote 194), p. 233.
199. *Ibid*., p. 234.

While the database prepared by Professor Brown Weiss includes both bilateral and multilateral treaties, she found that bilateral treaties comprise over 70 percent of the new treaties negotiated in a given period, although the share of multilateral agreements has increased recently [200]. This is in line with the trend since the end of the Second World War toward international governance through multilateral treaties – something that had not been the case prior to World War II, the main exceptions being the major peace treaties [201].

Professor Brown Weiss found that boundary demarcation figured prominently in water treaties until 1930 [202], which is understandable in light of the reorganization of many States and boundaries following World War I. She also found that the percentage of treaties dealing with navigation on international watercourses peaked during the period from 1700 to 1930, then declined sharply. Perhaps correspondingly, the percentage of treaties dealing with the allocation and use of shared freshwater resources "were most significant as a percentage of total agreements negotiated during the period 1931-2000" [203]. This underscores both the decline in the *relative* [204] importance of navigation and the rise in that of non-navigational uses and the protection of international watercourses and their ecosystems. The rise in the number of treaties dealing with allocation and use also demonstrates that States have increasingly sought to stabilize their relations with respect to non-navigational uses of shared freshwater resources by concluding treaties to protect their interests in those resources. Countries are thus continuing, and refining, a practice that is reflected in the Umma-Lagash Treaty of 3100 BC.

Professor Brown Weiss concludes on the basis of her survey that during both the eighteenth and nineteenth centuries, and prior to that period, as well, international rivers were seen as important boundaries between countries and as highways for commerce. She reports that

---

200. *Ibid.*, pp. 234-235.
201. Perhaps foremost among these are the Peace of Versailles and its associated agreements, which ended the First World War. *See* the Treaties of Versailles (1919), 225 CTS, p. 188, 2 MPT, p. 1265, Neuilly (1919), 2 MPT, p. 1727, Trianon (1920), 3 MPT, p. 1863, and Sèvres (1920), 3 MPT, p. 2055. These agreements may also be found at 28 LNTS, p. 11.
202. Brown Weiss (*above* footnote 194), p. 235.
203. *Ibid.*
204. The word "relative" is emphasized because navigation is still a very important use of international watercourses for both developing and developed countries in many regions of the world. The point is simply that as measured by the number of agreements concluded, States have been more concerned recently with non-navigational uses than with navigational ones.

The Evolution of the Law of International Watercourses 317

during this period, "[a] majority of the [international water] agreements were negotiated between European countries over European waters: approximately 75 percent of the agreements in the eighteenth century and almost 50 percent in the nineteenth century"[205]. That the use of rivers to demarcate boundaries between countries is a common and important practice is well known. Western Europe is a well-watered region with many rivers[206]. Stabilization of international boundaries using those rivers, as appropriate, is a convenient device. The emergence of modern international law in Europe with the Peace of Westphalia may also contribute to the explanation for the high percentage of water treaties concluded in Europe[207], though the role of that factor seems less important than the hydrographic one.

Professor Brown Weiss finds that "[t]he most striking developments in the evolution of international water agreements have taken place during the latter half of the twentieth century", when the number of treaties concerning issues other than navigation and boundary demarcation "increased dramatically"[208]. This evidence is not surprising in view of the greater pressure being placed on limited freshwater resources as well as the heightened consciousness of the importance of safeguarding clean water and freshwater ecosystems.

In sum, this very brief overview of Professor Brown Weiss's findings confirms that countries have sought over time to stabilize their relations with respect to shared freshwater resources through the conclusion of agreements concerning those resources. Again, the evidence supporting this proposition begins with the earliest known document of any kind, that found on the Stele of the Vultures, and runs up to the present day. It seems impossible to overemphasize the significance of this treaty between Umma and Lagash because it suggests that certain practices – such as written (here in cuneiform inscriptions on limestone[209]) documentation of agreements that settle water disputes – could well have been entrenched by the time the stele was prepared. It may therefore be assumed with some confidence that this practice extended backwards into prerecorded history, strongly suggesting human societies' determination to stabilize their water relations with other

---

205. Brown Weiss (*above* footnote 194), p. 237 (emphasis added).
206. The catastrophic flooding of Germany and Belgium, in particular, in July of 2021 underscores this fact. See e.g. S. Sengupta, "Climate Change Comes for the Wealthy Nations", *New York Times*, 18 July 2021, p. 1.
207. Brown Weiss (*above* footnote 194), p. 238.
208. *Ibid.*, p. 240.
209. Sand (*above* footnote 7).

political units by the conclusion of agreements, at least some of which were in very early times, quite literally, carved in stone.

V. Lessons from the fate of the "Harmon Doctrine"

Now let us skip ahead six millennia or so, to the late nineteenth century, for an illustration of how an important State official's determination that it was legitimate to act unilaterally with respect to freshwater resources shared with another State was ultimately overwhelmed by forces compelling cooperation rather than conflict. I am referring here to the so-called "Harmon Doctrine", known throughout the world by international water law aficionados as the assertion that a State has absolute territorial sovereignty over the portion of an international watercourse that lies within its territory. If true, this theory would, of course, negate the idea that international law, beyond that which confers sovereignty on States in the first place, has something to say about one State's obligations owed to another State with respect to international watercourses they share.

1. Background

First, some background concerning the dispute between Mexico and the United States over the use of Rio Grande waters in the late nineteenth century. The Rio Grande, while a rather long river, is not known for carrying a large volume of water [210]. It is situated in a largely arid and semi-arid geographical area in the southwestern United States, flowing from its origin in the San Juan Mountains in southwestern Colorado through that State, then New Mexico, until it reaches the sister cities of El Paso, Texas, in the United States, and Ciudad Juarez, in Mexico. Here, the river begins to form the boundary between the two countries [211], continuing for 1,240 miles (or some 1,996 kilometers) until it flows – or should flow, if it is still carrying any water at that point – into the Gulf of Mexico. Mexican tributaries also contribute significantly to the Rio Grande's flow in the area where it forms the border between the two countries, the Rio Grande Valley.

By the late nineteenth century, agricultural and municipal uses of Rio Grande waters had become entrenched on the Mexican side of the

---

210. Estimates of its flow range from 82 to 120 cubic meters per second. *Water in Crisis* (*above* footnote 2), pp. 146, 147.

211. Specifically, the river forms the boundary between the US State of Texas and the Mexican States of Chihuahua, Coahuila, Nuevo Leon and Tamaulipas.

border around Ciudad Juarez. Also at that time, Americans settling in Colorado and New Mexico began to divert significant quantities of water from the Rio Grande's upper reaches for agricultural and other purposes. This gave rise to a diplomatic note from the Mexican Ambassador to the United States, Matías Romero, to the American Secretary of State, W. Q. Gresham. In his note, Romero emphasized the urgent need for a solution to the problem of the

> "taking of water from the [Rio Grande] in the State of Colorado and the Territory of New Mexico, which has so seriously affected the existence of the frontier communities for several miles below [Ciudad Juarez] [in view of] the danger [that] otherwise those communities may be annihilated"[212].

The Mexican consul at El Paso, Texas, believed that the disposition of this question would decide "the existence or the disappearance of the [border] towns" of both Ciudad Juarez and El Paso, Texas. He therefore pleaded for what he called "the equitable division of the waters of the river"[213]. It is worthy of note that this invocation of the principle of equitable allocation occurred in 1894.

This problem was sufficiently serious that it came to the attention of the United States Congress. As early as 1878, the US Secretary of War warned in a report to the House of Representatives that the taking of water from the Rio Grande for irrigation means that "there will not be enough water for all, and both sides have an equal right . . ."[214]. And the US Army General in charge of the Department of Texas observed that:

> "our neighbors . . . are a good deal excited over what they deem the violation of their riparian rights, through our people taking all the water of the Rio Grande for the irrigation of the San Luis Valley [in Colorado], which leaves the Rio Grande a dry bed for 500 miles"[215]. He warned, rather ominously, that "thus far there has been no call for military force", and suggested that "[t]he remedy

---

212. Minister Romero to Secretary Gresham, 12 October 1894, *Foreign Relations of the United States*, p. 395 (1894).
213. Mr Guarneros to Mr Romero, 4 October 1894, *Foreign Relations of the United States*, pp. 395-396 (1894).
214. Report of Col. Hatch transmitted to the House of Representatives by the Secretary of War, Ex. Doc. No. 84, 45th Cong., 2nd Sess., referred to in "Irrigation of Arid Lands – International Boundary – Mexican Relations", Report to accompany Bill H.R. 3924 by Mr. Lanham, 27 February 1890, HR Rep. No. 490, 51st Cong., 1st Sess., Serial Set 2808-2, p. 2 (1890).
215. Report of General Stanley to the Secretary of War, 12 September 1889, quoted in *ibid.*, p. 3.

for this water famine and consequent ruin to the inhabitants of the Rio Grande Valley must be found in storage reservoirs..."[216].

The report by the Secretary of War led to the introduction in Congress of proposed legislation in February, 1890, that would have authorized the President to negotiate a solution to the water problem with Mexico. It would further have authorized the President to discuss with Mexico the construction of an international dam on the Rio Grande in the vicinity of El Paso, and the formation of a joint commission whose authority would include "the adjust[ment] and determin[ation] of the respective water rights of the citizens of the two countries..."[217]. While this proposed legislation was not enacted, these ideas would bear fruit later.

Notably, the report accompanying the proposed law referred to Mexico as "a neighbor with whom we shall always have to deal, and whom it is both our duty and policy to treat and cultivate in a neighborly way"[218]. The report also quoted from a letter from a former Speaker of the House of Representatives that recognized that while the legal obligations of the United States "may be a disputed question[,] . . . there certainly is a moral obligation upon our part to cooperate with the Government of [Mexico] in such measures as may be necessary to prevent injury in the future"[219].

Later in 1890, Congress adopted a joint resolution recognizing the problem, which it characterized as a "standing menace to the harmony and prosperity of the citizens of [the two] countries..."[220].

Meanwhile, Mexico having received no satisfaction from the United States, Ambassador Romero sent another note in October 1895, carefully describing the arid condition of the Ciudad Juarez region, and stating that during the nearly 300-year existence of Ciudad Juarez, its

---

216. *Ibid.*
217. Concurrent Resolution of 29 April 1890 "concerning the irrigation of arid lands in the valley of the Rio Grande River, the construction of a dam across said river at or near El Paso, Tex., for the storage of its waste waters, and for other purposes", Sect. 3, annexed to *ibid.*, at p. 9.
218. Report to accompany Bill HR 3924 by Mr Lanham, 27 February 1890, HR Rep. No. 490, 51st Cong., 1st Sess., Serial Set 2808-2, p. 2 (1890).
219. John G. Carlisle to Mr Lanham, *ibid.*, at p. 7.
220. Concurrent Resolution of 29 April 1890 "concerning the irrigation of arid lands in the valley of the Rio Grande River, the construction of a dam across said river at or near El Paso, Tex., for the storage of its waste waters, and for other purposes", Con. Rec. – Senate, 29 April 1890, p. 3963, Con. Rec. – House, 29 April 1890, p. 3977; US Appendix, p. 145.

inhabitants had irrigated their land with water from the Rio Grande. He stated that the city and surrounding districts had had sufficient water for their crops until about 1885, "when a great many trenches were dug in the State of Colorado (especially in the [San Luis] Valley), and in the Territory of New Mexico . . ."[221]. Ambassador Romero added that in 1894 "the river became dried up entirely by the fifteenth of June", making it impossible to grow a number of the usual crops [222]. This situation led to a decrease in land values and a cutting in half of the population, from 20,000 in 1875 to 10,000 in 1894 [223].

Ambassador Romero then laid out Mexico's legal position. He first drew attention to the 1848 Treaty of Guadalupe Hidalgo between the two countries, Article VII of which provides that navigation of the Rio Grande below the southern boundary of New Mexico "shall be free and common to the vessels and citizens of both countries; and neither shall, without the consent of the other, construct any work that may impede or interrupt, in whole or in part, the exercise of this right . . ." [224]. Ambassador Romero referred to a US Army report of 1850 indicating that an army officer had traveled up the Rio Grande "with a vessel, reaching a point several kilometers above [El Paso], which shows that it was navigable at that time" [225]. He then stated Mexico's position that the irrigation ditches in Colorado and New Mexico fell within the treaty's prohibition of works that would interfere with navigation, since "nothing could impede it more absolutely than works which wholly turn aside the water of these rivers" [226]. Ambassador Romero also invoked "principles of international law", which he said would "form a sufficient basis for the rights of the Mexican inhabitants of the bank of the Rio Grande". Those inhabitants, he continued, would have an "[incontestable] claim to the use of the water of that river", that use "being prior to that of the inhabitants of Colorado by hundreds of years, and, according to the principles of civil law, a prior claim takes precedence in case of dispute" [227]. Having said this, Ambassador Romero concluded his note by expressing Mexico's strong interest in

---

221. Matías Romero, Mexican Minister, to Richard Olney, Secretary of State, 21 October 1895, US Appendix, p. 201.
222. *Ibid.*
223. *Ibid.*
224. 2 February 1848, 1 *Malloy,* p. 1107.
225. Romero to Olney, footnote 193 *above,* US Appendix, p. 201.
226. US Appendix, p. 202; also quoted in 21 Op. Att'y Gen., p. 277 (1895).
227. *Ibid.*

negotiating with the United States an arrangement for the distribution of Rio Grande waters [228].

At the time, the US Department of State did not have its own, in-house, legal adviser. It therefore referred all legal questions to the Department of Justice, headed by the Attorney-General. Secretary of State Richard Olney therefore referred Ambassador Romero's note to Attorney General Judson Harmon. Olney stated that the negotiations that the joint resolution of Congress had charged the President to conduct "can not be intelligently conducted unless the legal rights and obligations of the two Governments concerned and the responsibility of either, if any, for the disastrous state of things depicted in the Mexican [Ambassador's] letter are first ascertained" [229]. Olney therefore requested Harmon to prepare an opinion on the soundness of Mexico's legal claims, including whether Mexico's claims were supported by principles of international law independent of any treaty obligation [230].

2. Harmon's opinion

Attorney General Harmon's opinion first addressed Mexico's treaty claim, finding no basis for it on the ground that Article VII of the treaty applied only to the part of the Rio Grande lying below the southern boundary of New Mexico. Since the activities in question – principally diversions in Colorado – occurred well north of that boundary, they were outside the scope of the treaty. While this seems a strained interpretation by today's standards, it is the portion of Harmon's opinion that deals with general principles of international law that is of greatest interest to us. It is these passages that have become known as the "Harmon Doctrine".

Harmon began by stating that "[a]n extended search affords no precedent or authority which has direct bearing on the case" [231]. While this seems incredible today, the law in the field of transboundary harm, and in particular of transboundary harm inflicted through the medium of an international watercourse, was not well-developed in Harmon's day. However, even in that time, there were a number of well-known authorities that addressed the question before Harmon, beginning

---

228. *Ibid.*
229. R. Olney, Secretary of State, to Judson Harmon, Attorney General, 5 November 1895, US Appendix, p. 204. The relevant portions of the Secretary of State's letter are quoted in Harmon's opinion, 21 Op. Att'y Gen. 274, at p. 275 (1895).
230. *Ibid.*
231. 21 Op. Att'y Gen. p. 280.

with Grotius and de Martens, and upon which he could have drawn, but he did not [232]. One hopes that the fact that these great figures in international law would in all likelihood have come out differently than Harmon on the question before him is not what led him to ignore them, but this remains a possibility.

Thus, faced with a *non liquet* that was arguably of his own creation, Harmon turned to an opinion of the US Supreme Court in a sovereign immunity case, *The Schooner Exchange* v. *McFaddon*[233], decided in 1812 in an opinion by the great jurist, Chief Justice John Marshall. Harmon wrote as follows:

> "The fundamental principle of international law is the absolute sovereignty of every nation, as against all others, within its own territory. Of the nature and scope of sovereignty with respect to judicial jurisdiction, which is one of its elements, Chief Justice Marshall said . . .:
>
> 'The jurisdiction of the nation within its own territory is necessarily exclusive and absolute. It is susceptible of no limitation not imposed by itself. Any restriction upon it, deriving validly from an external source, would imply a diminution of its sovereignty to the extent of the restriction, and an investment of that sovereignty to the same extent in that power which would impose such restriction.
>
> All exceptions, therefore, to the full and complete power of a nation within its own territories must be traced up to the consent of the nation itself. They can flow from no other legitimate source.'" [234]

Even assuming these statements were generally correct in the early part of the nineteenth century in respect of the doctrine of sovereign immunity, which is what was involved in the *Schooner Exchange* case, Harmon failed to even attempt to explain how they applied to shared freshwater resources. As to that subject matter, Harmon's opinion would seem to land the United States, in respect of Mexico, squarely in Hobbes' "state of nature", and the *bellum omnium contra omnes* that

---

232. See e.g. H. Grotius, *De Juri Belli ac Pacis*, Lib. II, Cap. II, XII; the Decree of the Provisory Executive Council of the French Republic of 16 Nov. 1792, referred to by P. Pradier-Fodéré, Traité de Droit International Public Européen et Américain, Vol. II, pp. 282 *et seq*. (No. 734) (Paris, 1885); and Caratheodory, Du droit international concernant les grands cours d'eau, p. 32 (1861).
233. *The Schooner Exch.* v. *McFaddon*, 11 US 116, 3 L. Ed. 287 (1812).
234. 21 Op. Att'y Gen. at pp. 281-282.

prevails there. This is the case because Harmon's declaration amounts to a finding that there is *no* law regulating what a country can do within its own territory with respect to the waters of an international watercourse. But, having made the strongest case he could for complete freedom of action, irrespective of the consequences upon other nations, Attorney General Harmon recognized that other factors – non-legal ones – might lead the Department of State to seek a less extreme solution. Harmon stated:

> "The case presented is a novel one. Whether the circumstances make it possible or proper to take any action from considerations of comity is a question which does not pertain to the Department [of Justice]; but that question should be decided as one of policy only, because, in my opinion, the rules, principles, and precedents of international law impose no liability or obligation upon the United States." [235]

The implication of this latter statement is that Harmon had made the strongest legal case possible, but that he recognized that his arguments need not necessarily be deployed in negotiations with Mexico. They could instead be kept in a back pocket, to be withdrawn only if the United States were somehow backed into a corner in such negotiations. In fact, Chief Justice Marshall does much the same thing in his opinion in *The Schooner Exchange*. After the fire and brimstone of his absolute sovereignty language, Marshall wrote, two sentences beyond the end of Harmon's quotation from his opinion, as follows:

> "The world being composed of distinct sovereignties, possessing equal rights and equal independence, whose mutual benefit is promoted by intercourse with each other, . . . all sovereigns have consented to a relaxation in practice, in cases under certain peculiar circumstances, of that absolute and complete jurisdiction within their respective territories which sovereignty confers.
>
> . . .
>
> A nation would justly be considered as violating its faith, although that faith might not be expressly plighted, which should suddenly and without previous notice, exercise its territorial powers in a manner not consonant to the usages and received obligations of the civilized world." [236]

---

235. 21 Op. Att'y Gen. p. 283 (emphasis added).
236. *The Schooner Exch.* v. *McFaddon*, 11 US 116, 3 L. Ed. 287 (1812).

Indeed, it is worth noting that the US Supreme Court did not actually apply the rule of absolute territorial sovereignty in the *Schooner Exchange* case itself: the Court held that the United States would not exercise jurisdiction over the schooner *Exchange* because it enjoyed sovereign immunity as a public armed vessel in the service of a foreign power, France. But this may have escaped Harmon's attention.

Would the United States, through its assertion of absolute territorial sovereignty to justify the drying up of a river that flowed to Mexico, be justly considered to have violated its faith, on the ground that it had "suddenly and without previous notice, exercise[d] its territorial powers in a manner not consonant to the usages and received obligations of the civilized world"? It would not be surprising if it were. After all, the United States had, abruptly and without previous notice, changed the manner in which it exercised its territorial powers through the greatly increased diversions in Colorado and New Mexico. But as we will see, the United States did not in the end rely on the doctrine of absolute territorial sovereignty in seeking a solution to the case.

It is particularly striking that Attorney General Harmon rested his entire case upon two brief paragraphs from an old Supreme Court decision that was not apposite to the Rio Grande situation, and that he did not do what any law student would have done, namely, apply the case to the facts before him – especially in view of the fact that this was a dispute that had attracted national attention and had been the subject of a joint resolution of Congress.

3. The events following the issuance of Harmon's opinion

The continuation of this story is crucial for understanding what States are willing to do in their quest for stability in their relations generally, and in their water relations, in particular. Did the United States wheel out Harmon's howitzer of absolute territorial sovereignty and blast away? I have already hinted that it did not. In fact, there is no record of the opinion even having been mentioned in diplomatic exchanges between the countries for a full decade following its issuance by the Attorney General. And even then, the countries were on the brink of concluding their 1906 treaty, which as we will see presently, provided for the "*equitable* distribution" of Rio Grande waters. Our question is, why did the United States not take full advantage of the Harmon opinion in its relations with Mexico? After all, the Rio Grande dispute was triggered in large part through extensive and rather abrupt diversions of Rio Grande water in Colorado and New Mexico, two areas of the country that were very much in the process of developing economically, which is something the US national Government would certainly have wanted to encourage and support.

There does not seem to be any documentary evidence directly on the point concerning why the United States did not deploy Harmon's howitzer, but we can make educated guesses. First of all, Americans were being affected by the upstream diversions as well as Mexicans, both in El Paso and in the Rio Grande Valley. This is clear from the US reports referred to earlier. Second, the United States may have been conscious of the fact that it is downstream on major watercourses shared with Canada, such as the Columbia River, and would not want its positions taken *vis-à-vis* Mexico to boomerang on it in its relations with Canada. And third, the United States clearly did not want to be seen as a bully. It wished to occupy the moral high ground and to maintain good relations with Mexico, which as US officials recognized was not going to go away [237]. The United States Government therefore had to find a solution that balanced the interests of the upstream diverters against those of Americans downstream who relied on Rio Grande waters, but one that would also be fair to Mexico, whose citizens according to Ambassador Romero had already been using Rio Grande waters for nearly two centuries by the time the United States declared its independence from Great Britain in 1776 [238]. The US Government therefore, while denying any legal liability for depriving Mexico of water, informed Mexico that it was preparing a draft treaty that would "adjust the question in accordance with the high principles of equity and comity which happily govern the relations between the United States and Mexico" [239].

In the same diplomatic note, the US State Department informed Mexico of a project to construct a storage dam on the Rio Grande at Engle, New Mexico, which would "hasten[s] the satisfactory solution of the whole question between the two governments" [240]. The idea of solving all of the various problems by constructing a storage dam on the

---

237. This is a reference to the statement in the report accompanying proposed legislation referring to Mexico as "a neighbor with whom we shall always have to deal . . .", Report to accompany Bill H.R. 3924 by Mr Lanham, 27 February 1890, HR Rep. No. 490, 51st Cong., 1st Sess., Serial Set 2808-2, p. 2 (1890).
238. This is inferred from Ambassador Romero's statement referred to above that Rio Grande waters had been used in Mexico for some 300 years.
239. Acting Secretary Adee to Chargé d'Affaires ad interim F. Gamboa, 1 May 1905, *ibid.*, p. 503.
240. *Ibid.*

The Evolution of the Law of International Watercourses 327

Rio Grande had emerged from the International Boundary Commission established by the two States in 1889, which they had instructed to report on "[t]he best and most feasible mode . . . of so regulating the use of the waters of [the Rio Grande] as to secure to each country concerned and to its inhabitants their legal and equitable rights and interests in said waters"[241]. The Commission, which was renamed the International Boundary and Water Commission and given new powers and duties in a pathbreaking 1944 treaty between the two States[242], submitted a remarkable joint report in 1896[243], which included the following statement:

> "It is the opinion of the joint commission that Mexico has been wrongfully deprived for many years of a portion of her equitable rights in the flow of one-half of the waters of the Rio Grande at the time of the treaty of Guadalupe Hidalgo; and if there were no other evidence of that fact than the records and measurements [the Commission had referred to], it is apparent to the eye of any visitor to the locality, where can be witnessed the dying fruit trees and vines; and abandoned fields; and dry canals for the greatest portion that has heretofore been cultivated; and while we are considering the equitable rights of Mexico, this is also true of the United States side, where almost the same abandonment and destruction of former prosperous farms may be witnessed."[244]

The Commission's report recommended that a storage dam be constructed at El Paso, and that a treaty be concluded to provide for the distribution of Rio Grande waters. The first recommendation was complicated by the fact that a private company, the Rio Grande Dam and Irrigation Company, had already been given a permit by the

---

241. Protocol contained in note from Minister Romero to Secretary Olney 6 May 1896, US Appendix, p. 226.
242. This commission had been established by the Convention between the United States and Mexico of 1 March 1889. 1 Malloy, p. 1167; Legislative Texts, Treaty No. 74, p. 229; 1974 *YB Int'l L. Comm'n*, Vol. 2, pt. 2, p. 76, para. 184. A later treaty changed the name of this body to the International Boundary and Water Commission, United States and Mexico and vested new powers and duties in the Commission. *See* Treaty between the United States and Mexico relating to the Utilization of the Waters of the Colorado and Tijuana Rivers, and of the Rio Grande (Rio Bravo) from Fort Quitman, Texas, to the Gulf of Mexico, 3 February 1944, and supplementary protocol, 14 November 1944, 3 *UNTS*, p. 314; Legislative Texts, Treaty No. 77, p. 236; 1974 *YB. Int'l L. Comm'n*, Vol. 2, pt. 2, p. 80, para. 212.
243. Report of 25 November 1896, *ibid.*, p. 264.
244. Col. Anson Mills, Commissioner, to Secretary Olney, 25 November 1896, *ibid.*, p. 261, at p. 268.

Secretary of the Interior to construct dams and other works on the Rio Grande at Elephant Butte, New Mexico. But the plot thickens. The Secretary of State requested the Secretary of the Interior to look into whether there were any legal means to cancel the rights granted to the private company. The Secretary of State also inquired of the Secretary of War whether a permit from that department would not be necessary. The Secretary of War had jurisdiction over the protection of navigable waters, and it had come to the attention of the Secretary of State that "the Rio Grande River in some parts above the international boundary line is, and has been used as, a waterway for navigation between the United States and Mexico . . ."[245]. The Secretary of War confirmed this, finding that "the Rio Grande from a point above Elephant Butte down is a navigable water of the United States" – which must have come as something of a surprise to the Rio Grande Dam and Irrigation Company since Attorney General Harmon had come to precisely the opposite conclusion only two years earlier. But the Secretary of War did not stop there. He found that the private company's proposed dam at Elephant Butte and the distribution of water from its reservoir for irrigation would have the result that "the Rio Grande will be practically destroyed as a stream for many miles below Elephant Butte"[246].

These findings led the US Government to sue the private company to prevent it from constructing a dam at Elephant Butte. The grounds for the suit? That the dam would "seriously obstruct the navigable capacity of the said river"[247], and that the company had not been authorized to construct the dam by the US Government. The company was ultimately enjoined permanently from constructing the dam at Elephant Butte. If any proof were needed for the proposition that there can be interrelationships between navigational and non-navigational uses of international watercourses, surely this story provides it.

Adding insult to injury – at least in what must have been the view of the Rio Grande Dam and Irrigation Company – the US Government had in the meantime, while the litigation against the company was pending, constructed a dam near Engle, New Mexico, approximately one mile

---

245. Secretary Olney to D. Francis, Secretary of the Interior, 11 January 1897, *ibid.*, p. 292, at p. 293.
246. Secretary of War to the Attorney General, 19 February 1897, *ibid.*, p. 313, at p. 314.
247. See *United States* v. *The Rio Grande Dam & Irrigation Company*, No. 140, Chancery, order granting temporary injunction of 24 May 1897, *ibid.*, p. 1; *United States* v. *Rio Grande Dam and Irrigation Co*, 174 US p. 690 (1899).

below the Elephant Butte Dam site [248]. This obviously made it all the more important that the private project at Elephant Butte not be allowed to proceed, since that project would have rendered the downstream Engle dam of little use.

It was most fortunate for the United States that there was an engineering solution to this dilemma that could largely satisfy all parties in one fell swoop: the upstream diverters could keep diverting (though some regulation was perhaps inevitable), the downstream farmers – in both countries – could resume farming, and the two countries involved could resume relating, in a friendly and mutually supportive way. Like many rivers in the southwestern United States, the Rio Grande is prone to alternating years of flood and drought. Such a pattern lends itself well to storage dams, since water can be stored in years of flood and released in years of drought. The former Engle Dam was renamed the Elephant Butte Dam and is owned and operated today by the United States Bureau of Reclamation. Perhaps appropriately, the dam is located near the small city of Truth or Consequences, New Mexico.

VI. The 1906 Treaty

A draft treaty for the settlement of the dispute over the Rio Grande was prepared by the US Geological Survey and submitted to Mexico through Secretary of State Elihu Root. The two countries moved quickly to agreement on the text. The Convention between the United States of America and Mexico concerning the Equitable Distribution of the Waters of the Rio Grande for Irrigation Purposes [249], the first treaty entered into by the United States that deals exclusively with international watercourses, was signed at Washington on 21 May 1906. This agreement is one of our "milestones", in the evolution of the law of international watercourses.

The treaty provides that after completion of the storage dam near Engle, New Mexico, the United States is to deliver without cost to Mexico 60,000 acre-feet of water to Mexico annually, in the bed of the Rio Grande, in accordance with an annexed schedule [250].

---

248. US Answer, p. 1. pp. 24-25.
249. 34 Stat. 2953 (emphasis added).
250. The treaty also provides, in typical boilerplate language, that Mexico waives all claims arising out of diversions in the United States and that in entering into the treaty the United States does not concede any legal basis for claims that may be brought against it concerning diversions in the United States, nor does the United States concede the establishment of any general principle or precedent by concluding the agreement.

VII. Conclusion

In conclusion, the story of the dispute between Mexico and the United States over Rio Grande water shows that while extreme positions can be taken on both sides – and in this case on one side in particular, that of the United States – those positions in the end do not typically carry the day. There is clear evidence that the United States realized that it was bound together with Mexico through the river they shared, and that Mexico was "a neighbor with whom we shall always have to deal, and whom it is both our duty and policy to treat and cultivate in a neighborly way"[251]. Under those circumstances, which apply to all international watercourses, the United States and Mexico clearly decided that an arrangement that would provide for an "equitable distribution" of the waters of the Rio Grande between them would benefit both parties and would stand the test of time.

The story is remarkable because it shows that within the course of one dispute covering around a decade, at a time when there was some uncertainty about the governing legal principles, the applicable standard in effect evolved from absolute territorial sovereignty – the "Harmon Doctrine" – to equitable distribution, which remains the basic normative principle today, 115 years later.

---

251. Report to accompany Bill HR 3924 by Mr Lanham, 27 February 1890, HR Rep. No. 490, 51st Cong., 1st Sess., Serial Set 2808-2, p. 2 (1890).

CHAPTER 4 [252]

NAVIGATION: NATURE'S HIGHWAYS IN A FORESTED LAND

I. Introduction

The focus in this chapter will be on the evolution of the legal regulation of navigation on international watercourses. We will first explore the historical background of the law of navigation – how ancient civilizations confronted this issue as far back as the fifth millennium BC. Next, we will survey the development, chiefly over the past two centuries, of the rules of international law governing navigation we know today. We will then continue our discussion of the law of navigation as it currently stands, with an emphasis on particularly pivotal case law and the general rules that are broadly recognized.

Before we delve any further into the topic, we should first make clear what is meant by the expression "navigation" or "navigational use", as those terms are used in international law. The term "navigation" refers to the use of a waterway by humans for the floating of any form of vessel – whether crude raft, papyrus boat, steamship, or any other floating conveyance. Although the term is thus used in its broadest sense, in practice the interest of States sharing waterways has been focused primarily on the *purpose* for which the vessel is being used (principally whether it is engaged in commerce), rather than the physical nature of it. It follows that the expression "navigational use" concerns the use of a waterway for navigation. One final observation is that in the field of navigation, the term "waterway" is generally more appropriate than "watercourse", since the river is being used as a "highway" for vessels. The two terms will largely be used interchangeably here, however.

II. Early practice

We may begin with a brief historical overview of navigation on what we would today call international waterways. There is evidence that people traveled in boats on the Tigris and Euphrates Rivers of

---

252. The author would like to express his appreciation to Ms Sierra Horton, 2L at the McGeorge School of Law, for her excellent assistance with this Chapter.

Mesopotamia in the fifth millennium BC and on the Nile in the fourth millennium [253]. As far as is known, there were no general rules applicable to navigation on these rivers in ancient times, but there was, in a sense, an "international" aspect to how fluvial highways were governed: the right to navigate on a waterway often depended on obtaining the permission of the ruler who controlled it [254]. During the Roman Empire, Roman law accorded freedom of navigation to all on rivers which were situated *within* the Empire. Navigation on the Danube and the Rhine, which marked the Empire's boundaries, was strictly controlled.

The Romans' principle of freedom of navigation within the boundaries of their empire stemmed from their overarching treatment of waters as public spaces more appropriately governed by the rules of the law of nature, rather than the law of humans. This notion of a natural right to navigation is a powerful one, and it has permeated international legal thought for centuries. For example, in 1792, Thomas Jefferson invoked this concept of natural law in a report to President George Washington concerning the right of the United States to the free navigation of the lower Mississippi River, which was at the time partially under Spanish sovereignty. In the same year, the principle of free navigation was also echoed in a French decree which has been characterized – perhaps somewhat extravagantly – as "a turning point in the history of international river law" [255]. However, the French decree did go even further than Jefferson's ideas by asserting the supremacy of the law of nature over *all* positive law, including treaties. The French theory served as a catalyst of sorts for the further development of the law governing navigation, subsequently finding expression in international instruments to be addressed later in the present Chapter.

While this principle of a natural right to free navigation is no doubt a significant one, it is not the only concept which has been of importance in the development of the law of navigation on international watercourses. The doctrine of *territorial sovereignty* we have encountered earlier – the idea of a State's exclusive jurisdiction and control over everything within its territory, including portions of international watercourses located there – has been a conflicting, albeit equally fundamental tenet

---

253. L. Teclaff, *Fiat or Custom: The Checkered Development of International Water Law*, 31 Nat. Res. J. 45, 46 (1991). See also L. Teclaff, *The River Basin in History and Law*, Martinus Nijhoff, The Hague, 1967, p. 42.
254. See Teclaff 1991 (*above* footnote 252), p. 46.
255. B. Vitányi, *The International Regime of River Navigation*, Alphen aan den Rijn, Sijthoff & Noordhoff, 1979, p. 31.

that has shaped the evolution of the law of navigation [256]. In fact, the doctrine of territorial sovereignty proved to be the undoing of the principle of freedom of navigation for all nations who were parties to the World War I peace treaties, which we will soon discuss in more detail.

The economic liberalism of the eighteenth and nineteenth centuries is yet another consideration – one of a more practical nature – which has impacted the evolution of the law of navigation on international watercourses. As we transition into a more focused discussion on the development of the law of navigational uses in Europe specifically, we will see how this principle of economic liberalism helped fuel the drive toward freedom of navigation in a variety of influential treaties and cases.

Let us now turn to the development of the law in this field in Western Europe.

III. Development of the law of navigational uses of international watercourses in Western Europe

To fully understand the evolution of the law of navigational uses of international watercourses, it is necessary to spend some time tracking its development in Western European nations. It is here that – given the region's geography and topography – navigation has historically overshadowed other uses of international watercourses and thus, where the law of navigational uses is the most highly developed. In this region, irrigation was unnecessary due to plentiful rainfall, and overland travel was often made difficult by dense forests. As in the case of arid regions, the use of rivers as avenues of communication and commerce played an important role in the development of political organization. In view of the historic importance of navigation in the more humid areas, it is perhaps not surprising that the earliest entry contained in a compilation of over 2,000 international legal instruments concerning water resources is a grant of freedom of navigation on the Rhine, made in the year 805 by Charlemagne to a monastery (this being the second milestone of our course) [257].

---

256. Caflisch (*above* footnote 36), p. 39, who refers to territorial sovereignty as a "dogma" in the context of navigation.

257. Food and Agriculture Organization of the United Nations, Systematic Index of International Water Resources Treaties, Declarations, Acts and Cases by Basin, FAO, Rome, 1978, p. 1 (hereafter referred to as FAO Index).

The evolution of the law of navigational uses in Western Europe is reflected in a series of foundational instruments. We will begin with the Peace of Westphalia in 1648, the third in our tour of influential, law-altering milestones [258]. The Peace of Westphalia is generally identified with the emergence of the modern nation-state and thus, the beginnings of the international legal system we know today. It consisted of the Treaties of Münster and Osnabrück – both of which contained important provisions concerning navigation on shared waterways. The Treaty of Münster granted the Dutch Republic independence from Spain and opened the Lower Rhine to free navigation [259]. However, it also declared the Scheldt River in the Spanish Netherlands *closed* to navigation as a concession to Amsterdam in its commercial rivalry with Antwerp [260]. As we continue our discussion of navigation in other major European peace treaties of the nineteenth and early twentieth centuries, you will see that those concerns surrounding commerce have continued to be a driving force, shaping the evolution of the law of the navigational uses of international watercourses in a substantial way.

The Congress of Vienna of 1815 is another pivotal milestone in the evolution of the law of navigational uses. Of course, its chief purpose was to establish a balance of power in Europe in order to maintain peace following the Napoleonic Wars. But it also laid down a model for the regulation of navigation on international waterways that was then followed in numerous agreements over at least the next century. Professor Lucius Caflisch observed that provisions of the Congress's Final Act established, for the first time, the opening of international watercourses on the multilateral level [261]. Article 109 of the Final Act provided that navigation on the rivers governed by the agreement "shall be entirely free, and shall not, in respect to Commerce, be prohibited to any one; it being understood that the Regulations established with regard to the Police of this navigation shall be respected, as they will be framed alike for all, and as favourable as possible to the Commerce of all nations" [262]. The principle of freedom of navigation laid down

---

258. Treaty of Peace between Sweden and the Empire, signed at Osnabrück, 14 October (24), 1648, 1 CTS 119 (English transl. at p. 198); Treaty of Peace between France and the Empire, signed at Münster, 14 October (24), 1648, 1 CTS 271.
259. Treaty of Münster, *ibid.*, Article XII.
260. *Ibid.*, Article XIV. See also Wescoat (*above* footnote 194).
261. Caflisch (*above* footnote 33). Caflisch refers to Articles 108-116 of the Final Act.
262. Congress of Vienna, 9 June 1815, Austria, France, Great Britain, Portugal, Prussia, Russia and Sweden, 1 MPT pp. 519, 567; French text in 64 CTS p. 453.

in the Congress of Vienna applied to the eight major States of Europe that were parties to the agreement, but their influence was such that it soon spread beyond their borders [263]. While Article 109 applied by its terms to all navigable rivers that separate or cross the territories of the contracting parties, the chief commercial thoroughfare of Western Europe to which those provisions granted access was the Rhine.

Some forty years later, the General Treaty of Peace of 1856, which ended the Crimean War, established freedom of navigation on the Danube. While clearly influenced by the Congress of Vienna of 1815, the General Treaty of Peace's grant of freedom of navigation went beyond the Congress of Vienna model by extending navigational rights to *all* nations, rather than solely the riparian States that were parties to the agreement [264]. This distinction between the Congress of Vienna and the 1856 General Treaty of Peace is an important one that reflects a continuing tension in the law of navigation to which we will return later. An innovative feature of both the Congress of Vienna and the 1856 treaty is that both established commissions charged with administering the rivers concerned [265]. The establishment of such commissions increasingly became a feature of treaties relating to international watercourses because of the important role these bodies can play in international river basin management.

A final set of major peace treaties containing provisions on navigation is the 1919 Treaty of Versailles and its associated agreements, concluded at the end of the First World War [266]. These treaties declared certain important rivers of Western and Eastern Europe, including the Rhine, Moselle, Meuse, Elbe, Oder and Danube, to be international, opening them to commerce and trade, and established commissions with extensive powers to administer them [267]. The World War I peace

---

263. Kaeckenbeeck (*above* footnote 17), p. 61. Kaeckenbeeck elucidates the "Applications of the principles of the Congress of Vienna", using the Rhine, the Danube and the Congo as examples.
264. General Treaty of Peace, Paris, Article 15, 30 March 1856, France, Great Britain, Prussia, Sardinia (Italy), Ottoman Empire (Turkey), Austria-Hungary, 10 Herstlet Comm'l Treaties, p. 533.
265. See Wescoat (*above* footnote 194), p. 54.
266. Treaty of Peace between the Allied and Associated Powers and Germany, Versailles, 28 June 1919, 11 Martens, 3rd ser., p. 323; Treaty of Saint-Germain, 10 September 1919, *ibid*., p. 691; Treaty of Neuilly, 27 November 1919, 12 Martens, 3rd ser., p. 325; and Treaty of Trianon, 4 June 1920, *ibid*., p. 423. See the discussion of the provisions relating to navigation on international rivers in Vitányi (*above* footnote 254), pp. 100-108. See also Wescoat (*above* footnote 194), pp. 64-70, where the influence of the League of Nations on multilateral water policy is also discussed.
267. Treaty of Versailles, Article 331; Treaty of Saint-Germain, art. 291; Treaty of Neuilly, Article 219; and Treaty of Trianon, Article 275. See Vitányi (*above* foot-

agreements were quite liberal with respect to matters of navigation on international waterways in Europe. The Treaty of Versailles expanded the principle of freedom of navigation on the rivers to which it applied, extending it to non-riparian States for merchant shipping [268]. The other peace treaties concluded after the First World War contained provisions similar to those of the Treaty of Versailles [269]. It is essential to note, however, that the Treaty of Versailles' liberal provisions were limited to waterways or parts thereof that were declared "international", meaning in this case *only* defined portions of the rivers specifically named, and to navigable portions of those of their tributaries that naturally provide more than one State with access to the sea [270].

The World War I peace treaties contemplated the development of a General Convention on freedom of navigation, to be approved by the League of Nations, which would supersede the regime they contained [271]. The Covenant of the League of Nations, in turn, specifically provided

---

note 254), p. 100; and *Jurisdiction of the European Commission of the Danube*, 1927, Adv. Op., PCIJ, Ser. B, No. 14., Article 331 of the Treaty of Versailles provides in relevant part as follows:

"The following rivers are declared international: the Elbe (Labe) from its confluence with the Vltava (Moldau), and the Vltava (Moldau) from Prague; the Oder (Odra) from its confluence with the Oppa; the Niemen (Russstrom-Memel-Niemen) from Grodno; the Danube from Ulm; and all navigable parts of these river systems which naturally provide more than one State with access to the sea, with or without transshipment from one vessel to another; together with lateral canals and channels constructed either to duplicate or to improve naturally navigable sections of the specified river systems, or to connect two naturally navigable sections of the same river."

268. See Articles 332-337 and 340-362 of the Treaty of Versailles; Articles 292-298 and 301-308 of the Treaty of Saint-Germain; Articles 276-282 and 285-291 of the Treaty of Trianon; and Articles 220-226 and 229-235 of the Treaty of Neuilly. See the discussion in Vitányi (*above* footnote 254), pp. 100-101.

269. See Article 292 of the Treaty of Saint-Germain, Article 276 of the Treaty of Trianon, and Article 220 of the Treaty of Neuilly. Vitányi notes that prescribing both national and most-favored-nation treatment seems redundant at first glance but observes that the latter may afford better treatment than the former in some cases. Vitányi (*above* footnote 254), p. 101.

270. Treaty of Versailles, Article 331 (*above* footnote 265).

271. Treaty of Versailles, Article 338; Treaty of Saint-Germain, Article 299; Treaty of Trianon, Article 283; and Treaty of Neuilly, Article 227. Article 338 of the Treaty of Versailles provides as follows:

"The regime set out in Articles 332 to 337 above shall be superseded by one to be laid down in a General Convention drawn up by the Allied and Associated Powers, and approved by the League of Nations, relating to the waterways recognised in such Convention as having an international character. This Convention shall apply in particular to the whole or part of the above-mentioned river systems of the Elbe (Labe), the Oder (Odra), the Niemen (Russtrom-Memel-Niemen), and the Danube, and such other parts of these river systems as may be covered by a general definition."

that the members of the organization would "make provision to secure and maintain the freedom of communication and of transit and equitable treatment for the commerce of all members of the League" [272].

Accordingly, the League of Nations invited forty-one States from Europe, Latin America and Asia – including the Allied and Associated Powers and neutral countries – to a Conference at Barcelona for the purpose of elaborating such an agreement. The result was the Convention and Statute on the Regime of Navigable Waterways of International Concern, which was concluded on 20 April 1921 and which I will hereafter refer to as "the Barcelona Convention" and "the Barcelona Statute" (the Statute is incorporated into the Convention by the terms of the latter) [273]. The provisions of this agreement are of particular interest because of the broad geographic distribution of the States that participated in its elaboration. A glaring omission, however, is that no African countries were among those invited to participate despite the importance of navigation on African rivers. This was no doubt due to the fact that the countries whose rivers were most heavily navigated were at the time under colonial domination. Nevertheless, the list of participating States constituted the bulk of the international community as it then stood. Given the breadth and overall inclusiveness of the convention, it is important to include in any discussion regarding the evolution of the law of navigation on international waterways. However, it is also necessary to note how the Barcelona Convention's relative inclusiveness came at a steep price, and ultimately led to its demise [274].

While European countries had just demonstrated a willingness to allow "vessels of all nations" to navigate on their rivers in the World War I peace treaties, the Barcelona Statute restricts the right of freedom of navigation to only other contracting States to the agreement. To quote it directly, Article 3 of the Statute states:

"[E]ach of the Contracting States shall accord free exercise of navigation to the vessels flying the flag of any one of the other Contracting States on those parts of navigable waterways specified

---

272. The Covenant of the League of Nations, 1919, *Yale Law School: The Avalon Project*, available at https://avalon.law.yale.edu/20th_century/leagcov.asp (last visited September 2021).
273. 20 April 1921, 7 *LNTS* 35 (hereafter referred to as the Barcelona Convention and Statute, respectively).
274. See the discussion in Vitányi (*above* footnote 254), pp. 103-106.

[in the Statute] which may be situated under its sovereignty or authority." [275]

The potential problems created by this restriction, particularly between States that are parties to both the Versailles and Barcelona regimes and those that are parties to *only* the Versailles system, are quite obvious. This is especially the case since the peace treaties contemplated that their liberal provisions on freedom of navigation would be superseded by what became the Barcelona Convention. The severe limitation of the Barcelona Convention to invited parties only reflects a concern on the part of a majority of members of the Commission of Enquiry that prepared the Barcelona conference's working document. This concern was that the preservation of freedom of navigation for *all* States would unduly interfere with the sovereignty and authority of riparian States. Again we see at play the clash between freedom of navigation and territorial sovereignty.

The retrogression from freedom of navigation for *all* nations under the peace treaties to such freedom *only* for the contracting States under the Barcelona Statute spelled the Statute's, and the Convention's, downfall. When the League of Nations was dissolved in 1946, only twenty-two States, a mere six of which were non-European [276], were parties to the Barcelona Convention and Statute. While Malta and Nigeria acceded to the Convention in 1966 and 1967, respectively, India denounced it in 1956 and Malawi in 1969 declared its wish "to terminate any connection with this Convention which it might have inherited" [277] – presumably from its colonizer, Great Britain. Thus, while the contracting parties to the Barcelona Convention began optimistically by expressing their desire to "carry ... further the development as regards the international regime of navigation on international waterways, which began more than a century ago" [278] (clearly referring to the Congress of Vienna), they may more accurately be characterized as having taken a step backwards [279].

IV. Influential cases and the law as it stands today

Before discussing cases that have contributed to the development of the law of navigation on international waterways, allow me to sum

---

275. Barcelona Statute, Article 3.
276. These were Chile, Colombia, India, Peru, Thailand and Turkey.
277. Multilateral Treaties Deposited with the Secretary-General, League of Nations Treaties, Treaty 17.
278. Barcelona Convention, preamble, 1st para.
279. To the same effect see R. R. Baxter, *The Law of International Waterways, With Particular Regard to Interoceanic Canals*, Cambridge, Massachusetts, Harvard University Press, 1964, p. 134. See also Vitányi (*above* footnote 254), p. 104.

The Evolution of the Law of International Watercourses 339

up what we have covered thus far: While navigation has been integral to the development of human social organization for millennia, it may be surprising that the development of legal norms governing the navigational use of international waterways is relatively recent – "recent" meaning chiefly over the past two centuries. While the Romans' principle of freedom of navigation for all has persisted, a look at major peace treaties from as far back as 1648 and up until 1921 tells us that this long-standing principle has often conflicted with others, principally that of territorial sovereignty. This conflict has often manifested itself as a dichotomy between treaties that truly allow for freedom of navigation for all, such as the General Treaty of Peace of 1856, and those that allow freedom of navigation solely for riparian States.

Now we may turn to the contributions of international courts and tribunals to the development of the law of navigation on international waterways, chiefly in three cases: the *River Oder* case, decided by the Permanent Court of International Justice in 1929 [280]; the *Oscar Chinn* case, also decided by the Permanent Court, but in 1934 [281]; and the *Navigational and Related Rights* case, decided by the International Court of Justice in 2009 [282]. We will review each decision briefly and highlight the way in which international tribunals have interpreted and applied the relevant rules of international law.

V. *The* River Oder *case*

The *River Oder* case grew out of the Treaty of Versailles, which, it will be recalled, declared to be "international" a number of rivers, including the Oder, from its confluence with the Oppa, and including "all navigable parts of these river systems which naturally provide more than one State with access to the sea . . ." [283]. Article 341 of the Treaty placed the Oder under the administration of an International Commission, which was mandated to "define the sections of the river or its tributaries to which the international regime shall be applied" [284]. The question arose whether two tributaries of the Oder, the Netze and the Warthe, both of which originated in Poland and flowed across the

---

280. Judgment of 10 September 1929, Germany, Denmark, France, Great Britain, Sweden, Czechoslovakia/Poland, PCIJ, Ser. A, No. 23, Ser. C, No. 17 (II).
281. Judgment of 12 December 1934, Great Britain/Belgium, PCIJ, Ser. A/B, No. 63, Ser. C, No. 75.
282. *Dispute regarding Navigational and Related Rights (Costa Rica v. Nicaragua), Judgment, ICJ Reports 2009*, p. 213.
283. Treaty of Versailles, Article 331, quoted in *above* footnote 265.
284. *Ibid.*, Article 341.

Polish border, should be within the jurisdiction of the Commission. Poland maintained that the Commission's jurisdiction with respect to these two tributaries should end at the Polish border; the other six members of the Commission believed that its jurisdiction should extend upstream to the point at which the two rivers ceased to be navigable, whether that was within Polish territory or not. Poland then argued that the portions of these tributaries which were situated in Polish territory provided *only* Poland "with access to the sea" and that those portions were therefore not "international" under the Treaty. The other six States took the contrary position, which the Court upheld. Interestingly, the six governments had relied on the 1921 Barcelona Statute to justify their position, but the Court held that Poland was not bound by the Barcelona Statute, because it was not a party to the Barcelona Convention. Thus, the Court instead focused on the Treaty of Versailles.

In a portion of the opinion that has since become well-known, the Court reasoned that the solution to the sort of problem the countries were faced with "has been sought not in the idea of a right of passage in favour of upstream States, but in that of a *community of interest* of riparian States. This community interest in a navigable river becomes the basis of a common legal right, the essential features of which are the *perfect equality* of all riparian States in the user of the whole course of the river and the exclusion of any preferential privilege of any riparian State in relation to the others" [285]. The Court declared that this "community of interest" theory is the concept upon which international river law, "as laid down by the Act of the Congress of Vienna" is "undoubtedly based". It is a powerful concept, which in the context of the *River Oder* case essentially meant that so long as the river was navigable, it was "international" in character, regardless of the country in which the river or its tributaries were located. The Permanent Court thus, in effect, finessed the requirements of the Treaty of Versailles under Article 331 that the river provide "more than one State with access to the sea". The community of interest doctrine made clear that freedom of navigation is a two-way street: not only can upstream States navigate freely through downstream States to the sea, but downstream States are permitted to navigate freely through the territories of upstream States, as well.

---

285. PCIJ, Ser. A, No. 23, pp. 27-28 (emphasis added).

VI. *The* Oscar Chinn *case*

The *Oscar Chinn*[286] case is certainly less well-known than the *Oder* case, but it is nevertheless significant for its interpretation of certain aspects of the law of navigation and its potential implications for future cases. The case involved a British citizen, Oscar Chinn, who in 1929 established a river transport and ship-building and repairing company in what was then the Belgian Congo. In 1921, the Belgian Government had transferred its transport services business on the Congo River to a company that it had formed and was under its management. In 1925, this company combined with a private enterprise and became known as Unatra (Union Nationale des Transports Fluviaux). Belgium owned more than half the shares of Unatra and also supervised it.

The Great Depression of the 1930s caused a collapse of prices obtained for colonial produce in the European markets; this seriously affected trade in the Congo Colony, which led the Belgian Minister for the Colonies to reduce the transport rates of the companies the Government was in a position to control, to one franc per ton – a nominal charge[287]. The Colony refused, at first, to extend the benefit of these measures to fluvial transport companies other than Unatra[288]. According to the United Kingdom, this arrangement ultimately ruined Mr Chinn, who was forced to suspend his businesses as a result. The British Government eventually espoused Chinn's claim and, when negotiations with Belgium proved fruitless, the two Governments agreed to submit the case to the Permanent Court. The first question put to the Court was whether the measures taken by Belgium in relation to fluvial transport on the waterways of the Belgian Congo were in conflict with the international obligations of Belgium owed to the United Kingdom. These international obligations, according to the Court, arose from the 1919 Convention of Saint-Germain-en-Laye, one of the group of Versailles treaties, and second, from the general principles of international law. Under Article 5 of the 1919 Convention, navigation on the rivers and lakes within the Congo River basin is to be "entirely free for merchant vessels and for the transport of goods

---

286. Judgment of 12 December 1934, Great Britain/Belgium, PCIJ, Ser. A/B, No. 63, Ser. C, No. 75.
287. Ser. A/B, p. 73.
288. However, in 1932, after Chinn suspended his operations, the Belgian Government announced that it would extend to Belgian or foreign ship-owners advances similar to those granted to Unatra. *Ibid.*, p. 76.

and passengers" [289]. It also provides that "craft of every kind belonging to nationals of the [parties] shall be treated in all respects on a footing of perfect equality" [290]. The United Kingdom argued an alleged "inconsistency between the measures taken by the Belgian Government and the principles of equality and freedom of trade and freedom of navigation" [291].

The Court explained the meaning of freedom of navigation as "freedom of movement for vessels, freedom to enter ports, and to make use of plant and docks, to load and unload goods and to transport goods and passengers" [292]. The Court continued:

> "From this point of view, freedom of navigation also implies, as far as the business side of maritime or fluvial transport is concerned, freedom of commerce. But it does not follow that in all other respects freedom of navigation entails and presupposes freedom of commerce." [293]

Ultimately, the Court held, by six votes to five, that Belgium had not violated either the freedom of commerce principle or that of non-discrimination. As to freedom of commerce, the Court reasoned that the freedom of trade, or the right to engage in any commercial activity, was never denied to Mr Chinn. It also maintained that this right to engage in any commercial activity presupposes the existence of commercial competition – something Mr Chinn must have known he would encounter in the form of Unatra [294]. The Court found that a concentration of business of the kind involved in respect of Unatra would only infringe freedom of commerce if a monopoly were established that others are bound to respect. This was not the case here, according to the Court, because the Belgian Government never *prohibited* commerce by other companies. Instead, the Court found that what the United Kingdom characterized as a "*de facto* monopoly" was merely a "natural consequence of the situation of the services under State supervision as compared with private concerns", and that the freedom of trade and of navigation provided for in the Convention did not "imply an obligation on the Belgian government to guarantee the success of each individual concern" [295].

---

289. As quoted in *ibid.*, p. 80.
290. *Ibid.*
291. *Ibid.*, pp. 82-83.
292. *Ibid.*, p. 83.
293. *Ibid.*
294. *Ibid.*, p. 84.
295. *Ibid.*, p. 85.

International law scholars have criticized the Permanent Court's decision in *Oscar Chinn*, arguing that the Court's holding "betrays such a narrow conception" of the notion of freedom of trade "as to reduce it to an empty phrase" [296]. Of course, the case may be a unique one, especially given its colonial context and the severe economic depression that led Belgium to take the measures in question. But the Court's decision does seem to allow a State to do indirectly what it cannot do directly, with the effect that freedom of navigation is rendered virtually meaningless.

VII. *The* Navigational and Related Rights *case*

We will consider next the *Navigational and Related Rights* case, decided in 2009 by the International Court of Justice. This case was brought by Costa Rica against Nicaragua, and largely involved the interpretation and application of the principal legal instruments governing the San Juan River: the 1858 Treaty of Limits between the two countries and an 1888 arbitral award of President Grover Cleveland concerning the Treaty, its interpretation and application. To put the case in geographical context, the San Juan River has its source in Lake Nicaragua and flows for some 205 kilometers before emptying into the Caribbean Sea. The main stem of the river is, in its entirety, situated within Nicaraguan territory. This is rather unusual in the case of regimes of borders formed by rivers, which more frequently locate the border in the river on the river's "thalweg" – its deepest navigable channel – or on its median line, rather than on one of its banks. In the case of the San Juan River, the placement of the boundary along the Costa Rican bank, rather than in the river, may be understood as part of a compromise struck in the 1858 Treaty of Limits in which Nicaragua relinquished its claim to the Nicoya/Guanacaste Peninsula, and Costa Rica recognized Nicaragua's full sovereignty over the San Juan River [297]. Thus, the 1858 Treaty "established Nicaragua's dominion and sovereign jurisdiction over the waters of the San Juan River, but at the same time affirmed Costa Rica's navigational rights *'con objetos de comercio'* on the lower course of the river (Art. VI)" [298].

---

296. Vitányi (*above* footnote 254), p. 253.
297. Nicaragua was anticipating use of the river by Cornelius Vanderbilt in connection with his plan to construct an inter-oceanic canal, taking advantage of both the river and the enormous Lake of Nicaragua, something that would presumably been lucrative for Nicaragua.
298. *Navigational and Related Rights*, p. 229, para. 19.

Here is where the issue of interest to us arises: During the mid-1990s, Nicaragua introduced certain measures concerning navigation by Costa Rica on the San Juan [299]. For example, one measure required the charging of fees "for passengers travelling on Costa Rican vessels navigating on the San Juan River and the requirement for Costa Rican vessels to stop at Nicaraguan Army posts along the river". Costa Rica argued that, in light of these measures, Nicaragua had not respected its right of navigation on the San Juan under the Treaty of Limits and Cleveland Award.

The expression *"con objetos de comercio"* became a principal focus of the case. In essence, Costa Rica argued that the term was entirely permissive, meaning broadly "for commercial purposes". For Nicaragua, on the other hand, the Spanish expression had a considerably more restrictive meaning, requiring that any navigation by Costa Rica be "with articles of trade" or words to that effect, meaning that Costa Rican vessels could navigate on the San Juan only if they were carrying commercial merchandise. The distinction was important, in particular due to Costa Rica's wish to bring tourists on boats from Costa Rica into the San Juan. Costa Rica argued that navigation for this purpose was commercial, and thus permitted by the Treaty of Limits. Costa Rica then took its interpretation of the term one step further by arguing that "commerce" also had a second and much broader meaning of "communication and dealings of some persons or peoples with others" – a definition Costa Rica adopted from nineteenth-century editions of the *Dictionary of the Royal Spanish Academy* [300]. According to Costa Rica, this meant that

> "'commerce' includes movement and contact between inhabitants of the villages on the Costa Rican bank of the San Juan, and the use of the river for purposes of navigation by Costa Rican public officials providing the local population with essential services, in areas such as health, education, and security" [301].

Nicaragua responded that, when the treaty was concluded in 1858, what was important to Costa Rica was the ability to bring its coffee out to the Caribbean via the San Juan for shipment to England, which

---

299. Other measures had been introduced in the 1980s which Nicaragua justified as temporary, exceptional measures to protect Nicaragua's national security in the context of the armed conflict that was going on at the time. *Ibid.*, p. 230, para. 24.
300. *Ibid.*, p. 241, para. 59.
301. *Ibid.*

was then the largest market for this commodity[302]. Thus, Nicaragua maintained that its interpretation of the term *"con objetos de comercio"* as meaning "with items of commerce" or "with articles of trade" was clearly the correct interpretation, because it reflected Costa Rica's interests *at the time the treaty was concluded*. This, of course, would mean that navigation by tourist boats, and certainly navigation for the purpose of resupplying and exchanging police personnel at Costa Rican border posts, would be excluded.

The Court declined to subscribe to either country's interpretation. It did acknowledge, however, a general rule that "the terms used in a treaty must be interpreted in light of what is determined to have been the parties' *common* intention, which is, by definition, contemporaneous with the treaty's conclusion"[303]. To make this determination of "common intention", the Court recognized that it may be necessary to ascertain the meaning of terms used by the parties when the treaty was drafted. The Court further recognized that it "has so proceeded in certain cases requiring it to interpret a term whose meaning had evolved since the conclusion of the treaty at issue, and in those cases the Court adhered to the original meaning . . ."[304]. But the Court also identified two kinds of situations in which a departure from the original intent of the parties could be justified. The first was subsequent practice, within the meaning of Article 31 (3) *(b)* of the Vienna Convention on the Law of Treaties[305]. Such practice by the parties, according to the Court, could potentially "result in a departure from the original intent on the basis of a tacit agreement between [them]"[306]. The second kind of situation arises when it is clear that the parties' intent "was, or may

---

302. "Costa Rica's other vital national aim was to secure for its products, mainly coffee, a way out to the Atlantic that would ensure faster and cheaper access to the European market, particularly Great Britain, which absorbed half of her production at a time when Costa Rica lacked ports on the Caribbean and her exports to Europe had to head for Cape Horn. That is what the Jerez-Cañas Treaty granted Costa Rica." Counter-Memorial of Nicaragua, vol. I, p. 161, para. 4.1.35, available at icj-cij.org/public/files/case-related/133/15086.pdf.
303. *Navigational and Related Rights*, p. 242, para. 63.
304. *Ibid.*, citing the Judgment of 27 August 1952 in the case concerning *Rights of Nationals of the United States of America in Morocco (France v. United States of America), ICJ Reports 1952*, p. 176, "on the question of the meaning of 'dispute' in the context of a treaty concluded in 1836, the Court having determined the meaning of this term in Morocco when the treaty was concluded"; and the Judgment of 13 December 1999 in the case concerning *Kasikili/Sedudu Island (Botswana/Namibia), ICJ Reports 1999 (II)*, p. 1062, para. 25, "in respect of the meaning of 'centre of the main channel' and 'thalweg' when the Anglo-German Agreement of 1890 was concluded".
305. *Ibid.*, para. 64.
306. *Ibid.*

be presumed to have been" to give certain terms used in the treaty a "meaning or content capable of evolving, not one fixed once and for all, so as to make allowance for, among other things, developments in international law" [307]. The Court continued to reason that the deliberate use of generic terms in a treaty implied that the parties necessarily were aware that "the meaning of the terms was likely to evolve over time, and where the treaty has been entered into for a very long period, the parties must be presumed, as a general rule, to have intended those terms to have an evolving meaning" [308].

The Court proceeded to find that *"comercio"* is a generic term which refers broadly to a class of activity [309]. It also noted that the 1858 Treaty was entered into for an unlimited duration, and therefore concluded that the present meaning of the term *"comercio"* is what ultimately must be accepted for the purposes of applying the treaty. The Court went on to find that "the right of free navigation in question applies to the transport of persons as well as the transport of goods, as the activity of transporting persons can be commercial in nature nowadays" [310].

The important contribution of this case for our purposes thus concerns the use of evolutionary interpretation of treaties by the Court. The technique has since been relied upon in subsequent cases concerning the law of international watercourses. The Court's judgment in *Navigational and Related Rights* has contributed importantly to the evolution of not only navigational law, but also in environmental cases, where it has been particularly influential [311].

VIII. The contributions of learned societies

Along with the contributions of significant cases, it is also essential in a discussion of the law of navigation on international waterways to acknowledge the contributions of learned societies, in particular, the Institute of International Law/Institut de Droit International (IIL/IDI), and the International Law Association (ILA). We will begin with the Institute of International Law [312], and its pioneering Draft Inter-

---

307. *Ibid.*
308. *Ibid.*, para. 66.
309. *Ibid.*, para. 67.
310. *Ibid.*, para. 71.
311. See e.g. *Pulp Mills on the River Uruguay (Argentina v. Uruguay), ICJ Reports 2010*, p. 14; and *Indus Waters Kishenganga Arbitration (Pakistan v. India), Record of Proceedings (2010-2013)*, Permanent Court of Arbitration Award Series, Case No. 2011-01 (2014).
312. Information on the IIL/IDI is available on its website, https://www.idi-iil.org/en/.

The Evolution of the Law of International Watercourses 347

national Regulation on River Navigation, adopted by the Institute at its Heidelberg meeting, in the year 1887. Articles 3 and 4 of the Regulation make clear that commercial navigation on "international rivers" – a term the Institute did not define – is free to all flags on the entire navigable course of those waterways, and that the subjects and flags of all nations, riparians and non-riparians alike, are to be treated equally [313].

Almost fifty years later, the Institute revisited the subject of navigation at its Paris meeting in 1934, at which time it adopted a Regulation on Navigation on International Rivers [314]. This time, the Institute also offered a definition of "rivers referred to as international", as meaning "those waterways which, in the naturally navigable part of their course, traverse or separate two or more States, and . . . any tributaries having the same characteristics; . . ." [315]. To this definition are added waterways connecting two international rivers and such works as "artificial navigable waterways" that are designed to avoid "the deficiencies of the naturally navigable waterway" [316]. These would presumably be chiefly canals, though there are in fact bridges that boats can navigate on, such as the famous Magdeburg Water Bridge in Germany.

The freedom of navigation spelled out in the Institute's Paris Regulation is even more liberal than that reflected in its Heidelberg Regulation of 1887. Article 2 of the Paris Regulation begins simply, "Movement on international waterways shall be free" [317]. The remainder of the article specifies what this freedom comprises, stating that it is "the right for all vessels, boats, timber-trains and other means of water transport to circulate freely throughout the navigable length of the waterway" [318]. This freedom is subject only to the condition that vessels comply with the appropriate policing and other rules contained in the Regulation or with those prescribed by the riparian States that are consistent with the Regulation. Article 3 of the Paris Regulation provides that "the citizens, property and flags (whether maritime or fluvial) of all nations shall, in all matters of direct or indirect concern to navigation, be treated on a

---

313. *Ibid.*, transl. adapted from Kaeckenbeeck (*above* footnote 17), pp. 175-176. The omitted portion of Article 3 provides that the boundary of States separated by a river is marked by the thalweg, i.e., the middle line of the channel. (Ordinarily the term "thalweg" refers to the deepest navigable channel rather than the middle line.)
314. *Annuaire de l'Institut de droit international*, Session de Paris, October 1934, pp. 713-719 (Brussels, 1934), available on the IIL's website, available at https://www.internationalwaterlaw.org/documents/intldocs/IIL/IIL-Resolution_of_Paris.pdf.
315. *Ibid.*, Article 1 (1).
316. *Ibid.*, Article 1 (2).
317. IIL Paris Regulation (*above* footnote 313), Article 2.
318. *Ibid.*, Article 2 *(a)*.

footing of perfect equality and in conformity with international law" [319]. While similar to the formula in Article 4 of the Heidelberg Regulation, Article 3 of the Paris Regulation adds "property", "maritime" flags, "matters of direct or indirect concern" and a reference to "international law" and omits any direct reference to citizens of non-riparian States [320].

Articles 12 and 13 of the Paris Regulation deal specifically with public vessels. Article 12 makes clear that "the police and navigation rules in force on any section of the river shall apply to military vessels or those assigned to a non-commercial public service on that section" [321]. Article 13 addresses other public vessels and makes the same protections applicable to State-owned or chartered vessels, other than those mentioned in Article 12, that apply to private merchant vessels. This provision might seem rather surprising, in light of the fact that the principle of freedom of navigation was developed with merchant shipping in mind. It may also be surprising in light of the recurrent preoccupations concerning the territorial sovereignty of riparian States which would, *prima facie*, be under greater threat in the case of publicly owned or chartered vessels than where purely private commercial ships were involved. It seems probable, however, that the Regulation sought to deal with vessels exercising forms of public authority in Article 12, and in Article 13 with those that may be State-owned or chartered, but which are engaged in commerce. Understood in this way, the presence of the latter kinds of vessels would likely not be significantly objectionable to the territorial state.

Also influential are the Helsinki Rules on the Uses of the Waters of International Rivers, adopted by the International Law Association (ILA) in 1966 [322]. The Helsinki Rules have since been revised and updated in the "Berlin Rules" adopted by the ILA in 2004, but we will maintain our focus on the Helsinki Rules because they are well known and have taken on significant authoritative value in what is now over a half-century since their adoption. The provisions of Chapter 4 of the Helsinki Rules focus entirely on navigation, and they appear to have

---

319. *Ibid.*, Article 3, para. 1.
320. *Ibid.*, para. 2.
321. *Ibid.*, Article 12.
322. Helsinki Rules on the Uses of Waters of International Rivers, International Law Association (ILA), Report of the Fifty-Second Conference, Helsinki, 1966, p. 484, International Law Association, London, 1966. While the Helsinki Rules have now been revised and updated in the "Berlin Rules" adopted by the ILA at its Berlin Conference in 2004, the Helsinki Rules are discussed here because they are well known and have taken on significant authoritative value in the years since their adoption.

been largely inspired by the 1921 Barcelona Statute – most obviously by the fact that the Helsinki Rules limit rights of free navigation to riparian States [323]. Article 13 (XIII) provides: "Subject to any limitations or qualifications referred to in these Chapters, each riparian State is entitled to enjoy rights of free navigation on the entire course of a river or lake." [324] Interestingly, the commentary to Article XIII acknowledges that, despite the fact that "some have advocated the extension of the principle of freedom of navigation to non-riparian States, the present state of the applicable law has not gone that far" [325]. Like the Barcelona Statute, the Helsinki Rules state that their provisions on navigation do not apply to vessels exercising public authority.

IX. Conclusions

This Chapter has surveyed the development of the law of navigation on international waterways, focusing on its basic principles. On the basis of this review, it is possible for us to draw several conclusions. The first of these is that, as we have seen, the rules of international law regarding navigation are most highly developed in Europe. The development occurred to some extent bilaterally, to be sure, but was consolidated and widely dispersed by the major peace treaties beginning with the Peace of Westphalia in 1648. These rules provided broadly for freedom of navigation, first for riparians, then for all nations.

Second, an attempt at the Barcelona Conference in 1921 to spread the applicability of the European regime beyond the countries of Europe and their colonies caused a clear and oft-criticized regression in the law's development, back to a reciprocity-based restriction of free navigation only to co-riparians.

While European rules remain liberal, those in other parts of the world are less clear. The spread of the European regime through colonialism and trade, and its retention in many countries after their

---

323. The commentary to Article XIII states that "Although some have advocated the extension of the principle of freedom of navigation to non-riparian States, the present state of the applicable law has not gone that far". Helsinki Rules, Article XIII, Comment *(b)*. The commentary does acknowledge a movement in the nineteenth century, especially in Latin America, to permit non-riparians to enjoy free navigation, and the regime of a number of European rivers (the Danube, Elbe, Oder and Rhine) allowing non-riparians such rights. *Ibid.*, Article XVII of the Rules states the obvious, viz., that "A riparian State may grant rights of navigation to non-riparian States on rivers or lakes within its territory." *Ibid.*
324. Helsinki Rules (*above* footnote 321), Article XIII.
325. Helsinki Rules (*above* footnote 321), Article XIII, Comment *(b)*.

independence, mean that some version of the regime remains in many regions of the world – at least in the form of treaties. Pronouncements of the International Court, particularly in the *Oder* case, suggest that the principle of freedom of navigation may be one of general international law.

It is also worth noting here the work of independent organizations of high repute such as the Institute of International Law and the International Law Association, both of which strongly support freedom of navigation for riparian States on international waterways. The studies of these organizations are global in scope, and the standing of the organizations and their careful work suggests that the rules reflected in their drafts are entitled to be accorded high authoritative value.

In the absence of any contrary treaty regime or inconsistent state practice regarding a particular waterway or area, it seems reasonable to conclude ultimately that the principle of freedom of navigation for riparian States to an international waterway should be presumed to be the prevailing standard under general international law. This principle, as we have seen, has developed through the consistent practice of States over nearly two centuries. And, while it is of course subject to important qualifications, such as those relating to the security of the territorial State, the principle is mutually advantageous to States sharing waterways and remains widely embraced.

CHAPTER 5

EVOLUTION OF THE LAW GOVERNING
THE NON-NAVIGATIONAL USES
OF INTERNATIONAL WATERCOURSES

I. Introduction

Having reviewed the evolution of the law of navigational uses of international watercourses in Chapter 4, the present chapter will focus on the evolution of the law concerning non-navigational uses of international watercourses. In preceding chapters much of this topic has actually already been covered, in one form or another. The effort here will be to bring a measure of coherence to the subject and to identify several indications of the way in which the law has evolved.

II. Ancient times

Even before the rise of the ancient fluvial civilizations, such as those in Mesopotamia and Egypt, evidence of early canals and dikes suggests that small communities and city-states had found it necessary to cooperate in order to control and utilize effectively the waters of major rivers [326]. As we have seen, however, cooperation was sometimes short-lived, even when provided for in ancient agreements such as that inscribed on the Stele of the Vultures [327]. Breakdowns in these cooperative relationships engendered conflicts that "eventually led to political consolidation and expansion" [328], resulting ultimately in the formation of empires. Therefore, it is probably not an exaggeration to conclude, as has one author, that the development of "[w]ater control for agriculture... gave rise to the so-called fluvial or irrigation civilizations..." [329]. Indeed, Karl August Wittfogel is well known for the theory that the need to organize human effort to harness water for irrigation

---

326. Teclaff (*above* footnote 71), pp. 20-21, discussing evidence of cooperation between such groups in pre-dynastic Egypt and between city states in Mesopotamia before unification.
327. See the discussion of the wars between the Mesopotamian city-states of Umma and Lagash in Chapter 1, and *below*.
328. Teclaff (*above* footnote 71), p. 21.
329. *Ibid.*, p. 15.

in arid areas led to the development of bureaucratic governmental structures (and even despotism)[330]. More generally, Berber argues that "the organisation of the state as known to us over the last six thousand years had its origins in water rights"[331]. Moreover, the consolidation and centralization of the fluvial civilizations was facilitated by navigation on the same rivers that made agriculture possible[332].

In tracing the development of the law of international watercourses, it is impossible to ignore these early arrangements, agreements and unilateral acts, even though they precede by hundreds and sometimes thousands of years the rise of the modern nation-state and the law of nations as we know it[333]. The very fact that co-riparian social and political units have found it expedient and even necessary to enter into cooperative relationships with regard to their shared water resources since ancient times, provides valuable insight into the way in which groups of humans have been brought together by, and have interacted with regard to, rivers throughout history. The simple fact is that the importance of water to humans, individually and in organized groups, has led them to seek stability in their fluvial relations through the

---

330. K. A. Wittfogel, *Oriental Despotism: A Comparative Study of Total Power*, New Haven & London, Yale University Press, 1957.
331. F. J. Berber, *Rivers in International Law*, p. 1 (Oceana Publications Inc. 1959).
332. Teclaff (*above* footnote 71), pp. 28-32; and 42-47, dealing with "the politically divided basin – a unit for navigation", specifically with regard to the Tigris-Euphrates basin and the Nile basin.
333. The modern nation-state, and modern international law itself, is often said to date generally from the Peace of Westphalia of 1648, ending the Thirty Years' War: 1 CTS, pp. 119 (Osnabrück) and 271 (Münster). The foundation of modern international law is commonly regarded as being Hugo Grotius' classic work, *De Jure Belli Ac Pacis* (*On the Law of War and Peace*) (1620-5). While these characterizations are no doubt somewhat oversimplified, seeming as they do to ignore developments in other regions of the world, they provide convenient points of reference. *See generally* Nussbaum (*above* footnote 10), pp. 102-114 (on Grotius), especially p. 113 (*On the Law of War and Peace* "initiated the doctrine of modern international law"), and p. 115 (on the effect of the Peace of Westphalia); 1 Restatement (3d) of the Foreign Relations Law of the United States, p. 17 (1987); Brierly (*above* footnote 15), pp. 1-7 (on the rise of modern states) and 27-35 (on Grotius); and Clive Parry *The Function of Law in the International Community*, pp. 14-15, in *Manual of Public International Law*, Max Sørensen ed., London, MacMillan, 1968. At the same time, however, it should be borne in mind that "rules of international law are to be found in the history both of the ancient and medieval worlds . . ."; Brierly (*above* footnote 15), p. 1. Indeed, according to one view, "'[m]odern times' begin customarily with 1492, the year of the discovery of America", and "[t]he growth of international law in the new era must be attributed, in the first place, to the rise of national states, especially of Spain, England, and France . . . which matured in the early stages of modern times". Nussbaum (*above* footnote 10), p. 61. But much depends on how one defines "modern". According to Nussbaum, "the modern law of nations as we know it today began to unfold only in the second half of the nineteenth century." *Ibid.*, p. ix. And, of course, Nussbaum's characterization seems quite Western-centric by today's standards.

The Evolution of the Law of International Watercourses 353

development and acceptance of customs, as well as through more formal acts such as agreements.

The FAO compilation referred to earlier, the 1978 *Systematic Index of international water resources Treaties* and other documents, lists no fewer than fifteen agreements relating to eight different river basins that were concluded before the foundations of the modern system of nation-states were laid by the Peace of Westphalia in 1648 [334]. Most of these instruments dealt with freedom of commerce and navigation, but other matters covered include the following: boundaries or territory (1312, 1554) [335], construction of dams (1588) [336], and river training works for sediment control (1604) [337].

Treaty activity increased significantly after 1648, with nearly as many agreements (thirteen) being concluded during the balance of that century as had been entered into during the preceding sixteen centuries [338]. But the real explosion of treaties concerning shared rivers and lakes began in the eighteenth century – coinciding, probably not coincidentally, with the beginning of the industrial revolution – during which eighty-one such agreements were concluded. It appears that, as is true in other fields, the more empires disintegrated and the system of nation-states flourished, the more States sharing watercourses found it to be in their interest to stabilize their fluvial relationships through agreements.

In all, the FAO collection lists over two thousand international legal instruments concerning water resources – an astonishing number, when

---

334. FAO Index (*above* footnote 256), pp. 1-4. The Peace of Westphalia is referred to in the immediately preceding footnote. Teclaff observes that during the seventeenth and eighteenth centuries, "inter-city agreements were replaced by intergovernmental treaties . . ."; Teclaff 1967 (*above* footnote 252), p. 59. Particularly noteworthy in the present context is the Treaty between Turkey and Austria of 1 May 1616, Testa, Rec. des Traités de la Porte Ottomane, p. 26, which according to Paul Fauchille is the earliest intergovernmental agreement providing for freedom of navigation. 1 Paul Fauchille, *Traité de Droit International Public*, 2d. pt., 8th ed., Paris, Rousseau, 1925, p. 467. That treaty recognized the right of the vessels of both states to navigate on the Danube.
335. Treaty of 1312 between Sweden (Finland) and the Principality of Novgorod (Russia) concerning Lake Ladoga, FAO Index (*above* footnote 256), p. 1; Treaty of 26 July 1554 between the Bishop of Constance and Switzerland concerning Lake Constance, *ibid.*, p. 2.
336. Treaty of 28 April 1588 between Austria and Switzerland concerning the Rhine River, *ibid.*, p. 3.
337. Treaty of 1604 between Milan and Switzerland concerning the Tresa River, *ibid.*, p. 3. "Training" refers to works designed to channel or direct the flow of rivers. River training, or regulation, is dealt with in Article 25 of the UN Watercourses Convention, Annex I.
338. See the FAO Index (*above* footnote 256). See also Fauchille (*above* footnote 333), pp. 467 *et seq.* for a survey of the early agreements.

it is borne in mind that all of these documents deal with the same natural resource[339]. Most of these instruments are agreements[340], and the vast majority of those are bilateral in character[341]. When viewed in this light, the sheer number of instruments reveals that States have tended to conclude not general conventions on international watercourses (although there are several exceptions[342]) but agreements concerning a specific watercourse (or sometimes watercourses) with other States sharing that watercourse.

The accelerating pace of the conclusion of treaties concerning international watercourses[343] is understandable not only in terms of the dissolution of empires – which "internationalized" additional watercourses[344] and made it necessary that the now independent States stabilize relations with each other – and the maturation of the community of nation-states, but also, and in particular, in light of the changes in the ways in which humans used fresh water. Its use as a source of motive power began at least 3,000 years ago[345]. The Romans used water to provide energy for various forms of industry. Its applications during this period seem to have been restricted only by the limits of human ingenuity, water having been used to make everything from iron to beer[346]. Water power was widely used in Europe and England in the twelfth and thirteenth centuries for milling flour, fulling, mining, the making of iron and other forms of industry[347]. Still, in terms of

---

339. As we have seen, Professor E. Brown Weiss also reviewed over 2,000 international water agreements in her Hague Lectures. Brown Weiss (*above* footnote 194).

340. There are a number of "unilateral acts" listed in the FAO Index (*above* footnote 256), viz., 121 up to the year 1899.

341. Of the agreements through 1899 listed in the FAO Index (*above* footnote 256), 621 are bilateral and 166 multilateral.

342. Convention and Statute on the Regime of Navigable Waterways of International Concern, 20 April 1921, 7 *LNTS*, p. 37; Convention Relating to the Development of Hydraulic Power Affecting More than One State, 9 December 1923, 36 *LNTS*, p. 77; ECE Convention on the Protection and Use of Transboundary Watercourses and International Lakes, 17 March 1992, 31 *ILM*, p. 1312 (1992), which has been open to global participation since March, 2016; and the 1997 UN Watercourses Convention, (*above* footnote 4).

343. For example, the FAO Index (*above* footnote 256), contains 357 entries from the first instrument listed (from the year 805 AD) through 1849, and 560 entries for the years 1850-99. And the pace continued to increase in the twentieth century.

344. This was also true, of course, of the dissolution of the Soviet Union, as well as smaller states such as Yugoslavia and Czechoslovakia.

345. Integrated River Basin Development, UN Doc. E/3066/Rev. 1, New York, United Nations, p. 2.

346. Teclaff notes that the Romans employed water "in the making of cloth, paper, iron, beer, and tools, as well as in the extraction of alluvial gold, tin, and other mineral deposits", Teclaff 1967 (*above* footnote 252), p. 75.

347. *Ibid.*, pp. 75-76.

their relative importance to States, navigation continued to hold sway over other uses until the late nineteenth and early twentieth centuries according to a report submitted in 1920 by a League of Nations Commission of Enquiry, which was responsible for preparatory work for the 1921 Barcelona Conference on Freedom of Communications and Transit [348]. This was in part a consequence of the Congress of Vienna of 1815, which as we have seen opened international watercourses to free navigation on a multilateral basis among the eight major States of Europe that were parties to the agreement. Given the dominance of the so-called "Great Powers" [349] of Europe in the nineteenth century, like other studies of the importance of navigation versus other uses, the report of the Commission of Enquiry may not take adequate account of practice in more arid regions, evidence of that practice perhaps not having been as readily available. Nonetheless, that the use of rivers for transport and commerce was the principal concern of States until that period is manifest in the treaty practice in relation to the utilization of international watercourses of which we have evidence, which was overwhelmingly devoted to navigation [350].

---

348. The report submitted in 1920 by the Commission of Enquiry stated: "A hundred years ago waterways were principally used for purposes of navigation; today this is no longer invariably the case. Waterways nowadays frequently serve other purposes . . . from this point of view the absolute priority of navigation is no longer invariably admissible . . .". League of Nations, Barcelona Conference, Verbatim Records and Texts relating to the Convention on the Regime of Navigable Waterways of International Concern and to the Declaration Recognising the Right to a Flag of States Having No Sea-Coast, (Draft Convention on the Regime of Navigable Waterways, text prepared by the Commission of Enquiry and submitted to the Conference), Report on the Draft Convention on the International Regime of Navigable Waterways, Presented to the General Communications and Transit Conference by the Commission of Enquiry, p. 414, at p. 415 (Geneva 1921). *See also* Economic Commission for Europe, Legal Aspects of Hydro-Electric Development of Rivers and Lakes of Common Interest (ECE Hydroelectric Study), UN Doc. E/ECE/136, pp. 21-37, especially 25-26, United Nations, Geneva 1952: "Hydro-economy in the present sense of the term dates only from the end of the last century and is the product of a rapid development in technique". *Ibid.*, p. 25. See the discussion of the dethroning of navigation as the preeminent use by non-navigational uses in Chap. 2, *above*.
349. Kaeckenbeeck (*above* footnote 17), p. 100.
350. The FAO Index lists approximately 600 instruments dealing with navigation up to the end of the nineteenth century (the exact number depends upon whether subjects such as customs, tolls and bridges are included in the category of "navigation"). It lists 357 instruments for the same period dealing with all other subjects, including boundary demarcation, flow, fishing, pollution and hydropower. On this treaty practice, see generally Vitányi (*above* footnote 254); and Kaeckenbeeck (*above* footnote 17). Water power was used extensively for industrial purposes in eighteenth-century England, allowing the Industrial Revolution to begin there long before the arrival of the steam engine: Teclaff 1967 (*above* footnote 252), p. 78. Non-navigational uses would doubtless have captured the attention of States much earlier had this occurred in a country on the Continent rather than on an island.

But from the mid-nineteenth century onward, the available evidence indicates that the use of water for other purposes escalated markedly [351].

"With the beginning of the industrial revolution water needs for irrigation, water-power, navigation, flood control and water supply experienced a sharp increase. New techniques made it possible for engineers to undertake larger and more spectacular works, such as huge irrigation dams in India and canal systems in Europe." [352]

To these examples could be added hydroelectric facilities, some of which impound vast quantities of water, for which the technology was developed by the late nineteenth century [353]. The growth in water use for such purposes was especially pronounced in Europe and the United States, to which the Industrial Revolution was spreading from England [354]. Figures for the United States during the first three decades of the twentieth century demonstrate that this trend continued well past the heyday of the Industrial Revolution: in 1900, the average aggregate daily use of water was 40 billion gallons. This quantity rose to 66 billion gallons in 1910, 91 billion in 1920 and 110 billion gallons in 1930 [355] – nearly a three-fold increase in only thirty years. It is true that much of this growth is attributable to the virtual doubling of irrigated acreage in the American West [356]. But irrigated acreage increased outside the United

---

351. Brown Weiss found that the percentage of international water agreements dealing principally with navigation "peaked in the period 1700-1930", while treaties focused on "allocation and use issues were most significant as a percentage of total [international water] agreements negotiated during the period 1931-2000". Brown Weiss (*above* footnote 194), p. 235. But this does not negate the growth in the number of treaties dealing with allocation and use beginning in the nineteenth century.
352. Integrated River Basin Development (*above* footnote 344), p. 2. See also Berber (*above* footnote 330), pp. 5-9.
353. "By the early 1900's, hydroelectric power accounted for more than 40 percent of the United States' supply of electricity . . . The years 1895 through 1915 saw rapid changes occur in hydroelectric design and a wide variety of plant styles built. Hydroelectric plant design became fairly well standardized after World War I . . . " United States Bureau of Reclamation, "The History of Hydropower Development in the United States", available at http://www.usbr.gov/power/edu/history.html.
354. Teclaff 1967 (*above* footnote 252), p. 80, using pig-iron production figures to illustrate the "considerable lead" British industry enjoyed over its European and American counterparts.
355. *Ibid.*, p. 83.
356. *Ibid.*, stating that at least half of the increase was attributable to irrigation, and noting that irrigated land in the Western US increased from 7,543,000 acres in 1900 to 14,086,000 in 1930.

The Evolution of the Law of International Watercourses 357

States as well [357]; and other factors [358] such as increasing urbanization [359] and industrialization [360], which were also present in other regions of the world, accounted, and continue to account, for the steady growth in water use by humans [361]. We should keep in mind, however, that as mentioned earlier, highly developed countries tend to use water more efficiently, to the extent that their water use generally declines in volume even as that of other countries increases.

As the intensity of non-navigational uses of international watercourses grew, a body of law and practice dealing with those uses began to develop. Professor Herbert Smith found that "the first diplomatic assertion of any rule of international law upon the question" of non-navigational uses of international watercourses was a protest by Holland in 1856 concerning a Belgian diversion of water from the Meuse to serve the Campine Canal [362] – our fourth milestone in the evolution of the law of international watercourses. The fact that streams, especially navigable ones, came to be "a valuable source of electric power" [363], or well-suited to other economically important uses not involving navigation, led to a reexamination of the notion that navigation should enjoy priority over other uses of international watercourses [364]. At the same time that

---

357. See e.g. *ibid.*, p. 82, describing the displacement of navigation by other uses in the Garonne basin of France in the second half of the nineteenth century.
358. These other factors are discussed in Chap. 1.
359. Teclaff 1967 (*above* footnote 252), providing figures on population density in the middle of the twentieth century in Europe and the United States at p. 86, and on the growth of the population in Europe and the United States in the first and second halves of the nineteenth century at p. 82.
360. As early as 1952 the US President's Materials Policy Commission (the "Paley Commission") reported that industrial water use would increase by 170 percent between 1950 and 1975, as contrasted with a 25 percent increase in irrigation withdrawals, nearly doubling the latter. See reprint of Ch. 10, vol. 1, of President's Materials Policy Commission of 1952 (Paley Commission), US Senate, Hearings before the Subcommittee on Air and Water Pollution of the Committee on Public Works, 92d Cong., 1st Sess., 22 and 23 June 1971, Serial No. 92-H27, p. 4377, especially Table 1, at p. 4379. Teclaff 1967 (*above* footnote 252) discusses "the growth of modern industrialization and water use", at pp. 80-87.
361. See Chap. 1, *above.*
362. Smith (*above* footnote 18), p. 137.
363. Report by the Commission of Enquiry to the Barcelona Conference (*above* footnote 347), p. 415.
364. See generally, Smith (*above* footnote 18), pp. 136-143; C.-A. Colliard, "Evolution et Aspects Actuels du Régime Juridique des Fleuves Internationaux", *Recueil des Cours*, vol. 125 (1968-III), pp. 362-372; and G. Sauser-Hall, "L'Utilisation Industrielle des Fleuves Internationaux", *Recueil des Cours*, Vol. 83 (1953), pp. 518-522. Even the two conferences on international watercourses convened by the League of Nations in the early 1920s, the results of which constituted the last general endorsement of a preference for navigational uses, are not necessarily inconsistent with this development. These were the First (Barcelona, 1921) and Second (Geneva, 1923) General Conferences on Freedom of Communications and Transit. While the Barcelona

industrial and other economic uses of watercourses were growing and their varieties proliferating, alternatives to navigation as a means of transport and communication were becoming more widespread, principally in the developed regions of the world. While Smith may be correct in stating that "[h]istorically the development of law in connection with international rivers has been almost entirely connected with questions of navigation rights"[365], it is also true that in the twentieth century States were concerned principally with non-navigational uses. "Law", Smith goes on to observe, "can only develop in time with its own subject-matter . . ."[366]. In this sense, navigation is, in terms of its development, the subject matter of the past[367]; the use of water for other purposes, together with the protection of freshwater ecosystems[368], is that of the present and future. Teclaff puts it well: "Water, a universal need, has become in the twentieth century as perhaps never before in history a universal problem."[369] The problem has only become more grave[370] and, within the first two decades of the twenty-first century, there are still few signs of solutions on the horizon. Maintaining harmony between nations sharing freshwater resources and providing for the equitable allocation of those resources while protecting

---

Conference was concerned with navigation, the Convention it adopted recognized the importance of non-navigational uses. See Convention and Statute on the Regime of Navigable Waterways of International Concern, Article 10, 20 April 1921, 7 *LNTS* 37. See Smith (*above* footnote 18), p. 142; and p. 149, where the author characterizes the "draftsmanship" of the Barcelona Convention, and in particular of its Article 10, as "unfortunate". The Geneva Conference adopted the Convention Relating to the Development of Hydraulic Power Affecting More than One State, 9 December 1923, 36 *LNTS* 77. The Convention made the development of hydraulic power subject to navigation (Art. 8) but it was, in effect, stillborn: it was ratified by some States from Africa, America, Asia and Europe, but only two of those (Austria and Hungary) shared a watercourse. Therefore, Convention has had virtually no practical application.

365. Smith (*above* footnote 18), p. 136. See also the IIL Madrid Resolution, adopted in 1911, which states in its "Statement of Reasons": "International law has dealt with the right of navigation with respect to international rivers but the use of water for the purposes of industry, agriculture, etc. was not foreseen by international law". Sauser-Hall (*above* footnote 363), p. 473, would add fishing to navigation as the sole uses of watercourses with which international law has been historically concerned.

366. Smith (*above* footnote 18), p. 137.

367. This is by no means to deny the continued importance of navigation, not only in the developing regions of the world, but also in the developed ones; for example, one need only visit the banks of the Rhine or the Mississippi for evidence of its current significance in many areas of the developed world. The statement in the text concerns the development of rules of law in the two areas. It is in this respect that most of the recent activity has been in the field of non-navigational uses.

368. O. Schachter, *Sharing the World's Resources*, New York, Columbia University Press, 1977, p.68 (discussing the consideration of environmental consequences as an important factor to be considered in arriving at an equitable apportionment).

369. Teclaff 1967 (*above* footnote 252), p. 1. This is, appropriately, the first sentence in Teclaff's book.

370. See generally Chap. 1.

The Evolution of the Law of International Watercourses 359

ecosystems and water quality is one of the great challenges facing international law and institutions in the twenty-first century. That non-navigational uses were increasing in importance was already evident in a 1920 report of the Commission of Enquiry formed under the auspices of the League of Nations, in which the Commission concluded that "the absolute priority of navigation is no longer invariably admissible . . ."[371].

For these reasons, navigation no longer enjoys inherent priority over other uses, absent agreement or custom to the contrary. In fact, according to the most recent and authoritative codification of the law in the field, the 1997 UN Watercourses Convention, no one kind of use enjoys inherent priority over others. Article 10 of the Convention provides as follows:

"Article 10
Relationship between different kinds of uses

1. In the absence of agreement or custom to the contrary, no use of an international watercourse enjoys inherent priority over other uses.

2. In the event of a conflict between uses of an international watercourse, it shall be resolved with reference to Articles 5 to 7, with special regard being given to the requirements of vital human needs."[372]

Thus if there is a conflict between different kinds of uses – such as navigation and hydropower production – it is to be resolved through the application of the principles of equitable and reasonable utilization (Arts. 5 and 6) and prevention of significant harm (Art. 7). The result of applying these provisions is likely to be a balanced outcome rather than one in which a particular kind of use prevails entirely over another kind. And it will be tailored to the international watercourse concerned, and the States sharing it. It is not clear from the text of Article 10 whether protection of watercourse ecosystems is considered a kind of "use". But obviously, many current non-navigational uses would not be served by

---

371. League of Nations, Barcelona Conference, Verbatim Records and Texts relating to the Convention on the Regime of Navigable Waterways of International Concern and to the Declaration Recognising the Right to a Flag of States Having No Sea-Coast, annex to Section IV (Draft Convention on the Regime of Navigable Waterways, text prepared by the Commission of Enquiry and submitted to the Conference), Report on the Draft Convention on the International Regime of Navigable Waterways, Presented to the General Communications and Transit Conference by the Commission of Enquiry, p. 414, at p. 415 (Geneva 1921). This report is also discussed in section E.1, *below*.
372. UN Watercourses Convention (*above* footnote 4), Article 10.

a dead or dying river. And the effective exception carved out for "vital human needs" in paragraph 2 would require at least minimal protection of fluvial ecosystems.

A "statement of understanding" adopted by the Working Group of the Whole in which the UN Convention was negotiated provides the following explanation of what is understood by the expression, "vital human needs": "In determining 'vital human needs', special attention is to be paid to providing sufficient water to sustain human life, including both drinking water and water required for production of food in order to prevent starvation."[373] This formulation is based on the commentary of the International Law Commission (ILC) on Article 10 (2)[374], which would in any event be relevant for the interpretation of that provision.

Let us turn now to the work of two non-governmental organizations. These organizations helped lay the foundation for the codification of the rules of general international law through the work of the International Law Commission. The ILC's work, in turn, formed the basis for the negotiation of the 1997 UN Convention on the Law of the Non-Navigational Uses of International Watercourses. Those two non-governmental organizations are, of course, the Institute of International Law and the International Law Association. We will begin with the Institute of International Law.

III. The Institute of International Law

Between 1911 and 1979 the Institute adopted three resolutions concerning shared water resources: the 1911 Madrid Resolution on International Regulations regarding the Use of International Watercourses[375], the 1961 Salzburg Resolution on the Use of International Non-Maritime Waters[376] and the 1979 Athens Resolution on the Pollution of Rivers and Lakes and International Law[377].

The seminal Madrid Resolution of 1911 is remarkable, not least for the principles it recognized in the early years of the twentieth century, when the law of the non-navigational uses of international watercourses was still in its formative stages. The "Statement of Reasons" accom-

---

373. Report of the Sixth Committee convening as the Working Group of the Whole, 11 April 1997, UN Doc. A/51/869, p. 5.
374. See 1994 *YB Int'l L. Comm'n*, Vol. II, pt. 2, p. 109.
375. IIL Madrid Resolution. English translation in [1974] *YB Int'l L. Comm'n*, Vol. 2, pt. 2, p. 200 (1976).
376. IIL Salzburg Resolution. English translation in [1974] *YB Int'l L. Comm'n*, Vol. 2, pt. 2, p. 202 (1976).
377. IIL Athens Resolution. English translation in *Environmental Protection and Sustainable Development*, p. 171.

panying the resolution declares that since international law had dealt with navigation but not

> "the use of water for the purposes of industry, agriculture, etc. . . . [i]t . . . seems expedient to remedy this lack by noting the rules of law resulting from the interdependence which undoubtedly exists between riparian States with a common stream and between States whose territories are crossed by a common stream" [378].

The resolution consists of two principal paragraphs, the first concerning contiguous watercourses and boundary lakes and the second relating to successive watercourses. The first paragraph provides that neither State on a contiguous watercourse may, without the other's consent, allow changes to be made to the watercourse that are detrimental to the opposite bank. It further states that neither State may utilize the water in such a way as to interfere seriously with the other State's utilization thereof. The second paragraph is broken down into seven sub-paragraphs. The most interesting provisions for present purposes are the following: a prohibition of alterations injurious to the water, as by discharges from factories; a prohibition of withdrawing so much water that the "utilizable character" of the stream, when it reaches the downstream State, is seriously modified; a prohibition of violating the right of navigation recognized in international law; a prohibition of flooding an upstream State by erecting works downstream; and a recommendation that permanent joint commissions be appointed to assist in avoiding and settling disputes.

It can be said without much exaggeration that this resolution of the Institute was a half-century ahead of its time. It blazed a trail that the Institute as well as other organizations were to follow, but only in the latter half of the twentieth century.

The Institute returned to the subject of international watercourses in 1961. Its Salzburg Resolution applies by its terms to "the utilization of waters which form part of a watercourse or hydrographic basin which extends over the territory of two or more States" [379]. The reference to a "hydrographic basin", and later, "watershed", marks an advance in the Institute's recognition of the functioning of watercourse systems. The resolution declares that a State's right to make use of shared waters "is

---

378. 1974 *YB Int'l L. Comm'n*, Vol. 2, pt. 2, p. 200. The resolution refers to contiguous (a "common stream") and successive international watercourses ("States whose territories are crossed by a common stream"), respectively.
379. *Ibid.*, Article 1, p. 202.

limited by the right of use by the other States concerned with the same river or watershed" [380]. The resolution then provides that any dispute as to the extent of the respective States' rights "shall be settled on the basis of equity, taking into consideration the respective needs of the States, as well as any other circumstances relevant to any particular case" [381]. This provision appears consistent with the principle of equitable utilization, although the latter is an obligation that applies precisely to the manner in which States use shared waters, not only to the resolution of disputes concerning them. The resolution goes on to provide, importantly, for advance notice of new uses and negotiations in the event of objections to such uses [382]. Prior notification of planned measures is an important procedural obligation that is the subject of a number of provisions of the Watercourses Convention, negotiated over thirty years later.

The Institute took up the subject of pollution of international watercourses almost two decades after adopting the Salzburg Resolution. The Institute's 1979 Athens Resolution recognizes the "common interest" of States sharing international rivers and lakes "in a rational and equitable utilization of such resources through the achievement of a reasonable balance between the various interests . . ." [383]. The resolution provides that States must "ensure" that activities within their borders "cause no pollution in the waters of international rivers and lakes beyond their boundaries" [384]. This appears on its face to be a surprisingly strict, and almost unrealistic obligation, even by today's standards. It is, however, moderated in a subsequent article, which provides that the obligation of prevention may be fulfilled by preventing new forms of pollution and increases in existing levels of pollution, and by abating existing pollution as soon as practicable [385]. The Athens Resolution also contains detailed provisions concerning forms of cooperation between States sharing the same basin, such as exchange of data concerning pollution, prior notification of potential polluting activities, consultation concerning pollution problems, and the establishment of international commissions competent to deal with basin-wide pollution issues [386].

Even this brief overview of the Institute's work in the field reveals a certain evolution in its approach to the subject. The 1911 resolution

---

380. *Ibid.*, Article 2.
381. *Ibid.*, Article 3.
382. *Ibid.*, Articles 5-7.
383. IIL Athens Resolution, preamble.
384. *Ibid.*, Article II.
385. *Ibid.*, Article III.
386. *Ibid.*, Article VII.

was characterized principally by prohibitions, and dealt separately with contiguous and successive watercourses. By 1961, the Institute was addressing its rules to the entire hydrographic basin, and had introduced the notion of equity into the legal regime. It is also here that procedural rules begin to appear, in the form of requirements of prior notification of new uses and negotiation of related disputes. The Institute's final resolution of 1979 also takes a "basin" approach. It refers specifically to the common interest of riparian States in equitable utilization of shared water resources and lays down a detailed set of procedures for the implementation of the duty to cooperate. Thus, several trends are observable in the work of the Institute: a trend toward applying legal rules to the entire hydrographic basin rather than merely to the surface water channel of the main stem of the river; one in favor of increased use of procedural rules, possibly culminating in the establishment of joint management mechanisms; and a trend toward the idea that it is in the interest of all riparians that shared water resources be utilized in an equitable and reasonable manner.

IV. The International Law Association [387]

Among the International Law Association's best-known products is the set of articles adopted at its meeting in Helsinki in 1966, the Helsinki Rules on the Uses of the Waters of International Rivers [388]. The Helsinki Rules represent a pioneering effort at comprehensive codification of the law of international watercourses. They address specific uses (pollution, navigation and timber floating) but their guiding principle is equitable utilization.

The Helsinki Rules apply to the use of waters of an "international drainage basin", which is defined as "a geographical area extending over two or more States determined by the watershed limits of the system of waters, including surface and underground waters, flowing into a common terminus" [389]. This definition is noteworthy not only for its broad approach, which is consistent with hydrological reality, but also for its specific mention of "underground waters". This increasingly important source of fresh water had largely escaped international legal regulation up to this point, probably in large part because governments

---

387. See especially the Helsinki Rules (*above* footnote 321).
388. Helsinki Rules (*above* footnote 321). The earlier work of the ILA on international watercourses is traced in 1974 *YB Int'l L. Comm'n*, Vol. 2, pt. 2, pp. 202-207.
389. Helsinki Rules (*above* footnote 321), Article II.

did not fully appreciate its characteristics, including its relationship to surface water systems.

The International Law Commission in 2008 adopted a set of draft articles on the Law of Transboundary Aquifers. Its earlier articles on international watercourses adopted in 1974 had covered groundwater that was related to surface water, since hydrologically the two form one system. As noted earlier, the 2008 articles unfortunately seem to ignore that, purporting to cover all forms of groundwater. While they, for the most part, simply apply the provisions of the 1997 UN Convention to groundwater, we have seen that they unfortunately include, as their first provision in Part Two, General Principles, an article entitled "Sovereignty of Aquifer States". This provision appears to turn back the clock to Harmon-Doctrine days in providing that each State in whose territory a part of a transboundary aquifer is situated "has sovereignty over the portion of a transboundary aquifer or aquifer system located within its territory". While it is undeniable that a State has sovereignty over the geologic formation underlying its territory, the notion that it has sovereignty over the water contained in the formation runs counter to the law of international watercourses that has been developed for more than a century, which as we have seen provides for equitable allocation of shared freshwater resources, not sovereignty over them.

Returning to the Helsinki Rules, along with the international drainage basin approach, the Helsinki Rules are known for having championed equitable utilization as the dominant principle of international watercourse law [390]. This is amply supported by State practice, as we have seen. Article IV of the Helsinki Rules provides simply as follows: "Each basin State is entitled, within its territory, to a reasonable and equitable share [391] in the beneficial uses of the waters of an international drainage basin". The following article contains a non-exhaustive list of factors to be taken into account in determining what amounts to a "reasonable and equitable share" in a specific case. The causing of harm to another State is not prohibited, but is dealt with

---

390. The commentary to the ILA's Montreal Rules on Water Pollution in an International Drainage Basin, adopted in 1982, states that 'the principle of equitable utilization . . . is the foundation on which the Helsinki Rules are built.' ILA, Report of the Sixtieth Conference, Montreal, 1982, ILA, London, 1983, pp. 535-546, at p. 536.

391. The author believes that the term "reasonable" has more to do with the manner of a State's utilization of the watercourse, than the quantitative "share" to which a State is entitled. That share must be equitable *vis-à-vis* co-riparian States. The manner in which the allocated water is used – e.g. avoiding wasteful uses – is more appropriately governed by the term "reasonable".

as a factor to be taken into account in determining whether a use is equitable [392]. The commentary to the Helsinki Rules makes clear that an existing use may have to give way to a new use in order to achieve an equitable apportionment of shared water resources; compensation would, however, have to be paid for the impairment or discontinuance of the existing use [393]. As to whether navigation enjoys priority over other uses, Article VI provides that no use or category of uses is entitled to "any inherent preference over any other use or category of uses".

In addition to Equitable Utilization (Chap. 2), the Helsinki Rules also contain chapters on Pollution (Chap. 3), Navigation (Chap. 4), Timber Floating (Chap. 5) and Procedures for the Prevention and Settlement of Disputes (Chap. 6). Chapter 3 on pollution does not ban pollution outright. It instead takes a nuanced approach, requiring the prevention of new pollution or increases in existing pollution, on the one hand, and the taking of "all reasonable measures to abate existing water pollution . . . to such an extent that no substantial damage is caused" to other States [394]. Even if a State fails to take reasonable measures to abate existing water pollution, it is not regarded as being *per se* in breach of its obligations, but is required to "enter into negotiations with the injured state with a view toward reaching a settlement equitable under the circumstances" [395]. Chapter 6 on the prevention and settlement of disputes includes procedures for prior notification of proposed projects and resolution of disputes by, *inter alia*, any joint institution that exists or may be established [396].

The Helsinki Rules obviously constitute a monumental work. They have had a major impact upon the development of the law of international watercourses, and reflect many principles and trends that later found expression in the UN Watercourses Convention. They take a holistic, basin approach, they deny any inherent priority to navigation, they are based on the doctrine of equitable utilization and they provide for the use of procedures to prevent disputes as well as to resolve them. It was in fact Judge E. J. Manner, the Finnish Chair of the ILA Committee that prepared the Rules who, in his capacity as a government delegate, proposed in the UN General Assembly that the International Law Commission take up the study of the law of the non-

---

392. See e.g. Article V (2) *(j)* and *(k)*.
393. Commentary to Article V.
394. Article X (1) *(b)*.
395. Article XI (2).
396. Article 31.

navigational uses of international watercourses, and that it consider using the Helsinki Rules as a model for its work [397]. While political considerations prevented the latter part of the proposal from being included in the General Assembly's referral of the topic to the ILC [398], it is clear that the Helsinki Rules are, in a very real sense, important precursors of the ILC's draft articles and thus of the UN Convention.

V. Indicia of the evolution of the law [399]

We will now, and finally, consider the manner in which the law of international watercourses has evolved from five different perspectives: First, the way in which kinds of uses are prioritized in the event they conflict; second, the way in which international watercourses are conceptualized for purposes of legal regulation; third, the approaches States have taken in treaty law to regulating their respective uses of international watercourses; fourth, the protection accorded to watercourses, including the flora and fauna associated with them; and fifth, the primacy of the obligation of equitable and reasonable utilization.

1. From preeminence of navigation to the absence of inherent priorities

We have seen that according to the available evidence, navigation received far more attention in the practice of States than non-navigational uses until the late nineteenth and early twentieth centuries. Particularly in well-watered Europe, navigation was generally accorded priority over non-navigational uses in the event the two came into conflict. This was no doubt the case largely because of the importance of navigation commercially, rivers having been the highways of the

---

397. Progressive Development and Codification of the Rules of International Law Relating to International Watercourses, UN GAOR, 6th Comm., 25th Sess., 1225th meeting, at p. 267, UN Doc. A/7991, A/C.6/SR.1225 (1970).

398. See generally Wescoat (*above* footnote 194).

399. The material in this section is adapted from Stephen McCaffrey, *The Evolution of the Law of International Watercourses*, Austrian J. Pub. & Int'l L., Vol. 45, 1993, pp. 87-111; S. McCaffrey, *The Progressive Development of International Law*, in The UN Watercourses Convention in Force: Strengthening International Law for Transboundary Water Management, Loures and Rieu-Clarke (eds.), Oxon, Routledge, 2013; and S. McCaffrey, *The Evolution of International Law Relating to Transboundary Waters*, in *Routledge Handbook of Water Law and Policy*, Rieu-Clarke, Allan and Hendry (eds.), London & New York, Routledge, 2017.

The Evolution of the Law of International Watercourses 367

past. In addition, as suggested earlier, it may be surmised that in Europe issues of allocation were of less import than in more arid areas because of the relatively abundant water supplies there [400].

But the Commission of Enquiry formed under the auspices of the League of Nations that produced the preparatory work for the 1921 Barcelona General Conference on Freedom of Communication and Transit, stated as follows in its report submitted in 1920:

> "A hundred years ago waterways were principally used for purposes of navigation; today this is no longer invariably the case. Waterways nowadays frequently serve other purposes . . . [F]rom this point of view the absolute priority of navigation is no longer invariably admissible . . ." [401].

This finding represents a tectonic shift from the historic priority given navigation over other uses to a recognition that at least under some circumstances it should yield to non-navigational uses.

Today it is not practical to attempt to identify a general rule concerning priorities because conditions and predominant uses are so varied in different parts of the world. Instead, the solution that has been arrived at in cases where different kinds of uses come into conflict is to determine how the conflict should be resolved on a case-by-case basis, in light of the obligations of equitable and reasonable utilization, and prevention of significant harm. This is the solution reflected in Article 10 of the UN Watercourses Convention, set forth above.

Suppose, for example, in facts like to those in the *Oder* case, Poland wished to construct a hydroelectric dam on one of the two tributaries of the Oder involved in the case. Downstream State X, on the other hand, had for some time navigated on that tributary to locations that would be upstream of the planned hydroelectric dam to trade with communities there. State X asserted that its navigational use took precedence over Poland's proposed non-navigational use. Article 10 would have Poland and State X resolve this conflict of uses by applying

---

400. But recall our fifth milestone, in which Holland protested a diversion by Belgium of waters from the Meuse River.
401. League of Nations, Barcelona Conference, Verbatim Records and Texts relating to the Convention on the Regime of Navigable Waterways of International Concern and to the Declaration Recognising the Right to a Flag of States Having No Sea-Coast, annex to Section IV (Draft Convention on the Regime of Navigable Waterways, text prepared by the Commission of Enquiry and submitted to the Conference), Report on the Draft Convention on the International Regime of Navigable Waterways, Presented to the General Communications and Transit Conference by the Commission of Enquiry, p. 414, at p. 415 (Geneva 1921).

the obligations of equitable and reasonable utilization (Arts. 5 and 6 of the Watercourses Convention) and prevention of significant harm (Art. 7 of the Convention). A possible solution could be for Poland to build ship locks adjoining the dam to permit passage of commercial shipping to portions of the tributary above the dam. Equity would suggest that State X (as well as any other States that wished to navigate to locations above the dam site) might contribute to the cost of the locks. Rather than according any particular kind of use inherent priority, overriding other uses, this approach seeks a balanced outcome. It may result in neither State getting everything it wants, but both States should be reasonably satisfied with the outcome in the end and persistent conflict should be avoided.

2. From the surface water channel to the system of waters

State practice relating to international watercourses until relatively recently dealt only with the surface portions of international watercourses, and even then, often only with the main stem of rivers. This approach in effect treated the watercourse as a pipe, or a canal, and thus attempted to regulate the use of something that does not exist in nature. Various explanations for this approach are plausible, including a lack of knowledge of hydrology on the part of governmental officials in charge of water relations with other States, leading them to conceptualize a river as being more akin to a canal or a pipe than a hydrological system [402]; and the historical importance of navigation, which might to some extent have led to a conceptualization of rivers as navigable channels, with no account being taken of the groundwater that feeds, and is fed by, most rivers. Moreover, agreements between States referred to a "river" or "lake", but seldom to tributaries of the main stem of a river or to a drainage basin [403]. The treaties that did

---

402. "[I]n the Western world philosophical reflection on water was overwhelmingly concerned with channels rather than basins up through the sixteenth century . . . Although local watershed processes have no doubt been appreciated from ancient times, scientific and practical attention has been focused on channels". Wescoat (*above* footnote 194), p. 320.

403. Exceptions may be found especially in European water treaties of the nineteenth century. See e.g. Convention entre la Suisse, le Grand-Duché de Bade et L'Alsace-Lorraine arrêtant des dispositions uniformes sur la pêche dans le Rhin et ses affleuts, y compris le Lac de Constance, Lucerne, 18 May 1887, Legislative Texts, Treaty No. 113, p. 397 (1964); and Convention entre la Suisse, l'Allemagne et les Pays-Bas pour régulariser la pêche du saumon dans le basin du Rhin, Berlin, 30 June 1885, Legislative Texts, Treaty No. 112, at p. 393.

extend to tributaries or river basins were often those that regulated fishing in the waters in question [404]. This may have been because it was clear that the purpose of the treaties (preservation of fish stocks) would be frustrated if entire basins were not protected. But whatever the explanation may be, the fact remains that State practice until relatively recently reflected very little recognition of the concept of a watercourse as a *system* of interrelated surface water and groundwater components.

As hydrology became better understood [405], treaties and drafts prepared by learned organizations began to employ a more holistic definition of the watercourse as a subject of legal regulation, and in at least one case, even political organization. In the second half of the nineteenth century, the American geologist and explorer John Wesley Powell (1834-1902) "realized that the limited water in the arid West would eventually lead to conflict between the states. Therefore, he suggested the boundaries of Western states be determined by watersheds . . ." [406].

But the territories of most countries do not correspond to drainage basins [407], and many of the world's great basins span one or more international borders [408]. Regulation and management of shared freshwater resources is most effectively done holistically, at the level of the basin,

---

404. See e.g. the agreements cited in the preceding footnote.
405. "Scientific controversies about drainage basins are . . . old but not ancient. Bernard de Palissy (1510-1590) is credited with elaborating the idea that rainfall over a catchment can produce streamflow . . . On a larger scale, French geographer Philippe Bauche (1700-1773) argued that mountain chains divided the earth's surface into large drainage basins that constitute 'natural regions'". Wescoat (*above* footnote 194), p. 321.
406. R. Wilson, "Map: The United States of Watersheds", *Washington Post* (19 November 2013), available at https://www.washingtonpost.com/blogs/govbeat/wp/2013/11/19/map-the-united-states-of-watersheds/. Wilson continues: "Why use watersheds to draw boundaries, instead of the sometimes-arbitrary, sometimes-geographical boundaries for states? Water usage, especially along the Colorado River, is the subject of innumerable state vs. state lawsuits, strict rationing and increasing conflict between urban areas and agricultural industries. Sorting states by watersheds would force the individual states to make their own decisions balancing water usage, rather than fighting among themselves. And those states would be able to use water within their own boundaries, rather than shipping water tens, even hundreds of miles away". *Ibid.*
407. See generally C. T. Smith, "The Drainage Basin as an Historical Basis for Human Activity", in *Water, Earth, and Man: A Synthesis of Hydrology, Geomorphology, and Socio-Economic Geography*, Richard J. Chorley and Roger G. Barry (eds.), London, Methuen, 1969, pp. 101-111.
408. Thirteen of the world's twenty longest rivers, or 65 percent, are international – including the two longest, the Nile and the Amazon. Asit Biswas, *Water for Sustainable Development*, D + C (Development and Cooperation), No. 5/1991, German Foundation for International Development, Berlin, 1991, p. 20.

or catchment. Yet the debates in the United Nations in the late 1960s over the referral to the International Law Commission of the study of international watercourses reveal some unease over the use of the drainage basin as the subject of legal regulation [409]. This seems to have been due in part to apprehension that such a remit could lead to the regulation of land areas in addition to the water contained in them. It is now understood that such regulation is necessary in order to effectively manage shared freshwater resources. Moreover, regulation of activities on land that may have transboundary consequences is in fact supported by accepted principles of international law [410]. However, a suggestion in the original draft of the resolution referring the watercourses topic to the ILC that the Commission use the International Law Association's 1966 Helsinki Rules and their drainage basin approach as a model for its work was rejected. This result seems to have been due, at least in part, precisely to the use by the Helsinki Rules of the drainage basin as the basis of its regulatory framework [411]. Finally, there is scant evidence that groundwater, a crucial component of watercourse systems, figured at all in the Assembly's consideration of the resolution.

But much has changed in the nearly five decades since 1970, and the evolution of the way in which the regulated subject matter is conceptualized is ongoing. Many older agreements – nearly all bilateral – focusing only on the surface water in a particular river are still in force, and some States continue to object on political grounds to a regulatory regime that would cover a drainage basin or watercourse system. But many modern agreements and other international instruments adopt what may be called a "system" approach, regulating not just the use of the water in the "pipe", or channel, that runs along or across a border, but also that of associated water in tributaries and aquifers. Examples of this trend from different regions are the following:

---

409. See Wescoat (*above* footnote 194), pp. 305-318.
410. These principles are reflected in a wide range of sources, including the *Island of Palmas Arbitration*, 2 UN RIAA, p. 839 (1928); the *Trail Smelter Arbitration (United States* v. *Canada)*, 3 UN RIAA 1911, 1938 (1941); the *Corfu Channel* case *(UK* v. *Albania)*, *ICJ Reports 1949*, 4, at p. 22; Principle 21 of the Stockholm Declaration on the Human Environment, UN doc. A/CONF.48/14 and Corr. 1 (1972); *Legality of the Threat or Use of Nuclear Weapons*, Advisory Opinion, *ICJ Reports 1996*, p. 226, at pp. 241-242; *Gabčíkovo-Nagymaros Project* (Hungary/Slovakia), *ICJ Reports 1997*, 7, at p. 41; *Pulp Mills on the River Uruguay (Argentina* v. *Uruguay)*, *ICJ Reports 2010*, 14, at p. 56; and the regulation of marine pollution from land-based sources, United Nations Convention on the Law of the Sea, Article 207, 10 December 1982, 1833 *UNTS* 397.
411. Wescoat (*above* footnote 194), p. 307.

The Evolution of the Law of International Watercourses

Africa

- The 1977 agreement concerning the Establishment of the Organization for the Management and Development of the Kagera River Basin [412];
- The 1987 Agreement on the Action Plan for the Environmentally Sound Management of the Common Zambezi River System [413];
- The 2000 Revised Protocol on Shared Watercourses in the Southern African Development Community (SADC) [414].

The Americas

- The 1961 Treaty relating to Cooperative Development of the Water Resources of the Columbia River Basin [415];
- The 1969 Treaty on the River Plate (La Plata River) Basin [416];
- The 1978 Great Lakes Water Quality Agreement, as amended by Protocols of 1983 and 1987 [417].

Asia

- The 1995 Agreement on the Cooperation for the Sustainable Development of the Mekong River Basin [418].

Europe

- The 2000 EU Water Framework Directive [419].

These agreements are complemented by the 1997 UN Watercourses Convention and the 1992 UNECE Convention on the Protection and

---

412. 1089 *UNTS* 165.
413. 26-28 May 1987, 28 *ILM* 1109 (1988).
414. 7 August 2000, available at http://www.internationalwaterlaw.org/documents/regionaldocs/Revised-SADC-SharedWatercourse-Protocol-2000.pdf.
415. Treaty between the United States and Canada relating to Cooperative Development of the Water Resources of the Columbia River Basin, 17 January 1961, available at http://faolex.fao.org/docs/pdf/bi-145062.pdf.
416. 875 *UNTS* 3.
417. 1978 Great Lakes Water Quality Agreement Between the United States and Canada as amended by the 1983 and 1987 Protocols, 22 November 1978, 30 UST 1383, TIAS 9257, as amended 16 October 1983, TIAS 10798 and 18 November 1987, TIAS 11551, consolidated in International Joint Commission, Revised Great Lakes Water Quality Agreement of 1978 (1988), available at http://www.ijc.org/files/tinymce/uploaded/GLWQA_e.pdf.
418. 5 April 1995, 34 *ILM* 864 (1995).
419. Directive 2000/60/EC of the European Parliament and of the Council establishing a framework for the Community action in the field of water policy, 22 December 2000, OJ L 327 (hereinafter "WFD").

Use of Transboundary Watercourses and International Lakes [420], both of which are open to accession by all States [421]. All of these treaties may be said to follow a "system" or drainage basin approach to the regulation of shared freshwater resources. The adoption of a broad conception of the term "watercourse" in the UN Convention, in particular, signals a general recognition that all parts of a freshwater system, including springs, tributaries, surface water and groundwater, must be included in regulatory frameworks if they are to be consistent with hydrologic reality.

3. From piecemeal problem-solving to integrated management and development

This trend parallels to some extent the one just discussed. But here the focus is more upon the increasing recourse to legal and institutional arrangements for the achievement of coordinated multipurpose river basin management, protection and development. The object of these regimes is to avoid conflicts between the multiple uses of shared river basins that are increasingly crowded by populations and industry. And there will be a growing need for such institutions to assist States in adapting to and ameliorating the impacts of climate change. The tool for achieving these objectives is integrated river basin management and development [422]. An illustration of this approach is the 2000 EU Water Framework Directive [423], which calls on all EU Member States to adopt river basin management plans. The EU explains the rationale for this approach as follows:

> "The best model for a single system of water management is management by river basin – the natural geographical and hydrological unit – instead of according to administrative or political boundaries . . . For each river basin district – some of which will traverse national frontiers – a 'river basin management plan' will need to be established and updated every six years, and

---

420. Helsinki, 17 March 1992, 31 *ILM* 1312 (1992).
421. As noted earlier, the latter treaty, while originally applicable in the ECE region, was amended in 2003 to allow accession by countries outside the UNECE region. The amendment entered into force on 6 February 2013, permitting all UN Member States to accede to the Convention beginning 1 March 2016, available at https://unece.org/DAM/env/water/publications/WAT_Text/ECE_MP.WAT_41.pdf.
422. See generally United Nations, Department of Economic and Social Affairs, Integrated River Basin Development, Report of a Panel of Experts, UN Doc. E/3066/Rev.1 (rev. ed. 1970).
423. WFD (*above* footnote 418).

this will provide the context for the co-ordination requirements [set forth in the Directive]."[424]

The integrated management approach contrasts with many early water treaties, which were often concluded for the purpose of dealing with a single issue, such as navigation [425] or fishing [426]. It is all the more necessary where the upper and lower parts of a drainage basin are located in different States:

> "The earlier and larger development [of a river basin] . . ., particularly by agriculture, takes place in the hotter, more nearly level areas of the lower basin, and population characteristically develops more rapidly there than in the upper basin, because of the greater food supply and easier navigation of the river's lower reaches. But this lower area, in many instances, is dependent upon the construction of dams in the upper and more mountainous areas for its protection against floods, for the storage of water for use in dry seasons and in dry years, and, nowadays, for power generation."[427]

Integrated management of shared basins is best achieved through the establishment of joint commissions or other similar mechanisms, which riparian States have increasingly done [428]. An early example of the use of a joint management mechanism is the 1909 Boundary Waters

---

424. WFD, *ibid.*, "Introduction to the EU Water Framework Directive", available at http://ec.europa.eu/environment/water/water-framework/info/intro_en.htm.
425. See e.g. the Treaty of Paris of 30 May 1814, Article 5 (Rhine), Martens Recueil 2, p. 1 (1887); the Final Act of the Congress of Vienna of 9 June 1815, Articles 108-116, *ibid.*, p. 379; the Navigation Act of 7 November 1857 (Danube), *ibid.*, pt. 2, Vol. 16, p. 75.
426. See e.g. Convention entre la Suisse, l'Allemagne et les Pays-Bas pour régulariser la pêche du saumon dans le bassin du Rhin, 30 June 1885, available at https://www.admin.ch/opc/fr/classified-compilation/18850013/index.html; and the Convention between Austria-Hungary, Baden, Bavaria, Liechtenstein, Switzerland and Württemberg Laying Down Uniform Provisions concerning Fishing in Lake Constance, with Protocol, 2 July 1893, Legislative Texts and Treaty Provisions concerning the Utilization of International Rivers for Other Purposes than Navigation, UN Doc. ST/LEG/SER.B/12, Treaty No. 114, p. 403.
427. N. Ely and A. Wolman, "Administration", in *The Law of International Drainage Basins*, A. Garretson, R. Hayton and C. Olmstead (eds.), Dobbs Ferry, NY, Oceana, 1967, p. 124.
428. See e.g. S. McCaffrey, "International Watercourses", in *Hague Academy of International Law, A Handbook on International Organizations*, R.-J. Dupuy (ed.), Dordrecht, Boston, London, 2nd ed., 1998; and McCaffrey, Sixth Report, 1990 *YB Int'l L. Comm'n*, Vol. 2, pt. 1, p. 42, noting with regard to joint management mechanisms that "Today there are nearly as many such joint bodies as there are international watercourses; . . .", *ibid.*, p. 43, para. 4.

Treaty between the United States and Canada [429], which established the International Joint Commission (IJC) between the two countries [430]. The IJC is often pointed to as an example of a successful joint mechanism. The same may be said of the Permanent Indus Commission established by the 1960 Indus Waters Treaty between India and Pakistan [431], which has continued to function through a number of conflicts between the two States. Both of the global treaties on international watercourses, the UN [432] and ECE [433] Conventions, envision the establishment of joint commissions, demonstrating a recognition of their utility by the international community. The same is effectively true of the EU's Water Framework Directive, which provides for the assignment of river basins covering the territory of more than one Member State to an international river basin district [434].

4. From protection of fisheries to protection of fish

The trend toward integrated river basin management parallels the growing realization that the protection of aquatic ecosystems is not only important as an element of sustainable development and intergenerational equity, but is in fact beneficial to humans [435]. Scientific progress has demonstrated, perhaps now unsurprisingly, that a dead or non-functioning watercourse benefits no one. And better understanding of phenomena such as tipping points and feedback loops have underscored the critical role of prevention, in contrast to the more traditional practice of waiting for environmental problems to manifest

---

429. Treaty between the United States and Great Britain relating to Boundary Waters, and Questions Arising between the United States and Canada, 12 Bevans, p. 319, 36 Stat. p. 2448, TS, p. 548, 102 BFSP, p. 137, available at https://legacyfiles.ijc.org/tinymce/uploaded/Boundary%20Waters%20Treaty%20of%201909_3.pdf.
430. *Ibid.*, Article III.
431. Karachi, 19 September 1960, 419 *UNTS* 290, Article VIII.
432. UN Watercourses Convention (*above* footnote 4).
433. Convention on the Protection and Use of Transboundary Watercourses and International Lakes, Helsinki, 17 March 1992, 31 *ILM* 1312 (1992), available at https://treaties.un.org/Pages/ViewDetails.aspx?src=IND&mtdsg_no=XXVII-5&chapter=27&clang=_en.
434. EU Water Framework Directive, Directive 2000/60/EC, 23 October 2000, OJ L 327, Article 3 (3), available at http://ec.europa.eu/environment/water/water-framework/index_en.html.
435. See generally O. McIntyre, *Environmental Protection of International Watercourses Under International Law*, Ashgate, 2007; Stephen McCaffrey, "Pollution of Shared Freshwater Resources in International Law", in *Transboundary Pollution: Evolving Issues of International Law and Policy*, S. Jayakumar, T. Koh, R. Beckman and H. Duy Phan (eds.), Edward Elgar, 2015, p. 81; and McCaffrey (*above* footnote 7), pp. 507-523.

The Evolution of the Law of International Watercourses 375

themselves before taking corrective action. As this is written, we are witnessing the tremendous cost of the latter behavior in relation to the havoc that is being unleashed by climate change, in the form of massive floods, droughts and wildfires, suggesting that the window for prevention is closing rapidly.

While human capacity to pollute watercourses has mushroomed to proportions that could hardly have been imagined a century ago, even in the Middle Ages freshwater pollution had grown to the point that it has been held responsible for widespread epidemics such as the Black Plague [436]. But treaty practice was for the most part concerned with the protection of fisheries – i.e. resources that were valuable to humans – rather than to protection of the fish themselves, their ecosystems or even of the quality of water for human consumption [437]. Protection was attempted in these agreements through strict prohibitions, e.g. of pollution harmful to fish, rather than through more flexible regulations or water quality standards – although the threshold of fish kills could of course be seen as an early form of standard.

It was only in the latter half of the twentieth century that agreements began to address protection of aquatic ecosystems. A leading example is the 1978 Agreement between Canada and the United States on Great Lakes Water Quality (GLWQA) [438], which states that its purpose is: "to restore and maintain the chemical, physical, and biological integrity of the waters of the Great Lakes Basin Ecosystem". Another example from the same period, also a bilateral treaty, is the 1975 Statute of the Uruguay River [439]. Article 36 of that treaty provides:

> "The Parties shall co-ordinate, through the Commission [440], the necessary measures to avoid any change in the ecological balance and to control pests and other harmful factors in the river and the areas affected by it." [441]

---

436. See J. Sette-Camara, "Pollution of International Rivers", *Recueil des Cours*, Vol. 186 (1984), p. 139.
437. See e.g. the 1904 Convention between France and Switzerland for the regulation of fishing in their frontier waters, Article 17, de Martens, *Noveau Recueil*, 2nd series, Vol. 33, p. 501. An early exception is the 1909 Boundary Waters Treaty between Canada and the United States (*above* footnote 428), which in Article IV (2) prohibits such water pollution as injuries health or property on the other side of the boundary.
438. 837 *UNTS* 213, available at https://treaties.un.org/doc/publication/unts/volume%201153/volume-1153-i-18177-english.pdf.
439. 635 *UNTS* 91 (hereinafter the "Statute of the River Uruguay").
440. This refers to the Administrative Commission of the River Uruguay established under Article 49 of the Statute (author's footnote).
441. Statute of the River Uruguay (*above* footnote 438), Article 36.

And according to Article 41 *(a)* of the Statute, the Parties undertake: "To protect and preserve the aquatic environment and, in particular, to prevent its pollution, by prescribing appropriate rules and measures in accordance with applicable international agreements and in keeping, where relevant, with the guidelines and recommendations of international technical bodies; ...."[442]. That these are obligations of due diligence was underlined by the International Court in the *Pulp Mills* case[443].

The importance of protecting the fluvial environment more broadly is recognized in Article 20 of the UN Watercourses Convention in the following terms: "Watercourse states shall, individually and, where appropriate, jointly, protect and preserve the ecosystems of international watercourses."

This is a broad provision that is not confined to protection of the ecology of the water in the watercourse only, but embraces the entire fluvial ecosystem. The commentary of the International Law Commission, which prepared the draft on the basis of which the UN Convention was negotiated, explains that the term "ecosystem" refers to an "ecological unit consisting of living and non-living components that are interdependent and function as a community"[444]. This is of great importance in that poor land-use practices, such as grazing and deforestation in the vicinity of watercourses, can do great harm to life in the watercourse itself, and to its banks and bed. This article was the subject of "complex negotiations" during the drawing up of the Convention but the term "ecosystem" was ultimately retained[445].

5. *From "no harm" to equitable utilization*

Holland's protest of Belgium's diversion of the Meuse in 1856, our fifth milestone, is typical of early diplomatic exchanges and treaties[446], in that it focuses on the avoidance of harm rather than allocation. The note contained the following statement:

---

442. *Ibid.*, Article 41 *(a)*.
443. *Pulp Mills on the River Uruguay (Argentina v. Uruguay)*, *ICJ Reports 2010*, 14, p. 55, para. 101.
444. 1994 *YB Int'l L. Comm'n*, Vol. 2, pt. 2, pp. 280-281.
445. See A. Tanzi and M. Acari, *The United Nations Convention on the Law of International Watercourses*, Kluwer, The Hague, 2001, p. 241.
446. See e.g. Article IV of the 1909 Boundary Waters Treaty between the United States and Canada (*above* footnote 428); the Exchange of Notes between the United Kingdom and Egypt of 7 May 1929, para. 4 *(b)*, 93 *LNTS* 44; and the Convention of 17 September 1955 between Italy and Switzerland concerning the regulation of Lake Lugano, 291 *UNTS* 213.

"The Meuse being a river common both to Holland and to Belgium, it goes without saying that both parties are entitled to make the natural use of the stream, but at the same time, following general principles of law, each is bound to abstain from any action which might cause damage to the other. In other words, they cannot be allowed to make themselves masters of the water by diverting it to serve their own needs, whether for purposes of navigation or irrigation." [447]

While this note postdates the treaty between Umma and Lagash, our first milestone, by over 4,000 years, it is of interest because it has been characterized as the earliest known record of an assertion of a rule of international law relating to non-navigational uses of international watercourses in the modern era [448]. Holland's protest was based on "general principles of law", according to which "each is bound to abstain from any action which might cause damage to the other". Holland's claim is therefore in conformity with the maxim, *sic utere tuo ut alienum non laedas* (so use your own as not to harm that of another). If the claim were given literal and strict effect, however, it would be highly problematic – especially in today's interconnected world, but even in the nineteenth century. For a categorical prohibition of the causing of harm would give absolute priority to the use claimed to be harmed, meaning that a State whose use was prior in time would have a veto over uses of co-riparian States that may harm the former State's uses. But State practice reveals a recognition that absolute entitlements are incompatible with the flexible cooperative relationships that are essential in respect of shared natural resources [449]. Thus the so-called "no-harm" principle has not generally been treated in practice as a prohibition of the causing of all factual harm [450]. Instead, in keeping

---

447. Smith (*above* footnote 18), p. 217.
448. *Ibid.*, p. 137.
449. See in particular, the treaty that resolved the dispute between Mexico and the United States that gave rise to the infamous "Harmon Doctrine", Convention concerning the Equitable Distribution of the Waters of the Rio Grande for Irrigation Purposes, 21 May 1906, United States Treaty Series No. 455, available at http://www.ibwc.gov/Files/1906Conv.pdf. See generally the exhaustive review of practice and literature in Charles Bourne, "The Right to Utilize the Waters of International Rivers", 3 *Can. YB Int'l L.* 187 (1965) (hereafter "Bourne").
450. See e.g. the Trail Smelter Arbitration, 3 UNRIAA 1911 ("serious consequence", *ibid.*, at 1965); and the Lake Lanoux Arbitration, 12 UNRIAA 281 ("serious injury to the lower riparian State", transl. from 1974 *YB Int'l L. Comm'n*, Vol. 2, pt. 2, para. 1065). Both of these decisions allowed the project in question to proceed, though subject to adjustments that either had already been made (*Lake Lanoux*) or were to be made (*Trail Smelter*) by the proposing State.

with the principle of equality of right, it has been seen as a prohibition of harm that is contrary to the rights of the harmed State. In the context of shared freshwater resources in particular, those rights would not extend to a categorical right to be free from all harm [451].

This proposition is supported by our eleventh milestone, the *"Donauversinkung"* case between the German States of Württemberg and Prussia, on the one hand, and Baden, on the other, decided by the Staatsgerichtshof in 1927 [452]. In that case, the two applicant States sought relief from the phenomenon of the "sinking of the Danube". The court stated:

> "The exercise of sovereign rights by every State in regard to international rivers traversing its territory is limited by the duty not to injure the interests of other members of the international community . . . The application of this principle is governed by the circumstances of each particular case. The interests of the States in question must be weighed in an equitable manner against one another. One must consider not only the absolute injury caused to the neighboring State, but also the relation of the advantage gained by one to the injury caused to the other." [453]

Thus, the court recognized that the "no-harm" principle of *sic utere tuo* does not constitute a categorical prohibition of harm but must be applied in a balanced way, to preserve what the United States Supreme Court has called the States' "relative rights" [454]. The objective of this process is the achievement of an equitable apportionment of uses and benefits of the watercourse in a manner that is sustainable.

This regime is reflected in the UN Watercourses Convention, in particular in Articles 5-7 [455]. Article 5 (1) provides that States are to "utilize an international watercourse in an equitable and reasonable manner", taking into account the interests of the co-riparian States

---

451. This principle is expressed well in the *Donauversinkung* case, decided by the German Staatsgerichtshof in 1927, discussed below. It is also supported by the authorities reviewed by Professor Bourne in Bourne (*above* footnote 448).

452. *Württemberg and Prussia* v. *Baden*, German Staatsgerichtshof, 18 June 1927, Entsch. des Reichsgerichts in Zivilsachen, Vol. 116, App., pp. 18-45. The present discussion is based on the report in *Annual Digest of Public International Law Cases: Years 1927 and 1928* (*above* footnote 170), pp. 131-132. This case is discussed in Chapter 6.

453. *Annual Digest of Public International Law Cases: Years 1927 and 1928* (*above* footnote 170), p. 131.

454. *Wyoming* v. *Colorado*, 259 US 419, at 484 (1922).

455. UN Watercourses Convention (*above* footnote 4), Articles 5-7.

concerned. Equitable and reasonable utilization requires taking into consideration all relevant factors, an indicative list of which is contained in Article 6. Article 7 (1) provides that States are to "take all appropriate measures to prevent the causing of significant harm to other watercourse States". It is noteworthy that the article does not say "shall not cause significant harm" to other States, but only that a State is to "take all appropriate measures to prevent the causing of significant harm" to other States. The formula "take all appropriate measures" connotes a due diligence obligation. Thus, a State must exercise due diligence to prevent the causing of significant harm to other States. If the State has exercised due diligence but harm is nevertheless caused, the State has still fulfilled its obligation.

Paragraph 2 of Article 7 recognizes such a situation, namely, that harm may nevertheless be caused despite a State's having exercised due diligence to prevent it. Paragraph 2 sets forth a process for dealing with this situation: first, the harming State must exercise due diligence to eliminate or mitigate the harm, but it is to do so "having due regard to" the principle of equitable and reasonable utilization, enshrined in Articles 5 and 6. An implication here is that some harm may have to be tolerated by the harmed State in order to achieve an equitable balance of uses as between the harming and harmed States. However, in such a case it may be "appropriate" for the harming State to provide some form of compensation to the harmed State for any harm sustained, and this the two States are to "discuss". These rules are based on the practice of States, which recognizes that a categorical prohibition of harm is both untenable and unworkable, and that there must be flexibility in the legal regime of rights of co-riparian States.

The UN Watercourses Convention may be considered to be a codification of the basic principles of the law in the field[456]. The way in which Article 7 melds the obligation of equitable and reasonable utilization with that of the prevention of significant harm, creating a process guided by the former and designed to reach an equitable outcome, signals the emergence of equitable and reasonable utilization as the core principle in the field. A State's perception that it has been harmed by uses in a co-riparian State will trigger the process of arriving

---

456. This is due both to the provenance of the Convention, which was based on 20 years' study by the International Law Commission, and to its treatment by the ICJ and in the literature. Four months after the Convention was concluded it was relied upon by the ICJ in the *Gabčíkovo-Nagymaros Project* case, *ICJ Reports 1997*, 7. See also Tanzi and Arcari (*above* footnote 444), p. 2.

at an equitable and reasonable resolution but will no longer be sufficient in and of itself to entitle the State to cessation of the allegedly harmful conduct. Of course, riparian States should continue to enjoy protection against the most extreme forms of harm, such as pollution by hazardous (e.g. radioactive) substances, the causing of which could not in any event be considered, *prima facie*, to be equitable.

CHAPTER 6

CONCLUSIONS AND OUTLOOK

I. Some conclusions

We may conclude this special course with the simple observation that the law of international watercourses has indeed evolved considerably since 3100 BC, the approximate date of a treaty that constitutes the earliest evidence presently available of something resembling that law. We have seen both increased sophistication in the development of rules of sharing, a process that can be difficult when such a precious and existential resource is involved, and at the same time stubborn persistence of tendencies driven by the same existential quality of water to revert to the lawless, Harmon-Doctrinesque assertion of "sovereignty" over the portion of an international watercourse located within the boundaries of a State. But these claims of sovereignty go further than an indisputable claim of sovereignty over territory. They imagine that territorial sovereignty also confers ultimate authority over water that happens to be situated for the moment within their territory, but which is destined to flow across a boundary into another State, which also depends upon it. The State within which the waters of an international watercourse are momentarily situated could only assert sovereignty over those waters to the extent that it had no other international obligations with respect to them. The foregoing chapters have demonstrated that the evolution of the law of international watercourses has given rise to obligations of States in this position concerning those waters.

We have noted the tension between sovereignty and international obligations with regard to both non-navigational and navigational uses of international watercourses. While assertions of sovereignty are usually associated with upstream States, something akin to those assertions has also been advanced by downstream States. We have seen that downstream areas on international watercourses tend to develop earlier, both economically and in terms of their use of international watercourses, have larger populations, and have often developed a strong dependence on international watercourses shared with upstream States. It is likewise typical that upstream States develop their water resources later than their downstream neighbors, since they are often mountainous and thus topographically less suited to large agricultural operations [457].

But these conditions relating to human settlement and economic development, which largely follow from natural ones, hold the potential for conflict when the upstream State begins to develop the portion of the international watercourse within its territory, for example, through the construction of dams. The technology permitting the construction of large dams, holding back immense quantities of water and often equipped with hydroelectric power plants, did not become available until the latter half of the nineteenth century, by which time downstream uses had often been entrenched for hundreds, if not thousands, of years. This has prompted downstream States to invoke an entitlement to receive the quantity of water they have historically received, and sometimes at the time they have historically received it. Such a claimed entitlement is, in its own way, effectively an assertion of "sovereignty" or, as it has been called in this context, absolute territorial *integrity* [458]. The doctrine of absolute territorial integrity is the theoretical opposite of absolute territorial *sovereignty*. According to this theory, the upstream State may do nothing that might affect the natural flow of the water into the downstream State. Something akin to this doctrine has long been asserted by Egypt, which relies almost entirely on the Nile for its fresh water. The doctrine has in effect surfaced again in the context of the controversy over the Grand Ethiopian Renaissance Dam, discussed in Chapter 2.

But surely the *Lake Lanoux* tribunal had it right when it declared: "Territorial sovereignty acts as a presumption. It must yield to all international obligations, whatever their origin, but only to them" [459]. The concept of territorial sovereignty as a rebuttable presumption, one that can be overcome by establishing an international obligation on the part of the territorial State, is a useful way of thinking about these situations. In the GERD case, for example, if Egypt wished to assert a sovereign right to continue to receive the same quantity of Nile water it had historically received, the question would be whether Egypt had international obligations that would affect such a right. As shown

---

457. For a discussion of this phenomenon, see Ely and Wolman (*above* footnote 426).

458. See generally Berber (*above* footnote 330), pp. 19-22; Caflisch (*above* footnote 36), pp. 51-54; and McCaffrey (*above* footnote 7), pp. 116-125.

459. 1974 *YB Int'l L. Comm'n*, Vol. 2, pt. 2, p. 195, para. 1063. The tribunal continued: "The question is, therefore, to determine what the obligations of the French Government are in this matter."

in the foregoing chapters, Egypt, like all States sharing international watercourses, would have an obligation of equitable and reasonable utilization of the River Nile. This obligation would presumably rebut the presumption of any sovereign right Egypt may have asserted to receive Nile waters, resulting in Egypt's having the obligation to use the Nile in a manner that is equitable and reasonable *vis-à-vis* other Nile riparian States. What constitutes equitable and reasonable utilization of the Nile by Egypt, *vis-à-vis* its co-riparians, would be determined through "taking into account all relevant factors and circumstances"[460], including those listed in Article 6 of the UN Watercourses Convention. Consideration of those factors and circumstances would certainly indicate that Egypt's equitable entitlement to Nile waters would be significant but would, equally certainly, reveal that Egypt's "[e]xisting . . . uses of the watercourse"[461] would not be the sole determinant of its entitlement.

An important overall conclusion of the present study is therefore that while assertions of sovereignty have not entirely disappeared from the landscape of the law of international watercourses, they occupy a much less significant space in the relations between States sharing watercourses than was the case in the nineteenth century. It will be recalled that the very State whose official gave the clearest expression of the doctrine of absolute territorial sovereignty in 1895[462] resolved the dispute in the context of which it was articulated in a treaty of 1906 providing for the "equitable distribution" of the waters of the river in question[463]. Thus the epitome of the doctrine of absolute territorial sovereignty, the "Harmon Doctrine", turned out to be nothing more than zealous advocacy by an attorney for a client, who wisely decided not to use it but to settle the dispute via a not-inexpensive compromise.

There is nothing in the 1997 UN Watercourses Convention that would support a claim of absolute territorial sovereignty – or its counterpart, absolute territorial integrity. As we have seen, that agreement is taken as reflecting the prevailing view among States as to the content of the

---

460. UN Watercourses Convention (*above* footnote 4), Article 6 (1).
461. *Ibid.*, Article 6 (1) *(e)*. The omitted portion of that sub-paragraph refers to "potential" uses of the watercourse, which would require considering such uses by Ethiopia and other upper riparian States.
462. The "official" was, of course, Judson Harmon, the US Attorney General at the time.
463. The treaty, our seventh milepost, is the Convention concerning the Equitable Distribution of the Waters of the Rio Grande for Irrigation Purposes of 21 May 1906, United States Treaty Series No. 455, available at http://www.ibwc.gov/Files/1906Conv.pdf.

law of the non-navigational uses of international watercourses, which is to say that it is generally accepted as reflecting the basic principles of customary international law on the subject.

II. Outlook

The threat that looms over the further positive development of this field of law is, of course, climate change. In fact, climate change is now more than a threat; it is very much with us, as the historic high temperatures, wildfires, floods and droughts we are currently experiencing as this is written in the summer of 2021 attest. Climate change promises further disruptions of ages-old water management techniques, which are generally built upon historic records of such things as precipitation, stream flow and climate. Those records are now being overwhelmed by the impacts of climate change.

Among the things that have seemed immutable in this field is the treaty. As the *Gabčíkovo-Nagymaros Project* case [464] showed, the treaty is the cornerstone of the stability the international legal system is designed to produce. And yet, in the era of climate change, the factual bases of water treaties can themselves quickly change. The international community must therefore bend its efforts toward the refinement of existing legal means, and development of new ones, to permit treaties to adapt without losing their stabilizing quality. Some of this flexibility can be supplied by the kind of evolutionary interpretation of treaties that was applied in some of the cases reviewed in these lectures. But that may not be enough. Just as adaptive management will be necessary for watercourses themselves, so also will the ability to adapt treaties to apply them in a world of changing conditions. This will be one of the major challenges facing international law in the coming decades. Since there can be no life without water, for the sake of humanity, let us hope that the international community is up to that challenge.

---

464. *ICJ Reports 1997*, p. 7.

PUBLICATIONS DE L'ACADÉMIE
DE DROIT INTERNATIONAL
DE LA HAYE

PUBLICATIONS OF THE
HAGUE ACADEMY OF INTERNATIONAL
LAW

RECUEIL DES COURS Depuis 1923, les plus grands noms du droit international ont professé à l'Académie de droit international de La Haye. Tous les tomes du *Recueil* qui ont été publiés depuis cette date sont disponibles, chaque tome étant, depuis les tout premiers, régulièrement réimprimé sous sa forme originale.
Depuis 2008, certains cours font l'objet d'une édition en livres de poche.
En outre, toute la collection existe en version électronique. Tous les ouvrages parus à ce jour ont été mis en ligne et peuvent être consultés moyennant un des abonnements proposés, qui offrent un éventail de tarifs et de possibilités.

INDEX A ce jour, il a paru sept index généraux. Ils couvrent les tomes suivants :

1 à 101	(1923-1960)	379 pages	ISBN 978-90-218-9948-0
102 à 125	(1961-1968)	204 pages	ISBN 978-90-286-0643-2
126 à 151	(1969-1976)	280 pages	ISBN 978-90-286-0630-2
152 à 178	(1976-1982)	416 pages	ISBN 978-0-7923-2955-8
179 à 200	(1983-1986)	260 pages	ISBN 978-90-411-0110-5
201 à 250	(1987-1994)	448 pages	ISBN 978-90-04-13700-4
251 à 300	(1995-2002)	580 pages	ISBN 978-90-04-15387-7

A partir du tome 210 il a été décidé de publier un index complet qui couvrira chaque fois dix tomes du *Recueil des cours*. Le dernier index paru couvre les tomes suivants :
311 à 320   (2004-2006)   392 pages   Tome 320A   ISBN 978-90-04-19695-7

COLLOQUES L'Académie organise également des colloques dont les débats sont publiés. Les derniers volumes parus de ces colloques portent les titres suivants : *Le règlement pacifique des différends internationaux en Europe : perspectives d'avenir* (1990) ; *Le développement du rôle du Conseil de sécurité* (1992) ; *La Convention sur l'interdiction et l'élimination des armes chimiques : une percée dans l'entreprise multilatérale du désarmement* (1994) ; *Actualité de la Conférence de La Haye de 1907, Deuxième Conférence de la Paix* (2007).

CENTRE D'ÉTUDE ET DE RECHERCHE Les travaux scientifiques du Centre d'étude et de recherche de droit international et de relations internationales de l'Académie de droit international de La Haye, dont les sujets sont choisis par le Curatorium de l'Académie, faisaient l'objet, depuis la session de 1985, d'une publication dans laquelle les directeurs d'études dressaient le bilan des recherches du Centre qu'ils avaient dirigé. Cette série a été arrêtée et la dernière brochure parue porte le titre suivant : *Les règles et les institutions du droit international humanitaire à l'épreuve des conflits armés récents*. Néanmoins, lorsque les travaux du Centre se révèlent particulièrement intéressants et originaux, les rapports des directeurs et les articles rédigés par les chercheurs font l'objet d'un ouvrage collectif.

Les demandes de renseignements ou de catalogues et les commandes doivent être adressées à

MARTINUS NIJHOFF PUBLISHERS

B.P. 9000, 2300 PA Leyde   Pays-Bas   **http://www.brill.nl**

COLLECTED COURSES Since 1923 the top names in international law have taught at The Hague Academy of International Law. All the volumes of the *Collected Courses* which have been published since 1923 are available, as, since the very first volume, they are reprinted regularly in their original format.
Since 2008, certain courses have been the subject of a pocketbook edition.
In addition, the total collection now exists in electronic form. All works already published have been put "on line" and can be consulted under one of the proposed subscription methods, which offer a range of tariffs and possibilities.

INDEXES Up till now seven General Indexes have been published. They cover the following volumes:

1 to 101	(1923-1960)	379 pages	ISBN 978-90-218-9948-0
102 to 125	(1961-1968)	204 pages	ISBN 978-90-286-0643-2
126 to 151	(1969-1976)	280 pages	ISBN 978-90-286-0630-2
152 to 178	(1976-1982)	416 pages	ISBN 978-0-7923-2955-8
179 to 200	(1983-1986)	260 pages	ISBN 978-90-411-0110-5
201 to 250	(1987-1994)	448 pages	ISBN 978-90-04-13700-4
251 to 300	(1995-2002)	580 pages	ISBN 978-90-04-15387-7

From Volume 210 onwards it has been decided to publish a full index covering, each time, ten volumes of the *Collected Courses*. The latest Index published covers the following volumes:
311 to 320   (2004-2006)   392 pages   Volume 320A   ISBN 978-90-04-19695-7

WORKSHOPS The Academy publishes the discussions from the Workshops which it organises. The latest titles of the Workshops already published are as follows: *The Peaceful Settlement of International Disputes in Europe: Future Prospects* (1990) ; *The Development of the Role of the Security Council* (1992); *The Convention on the Prohibition and Elimination of Chemical Weapons : A Breakthrough in Multilateral Disarmament* (1994); *Topicality of the 1907 Hague Conference, the Second Peace Conference* (2007).

CENTRE FOR STUDIES AND RESEARCH The scientific works of the Centre for Studies and Research in International Law and International Relations of The Hague Academy of International Law, the subjects of which are chosen by the Curatorium of the Academy, have been published, since the Centre's 1985 session, in a publication in which the Directors of Studies reported on the state of research of the Centre under their direction. This series has been discontinued and the title of the latest booklet published is as follows: *Rules and Institutions of International Humanitarian Law Put to the Test of Recent Armed Conflicts.* Nevertheless, when the work of the Centre has been of particular interest and originality, the reports of the Directors of Studies together with the articles by the researchers form the subject of a collection published by the Academy.

Requests for information, catalogues and orders for publications must be addressed to

MARTINUS NIJHOFF PUBLISHERS

P.O. Box 9000, 2300 PA Leiden   The Netherlands   **http://www.brill.nl**

TABLE PAR TOME DES COURS PUBLIÉS CES DERNIÈRES ANNÉES
INDEX BY VOLUME OF THE COURSES PUBLISHED THESE LAST YEARS

Tome/Volume 363 (2012)

Sur, S. : La créativité du droit international. Cours général de droit international public, 9-332.
Turp, D. : La contribution du droit international au maintien de la diversité culturelle, 333-454. (ISBN 978-90-04-25556-2)

Tome/Volume 364 (2012)

Gaja, G. : The Protection of General Interests in the International Community. General Course on Public International Law (2011), 9-186.
Glenn, H. P. : La conciliation des lois. Cours général de droit international privé (2011), 187-470. (ISBN 978-90-04-25557-9)

Tome/Volume 365 (2013)

Crawford, J. : Chance, Order, Change: The Course of International Law. General Course on Public International Law, 9-390.
(ISBN 978-90-04-25560-9)

Tome/Volume 366 (2013)

Hayton, D. : "Trusts" in Private International Law, 9-98.
Hobér, K. : Res Judicata and Lis Pendens in International Arbitration, 99-406.
(ISBN 978-90-04-26395-6)

Tome/Volume 367 (2013)

Kolb, R. : L'article 103 de la Charte des Nations Unies, 9-252.
Nascimbene, B. : Le droit de la nationalité et le droit des organisations d'intégration régionales. Vers de nouveaux statuts de résidents?, 253-454.
(ISBN 978-90-04-26793-0)

Tome/Volume 368 (2013)

Caflisch, L : Frontières nationales, limites et délimitations. — Quelle importance aujourd'hui? (conférence inaugurale), 9-46.
Benvenisti, E. : The International Law of Global Governance, 47-280.
Park, K. G. : La protection des personnes en cas de catastrophes, 281-456.
(ISBN 978-90-04-26795-4)

Tome/Volume 369 (2013)

Kronke, H. : Transnational Commercial Law and Conflict of Laws: Institutional Co-operation and Substantive Complementarity (Opening Lecture), 9-42.
Ortiz Ahlf, L. : The Human Rights of Undocumented Migrants, 43-160.
Kono, T. : Efficiency in Private International Law, 161-360.
Yusuf, A. A. : Pan-Africanism and International Law, 361-512.
(ISBN 978-90-04-26797-8)

Tome/Volume 370 (2013)

Dominicé, Ch. : La société internationale à la recherche de son équilibre. Cours général de droit international public, 9-392. (ISBN 978-90-04-26799-2)

Tome/Volume 371 (2014)

Lagarde, P. : La méthode de la reconnaissance est-elle l'avenir du droit international privé?, 9-42.
Charlesworth, H. : Democracy and International Law, 43-152.
de Vareilles-Sommières, P. : L'exception d'ordre public et la régularité substantielle internationale de la loi étrangère, 153-272.
Yanagihara, M. : Significance of the History of the Law of Nations in Europe and East Asia, 273-435.
(ISBN 978-90-04-28936-9)

Tome/Volume 372 (2014)

Bucher, A. : La compétence universelle civile, 9-128.
Cordero-Moss, G. : Limitations on Party Autonomy in International Commercial Arbitration, 129-326.
Sinjela, M. : Intellectual Property: Cross-Border Recognition of Rights and National Development, 327-394.
Dolzer, R. : International Co-operation in Energy Affairs, 395-504.
(ISBN 978-90-04-28937-6)

Tome/Volume 373 (2014)

Cachard, O. : Le transport international aérien de passagers, 9-216.
Audit, M. : Bioéthique et droit international privé, 217-447.
(ISBN 978-90-04-28938-3)

Tome/Volume 374 (2014)

Struycken, A. V. M. : Arbitration and State Contract, 9-52.
Corten, O., La rébellion et le droit international : le principe de neutralité en tension, 53-312.
Parra, A. : The Convention and Centre for Settlement of Investment Disputes, 313-410. (ISBN 978-90-04-29764-7)

Tome/Volume 374 (2014)

Struycken, A. V. M. : Arbitration and State Contract, 9-52.
Corten, O., La rébellion et le droit international : le principe de neutralité en tension, 53-312.
Parra, A. : The Convention and Centre for Settlement of Investment Disputes, 313-410. (ISBN 978-90-04-29764-7)

Tome/Volume 375 (2014)

Jayme, E. : Narrative Norms in Private International Law – The Example of Art Law, 9-52.
De Boer, Th. M. : Choice of Law in Arbitration Proceedings, 53-88.
Frigo, M. : Circulation des biens culturels, détermination de la loi applicable et méthodes de règlement des litiges, 89-474.
(ISBN 978-90-04-29766-1)

Tome/Volume 376 (2014)

Cançado Trindade, A. A.: The Contribution of Latin American Legal Doctrine to the Progressive Development of International Law, 9-92.
Gray, C.: The Limits of Force, 93-198.
Najurieta, M. S.: L'adoption internationale des mineurs et les droits de l'enfant, 199-494. (ISBN 978-90-04-29768-5)

Tome/Volume 377 (2015)

Kassir, W. J.: Le renvoi en droit international privé – technique de dialogue entre les cultures juridiques, 9-120.
Noodt Taquela, M. B.: Applying the Most Favourable Treaty or Domestic Rules to Facilitate Private International Law Co-operation, 121-318.
Tuzmukhamedov, B.: Legal Dimensions of Arms Control Agreements, An Introductory Overview, 319-468.
(ISBN 978-90-04-29770-8)

Tome/Volume 378 (2015)

Iwasawa, Y.: Domestic Application of International Law, 9-262.
Carrascosa Gonzalez, J.: The Internet – Privacy and Rights relating to Personality, 263-486.
(ISBN 978-90-04-32125-0)

Tome/Volume 379 (2015)

Lowe, V.: The Limits of the Law.
Boele-Woelki, K.: Party Autonomy in Litigation and Arbitration in View of The Hague Principles on Choice of Law in International Commercial Contracts.
Fresnedo de Aguirre, C.: Public Policy: Common Principles in the American States.
Ben Achour, R.: Changements anticonstitutionnels de gouvernement et droit international. (ISBN 978-90-04-32127-4)

Tome/Volume 380 (2015)

Van Loon, J. H. A.: The Global Horizon of Private International Law.
Pougoué, P.-G.: L'arbitrage dans l'espace OHADA.
Kruger, T.: The Quest for Legal Certainty in International Civil Cases.
(ISBN 978-90-04-32131-1)

Tome/Volume 381 (2015)

Jayme, E.: Les langues et le droit international privé, 11-39.
Bermann, G.: Arbitrage and Private International Law. General Course on Private International Law (2015), 41-484.
(ISBN 978-90-04-33828-9)

Tome/Volume 382 (2015)

Cooper, D., and C. Kuner: Data Protection Law and International Dispute Resolution, 9-174.
Jia, B. B.: International Case Law in the Development of International Law, 175-397.
(ISBN 978-90-04-33830-2)

Tome/Volume 383 (2016)

Bennouna, M. : Le droit international entre la lettre et l'esprit, 9-231.
Iovane, M. : L'influence de la multiplication des juridictions internationales sur l'application du droit international, 233-446. (ISBN 978-90-04-34648-2)

Tome/Volume 384 (2016)

Symeonides, S. C. : Private International Law Idealism, Pragmatism, Eclecticism, 9-385. (ISBN 978-90-04-35131-8)

Tome/Volume 385 (2016)

Berman, Sir F. : Why Do we Need a Law of Treaties?, 9-31.
Marrella, F. : Protection internationale des droits de l'homme et activités des sociétés transnationales, 33-435.(ISBN 978-90-04-35132-5)

Tome/Volume 386 (2016)

Murphy, S. D. : International Law relating to Islands, 9-266.
Cataldi, G. : La mise en œuvre des décisions des tribunaux internationaux dans l'ordre interne, 267-428. (ISBN 978-90-04-35133-2)

Tome/Volume 387 (2016)

Lequette, Y. : Les mutations du droit international privé : vers un changement de paradigme?, 9-644. (ISBN 978-90-04-36118-8)

Tome/Volume 388 (2016)

Bonell, M. J. : The Law Governing International Commercial Contracts : Hard Law versus Soft Law, 9-48.
Hess, B. : The Private-Public Divide in International Dispute Resolution, 49-266. (ISBN 978-90-04-36120-1)

Tome/Volume 389 (2017)

Muir Watt, H. : Discours sur les méthodes du droit international privé (des formes juridiques de l'inter-altérité). Cours général de droit international privé, 9-410. (ISBN 978-90-04-36122-5)

Tome/Volume 390 (2017)

Rau, A. S. : The Allocation of Power between Arbitral Tribunals and State Courts, 9-396. (ISBN 978-90-04-36475-2)

Tome/Volume 391 (2017)

Cançado Trindade, A. A. : Les tribunaux internationaux et leur mission commune de réalisation de la justice : développements, état actuel et perspectives, Conférence spéciale (2017), 9-101.
Mariño Menéndez, F. M. : The Prohibition of Torture in Public International Law, 103-185.
Swinarski, C. : Effets pour l'individu des régimes de protection de droit international, 187-369.
Cot, J.-P. : L'éthique du procès international (leçon inaugurale), 371-384.
(ISBN 978-90-04-37781-3)

Tome/Volume 392 (2017)

Novak, F.: The System of Reparations in the Jurisprudence of the Inter-American Court of Human Rights, 9-203.
Nolte, G.: Treaties and their Practice – Symptoms of their Rise or Decline, 205-397. (ISBN 978-90-04-39273-1)

Tome/Volume 393 (2017)

Tiburcio, C.: The Current Practice of International Co-Operation in Civil Matters, 9-310.
Ruiz De Santiago, J.: Aspects juridiques des mouvements forcés de personnes, 311-468. (ISBN 978-90-04-39274-8)

Tome/Volume 394 (2017)

Kostin, A. A.: International Commercial Arbitration, with Special Focus on Russia, 9-86.
Cuniberti, G.: Le fondement de l'effet des jugements étrangers, 87-283. (ISBN 978-90-04-39275-5)

Tome/Volume 395 (2018)

Salerno, F.: The Identity and Continuity of Personal Status in Contemporary Private International Law, 9-198.
Chinkin, C. M.: United Nations Accountability for Violations of International Human Rights Law, 199-320. (ISBN 978-90-04-40710-7)

Tome/Volume 396 (2018)

Jacquet, J.-M.: Droit international privé et arbitrage commercial international, 9-36.
Brown Weiss, E.: Establishing Norms in a Kaleidoscopic World. General Course on Public International Law, 37-415. (ISBN 978-90-04-41002-2)

Tome/Volume 397 (2018)

D'Avout, L.: L'entreprise et les conflits internationaux de lois, 9-612. (ISBN 978-90-04-41221-7)

Tome/Volume 398 (2018)

Treves, T.: The Expansion of International Law, General Course on Public International Law (2015), 9-398. (ISBN 978-90-04-41224-8)

Tome/Volume 399 (2018)

Kanehara, A.: Reassessment of the Acts of the State in the Law of State Responsibility, 9-266.
Buxbaum, H. L.: Public Regulation and Private Enforcement in a Global Economy: Strategies for Managing Conflict, 267-442. (ISBN 978-90-04-41670-3)

Tome/Volume 400 (2018)

Chedly, L.: L'efficacité de l'arbitrage commercial international, 9-624. (ISBN 978-90-04-42388-6)

Tome/Volume 401 (2019)

Wood, P. : Extraterritorial Enforcement of Regulatory Laws, 9-126.
Nishitani, Yuko : Identité culturelle en droit international privé de la famille, 127-450.
(ISBN 978-90-04-42389-3)

Tome/Volume 402 (2019)

Kinsch, P. : Le rôle du politique en droit international privé. Cours général de droit international privé, 9-384.
Dasser, F. : "Soft Law" in International Commercial Arbitration, 385-596.
(ISBN 978-90-04-42392-3)

Tome/Volume 403 (2019)

Daudet, Y. : 1919-2019, le flux du multilatéralisme, 9-48.
Kessedjian, C. : Le tiers impartial et indépendant en droit international, juge, arbitre, médiateur, conciliateur, 49-643.
(ISBN 978-90-04-42468-5)

Tome/Volume 404 (2019)

Rajamani, L. : Innovation and Experimentation in the International Climate Change Regime, 9-234.
Sorel, J.-M. : Quelle normativité pour le droit des relations monétaires et financières internationales?, 235-403. (ISBN 978-90-04-43142-3)

Tome/Volume 405 (2019)

Paulsson, J. : Issues arising from Findings of Denial of Justice, 9-74.
Brunée, J. : Procedure and Substance in International Environmental Law, 75-240.
(ISBN 978-90-04-43300-7)

Tome/Volume 406 (2019)

Bundy, R. : The Practice of International Law, Inaugural Lecture, 9-26.
Gama, L. : Les principes d'UNIDROIT et la loi régissant les contrats de commerce, 27-343.
(ISBN 978-90-04-43611-4)

Tome/Volume 407 (2020)

Wouters, J. : Le statut juridique des standards publics et privés dans les relations économiques internationales, 9-122.
Maljean-Dubois, S. : Le droit international de la biodiversité, 123-538.
(ISBN 978-90-04-43643-5)

Tome/Volume 408 (2020)

Cançado Trindade, A. A. : Reflections on the Realization of Justice in the Era of Contemporary International Tribunals, 9-88.
González, C. : Party Autonomy in International Family Law, 89-361.
(ISBN 978-90-04-44504-8)

Tome/Volume 409 (2020)

Shany, Y: The Extraterritorial Application of International Human Rights Law, 9-152.
Besson, S.: La *due diligence* en droit international, 153-398.
(ISBN 978-90-04-44505-5)

Tome/Volume 410 (2020)

Koh, H. H.: American Schools of International Law, 9-93.
Peters, A.: Animals in International Law, 95-544.
(ISBN 978-90-04-44897-1)

Tome/Volume 411 (2020)

Cahin, G: Reconstrution et construction de l'Etat en droit international, 9-573.
(ISBN 978-90-04-44898-8)

Tome/Volume 412 (2020)

Momtaz, D: La hiérarchisation de l'ordre juridique international, cours général de droit international public, 9-252.
Grammaticaki-Alexiou, A.: Best Interests of the Child in Private International Law, 253-434.
(ISBN 978-90-04-44899-5)

Tome/Volume 413 (2021)

Ferrari, F.: Forum Shopping Despite Unification of Law, 9-290.
(ISBN 978-90-04-46100-0)

Tome/Volume 414 (2021)

Pellet, A.: Le droit international à la lumière de la pratique: l'introuvable théorie de la réalité. Cours général de droit international public, 9-547.
(ISBN 978-90-04-46547-3)

Tome/Volume 415 (2021)

Trooboff, P. D.: Globalization, Personal Jurisdiction and the Internet. Responding to the Challenge of adapting settled Principles and Precedents. General Course of Private International Law, 9-321.
(ISBN 978-90-04-46730-9)

Tome/Volume 416 (2021)

Wolfrum, R: Solidarity and Community Interests: Driving Forces for the Interpretation and Development of International Law. General Course on Public International Law, 9-479. (ISBN 978-90-04-46827-6)

Tome/Volume 417 (2021)

d'Argent, P.: Les obligations internationales, 9-210.
Schabas, W. A.: Relationships Between International Criminal Law and Other Branches of International Law, 211-392.
(ISBN 978-90-04-47239-6)

Tome/Volume 418 (2021)

Bollée, S. : Les pouvoirs inhérents des arbitres internationaux, 9-224.
Tladi, D. : The Extraterritorial Use of Force against Non-State Actors, 225-360.
(ISBN 978-90-04-50380-9)

Tome/Volume 419 (2021)

Kolb, R. : Le droit international comme corps de «droit privé» et de «droit public». Cours général de droit international public, 9-668.
(ISBN 978-90-04-50381-6)

Tome/Volume 420 (2021)

Perrakis, S. : La protection internationale au profit des personnes vulnérables en droit international des droits de l'homme, 9-497.
(ISBN 978-90-04-50382-3)

Tome/Volume 421 (2021)

Estrella Faria, J. A. : La protection des biens culturels d'intérêt religieux en droit international public et en droit international privé, 9-333.
(ISBN 978-90-04-50829-3)

Tome/Volume 422 (2021)

Karayanni, M. : The Private International Law of Class Actions: A Functional approach, 9-248.
Mahmoudi, S. : Self-Defence and "Unwilling or Unable" States, 249-399.
(ISBN 978-90-04-50830-9)

Tome/Volume 423 (2022)

Kinnear, M. : The Growth, Challenges and Future Prospects for Investment Dispute Settlement, 9-36.
Weller, M. : "Mutual Trust": A Suitable Foundation for Private International Law in Regional Integration Communities and Beyond?, 37-378.
(ISBN 978-90-04-51411-9)

Tome/Volume 424 (2022)

Asada, M. : International Law of Nuclear Non-proliferation and Disarmament, 9-726.
(ISBN 978-90-04-51769-1)

Tome/Volume 425 (2022)

Metou, B. M. : Le contrôle international des dérogations aux droits de l'homme, 9-294.
Silva Romero, E. : Legal Fictions in the Language of International Arbitration, 295-423.
(ISBN 978-90-04-51770-7)

LES LIVRES DE POCHE DE L'ACADÉMIE
POCKETBOOKS OF THE ACADEMY
(Par ordre chronologique de parution) (By chronological order of publication)

Gaillard, E.: Aspects philosophiques du droit de l'arbitrage international, 2008, 252 pages.
(ISBN 978-90-04-17148-0)

Schrijver, N.: The Evolution of Sustainable Development in International Law: Inception, Meaning and Status, 2008, 276 pages.
(ISBN 978-90-04-17407-8)

Moura Vicente, D.: La propriété intellectuelle en droit international privé, 2009, 516 pages.
(ISBN 978-90-04-17907-3)

Decaux, E.: Les formes contemporaines de l'esclavage, 2009, 272 pages.
(ISBN 978-90-04-17908-0)

McLachlan, C.: Lis Pendens in International Litigation, 2009, 492 pages.
(ISBN 978-90-04-17909-7)

Carbone, S. M.: Conflits de lois en droit maritime, 2010, 312 pages.
(ISBN 978-90-04-18688-0)

Boele-Woelki, K.: Unifying and Harmonizing Substantive Law and the Role of Conflict of Laws, 2010, 288 pages.
(ISBN 978-90-04-18683-5)

Onuma, Y.: A Transcivilizational Perspective in International Law, 2010, 492 pages.
(ISBN 978-90-04-18689-7)

Bucher, A.: La dimension sociale du droit international privé. Cours général, 2011, 552 pages.
(ISBN 978-90-04-20917-6)

Thürer, D.: International Humanitarian Law: Theory, Practice, Context, 2011, 504 pages.
(ISBN 978-90-04-17910-3)

Alvarez, J. E.: The Public International Law Regime Governing International Investment, 2011, 504 pages.
(ISBN 978-90-04-18682-8)

Wang, G.: Radiating Impact of WTO on Its Members' Legal System: The Chinese Perspective, 2011, 384 pages.
(ISBN 978-90-04-21854-3)

Bogdan, M.: Private International Law as Component of the Law of the Forum, 2012, 360 pages.
(ISBN 978-90-04-22634-0)

Davey, W. J.: Non-discrimination in the World Trade Organization: The Rules and Exceptions, 2012, 360 pages.
(ISBN 978-90-04-23314-0)

Xue Hanqin: Chinese Contemporary Perspectives on International Law — History, Culture and International Law, 2012, 288 pages.
(ISBN 978-90-04-23613-4)

Reisman, W. M.: The Quest for World Order and Human Dignity in the Twenty-first Century: Constitutive Process and Individual Commitment. General Course on Public International Law, 2012, 504 pages.
(ISBN 978-90-04-23615-8)

Dugard, J.: The Secession of States and Their Recognition in the Wake of Kosovo, 2013, 312 pages.
(ISBN 978-90-04-25748-1)

Gannagé, L.: Les méthodes du droit international privé à l'épreuve des conflits de cultures, 2013, 372 pages.
(ISBN 978-90-04-25750-4)

Kohler, Ch.: L'autonomie de la volonté en droit international privé : un principe universel entre libéralisme et étatisme, 2013, 288 pages.
(ISBN 978-90-04-25752-8)

Kreindler, R.: Competence-Competence in the Face of Illegality in Contracts and Arbitration Agreements, 2013, 504 pages.
(ISBN 978-90-04-25754-2)

Crawford, J.: Chance, Order, Change: The Course of International Law. General Course on Public International Law, 2014, 540 pages.
(ISBN 978-90-04-26808-1)

Brand, R. A.: Transaction Planning Using Rules on Jurisdiction and the Recognition and Enforcement of Judgments, 2014, 360 pages.
(ISBN 978-90-04-26810-4)

Kolb, R.: L'article 103 de la Charte des Nations Unies, 2014, 416 pages.
(ISBN 978-90-04-27836-3)

Benvenisti, E.: The Law of Global Governance, 2014, 336 pages.
(ISBN 978-90-04-27911-7)

Yusuf, A. A.: Pan-Africanism and International Law, 2014, 288 pages.
(ISBN 978-90-04-28504-0)

Kono, T.: Efficiency in Private International Law, 2014, 216 pages.
(ISBN 978-90-04-28506-4)

Cachard, O.: Le transport international aérien de passagers, 2015, 292 pages.
(ISBN 978-90-04-29773-9)

Corten, O.: La rébellion et le droit international, 2015, 376 pages.
(ISBN 978-90-04-29775-3)

Frigo, M.: Circulation des biens culturels, détermination de la loi applicable et méthodes de règlement des litiges, 2016, 552 pages.
(ISBN 978-90-04-32129-8)

Bermann, G. A.: International Arbitration and Private International Law, 2017, 648 pages.
(ISBN 978-90-04-34825-7)

Bennouna, M.: Le droit international entre la lettre et l'esprit, 2017, 304 pages.
(ISBN 978-90-04-34846-2)

Murphy, S. D.: International Law relating to Islands, 2017, 376 pages.
(ISBN 978-90-04-36153-9)

Hess, B: The Private-Public Divide in International Dispute Resolution, 2018, 328 pages.
(ISBN 978-90-04-38488-0)

Rau, A.: The Allocation of Power between Arbitral Tribunals and State Courts, 2018, 608 pages.
(ISBN 978-90-04-38891-8)

Nolte, G.: Treaties and Their Practice – Symptoms of Their Rise or Decline, 2018, 288 pages.
(ISBN 978-90-04-39456-8)

Muir Watt, H.: Discours sur les méthodes du droit international privé (des formes juridiques de l'inter-altérité, 2019, 608 pages.
(ISBN 978-90-04-39558-9)

Cuniberti, G.: Le fondement de l'effet des jugements étrangers, 2019, 288 pages.
(ISBN 978-90-04-41180-7)

D'Avout, L.: L'entreprise et les conflits internationaux de lois, 2019, 880 pages.
(ISBN 978-90-04-41668-0)

Brown Weiss, E.: Establishing Norms in a Kaleidoscopic World, 2020, 536 pages.
(ISBN 978-90-04-42200-1)

Rajamani, L.: Innovation and Experimentation in the International Climate Change Regime, 2020, 336 pages.
(ISBN 978-90-04-44439-3)

Kessedjian, C.: Le tiers impartial et indépendant en droit international, juge, arbitre, médiateur, conciliateur, 2020, 832 pages.
(ISBN 978-90-04-44880-3)

Brunnée, J.: Procedure and Substance in International Environmental Law, 2020, 240 pages.
(ISBN 978-90-04-44437-9)

Dasser, F.: "Soft Law" in International Commercial Arbitration, 2021, 300 pages.
(ISBN 978-90-04-46289-2)

Maljean-Dubois, S.: Le droit international de la biodiversité, 2021, 590 pages.
(ISBN 978-90-04-46287-8)

Peters, A.: Animals in International Law, 2021, 641 pages.
(ISBN 978-90-04-46624-1)

Besson, S.: La *due diligence* en droit international, 363 pages.
(ISBN 978-90-04-46626-5)

Ferrari, F.: Forum Shopping Despite Unification of Law, 446 pages.
(ISBN 978-90-04-46626-5)

Wolfrum, R.: Solidarity and Community Interests: Driving Forces for the Interpretation and Development of International Law. General Course on Public International Law, 2022. (ISBN 978-90-04-50832-3)

Kolb, R.: Le droit international comme corps de «droit privé» et de «droit public», 2022. (ISBN 978-90-04-51836-0)